Playing SCENES

A sourcebook for performers

GERALD LEE RATLIFF

MERIWETHER PUBLISHING LTD.
Colorado Springs, Colorado

Meriwether Publishing Ltd., Publisher
P.O. Box 7710
Colorado Springs, CO 80933-7710

Executive editor: Theodore O. Zapel
Typesetting: Sharon E. Garlock
Cover design: Tom Myers

© Copyright MCMXCIII Meriwether Publishing Ltd.
Printed in the United States of America
First Edition

Library of Congress Cataloging-in-Publication Data

Ratliff, Gerald Lee.
    Playing scenes : a sourcebook for performers / Gerald Lee Ratliff.
  --1st ed.
       p.   cm.
    Includes bibliographical references.
    Summary: Performance hints and vocal and physical exercises for playing a variety of scenes from modern and classical theater.
    ISBN 0-916260-89-5
    1. Acting. [1. Acting.] I. Title.
PN2061.R37   1993
792'.028--dc20
                                                      93-11356
                                                        CIP
                                                       AC

3   4   5   01 02 03

TABLE OF CONTENTS

ACKNOWLEDGEMENTS

The use of the excerpts contained in this volume are fully protected under the copyright laws of the United States of America, the British Empire, the Dominion of Canada and all other countries of the Copyright Union. All rights, including professional, amateur, motion pictures, recitation, lecturing, public reading, radio broadcasting, television and the rights of translation into foreign languages are restricted. For more information related to full-scale productions contact the author's agents in writing. If no agent is listed, inquiry should be sent to the listed publisher.

And the Rain Came to Mayfield by Jason Milligan. Copyright © 1988, 1990, 1992 by Jason Milligan. Reprinted by permission of the author and The Tantleff Office, 375 Greenwich Street, Suite 700, New York, New York 10013. ALL RIGHTS RESERVED. CAUTION: Professionals and amateurs are hereby warned . . . *And the Rain Came to Mayfield* is subject to a royalty. It is fully protected under the copyright laws of the United States of America, the British Commonwealth, including Canada, and all other countries of the Copyright Union. All rights, including professional, amateur, motion picture, recitation, lecturing, public reading, radio broadcasting, television and the rights of translation into foreign languages are strictly reserved.

La Ronde by Arthur Schnitzler. English version by Eric Bentley, from *Before Brecht: Four German Plays,* edited and translated by Eric Bentley. Copyright © 1954, 1982 by Eric Bentley. Reprinted by permission of Applause Theatre Book Publishers, 211 West 71st Street, New York, New York 10023.

Cousins by Horton Foote. Copyright © 1979, 1989 by Horton Foote. Introduction copyright © 1986 by *The New York Times Company*. All rights reserved. No part of this book may be reproduced, stored in a retrieval system, or transmitted in any form, by any means, including mechanical, electronic, photocopying, recording or otherwise, without prior written permission of the publisher. The name Grove Press and the colophon printed on the title page and the outside of this book are trademarks registered in the U.S. Patent and Trademark Office and in other countries. Published by Grove Press, a division of Wheatland Corporation, 841 Broadway, New York, New York 10003. The introduction appeared in slightly different form in *The New York Times Magazine* on February 9, 1986 and is reprinted by permission. The author wishes to express his gratitude to Gerald Walker, who edited the original article. Also reprinted by permission of the author's agent, Lucy Kroll Agency, 390 West End Avenue, New York, New York 10024.

Dancing at Lughnasa by Brian Friel. Copyright © 1990 by Brian Friel. Reprinted by permission of Faber and Faber, Inc., 50 Cross Street, Winchester, Massachusetts 01890.

Album by David Rimmer. Copyright © 1981 by David Rimmer. Permission granted by Rosenstone/Wender, 3 East 48th Street, New York, New York 10017. Attention: Howard Rosenstone.

The Marriage of Bette and Boo by Christopher Durang. Copyright © 1985 by Christopher Durang. Reprinted by permission of the author's agent, Helen Merrill, 435 W. 23rd Street, #1 A, New York, New York 10011. Professionals and amateurs are hereby warned that all plays contained in this volume are fully protected under the Copyright Laws of the United States of America, the British Commonwealth, including the Dominion of Canada, and all other countries of the International Copyright Union and Universal Copyright Convention, and are subject to

PHOTOGRAPHS

A very special "thank you" to D. Terry Williams, Western Michigan University, and Harold Nichols, Kansas State University, for providing photographs for both *A Midsummer Night's Dream* and *Medea*. Individual production credits include Western Michigan University's production of *A Midsummer Night's Dream* director, James Daniels; scenic designer, John Jensen; costume designer, Gwen Nagle; and lighting designer, Matthew Knewtson. Kansas State University's production of *A Midsummer Night's Dream* director, Lew Shelton; sets, Mary Ann Lewis; lights, Brad Reissig; costumes, Marta Gilberd; and photography, Joe Nisil. Western Michigan University's production of *Medea* director David Karsten; scenic designer, Greg Roehrick; costume designer, Kristine Flonescheski; and lighting designer, David Morkel. Kansas State University's production of *Medea* director, Charlotte MacFarland; sets, Joel Herndon; lights, Tony Bish; costumes, Dana Pinkston; and photography, Joe Nisil.

All other photographs in this scene study book are from faculty and student productions at Montclair State College that are part of the Mainstage Theatre Series. I am deeply indebted to the kindness and the support of Joanne Owens, Managing Director of the Mainstage Theatre Series, for use of the theatre library and the production files in framing both the selected scenes as well as the descriptive photographs. This sourcebook would also not have been possible without the high quality performance and production approaches of the faculty and students that provided the inspiration for this publication.

Introduction

The fundamental principle that brings together this source-book for performance is that the actor is a creative artist and that the essential ingredient of creativity is imagination. The scenes and monologs that comprise this sourcebook are conveniently grouped in historical sequence from the classical to the contemporary. The scenes and monologs also progress in performance style and approach from the rather formal Greek tragedy to the more spontaneous contemporary realism. There is an introductory essay on the historical dimensions of each period surveyed and selected performance exercises that help to promote a relaxed approach to each scene or monolog in classroom or audition setting. It is important to understand the basic principles of the sourcebook so that you can cultivate the critical skills necessary to read a playscript with a keen and discerning insight and that you explore the suggested performance techniques to "visualize" the dramatic and theatrical elements inherent in each selected scene or monolog.

In approaching each scene or monolog the actor should have a clear set of performance objectives in mind for characterization and for movement but should also be flexible in approach so that there is no preconceived or rigid system of anticipated discoveries guiding the desired response. The sourcebook recognizes the actor's need to be knowledgeable about the scene or the monolog to be performed and provides the essential events and details necessary for an informed interpretation. The sourcebook also suggests imaginative performance clues to pursue related to both characterization and movement. The actor should approach suggested performance techniques in a manner that is comfortable and appropriate for an individual style of character development and delivery of dialog.

Another consideration is that the actor should engage in daily observation and studied investigation in approaching the scenes and monologs for a wider range of example from which to draw sensitive and complex performance portraits. The actor is also responsible for gathering as much supporting material for the performance as possible and to read the *complete* playscript before concentrating on either the selected scene or the edited monolog so that the interpretation that emerges is both informed and inventive. The sourcebook makes every effort to enlarge and to enrich the actor's natural comic or dramatic potential for achieving meaningful characterization in performance by encouraging original interpretations and fresh characterizations. Begin slowly at first and cultivate self-discipline and a willingness to experiment before proceeding to the more complex scenes and monologs that follow in the second half of the sourcebook. Remember, also, that with a foundation of knowledge about the historical period and the playscript, as well as an understanding of the styles and techniques of performance, it is possible to achieve a memorable comic or dramatic visualization.

Gerald Lee Ratliff
Indiana-Purdue University
Fort Wayne, Indiana

CHAPTER ONE

PLAYING CLASSICAL SCENES

*"Beauty of style and harmony and grace
and good rhythm depend on simplicity."*
— Plato, *The Republic*

The actor's basic approach to playing classical scenes depends upon a knowledge of the historical times in which the playscript was written as well as upon individual personality that suggests both the historical period and the character being portrayed. Although there is less information on the Greek theatre and on the acting style of the classical period than any other era in theatre history, what is traditionally known and accepted about typical theatre productions in ancient Greece may help the actor understand what is to be learned from the paintings, sculpture and theatre productions of the fifth and fourth centuries B.C.

The size of the Greek auditorium, ranging in size from several thousand at Oropus to more than 15,000 at Epidarius, suggests the need for the actor to exaggerate height in order to be seen by the spectators and the need to project the voice as well so that the dialog could be precisely understood in such a large, open space as the typical amphitheatre. While masks were used to provide facial expression that could be suggestive of the character's mood and attitude, the Greek actor was required to convey the supporting emotion of the character in body tension, statuesque poses or in highly stylized attitudes that involved broad gesture and formalized movement to reinforce character development.

Not only did the actor need an expressive body to convey the character being portrayed, but it was also necessary to have an articulate, resonant voice to express the emotions and the sentiments of the character as well. Vocally, the classical actor would have been a master in the art of persuasive speaking and oral declamation with an extensive speech training that promoted the principles of oratorical styles of public speaking and debate. Aristotle, the classical critic whose text the *Poetics* defines ancient Greek drama and literary criticism, also defines "acting" in the period as "... the proper management

3

of voice to express several emotions" and suggests that the voice is the primary instrument for the actor in creating character for performance.

Classical actor training also appears to have included singing as well as speaking, and there are a number of Greek tragedies and comedies that suggest "song-speech," or dialog that is alternatively spoken or sung in a chant-like or rhythmic intonation that helps to establish the mood or the attitude of the character. Consequently, it is apparent that the actor of the period would have needed to cultivate a catalog of tonal ranges in both speaking and singing that could depict mental and emotional states of mind. It would also have been necessary for the actor of the period to play more than one role per playscript given the number of speaking characters involved in most of the comedies and tragedies. The "three-actor" blueprint subscribed to by most theatre scholars suggests that only three performers were necessary to play the more than eight primary characters in most classical playscripts and that such a performance scheme demanded that each of the three classical actors be versatile in voice and body, agile in movement and more flexible in charcterization than the normal range of performance technique that would have been needed to portray a single character being played by a single actor.

Playing the Role

The actor who engages in scene study and playscript interpretation should be knowledgeable, and that implies an understanding of the basic theatrical techniques and conventions that give credibility to any creative performance. Being knowledgeable also suggests a familiarity with the historical manners and customs associated with the style of the performance. Having gathered all of the information available regarding the performance style of the classical period, including vocal and physical demands, the actor begins to reveal the preparation by incorporating the documented traits and mannerisms into an interpretation of the role that suggests both the period and the character being portrayed.

That is not to say, however, that the actor merely does historical research, "copies" what has been observed or discovered and then submits that to the audience for favorable comparison with the original sources. To take this approach to playing classical roles would undoubtedly result in a static, uninspired performance that would neither mirror the historical times nor reflect the skill of the performer. Perhaps that is the warning Socrates had in mind when he questioned the classical actor Ion on the role that inspiration played in the creation of unique, original character portraits:

SOCRATES: **I wish you would frankly tell me, Ion, what I am going to ask of you: When you produce the greatest effect upon the audience in the recitation of some striking passage are you in your right mind? Are you not carried out of yourself, and does not your soul in an ecstasy seem to be among the persons or the places of which you are speaking?**

ION: **I must confess that at the tale of pity my eyes are filled with tears, and when I speak of horrors, my hair stands on end and my heart throbs.**

— Plato, *The Dialogues*

Because the actor is a creative artist, relying on inspiration as well as technique to sketch three-dimensional character portraits, it is important to not only faithfully reproduce the historical style in performance but also to complement that creation with personal, unique traits and mannerisms that help to promote the authenticity and the texture of the portrait. To be both natural and credible is a noble goal in approaching classical scenes that appear to rely almost exclusively on the voice to convey character rather than on any other well-defined, systematic approach to performance style.

The actor of classical scenes should also be disciplined, and that implies a self-controlled and orderly system of preparation as well as an efficiency of simple technique that suggests to the audience that the final performance appears to be "spontaneous" and true-to-life rather than artificial and contrived. The simple technique to be pursued in classical scenes may be illustrated by an episode chronicled by the Roman grammarian Aulus Gellius. The Greek tragic actor Polus, in his portrayal of the heroine Electra, actually used the ashes of his own dead son in the scene in which the character Electra tearfully mourned the death of her brother while caressing the urn holding his cremated remains. The sincerity and simplicity of the portrayal, including the convention of a male playing a female role in classical tragedy, was incisive according to the account of Aulus Gellius and true sorrow and grief were mirrored on the actor's face and the audience of spectators was moved to tears at this unadorned, honest portrayal of apparent grief and sorrow.

5

The ancient Greek theatre of Epidarius suggests the need for the classical actor to project voice and to exaggerate height to be seen and heard in such a large, open space as the typical amphitheatre.

The innovation of performance technique implied by the incident of the actor Polus should also suggest that classical playscripts and performances may be given added dimension by original inventions and fresh interpretations. This ingredient of creativity, necessary for dynamic role-playing in any historical period of performance, is essential if the actor is to master the technical skills of believable stage characterization and to project himself as the fictitious character he is portraying. A truly inspired performance also suggests that it is through the actor's own personality that the character has been molded and given life. That is why it is important for the actor of classical scenes to explore their own personality as a key to creative role-playing and to incorporate imaginative performance ideas and potential character actions into scene study and subsequent performance that are both natural and believable.

It should also be obvious to the conscientious actor that the wider the range of experience and personal example from which to draw, the more sensitive and complex the probable performance portrait is likely to be; and the more three-dimensional and rewarding the creation. The initial responsibility, therefore, is a daily affair of keen observation and studied investigation that strengthens and reinforces the interpretation of the selected playscript and the individual character being portrayed. Sources of potential performance material will be discussed later in the chapter as they are related to the classical period but in all cases, and in all periods being studied, the material selected should be carefully woven into the performance so that it appears logical and spontaneous. Remember that the primary objective of the actor in classical scenes is to translate the given facts into a performance that is representative of the actual patterns of behavior observed in the society of the times or suggested in the playscript, and to remain faithful to these sources so that the audience may glimpse the suggested historical style and the individual character in performance.

Playing the Style

To speak of "style" is to promote an initial level of competence and characterization that arises from detailed scene study, and to discover the historical intricacies of interpretation and characterization that distinguish the art of the performance. Much of the responsibility for discerning style must rest with the actor having complete knowledge of the playscript, the period and the perspective necessary to view the character in relationship to the others in the scene. Whether the classical interludes of the farcical playwright Aristophanes or the absurd intrigues of the contemporary realist playwright Sam Shepard, each period of theatre history is distinguished by the individual style of its performance and production approaches.

If the actor in classical scenes has only a passing acquaintance with the dramatic literature and theory of the historical period, and may never have come in contact with the understood style of performance common in the period, that actor has a very narrow, limited vision of the historical dimensions of the playscript and a very superficial understanding of the attention to detail that is imperative to sustain an honest and believable interpretation of a character in a classical scene.

The classical style in performance is a reflection of the special demands made upon the actors of ancient Greece during the fourth and fifth centuries B.C. Although the ancient actors initially began their profession as amateur, strolling players they developed into highly skilled, professional performers during the "Golden Age" of drama. As "craftsmen of Dionysius," early actors appear to have formed their own professional unions with standard policies related to wages and conditions of employment. It is reported that Polus, the tragic actor who portrayed Electra holding the ashes of his own dead son, was paid the equivalent of $1,500 for two days' performances!

Greek audiences appear to have held actors in high esteem, and it was common practice in the period for specific actors like Thespis to attract sizable audiences for his interpretations of the major tragic heroines in the City Dionysia festival held to celebrate the harvest each year. It was also common practice to loudly ridicule actors whose interpretations were not appreciated and it is reported that the actor Aeschines performed so poorly that he was actually "stoned" out of the business! What emerges from these isolated examples, of course, is that people from all walks of life were devout theatre goers in ancient Greece and placed a high premium on actors who exhibited exceptional skill in mime, dance, gesture and voice.

The historical style of performance also relied quite heavily upon interpretation of the character. Greek actors had to develop an enormous range of vocal quality to effectively voice the declamatory style of vocal delivery that placed special emphasis upon articulation and enunciation of the verse dialog. There was an additional vocal requirement to cultivate a lyrical quality in the voice that would permit the singing of choral odes or recitative written as solo or as duet accompaniment to the character's development. In addition, it appears that the physical body was an important, expressive tool used to convey the mood and the attitude of the character. The classical actor, therefore, was required to have at command a more complete and detailed inventory of movement, gesture and physicalization than has been generally associated with ancient Greek performance style.

The need for an expressive, flexible physical body is perhaps best seen in the ornamented costumes worn by the tragic actors. Most contemporary scholars agree that classical actors wore *cothurni*, thick-soled boots similar to those worn today by Chinese actors, as well as *onkus*, a high headdress, as part of their stylistic approach to visual suggestion of character. When added to the ornaments, the masks and the body padding also worn by classical actors, the image of statuesque, imposing and awesome begins to emerge as part of the presentational style of performance. These commanding figures were aided in their impersonations with wood or cork masks that were designed to be placed entirely over the head to help elevate and stylize the depicted mood, emotion or attitude. To the ancient Greeks, these stylized masks were the ultimate expression of the character, the projection of their inner feelings.

A final principle of style in classical theatre is that all roles were assumed by men, including the great female characters Medea, Antigone, Hecuba and Electra. While it was possible for the mask and the costume to transform the classical actor into a crystallized image of the female character being portrayed, there is no evidence to suggest that ancient actors were "impersonators" of the leading heroines in either tragedy or comedy. It is more likely that men playing women was *artistically* truthful for the ancient Greeks, suggesting the universality of character rather than the gender of the character. It is also likely that such a performance style promoted a simplicity and a precision in the development of the character to avoid excessive exaggeration and to suggest the illusion of truthfulness.

Playing the Performance

To communicate the basic classical style that represents the historical period, and to also remain faithful to the principles of being natural and credible, it is important to understand the special nature of playing "performance." Having analyzed the playscript, researched the historical times in which the playscript was written, understood the situation depicted in the scene and detailed the primary forces at work in your individual character, it is now appropriate to add the finishing touches of theatricality and individuality to the character portrait being drawn. Playing the performance, then, relates to the specific performance technique each actor embraces to give life and dimension to the classical scene.

Some classical scenes may lend themselves to a performance that is representative of the actual patterns of behavior or custom chronicled in the society of the historical times; other classical scenes may remain so faithful and "authentic" to historical sources that the audience may actually catch a fleeting glimpse of period style in performance. There may also be opportunities to incorporate performance approaches based upon keen observation of ancient vase paintings or classical statues that depict heroic postures and poses. This scene book makes every effort to enrich the historical dimension of performance style by suggesting character actions and interpretative approaches as part of the introduction to the selected scenes which follow. The scene book also provides basic patterns of movement and thought that encourage classical actors to experiment with recommended "character hints" as a sounding board for creative exploration in performance.

Playing the performance also involves a period of detailed observation and analysis of the character being portrayed in the selected scene as reflected in the mannerisms, the gestures, the movements, the vocal qualities and the *distinguishing* personal habits which best suggest the dimension of the role-playing that will be necessary to accurately visualize the character for the audience. It may be of value in this approach to performance to discover in the analysis of the character and the selected scene a "metaphor," or implied comparison between the character and something inventive, and to incorporate those complementary performance features into the performance blueprint. For example, an analysis of Oedipus the King might suggest the performance metaphor of "knight errant" or "an uncurried horse awaiting death."

Honesty and simplicity are the keys to creative role-playing in the classical period. This is especially important to recall in light of the period costumes and masks that add the ingredients of magic, ritual and mystery to the actions of the individual characters. It is important, therefore, to approach each selected scene with sensitivity and objectivity; a relaxed and natural sense of movement; and an animation that suggests concentration and energy. Always be aware of possible interaction to the other performers in the scene and with the audience whenever possible.

In playing the performance each actor of classical scenes should seek to become an extension of what the dialog suggests about the

The acting style of the Greeks appears to have been vast in scope, but individual and personal in nature; larger than life, but intimate and isolated in nature.

character. The acting style of the Greeks appears to have been vast in scope, but individual and personal in nature; larger than life, but intimate and isolated in nature. It is important, therefore, that the performance approach enrich the poetic beauty of the rhythmic lines of dialog but also speak urgently, directly to the heart and to the soul of the spectator without appearing pretentious or artificial. That is why a truly inspired and creative performance of a classical scene is more likely to be natural and simple with the emphasis upon human nature rather than ancient history.

Classical Exercises

One of the special features of this scene study book is the use of exercises to prepare the performer for the selected scenes that follow each period of discussion. Since the primary tool of performance for the actor in classical scenes is an expressive voice, the following exercises are designed to "tune" the vocal instrument and to promote relaxation that frees the voice from tension and anxiety. The selected

11

vocal exercises also help the actor of classical scenes to explore the range of voice needed to express character accurately and creatively. The exercises should be repeated in the sequence given to help construct a performance routine that builds on increasingly complex vocal techniques to lessen stress and strain in the performance of the selected scenes that follow.

THE TONGUE THRUST

The preciseness with which speech sounds are formed depends upon the actor's use of the lips, tongue, teeth, hard palate, soft palate (velum) and jaw. The correct use of each of these vocal tools enables the actor of classical scenes to form the sounds, syllables and words that are necessary to effectively communicate to an audience. Nervousness or anxiety, however, may initially interfere with the ability to sustain sound or to form syllables precisely.

In order to discipline yourself so that nervousness and anxiety do not impair your ability to communicte effectively the words of the dialog or the mood of the character, you should cultivate a precise use of lip and tongue movement so that the words of the classical scene are uttered correctly. Begin this exercise by standing in front of a mirror and opening your mouth as wide as possible. Pull your tongue to the *center* of your open mouth and point it toward the mirror. With the tip of your extended tongue, touch the outside edge of your upper lip; then "outline" the outside of your lower lip; and, finally, rotate the tip of your tongue from the right to the left side of your open mouth. It is important in this part of the exercise to keep your mouth *open* and the tip of your tongue *pointed* so that proper pronunciation may follow in the second part of the exercise.

Next, repeat the following passage from Sophocles's *Oedipus the King,* using only your open mouth and the tip of your tongue to correctly pronounce the sounds. Make sure that the tip of your tongue is actively involved in pronunciation of all the *d*s, *t*s and *ing*s.

OEDIPUS: **Where are you, children? Where? O, come to me!**
Come, let me clasp you with a brother's arms,
These hands, which helped your father's eyes, once
bright,
To look upon you as they see you now —
Your father who, not seeing, nor inquiring,
Gave you for mother her who bore himself.

See you I cannot; but I weep for you,

For the unhappiness that must be yours,

And for the bitter life that you must lead.

What gathering of the citizens, what festivals,

Will you have part in? Your high celebrations

Will be to go back home, and sit in tears.

And when the time for marriage comes, what man

Will stake upon the ruin and the shame

That I am to my parents and to you?

Now, look again into the mirror and stretch your tongue as far as possible toward the tip of your nose. Relax and allow your tongue to slip back into your mouth. Then stretch your tongue downward as far as possible toward your chin. Relax and allow your tongue to slip back into your mouth. Now, repeat both "stretching" exercises in quick succession, alternating the movement of the tongue toward the tip of the nose and then toward the chin. After 15 stretching movements in each direction, relax for a moment. Then recite the following passages from Aeschylus's *Agamemnon,* using the tip of your tongue to voice correctly and precisely all of the *d*s, *t*s and *ing*s.

O, treat me not like a soft and delicate woman,

Or gazing open-mouthed, give me acclaim,

As though I were barbarian. These tapestries here

Will draw the envy of wide heaven should I touch them.

So are the gods worshipped.

No mortal ever walks on rich embroideries.

So treat me as a man, with a man's honouring,

Not as a God. The voice of rumour takes

These gifts and spreads them wide.

To be of humble mind is God's best gift.

OPEN YOUR THROAT!

No performer of classical scenes can afford the luxury of sloppy or slurred speech. Although faulty speech in performance has many possible sources, ranging from physical trauma to poor role-model imitations developed during childhood, understanding the correct production of sound is the first step toward vocal improvement. It is important, therefore, that you review the process of *resonation*, the amplification and enrichment of sound as it passes along the vocal folds. It is resonation that gives classical vocal performance flexibility and dimension.

Begin the exercise by locating your larynx (voice box) in order to feel the vibrations produced by the vocal folds in forming specific sounds. Place the tips of your fingers lightly on your Adam's apple as you voice the letters *b, p* and *d*. Do you feel the vibrations? Now, voice the following words as you notice the vibrations produced by the vocal folds: *baby, pretty, devil, bought, present* and *daring*.

Next, voice the letters *t, v, z, f* and *s*. What differences in the vibrations do you now feel? When you can distinguish the vibrations that result from each of the letters above, voice the following words as distinctly as possible: *team, vicar, zoo, final, sure, total, victory, zest, fame,* and *simple*. Now explore the vibrations produced by voicing the vowel sounds *a, e, i, o* and *u*. What vocal differences do you notice?

In "opening your throat" to produce the vibration needed to voice each letter, you should notice the quality of resonance that gives vitality and meaning to vocal performance. When the resonating cavities are open and flexible, speech sounds become amplified and vibrant. To demonstrate the need for resonation, pinch your nose closed and "hum" the following phrase: "Now is the time for all good men to come to the aid of their country." Do you notice the obstruction caused when the nasal cavity is closed? This creates the "nasal twang" of actors who are unable to resonate correctly under stress or strain.

Now set your teeth tightly together and repeat the following quotation from William Congreve's *The Mourning Bride:* "Heaven has no rage like love to hatred turned." Do you notice the obstruction caused when the teeth are tightly set together and the jaw is "locked" in an inflexible position? This results in the "tight lip" of actors who are extremely nervous. In order to cultivate the open throat and relaxed jaw necessary for resonant sound production in classical scenes, *sing* the following selection from Alfred, Lord Tennyson's "Choric Song" verses to feel the resonant vibrations. Note where your individual vibrations fall on the musical scale, and then repeat the exercise *humming* the same selection. What differences do you notice in your resonant vibrations?

There is sweet music here that softer falls

Than petals from blown roses on the grass,

Or night-dews on still waters between walls

Of shadowy granite, in a gleaming pass;

Music that gentlier on the spirit lies,

Than tired eyelids upon tired eyes;

Music that brings sweet sleep down from the blissful

skies.

When you are confident that your throat is open and your jaw is relaxed, recite the following passages from Sophocles's *Antigone* as you relate as many *vowel* and *consonant* sounds as possible to the musical scale. Keep your mouth "open" and resonate as fully and completely as possible without producing tension in the jaw.

Many wonders there are, but none so wondrous as man,

Who by his power channels the white seas

With ships driven by storm-winds

From the south, and the breaking waves

Beneath his paths are perilous.

Yet man wears upon himself the earth,

Eldest of the gods, immortal, never-sleeping,

Turning his furrows by his horse-teams:

So does the plowshare travel year by year.

* * *

Cunning beyond the wildest dreams man has,

Such is his fertile brain which leads him to evil and

good;

When he honours the laws of the land and has justice

Upheld by a solemn oath sworn before the gods,

Then proudly his city shall stand; but cityless is he

Who departs from the just ways by reason of his pride.

Never may such a man sit by my hearth or share

My thoughts, who sins unreasonably.

When you have completed this exercise you will have a better understanding of the resonation needed to play classical scenes that demand amplification and enrichment of sound to voice language rich in poetic imagery. Knowing how to reduce tension in your voice will also help to promote better communication of the dialog to the audience and enhance your classical poise and self-confidence in performance.

THE CLASSICAL SCENES

The following edited classical scenes are representative of the comedies and tragedies of the ancient Greek period. Each scene should be approached with a sense of historical accuracy and also a natural, spontaneous performance style that gives the presentation vitality. The actor should be innovative as well, and that might include the use of masks and bed sheets to suggest the historical period; or the current fashion of high-soled shoes might be an excellent suggestion of the classical *cothornus* worn to elevate the ancient performer and to give stature to the character being portrayed. An interesting convention of the period that might stimulate the audience reception would be the casting of men in some of the women's roles or the use of excessive padding in the comedies to help provoke the humor of the dialog and the action described. There is, also, the historically accurate practice of staging scenes out-of-doors, with the audience seated on a sloping hillside.

from **Lysistrata** (411 B.C.)

*Aristophanes**

By its very nature, coming as it does after epic and lyric poetry and still later than classical tragedy, Greek "Old Comedy" enjoys much of the liberty of choice in subject matter and license of method and approach that mark present day burlesque and satire. The range and variety of subjects treated suggests a frank, uncompromising spirit of ribald humor and reckless high spirits that is intended to provoke hearty, side-splitting laughter. Indeed, whatever lends itself to satire is instantly seized upon for caricature and ridicule. Eccentric and grotesque personalities are rather crudely parodied, social vices are quickly embraced and pomposity or virtue are savagely lampooned.

An unchecked, uncensored freedom of speech and suggestive language that is both harsh and vulgar is also found within the classical period of "Old Comedy." But it must not be forgotten that

*adapted by Gerald Lee Ratliff

such language and apparent license were part of the expected good fun and that such burlesque humor was forbidden to women and children, who were initially barred from public theatrical performances. That is why the rather simple plot and action of this scene would not have been offensive to the spectator. Quite simply stated, to force the men to stop the war between Athens and Sparta — which has raged for more than 20 years — Lysistrata urges the women of Greece to engage in a "sex strike" until the men agree to sue for peace. Although the women are at first reluctant, they finally agree and immediately capture the sacred Acropolis, forcing the men to surrender and make peace with Sparta.

The historical period of classical comedy demands that the actor have at command an arsenal of formalized gestures, stylized facial expressions and a well-developed range of vocal variety.

When playing the classical comedy scene the actor may wish to slightly exaggerate the movement and the action, suggesting the animation and the vitality of the characters. The historical period also demands that the actor have at command an arsenal of formalized gestures, stylized facial expressions and well developed range of vocal variety. Above all, the actor should not be timid or squeamish in executing the suggested dialog or to engage in the amusing insults or innuendo with the audience. This is especially true in the portrayal of Lysistrata, who should emerge as a crafty, forceful woman of incredible strength of will and determination.

CAST

LYSISTRATA
CALOCINE
VOLUPTIA

SCENE

Athens. A public square in early morning.

APPROACH

The scene opens with Lysistrata discovered asleep upon the *thymele,* or sacred altar, snoring loudly. She had been awaiting the tardy arrival of some Athenian women summoned to the public square before sunrise to discuss a strategy for ending the Peloponnesian War. Lysistrata's primary concern in the episode is to rouse the women's moral indignation and sense of outrage and to provoke them to engage in a marital strike that might bring the absent men home. She is not above intrigue, deception or insult to achieve her aim. Pacing of the scene should be rapid, especially on the initial series of entrances and exits by Calocine and the surprise appearance of Voluptia; and there should be frequent movement toward the spectators to draw them into the action or to share confidences with them.

1	LYSISTRATA: Soft, who goes there? By Athene, I could have
2	sworn I hear the women come! O, I must have dreamed it
3	all. That it should come to this: asleep here all the long night
4	in order to greet my sisters of Greece, who speed to assist
5	me in a most daring plan to end the war which has ravaged
6	our lands for thirty years!
7	O, good morning to you, gentle Athenians! By Apollo,
8	you have risen early to witness this spectacle! But why do
9	you sit there with folded arms and knitted brows, while all
10	around you dear Greece pulses and throbs? O, now I see!
11	'Tis no small wonder. Most of you be men! But that is wise
12	and to the point. For it is to you we would speak when all
13	have come together here. By Eros, it is an omen sure!
14	O, sweet friends, listen to the wise counsel I am about
15	to impart to you and take care that it is not lost upon you.
16	'Twould be the work of vulgar spectators if that were so;
17	not that of such an audience as this, by Jupiter! Lend me
18	your ears if you love frank speaking. If you do not love frank
19	speaking, stick your foot in your ear until I am done!
20	To be blunt, men are like children twice over and it is
21	far more fitting to soundly chastise them than to beat them;
22	for there is more excuse for their faults! That is why I
23	summon the women of Greece here this very morning. Our
24	leadership is in fumbling hands. They are incompetent and
25	impotent. They press too hard and are now overextended.
26	They force affairs, come late and their efforts are piecemeal
27	to say the least. They do not discharge their obligations,
28	will not give an inch and their tongues are like double-edged
29	swords.
30	And, O how they love wars! They come grunting and
31	humping home from the hunt, throw a raw piece of meat at
32	you, bark a command or two and expect the poor wife to sit
33	up and beg like a common cur! O, a plague on the blanket
34	infantry!
35	CALOCINE: Lysistrata, I am come! It is time!

1 LYSISTRATA: Away with you! I have not yet reached my climax!
2 CALOCINE: But you know the ancient proverb: "Speedy
3   execution is greatly esteemed by the public."
4 LYSISTRATA: I know the ancient proverb, twit! But I have not
5   yet set sail all that is writ down for me. The playwright will
6   be at wit's end if I do not reach my climax! He bids me here
7   to lay the men low, and to weave a seductive web to entrap
8   them.
9 CALOCINE: Can't he weave his own web, and allow us to get
10   down to our parts?
11 LYSISTRATA: 'Tis not a man's art! Besides, it is well known that
12   he writes his Prologues in a limping meter and does not run
13   erect until half way home.
14 CALOCINE: How far is he from home now?
15 LYSISTRATA: To judge from the sweetness of his words, I
16   would say just above the hill of Pisander.
17 CALOCINE: Stick to him, then. I shall come again when he is in
18   hand behind the door.
19 LYSISTRATA: Now, where was I? O, yes. And how his moods
20   change without rhyme or reason. If a man is to be believed,
21   a woman is a plague on him! If a man is to be believed,
22   through us come all his troubles, quarrels, disputes,
23   frustrations and griefs! But, sweet sisters, if we are truly
24   such a pest, why does he court us? Why, by Aphrodite, does
25   he marry us?
26   You, sir. If your wife goes out and you meet her away
27   from the house, why do you fly into a fury? Ought you not
28   rather to rejoice and give thanks to Zeus, for the pest has
29   disappeared and you will no longer have her about the
30   house? And you, sir. When your wife falls asleep at a friend's
31   house from too much wine or too much sporting, why do
32   you carry her home and then tiptoe round the house so as
33   not to wake this pest? Why do you bring her breakfast in
34   bed? Why do you hold her head and put cold cloth to her
35   face? Should you not have been glad that the pest nodded off?

1   O, by Menelaos, 'tis true! 'Tis true! If we but seat
2   ourselves at the window each of you cranes his neck to see
3   the pest! If we but stand in the doorway each of you walks
4   up and down, down and up, strutting like a proud peacock
5   to see the pest!
6 CALOCINE: Lysistrata, Lysistrata! By Poseidon, I am come
7   again!
8 LYSISTRATA: Away! Away with you again! I am just now
9   reaching my climax!
10 CALOCINE: Before you reach home?
11 LYSISTRATA: I am at the front door this very minute!
12 CALOCINE: I hope the door is not locked, by Ajax!
13 LYSISTRATA: Now, where am I? O, yes! This part of the Prologue
14   is so dear to me that I have committed it to memory. No
15   need for reference here.
16   Women of Athens, do you remember how long it has
17   been? O, no, sisters, not that! Do you remember how many
18   peaceful moments you have known? O, no, my dainties, not
19   that! Do you remember the beauty and serenity of life in
20   Greece before the men grew fond of war? Yes, comrades,
21   that's it!
22   Well, by a stroke of inspiration I have devised an
23   ingenious strategy to secure the much needed salvation of
24   Greece. And here is the plan. I propose to call all of the
25   women of Greece to arms, and to invite representatives of
26   our sex to meet here this very morning so that we may
27   resolve to end the war by —
28 CALOCINE: Lysistrata, this is the last time I come! If you have
29   not reached your climax by this time it is plain that the
30   playwright did not reach his either!
31 LYSISTRATA: But he seized every favorable opportunity. He
32   advanced every new position. I have it from his own mouth!
33 CALOCINE: Hold, Lysistrata! Or the spectators will get wind of
34   it! Remember what the ancients teach: "Whatever would
35   offend is best left unsaid."

21

1   LYSISTRATA: Right, by Artemis! But how shall we begin?

2   CALOCINE: At the beginning! I shall run on, again, and you

3   shall tell me of the ingenious plan you have devised to secure

4   the peace of Greece.

5   LYSISTRATA: Right, by Hymen!

6   CALOCINE: Well?

7   LYSISTRATA: Well, what?

8   CALOCINE: Thank the spectators and then be off? You have

9   already overstayed your welcome.

10   LYSISTRATA: Ladies and gentlemen, thank you for your

11   indulgence! I must now shoot off to do the bidding of the

12   playwright. Before I leave, however, I am sure that he would

13   want me to say this to you. It was writ down before he

14   misplaced his climax to the Prologue. "Let the wise judge

15   because of whatever is wise in this piece; and those who

16   like a laugh by whatever has made them laugh. In this way

17   I address most everyone here." Adieu, for now!

18   CALOCINE: Women of Athens, behold! I have at no time spoken.

19   I do so now! For ourselves, we shall no doubt persuade our

20   husbands to conclude a swift and lasting peace. But now,

21   in the name of Athene, are we to cure the hot-blooded and

22   frenzied Greek populace from waging war?

23   LYSISTRATA: Have no fear, Calocine! I have undertaken this

24   very day to force our people to lay down their arms and to

25   receive the message of peace. At dawn, under the pretense

26   of sacrificing a goat to Hermes, the old women of Athens

27   have gone afoot to seize the Acropolis! If all goes well, the

28   citadel should be ours by high noon! Then, the men will

29   have to mount *our* fortress if they want to reclaim the

30   treasure of the temple. And it is at that time we shall force

31   them to sue for peace!

32   CALOCINE: Well said, Lysistrata! And from our vantage point

33   above the city we shall rain down fire upon their heads and

34   rocks upon their swords!

35   LYSISTRATA: But come quickly, comrade! You must now learn

1   how to stand the test, to hold your own and to go forward

2   without feeling fatigue in the long battle ahead. And so that

3   you may prove fruitful in your quest, I have arranged for

4   some special instruction. Call forth Voluptia, fair peach of

5   Athens! She shall instruct us all in the art of women's

6   warfare!

7   CALOCINE: O, no! Not Voluptia! You're not going to believe this

8   tale!

9   VOLUPTIA: O, Ladies of Greece! You do me praise to call me

10   forth from my labors to here instruct you in my special

11   crafts. I speak as one who has given much, and often, to her

12   country. I speak as one who knows full well the secrets of

13   formations, desirable positions, size of reinforcements and

14   all of the military chatter relating to involuntary

15   movements on the parts of our enemies.

16   CALOCINE: With all fifty of his Majesty's legions no doubt!

17   VOLUPTIA: For you, however, I shall be brief! Come, sisters!

18   Pain and suffering are yours. Accept them! You must be

19   zealous and silent and endure! Why hoard for death your

20   maidenhood?

21   LYSISTRATA: Voluptia, that's the wrong speech!

22   VOLUPTIA: O, by Pisander! Pardon me, sisters! My passion is

23   such that I forget my purpose. Women of Greece, if you

24   would end the war and secure the peace for which you lay

25   awake each night you must wipe all decency from your face!

26   Steady, sisters!

27   A dose of hellbore to give you a brainwash, that's what

28   you need! And not the common stuff the apothecaries peddle

29   in the marketplace either, but the special brand from

30   Antigua! Steady, sisters!

31   Eyes emphasized with kohl and false hair, painted lips

32   and lined brows! Wax and Tarentine wraps and earrings.

33   Snake-winding bracelets, anklets, chains and lockets!

34   Steady, sisters! But no roses! O, by Pluto, no roses! When

35   they lose their fragrance both men and gods stay away, for

1   the odor has a marvelous capacity to drive away all repose!
2   What you don't possess by Nature you may acquire by
3   imitation, and a little padding! And don't forget that a
4   woman cannot possibly be loved without perfume! So put
5   it here and there and everywhere! And when you walk
6   spring forward with a light step. See, walk as I and men will
7   gaze at you with wonder, their heads erect and their faces
8   beaming with delight at the sight!
9   And don't forget to let your hands interlace, as though
10   you were praying with each step! And, O, face without chalk!
11   Remember, my dainties, for a woman redness of face is the
12   shining flower of charm. To rouge, my sweets, to rouge! But
13   do not be harsh or frightening, and do not seal your beauty
14   away in scarf or veil! O, sisters, throw off those nets that
15   sore beset you, and reveal your loveliness!
16   CALOCINE: At last she has hit upon something which strikes
17   home!
18   VOLUPTIA: There's not a part of you but snares men to their
19   doom! Love beckons in your eyes, your mouths are songs of
20   grace, your hands are scions of strength and flowers blossom
21   in your cheeks! If you do not believe my craft, take up your
22   mirror and see how your face has changed. O, receive them
23   with scented hair, in fragrant delicto at the half moon! O,
24   my sweets, what a noble work of art is Woman!
25   And don't forget to imitate the twelve postures of
26   Cyrone!
27   LYSISTRATA: Come quickly, sisters! While the fit of passion is
28   upon us let each swear an inviolable oath of abstinence! We
29   will swear!
30   CALOCINE: We will swear!
31   VOLUPTIA: We will swear!
32   ALL: We will swear!
33
34
35

24

from **Antigone** (442 B.C.)

Sophocles

Antigone was a popular play in the classical period and was frequently staged at the festival of Dionysus as part of the celebration of the seasons. Much of the play's success was due to the tragic characterizations of Creon and Antigone, two of the most fully drawn character portraits of the playwright Sophocles. Creon, a pathetic man more patriotic and sincere than intentionally harmful, is a fine example of the authority figure who is too rigid and inflexible to admit mistakes or errors in judgment until it is too late. Antigone, a headstrong and passionate young woman, more stubborn than sensible, is a fine example of the youthful and energetic crusader for right who refuses to compromise her principles even when her life is threatened.

Sophocles represents Greek tragedy at its best and most persuasive. His playscripts are rich in imagery, dramatic technique and characterization. His characters may be less "heroic" and more "human" than those of the other classical dramatists but they still exhibit a lofty dignity and an individuality that distinguish them from other tragic figures of this historical period. When you read the playscripts of Sophocles you will discover that he predicted the impending decline of Athens, pointing to the city's moral decay and religious hypocrisy. He also foretold the injustice and prejudice that would arise if the Athenian democracy did not protect the rights of minorities. He was ashamed of the cruel treatment of war slaves and was saddened by the poverty of the peasants and hired workers. Like a modern-day Abraham Lincoln, Sophocles issued an "Athenian Address" in playscripts like *Antigone* and warned the audience of impending doom if they didn't change their ways.

In terms of plot and action, this tragedy is direct and immediate. The story revolves around Oedipus's daughter, Antigone, and Creon, Oedipus's brother-in-law who becomes King of Thebes. The opening of the story depicts in narrative a great battle that has just been fought. Although the city of Thebes has triumphed, it has lost its king in the fighting. Creon, the new king, decrees as his first official act that the body of Polyneices, the defeated invader, shall remain unburied as a symbol of corruption.

Creon's decree has barely been made public when he receives word that an attempt has been made to bury the corpse by the princess Antigone, sister of the dead Polyneices and niece of Creon. When Antigone is accused, she makes no attempt to conceal her deed and

A number of modern versions of Antigone *portray Creon as an authority figure more patriotic than sincere and Antigone as a headstrong and passionate young woman more stubborn than sensible.*

challenges Creon's right to make laws that are in conflict with the will of the gods, who have provided for religious burial and atonement for those killed in battle. Creon, however, refuses to pardon Antigone for breaking his law and the rest of the playscript details the verbal battles and emotional assaults that lead inevitably to Antigone's death and the tragic demise of Creon's family.

When playing the classical tragedy scene the actor should seek to maintain an air of decorum and energy that suggests the dramatic tension inherent in the selected scenes that follow. There should be no effort made here to exaggerate the movement of the characters, but attention should be paid to voicing the "arguments" made by both Antigone and Creon as they each seek to persuade their individual point of view. The quality of the lyrical tragedy inherent in the verse of the playscript should also be maintained with a resonant, articulate approach to voice.

CAST

GUARD

CREON

ANTIGONE

ISMENE

TEIRESIAS

SCENE

An open space before the house of Creon.

APPROACH

The scene opens when the Guard enters quickly with Antigone, who has been caught at the graveside of Polyneices. Antigone admits that she knew of Creon's edict but refuses to obey it because it did not come from "God." Creon at first cannot believe that his own niece would be the rebel who tried to bury the traitor Polyneices. The strong-willed Antigone and the equally determined Creon exchange angry accusations and the scene explodes in threats and recriminations that prompt Creon to have Antigone arrested and charged with treason.

1 CREON: Stay! How and where did you take her?
2 GUARD: She was burying the man; that's all there is to tell you.
3 CREON: Do you mean what you say? Are you telling the truth?
4 GUARD: It happened this way. When we came to the place
5   where he lay, worrying over your threats, we swept away
6   all the dirt, leaving the rotting corpse bare. Then we sat
7   down on the bank of the hill toward the wind, so that the
8   smell would not stifle us. We kept each other awake by
9   thinking what you would do to us if we didn't carry out your
10   orders. Suddenly, a wind came roaring down from the sky
11   and clouds of choking dust and leaves filled our eyes.
12   After the storm had passed, we saw this girl in the
13   distance. She was crying aloud like a wounded bird in grief
14   and misery; and she cried like a bird cries when it sees its
15   nest bare and the nestlings gone. Then straightaway she
16   scooped up some dust in her hands and then held it high
17   while she sprinkled it over the corpse. We all rushed toward
18   her but she was not at all frightened of us. We bound her
19   and charged her with the present offence, but she denied
20   nothing.
21 CREON: You, then — you whose face is bent to the earth — do
22   you confess or do you deny the deed?
23 ANTIGONE: I did it. I make no denial.
24 CREON: *(To GUARD)* You may go away, wherever you will.
25   *(To ANTIGONE)* Now tell me — not in many words, but
26   briefly — did you know of the edict that forbade what you
27   did?
28 ANTIGONE: I knew it. How could I help but know? It was public.
29 CREON: And you had the boldness to transgress that law?
30 ANTIGONE: Yes, for it was not Zeus that made such a law; such
31   is not the justice of the gods. Nor did I think that your
32   decrees had so much force that a mortal could override the
33   unwritten and unchanging statutes of heaven. For their
34   authority is not of today nor yesterday, but from all time;
35   and no man knows when they were first put forth.

1   Not through dread of any human power could I answer
2   to the gods for breaking these. That I must die I knew
3   without your edict. But if I am to die before my time, I count
4   that a gain; for who, living as I do in the midst of many
5   woes, would not call death a friend?
6   It saddens me little, therefore, to come to my end. If I
7   had let my mother's son lie in death an unburied corpse,
8   that would have saddened me, but for myself I do not grieve.
9   And if my acts are foolish in your eyes, it may be that a
10   foolish judge condemns my folly.
11 CREON: Let me remind you that those who are too stiff and
12   stubborn are most often humbled; it is the hardened that
13   most often snap and splinter. I have seen wild horses that
14   show too much temper brought to calm by a little force. Too
15   much pride is out of place in one who lives subject to
16   another. This girl was already versed in insolence when she
17   transgressed the law that had been published; and now,
18   behold, a second insult — to boast about it, to exult in her
19   misdeed!
20   But I am no man, she is the man, if she carry this off
21   unpunished. No! She is my sister's child, but if she were
22   nearer to me in blood than any who worships Zeus at the
23   altar of my house, she should not escape a dreadful doom —
24   nor her sister either, for indeed I charge her too with
25   plotting his burial.
26   And summon that sister — for I saw her just now
27   within, raving and out of her wits. That is the way minds
28   plotting evil in the dark give away their secret and convict
29   themselves even before they are found out. But the most
30   intolerable thing is that one who has been caught in
31   wickedness should glory in the crime.
32 ANTIGONE: Would you do more than slay me?
33 CREON: No more than that — no, and nothing less.
34 ANTIGONE: Then why do you delay? Your speeches give me no
35   pleasure, and never will; and my words, I suppose, buzz

1   hatefully in your ear. I am ready; for there is no better way
2   I could prepare for death than by giving burial to my
3   brother. Everyone would say so if their lips were not sealed
4   by fear. But a king has many advantages, he can do and say
5   what he pleases.
6 CREON: You slander the race of Cadmus; not one of them
7   shares your view of this deed.
8 ANTIGONE: They see it as I do, but their tails are between their
9   legs.
10 CREON: They are loyal to their king; are you not ashamed to be
11   otherwise?
12 ANTIGONE: No; there is nothing shameful in piety to a brother.
13 CREON: Was it not a brother also who died in the good cause?
14 ANTIGONE: Born of the same mother and sired by the same
15   father.
16 CREON: Why then do you dishonor him by honoring that other?
17 ANTIGONE: The dead will not look upon it that way.
18 CREON: Yes, if you honor the wicked equally with the virtuous.
19 ANTIGONE: It was his brother, not his slave, that died.
20 CREON: One perished ravaging his fatherland, the other
21   defending it.
22 ANTIGONE: Nevertheless, Hades desires these rites.
23 CREON: Surely the gods are not pleased to be made equal with
24   the evil!
25 ANTIGONE: Who knows how the gods see good and evil.
26 CREON: A foe is never a friend — even in death.
27 ANTIGONE: It is not my nature to join in hating, but in loving.
28 CREON: Your place, then, is with the dead. If you must love,
29   love them. While I live, no woman shall overbear me. Guard!
30   Come, take her away!
31 GUARD: Your majesty! See where Ismene creeps through
32   yonder gate shedding such tears as only loving sisters weep.
33   It seems as if a cloud gathers about her brow and breaks in
34   rain upon her cheek.
35 CREON: And you, who lurked like a viper in my house, sucking

the blood of my honor, while I knew not that I was nursing
two reptiles ready to strike at my throne — come, tell me
now, will you confess your part in this guilty burial, or will
you swear you knew nothing of it?

ISMENE: I am guilty if she is, and share the blame.

ANTIGONE: No, no! Justice will not permit this. You did not
consent to the deed, nor would I let you have part in it.

ISMENE: But now that danger threatens you, I am not ashamed
to come to your side.

ANTIGONE: Who did the deed, the gods and the dead know; a
friend in words is not the friend I love.

ISMENE: Sister, do not reject me, but let me die with you, and
duly honor the dead.

ANTIGONE: Do not court death, not claim a deed to which you
did not put your hand. My death will suffice.

ISMENE: How could life be dear to me without you?

ANTIGONE: Ask Creon, you think highly on his word.

ISMENE: Why taunt me so, when it does you no good?

ANTIGONE: Ah, if I mock you, it is with pain I do it.

ISMENE: Oh tell me, how can I serve you, even now?

ANTIGONE: Save yourself; I do not grudge your escape.

ISMENE: Oh, my grief! Can I not share your fate?

ANTIGONE: You chose to live, and I to die.

ISMENE: At least I begged you not to make that choice.

ANTIGONE: This world approved your caution, but the gods my
courage.

ISMENE: But now I approve, and so I am guilty too.

ANTIGONE: O, little sister. Be of good cheer, and live. My life
has long been given to death, that I might serve the dead.

CREON: Behold, one of these girls turns to folly now, as the
other one has ever since she was born.

ISMENE: Yes, sire, such reason as nature gives us may break
under misfortune and go astray.

CREON: Yours did, when you chose to share evil deeds with the
evil.

1 ISMENE: But I cannot live without her.
2 CREON: You mistake; she lives no more.
3 ISMENE: Surely you will not slay your own son's betrothed?
4 CREON: He can plough other fields.
5 ISMENE: But he cannot find such love again.
6 CREON: I will not have an evil wife for my son.
7 ANTIGONE: Ah, Haemon, my beloved! Dishonored by your
8 father!
9 CREON: Enough! I'll hear no more of you and your marriage!
10 No more delay. Take them within. Let them know that they
11 are women, not meant to roam abroad. For even the boldest
12 seek to fly when they see Death stretching his hand their
13 way.
14 *(As the GUARD leads ANTIGONE and ISMENE away, the blind*
15 *prophet TEIRESIAS now enters to warn CREON that the gods are*
16 *offended by his treatment of POLYNEICES and will avenge*
17 *themselves on the city.)*
18 TEIRESIAS: Princes of Thebes, it is a hard journey for me to
19 come here, for the blind must walk by another's steps and
20 see with another's eyes; yet I have come.
21 CREON: And what, Teiresias, are your tidings?
22 TEIRESIAS: I shall tell you; and listen well to the seer.
23 CREON: I have never slighted your counsel.
24 TEIRESIAS: It is that way you have steered the city well.
25 CREON: I know, and bear witness, to the worth of your words.
26 TEIRESIAS: Then mark them now: for I tell you, you stand on
27 fate's thin edge.
28 CREON: What do you mean? I shudder at your message.
29 TEIRESIAS: You will know, when you hear the signs my art has
30 disclosed. For lately, as I took my place in my ancient seat
31 of augury, where all the birds of the air gather about me, I
32 heard strange things. They were screaming with feverish
33 rage, their usual clear notes were a frightful jargon; and I
34 knew they were rending each other murderously with their
35 talons: the whir of their wings told an angry tale.

1   Straightway, these things filling me with fear, I kindled
2   fire upon an altar, with due ceremony, and laid a sacrifice
3   among the fire; but moisture came oozing out from the bones
4   and flesh trickled upon the embers, making them smoke
5   and sputter. Then the gall burst and scattered on the air,
6   and the steaming thighs lay bared of the fat that had
7   wrapped them. And I tell you, it is your deeds that have
8   brought a sickness of the state. For the altars of our city
9   and the altars of our hearths have been polluted, one and
10   all, by birds and dogs who have fed on that outraged corpse
11   that was the son of Oedipus. It is for this reason that the
12   gods refuse prayer and sacrifice at our hands, and will not
13   consume the meat-offering with flame; nor does any bird
14   give a clear sign by its shrill cry, for they have tasted the
15   fatness of a slain man's blood.

16   Think then on these things, my son. All men are liable
17   to err; but he shows wisdom and earns blessings who heals
18   the ills his errors caused, being not too stubborn; too stiff
19   a will is folly. Yield to the dead, I counsel you, and do not
20   stab the fallen; what prowess is it to slay the slain anew? I
21   have sought your welfare, it is for your good I speak; and
22   it should be a pleasant thing to hear a good counsellor when
23   he counsels for your own gain.

24 CREON: Old man, you shoot all your shafts at me! But there is
25   no need to practice your prophecies on me! Go, seek your
26   price; but you shall not buy that corpse a grave! I know that
27   no mortal can pollute the gods. So, hoary prophet, the wisest
28   come to a shameful fall when they clothe shameful counsels
29   in fair words to earn a bribe!

30 TEIRESIAS: Alas! Does no man know, does none consider?
31 CREON: What pompous precept now?
32 TEIRESIAS: That honest counsel is the most priceless gift.
33 CREON: Yes, and folly the most worthless.
34 TEIRESIAS: True, and you are infected with that disease.
35 CREON: This wise man's taunts I shall not answer in kind.

33

1   TEIRESIAS: Yet you slander me, saying I swear falsely.

2   CREON: Well, the tribe of seers always liked money.

3   TEIRESIAS: And the race of tyrants was ever proud and
4   covetous.

5   CREON: Do you know you are speaking to your king?

6   TEIRESIAS: I know it: you saved the city when you followed my
7   advice.

8   CREON: You have your gifts, but you love evil deeds.

9   TEIRESIAS: Ah, you will sting me to utter the dread secret I
10   have kept hidden in my soul.

11   CREON: Out with it! But if you hope to earn a fee by shaking my
12   purpose, you babble in vain.

13   TEIRESIAS: Indeed I think I shall earn no reward from you.

14   CREON: Be sure you shall not trade on my resolve.

15   TEIRESIAS: Know then — aye, know it well! — you will not
16   live through many days, seeing the sun's swift chariot
17   sweeping heaven, 'til one whose blood comes from your own
18   heart shall be a corpse, matching two other corpses; because
19   you have given to the shadows one who belongs to the sun,
20   you have lodged a living soul in the grave; yet in this world
21   you detain one who belongs to the world below, a corpse
22   unburied, unhonored and unblest. These things outrage the
23   gods; therefore the furies of the gods lie now in wait for
24   you, preparing a vengeance equal to your guilt.

25   And mark well if I speak these things as a hireling. A
26   time not long delayed will waken the wailing of men and
27   women in your house. But after these cries I hear a more
28   dreadful tumult. For wrath and hatred will stir to arms
29   against you every city whose mangled sons had the burial-
30   rite from dogs and wild beasts, or from birds that will bear
31   the taint of this crime even to the startled hearths of the
32   unburied dead.

33   Such arrows I do indeed aim at your heart, since you
34   provoked me — they will find their mark, and you shall not
35   escape the sting. Lead me home, that he may spend his rage

1   on younger men, or learn to curb his bitter tongue and
2   temper his violent mind.
3
4
5
6
7
8
9
10
11
12
13
14
15
16
17
18
19
20
21
22
23
24
25
26
27
28
29
30
31
32
33
34
35

from **Oedipus the King** (425 B.C.)

Sophocles

The classical legend of Oedipus first appears in Greek literature as early as the writings of Homer (700 B.C.), author of the *Iliad* and the *Odyssey*. It would have also been well known to the Athenians of Sophocles's time from popular poems and short stories of the historical period. The playscript *Oedipus the King* is generally regarded as the finest of all Greek tragedies that detail the role that "fate" plays shaping human destiny. Fix the legend in your mind before you play the following scenes related to Oedipus and Creon.

In terms of plot and action, the Oedipus legend prophesied that Laios and Iocaste, king and queen of Thebes, would give birth to a child who would grow up to murder his father and marry his mother. Fearing this dreadful prophecy, the parents nailed their first son's feet together — hence the name Oedipus, which means "swollen-foot" — and left him to die on a lonely mountainside outside the city. However, he was found by a wandering shepherd who took the baby to the nearby city of Corinth. There he was adopted by the childless King Polybos and Queen Merope, who then raised him as a prince of the royal household. He never knew they were not his real parents.

When he was a young adult, Oedipus first heard the prophecy. Assuming that this applied to Polybos and Merope, the only parents Oedipus had ever known, he fled Corinth and wandered around Greece for almost 20 years. During his wandering he met a group of travelers and killed an old man who, unknown to him, was his *real* father, King Laios. Later, Oedipus arrived at Thebes and met the Sphinx, a monster who guarded the gates of the city. When Oedipus correctly answered the riddle asked by the Sphinx, he was rewarded with the title of King of Thebes and was given the hand of the recently widowed queen, Iocaste. Needless to say, no one knew that she was his real mother. They had four children — Antigone, Ismene, Eteocles and Polyneices — and enjoyed considerable wealth and prosperity for some time.

As the playscript *Oedipus the King* begins, however, a mysterious plague is sweeping the city. The sacred oracles have foretold that the plague can only be relieved by the discovery of the murderer of old King Laios. Oedipus — proud, impetuous man that he has become — is quick-tempered and frequently acts impulsively or violently in his desperate search to reveal the murderer. His passion for the truth and high moral standards leads him on a fatal journey for

A first principle of performance style in classical theatre was that all roles were assumed by men, including great female characters like Medea and Antigone. While men playing women was "artistically" truthful for the ancient Greeks, contemporary theatre practice enriches the image of female characters in Greek tragedy by casting women in female roles. (From the Western Michigan University production of Medea.*)*

the resolution of the problem and leads him inevitably to himself as the murderer of his own father.

When playing the classical scenes that follow, the actor should suggest Oedipus as a forceful, powerful ruler who begins the scene in absolute control of the situation and in control of Creon. As the scene progresses, however, the power and pride of Oedipus should begin to falter and the strength of Creon should begin to emerge. The character of Oedipus is not given a great deal of physical action in either of the scenes so it is important to suggest noble posture, authority in stance and heroic attitude early in the performance so that the later portrayal — after Oedipus discovers the truth of his actions — gradually presents him in a more human, compassionate mood.

CAST

OEDIPUS
CREON

SCENE

Thebes, before the royal palace.

APPROACH

The scene opens when Creon enters to address the audience and to plead his innocence after Oedipus had earlier accused him and the prophet Teiresias of conspiring to seize power. Tension builds when Oedipus himself enters the scene and attacks the character and the reputation of his brother-in-law. Creon responds in anger mingled with fear as Oedipus behaves in a forceful, tyrannical manner and demands that his brother-in-law pay for this treason with his life. Creon remains calm throughout these later outbursts and allows his own self-control to highlight the irrational, rash attitude of Oedipus.

1   OEDIPUS: What, *you*? You are come here? How can you find
2   The impudence to show yourself before
3   My house, when you are clearly proven
4   To have sought my life and tried to steal my crown?
5   Why, do you think me then a coward, or
6   A fool, that you should try to lay this plot?
7   Or that I should not see what you were scheming,
8   And so fall unresisting, blindly, to you?
9   But you were mad, so to attempt the throne,
10   Poor and unaided; this is not encompassed
11   Without the strong support of friends and money!
12   CREON: This is what you must do: now you have had your say
13   Hear my reply; then yourself shall judge.
14   OEDIPUS: A ready tongue! But I am bad at listening —
15   To you. For I have found how much you hate me.
16   CREON: One thing: first listen to what I have to say.
17   OEDIPUS: One thing: do not pretend you're not a villain.
18   CREON: If you believe it is a thing worth having,
19   Insensate stubbornness, then you are wrong.
20   OEDIPUS: If you believe that one can harm a kinsman
21   Without retaliation, you are wrong.
22   CREON: With this I have no quarrel; but explain
23   What injury you say that I have done you.
24   OEDIPUS: Did you advise, or did you not, that I
25   Should send a man for that most reverend prophet?
26   CREON: I did, and I am still of that advice.
27   OEDIPUS: How long a time is it since Laios ...
28   CREON: Since Laios did *what*? How can I say?
29   OEDIPUS: Was seen no more, but met a violent death?
30   CREON: It would be many years now past and gone.
31   OEDIPUS: And had this prophet learned his art already?
32   CREON: Yes, his repute was great — as it is now.
33   OEDIPUS: Did he make any mention then of me?
34   CREON: He never spoke of you within my hearing.
35   OEDIPUS: Touching the murder: did you make no search?

1   CREON: No search? Of course we did; but we found nothing.

2   OEDIPUS: And why did this wise prophet not speak *then*?

3   CREON: Who knows? Where I know nothing I say nothing.

4   OEDIPUS: This much you do know — and you'll do well to
5   answer.

6   CREON: What is it? If I know, I'll tell you freely.

7   OEDIPUS: That if he had not joined with you, he'd not
8   Have said that I was Laios' murderer.

9   CREON: If he said this, I did not know. But I
10   May rightly question you, as you have me.

11   OEDIPUS: Ask what you will. You'll never prove *I* killed him.

12   CREON: Why then: are you not married to my sister?

13   OEDIPUS: I am indeed; it cannot be denied.

14   CREON: You share with her the sovereignty of Thebes?

15   OEDIPUS: She need but ask, and anything is hers.

16   CREON: And am I not myself conjoined with you?

17   OEDIPUS: You are; not rebel therefore, but a traitor!

18   CREON: Not so, if you will reason with yourself,
19   As I with you. This first: would any man
20   To gain no increase of authority,
21   Choose kingship, with its fears and sleepless nights?
22   Not I. What I desire, what every man
23   Desires, if he has wisdom, is to take
24   The substance, not the show, of royalty.
25   For now, through you, I have both power and ease,
26   But were I King, I'd be oppressed with cares.
27   Not so: while I have ample sovereignty
28   And rule in peace, why should I want the crown?
29   I am not yet so mad as to give up
30   All that which brings me honor and advantage.
31   Now, every man greets me, and I greet him;
32   Those who have need of you make much of me,
33   Since I can make or mar them. Why should I
34   Surrender this to load myself with that?
35   A man of sense was never yet a traitor;

1	I have no taste for that, nor could I force
2	Myself to aid another's treachery.
3	But you can test me: go to Delphi; ask
4	If I reported rightly what was said.
5	And further: if you find that I had dealings
6	With that diviner, you may take and kill me
7	Not with your single vote, but yours and mine,
8	But not on bare suspicion, unsupported.
9	How wrong it is, to use a random judgment
10	And think the false man true, the true man false!
11	To spurn a loyal friend, that is no better
12	Than to destroy the life to which we cling.
13	This you will learn in time, for Time alone
14	Reveals the upright man; a single day
15	Suffices to unmask the treacherous.
16	OEDIPUS: When an enemy is quick to plot
17	And strike, I must be quick in answer.
18	If I am slow, and wait, I shall find
19	That you have gained your end, and I am lost.
20	CREON: What do you wish? To drive me into exile?
21	OEDIPUS: No, more than exile: I will have your life.
22	CREON: When will it cease, this monstrous rage of yours?
23	OEDIPUS: When your example shows what comes of envy?
24	CREON: Must you be stubborn? Cannot you believe me?
25	OEDIPUS: You speak to me as if I were a fool!
26	CREON: Because I know you are wrong.
27	OEDIPUS: Right, for myself!
28	CREON: It is not right for me!
29	OEDIPUS: But you are a traitor!
30	CREON: What if your charge is false?
31	OEDIPUS: I have to govern.
32	CREON: Not govern badly!
33	OEDIPUS: Listen to him, Thebes!
34	CREON: You're not the city! I am Theban too!
35	If I am guilty in a single point

41

1   Of such crimes you accuse me,

2   Then may I die accursed.

3   OEDIPUS: O, let me be! Get from my sight.

4   CREON: I go,

5   Misjudged by you — but not by the people,

6   Who will judge me better.

7   *(Following the exit of CREON, the playscript moves swiftly to its*

8   *tragic conclusion. All of the traditional classical legend of OEDIPUS*

9   *and the oracles' prophecies are unveiled with the appearance of the*

10   *SHEPHERD, who reveals the true origin of OEDIPUS' birth. With*

11   *a final cry of recognition and despair both IOCASTE and OEDIPUS*

12   *exit. A MESSENGER then enters to inform that the queen has killed*

13   *herself in her bedroom and that OEDIPUS has blinded himself with*

14   *the golden pins from his mother's gown.)*

15   *(This final scene presents OEDIPUS as a changed, humble man.*

16   *In stark contrast to the first episode between CREON and OEDIPUS,*

17   *we now see the terrifying sight of the once proud and noble king*

18   *staggering forth with blood still dripping from his face as he leans*

19   *heavily upon a wooden staff for support. It is a moment of irony*

20   *when OEDIPUS learns that CREON, who has returned to be the*

21   *new ruler of the city, is to be the one who judges his punishment*

22   *because he is the only one of the royal household left to protect the*

23   *city now that IOCASTE is dead and OEDIPUS is disgraced.)*

24   OEDIPUS: Alas! Alas! How can I speak to him?

25   What word of credit find? In all my commerce

26   With him aforetime I am proved false.

27   CREON: No exultation, Oedipus, and no reproach

28   Of injuries inflicted brings me here;

29   But if the face of men moves not your shame,

30   Then reverence show to that all-nurturing fire,

31   The holy Sun, that he be not polluted

32   By such accursed sight, which neither Earth

33   Nor rain from Heaven nor sunlight can endure.

34   Take him within, and quickly: it is right

35   His kinsmen only should behold and hear

1   Evils that chiefly on his kinsmen fall.

2   OEDIPUS: Drive me at once beyond your bounds, where I

3   Shall be alone, and no one speak to me,

4   CREON: I would have done it; but I first desired

5   To ask the gods what they would have me do.

6   OEDIPUS: No, their command was already given in full; to slay

7   Me, the polluter and the parricide.

8   CREON: Those were the words; but in our present need

9   It would be wise to ask what we should do.

10   OEDIPUS: You will inquire for such a wretch as I?

11   CREON: I will; for now *you* may even believe the gods.

12   OEDIPUS: Yes; and on you I lay this charge and duty:

13   Give burial, as you will, to her who lies

14   Within — for she is yours, and this is proper;

15   And, while I live, let not my father's city

16   Endure to have me as a citizen.

17   My home must be the mountains — on Cithacron —

18   Which, while they lived, my parents chose to be my tomb.

19   They wished to slay me; now they shall.

20   For this I know: sickness can never kill me,

21   Nor any other evil; I was not saved

22   That day from death, except for some strange doom.

23   My fate must take the course it will.

24   Now, for my sons,

25   Be not concerned for them: they can, being men,

26   Fend for themselves, wherever they may be.

27   But for my unhappy daughters, my two girls,

28   Whose chairs were always set beside my own

29   At table — they who shared in every dish

30   That was prepared for me — O, Creon!

31   These do I commend to you! And grant me this:

32   To take them in my arms, and weep for them.

33   My lord! most noble Creon! could I now

34   But hold them in my arms, then I should

35   I had them

1	As I had them when I could see them.
2	Ah! What is this?
3	O, Heaven! do I hear my dear ones sobbing?
4	Has Creon, in his pity, sent to me
5	My darling children? Has he? Is it true?
6	CREON: It is; they have always been your delight;
7	So, knowing this, I had them brought to you.
8	OEDIPUS: Then Heaven reward you, and for this kind service
9	Protect you better than it protected me!
10	Where are you, children? Where? O, come to me!
11	Come, let me clasp you with a brother's arms,
12	These hands, which helped your father's eyes, once more
13	bright,
14	To look upon you as they see you now —
15	Your father who, not seeing, nor inquiring,
16	Gave you for mother her who bore himself.
17	See you I cannot; but I weep for you,
18	For the unhappiness that must be yours,
19	And for the bitter life that you must lead.
20	What gathering of the citizens, what festivals,
21	Will you have part in? Your high celebrations
22	Will be to go back home, and sit in tears.
23	And when the time for marriage comes, what man will stake
24	Upon the ruin and the shame
25	That *I* am to my parents and to you?
26	Nothing is wanting there: your father slew
27	His father, married her who gave him birth,
28	And then, from that same source whence he himself
29	Had sprung, got you! With these things they will taunt you;
30	And who will then take you in marriage?
31	Nobody! But you must waste, unwedded and unfruitful.
32	O, Creon! Since they have no parent now
33	But you — for both of us who gave them life
34	Have perished — suffer them not to be cast out
35	Homeless and beggars; for they are your kin.

1   Have pity on them, for they are so young,

2   So desolate, except for you alone.

3   Say "Yes," good Creon! Let your hand confirm it.

4   And now, my children, for my exhortation

5   You are too young; but you can pray that I

6   May live henceforward — where I should.

7   And you more happily than the father who begot you.

8 CREON: Now make an end of tears, and go within.

9 OEDIPUS: Then I must go — against my will.

10 CREON: There is a time for everything.

11 OEDIPUS: You know what I would have you do?

12 CREON: If you will tell me, I shall know.

13 OEDIPUS: Send me away, away from Thebes.

14 CREON: The gods, not I, must grant you this.

15 OEDIPUS: The gods hate no man more than me!

16 CREON: Then what you ask they will soon give.

17 OEDIPUS: You promise this?

18 CREON: Ah, no! When I am ignorant, I do not speak.

19 OEDIPUS: Then lead me in; I say no more.

20 CREON: Release the children then, and come inside.

21 OEDIPUS: What? Take these children from me? no!

22 CREON: Seek not to have your way in all things:

23   Where you had your way before,

24   Your mastery broke before the end.

25

26

27

28

29

30

31

32

33

34

35

SELECTED BIBLIOGRAPHY

The following textbooks and suggested readings are recommended for the beginning actor who may wish to become acquainted with the historical period and style related to the classical performance of scenes. The suggested readings also provide meaningful information on practical approaches to explore scene study as well as playscript interpretation. A serious application of the theories and the selected exercises presented in these recommended sources should provide a solid foundation for approaching more difficult and complex scene performance in the chapters that follow.

Allen, James. *Greek Acting in the Fifth Century.* Berkeley, California: University of California Press, 1916.

Arnott, Peter. *The Ancient Greek and Roman Theatre.* New York: Random House, 1971.

Barton, Robert. *Style for Actors.* Mountain View, California: Mayfield Publishing Company, 1988.

Benedetti, Robert. *The Actor at Work.* 3rd edition. Englewood Cliffs, New Jersey: Prentice-Hall, 1981.

Bennett, Susan. *Theatre Audiences: A Theory of Production and Reception.* London: Routledge Press, 1990.

Berry, Cicely. *Voice and the Actor.* New York: Macmillan and Company, 1973.

Brockett, Oscar. *History of the Theatre.* 6th edition. Boston: Allyn and Bacon, 1987.

Colyer, Carlton. *The Art of Acting.* Colorado Springs: Meriwether Publishing, 1989.

Deardon, C. W. *The Stage of Aristophanes.* London: Athlone Press, 1976.

Glenn, Stanley. *The Complete Actor.* Boston: Allyn and Bacon, 1977.

Goldman, Michael. *The Actor's Freedom.* New York: Viking Press, 1975.

Hagen, Uta. *Respect for Acting.* New York: Macmillan and Company, 1973.

Hamilton, Edith. *The Greek Way.* New York: Norton, 1983.

Harriott, Rosemary. *Aristophanes: Poet and Dramatist.* Baltimore: Johns Hopkins University Press, 1986.

Harrop, John and Sabin Epstein. *Acting With Style.* Englewood Cliffs,

New Jersey: Prentice-Hall, 1982.

Hunter, R. L. *The New Comedy of Greece and Rome.* New York: Twayne Publishers, 1985.

Kahan, Stanley. *Introduction to Acting.* 2nd edition. Boston: Allyn and Bacon, 1985.

Kurtz, Paul. *Playing: An Introduction to Acting.* Boston: Allyn and Bacon, 1985.

McGaw, Charles. *Working a Scene: An Actor's Approach.* New York: Holt, Rinehart and Wilson, 1977.

Pisk, Litz. *The Actor and His Body.* New York: Theatre Arts Books, 1975.

Taplin, Oliver. *Greek Tragedy in Action.* Berkeley, California: University of California Press, 1978.

Winnington-Ingram, R. P. *Sophocles: An Interpretation.* New York: Cambridge University Press, 1980.

CHAPTER TWO

PLAYING
SHAKESPEAREAN SCENES

"To thine own self be true,
And it must follow as the night the day,
Thou canst not then be false to any man."

— Shakespeare, *Hamlet*

The actor's basic approach to playing Shakespearean scenes is more clearly different than that suggested for playing classical scenes. As a general performance rule, Shakespearean acting makes its greatest demands on the emotional and the physical resources of the actor. In contrast to the classical period, the Elizabethan period of Shakespeare included dramatic efforts to paint upon a broad canvas and to promote active audience participation.

Shakespeare's comic and dramatic characters are three dimensional portraits of men and women in action, driven by forces that at once compel and corrupt them. Yet despite the enormous range of complex characterization found in the playscripts, Shakespeare appears to treat his creations sympathetically as flesh-and-blood individuals who are human beings rather than mere shadows or stage figures. Typically, these characters arouse heightened emotional associations and provoke physical outbursts that create memorable stage portraits of men and women in heroic quests to resolve ancient wounds or to avenge current wrongs.

In his own historical time, it is believed that Shakespeare's playscripts were performed in the "presentational," or full-front and audience centered, style and that very little effort was made by the actors to suggest an illusion of reality. It should be noted, however, that while the actors may have been conscious that their performance was primarily directed *toward* the audience there is also ample historical evidence to suggest that there was an evident attempt made to suggest "believable" actions and attitudes in performance. Perhaps that is the suggestion Shakespeare had in mind in his advice to the actors in Hamlet's now famous Players' speech:

"Speak the speech, I pray you, as I pronounc'd it to you, trippingly on the tongue; but if you mouth it, as

many of our players do, I had as lief the town crier spoke my lines. Nor do not saw the air too much with your hand, thus, but use all gently; for in the very torrent, tempest, and, as I may say, whirlwind of your passion, you must acquire and beget a temperance that may give it smoothness.

* * *

Be not too tame neither, but let your own discretion be your tutor. Suit the action to the word, the word to the action; with this special observance, that you o'erstep not the modesty of nature; for anything so o'erdone is from the purpose of playing, whose end, both at the first and now, was and is to hold, as 'twere, the mirror up to nature; to show virtue her own feature, scorn her own image, and the very age and body of the time his form and pressure."

(Hamlet, III, ii)

Actor training for the typical Shakespearean performer was evidently extremely thorough and included music training, dancing, fencing, stage combat and wrestling. Because the playscripts were generally performed in outdoor theatres like Shakespeare's *Globe,* the actor would have needed to cultivate a resonant, well-projected voice that would be capable of not only being heard in a noisy playhouse that encouraged audience participation but also capable of giving subtle expression and nuance to the poetic dialog of the characters.

The Shakespearean actor, then, appears to have been an intelligent, well-rounded performer trained in physicalization and vocalization to express with some detail and accuracy the deep emotion and complex motivation of Shakespeare's characters. The Shakespearean actor was also a highly flexible and agile performer, capable of playing both comic and tragic roles as well as female roles. The ability to portray women in a believable and honest character portrait is also strong testimony to the Shakespearean actor's versatility and sensitivity. That same performance approach of versatility and sensitivity should also hold true for the contemporary actor of Shakespearean scenes.

Playing the Role

The actor who engages in Shakespearean scene study and play-script interpretation should begin by cultivating the basic principles of dramatic visualization. The dramatic visualization of a playscript, like the musical interpretation of a printed score, depends upon the actor's creative ability to envision a performance based solely upon words or actions. Since there are very few suggested stage directions in the playscripts of Shakespeare, the fullest and most rewarding understanding of a potential performance of a scene will be determined by the actor's ability to grasp the inherent performance principles implied in the playscript and to then translate them into an imaginative and yet critical perception of the character being portrayed.

It is important to approach each Shakespearean scene not as an historic relic but, rather, as an exciting flesh-and-blood episode that dramatizes a significant moment in the life of the character being portrayed. That is why the actor of Shakespearean scenes should be aware of the playwright's description of "character" and of the "action" of the character from the first entrance to the last exit of the scene.

Character is revealed by the physical qualities, the dialog and the action of the person being represented by the actor in the selected scene. A detailed evaluation of character may help the actor to discover both the human nature and the motivation that leads the character to perform specific actions. To be credible and convincing in Shakespearean scenes, the actor must study human behavior carefully to present the outward appearance of the character as accurately as it has been suggested by the lines of dialog that describe the character.

Actions of a character help to mirror and reflect individual thoughts and attitudes and help the actor to understand why a character speaks or responds in a particular manner at a particular moment. A detailed evaluation of a character's actions may help the actor understand the nuances of meaning suggested in the dialog and may also help to transmit the inner feelings of the character being portrayed. When the actor understands the actions he better understands the character and the dramatic or comic situation of the playscript.

The staged theatricality the actor must imagine in an initial reading of the Shakespearean scene should also include careful attention to implied notations for movement, relationship between charac-

51

ters, vocal characteristics suggested for individual speakers and the scene's building to a climax as it is structured through the actions of the characters. The demands made in an initial reading of the scene also call for an attentive attitude to potential performance accessories such as costumes, props or make-up that may help to add dimension to the character portrait. As the beginning actor's skills in playscript interpretation and scene study in Shakespearean comedy and tragedy become more critical and creative, it should become easier to visualize from an initial reading such performance approaches as the vocal tone of the "dour speech" by Jacques in *As You Like It*; the physical portrayal of the "lean-faced, hollow-eyed" Pinch in *The Comedy of Errors*; the character attitude of the "too wild, too rude," Gratiano in *The Merchant of Venice*; or the mental disposition of the "unbridled, too headstrong" Cressida in *Troilus and Cressida*.

Like the actor of classical scenes, the actor of Shakespearean scenes should cultivate a wide range of experience and personal example from which to draw in etching sensitive, complex character portraits that suggest the historical period. The actor is asked to translate the given facts available regarding the performance style of the period — including the vocal and physical demands of the scene — into a faithful, authentic suggestion of the traits and mannerisms of the characters depicted in the selected scene. It is equally important to also set aside a time for vocal and physical warm-ups that will prepare the actor for the physical demands of the selected scenes that follow, and to repeat the basic exercises included until a level of vocal and physical competence is achieved before moving to the performance of the scenes.

This scene study sourcebook recognizes the actor's limitations in terms of time available for rehearsal, and offers for consideration performance guidelines and character expectations that may be of value in the performance of the selected scene. The guidelines give the background narrative necessary to interpret the scene with confidence. The scene study sourcebook is also arranged so that the initial preparation and rehearsal periods lead naturally and easily to an investigation of the next scene in sequence. This blueprint for performance provides a series of "building blocks" with which the actor of Shakespearean scenes can construct an inspired performance. In addition, the selected scenes are of such inherent diversity in range of style and performance expectation that it is quite possible to test one's emerging acting technique by testing its economy and efficiency in realizing the objectives spelled out as a prelude to each scene.

Playing the Style

The Shakespearean style in performance appears to have reflected the historical times in which the drama flourished. Initially, the Elizabethan actor began as a rogue or vagabond performer who presented interludes or comic skits in town squares or small meeting halls, but by the end of the 16th century most actors were professional or under the patronage of royalty. Although the history of individual acting troupes is difficult to follow because the calamitous plagues that harried England throughout the Elizabethan period disrupted record-keeping, enough is known of Shakespeare's company — the King's Men — to suggest the playing style of the period.

A study of the typical Elizabethan playhouse reveals how flexible the stage had to be to accommodate the many changes of scenes demanded in each playscript. In most of Shakespeare's comedies and tragedies there are no indications of acts and scenes so when the actor left one locale that scene was ended and a new setting had to be imagined in another locale located in a separate playing area on the stage. This "transition" approach to staging — much like modern film making — promoted simultaneous action on a number of levels of the theatre playhouse and required that the actors be athletic and agile in their movement and in their physicalization.

The *Globe*, Shakespeare's playhouse, is thought to have held no more than 3,000 spectators and the audience to have been both varied and volatile. In the "gentlemen's room," or gallery, were titled lords and their ladies while in the "pit," a flat area between gallery walls, were the tradesmen, apprentices and servants. These "groundlings," who stood surrounding the stage throughout a production, were frequently rowdy and often punctuated their critical views of an individual performance with apple-eating, nut-cracking or beer-drinking that apparently went on throughout the afternoon. But the high quality of Shakespeare's poetic genius also suggests that the Elizabethan audience had sensibility and native intelligence even though few could read or write because they appear to have been attentive and to have had sharp ears that grasp the complex ideas being presented on the stage.

Most scholars agree that the historical style of performance was more natural than the classical period, and that it must have been both spirited and inspired to hold the interest of the audience for more than two hours without an intermission. Gesture and movement must also have played a major role in characterization if we are to

The typical Elizabethan playhouse reveals a flexible stage with a number of playing areas. Shakespeare's Globe Theatre *is thought to have included a gallery, a "pit" for standing and a limited number of boxes for dignitaries.*

believe the warning of the actor and playwright Thomas Heywood, who urged his fellow performers "not to use any impudent or forced motion in any part of the body, no rough or other violent gesture; nor on the contrary to stand like a stiff starched man." There is also a suggestion that the long, intricate speeches or soliloquies would have had to incorporate meaningful vocal variety and inflection to have been understood by the multitudes.

There are also persuasive arguments in favor of the Shakespearean style being more "subtle" and "intimate" than the classical period. The *Globe* playhouse could be dropped into the auditorium of almost any contemporary theatre and not touch the stage if we are to believe the modern "reconstruction" theories of the leading theatre scholars C. Walter Hodges and John Cranford Adams. The intimacy suggested by the smaller playhouse would have reduced the need for Shakespearean actors to "project" their voices in order to be understood and would have promoted a more natural approach to conversational dialog. This suggestion is inherent in Hamlet's famous advice in the Players' speech and reinforces modern interpretations that professional acting companies with popular actors were *not* oratorical in their vocal presentation during the later Elizabethan period.

The need for an expressive, athletic physical body in the acting of Shakespearean scenes is suggested by the rather "heroic" nature of the characters who appear in the playscripts. The frequent references to the "stature" and the "nature" of the heroes who engage in mortal combat suggest a performer supple in body and agile in movement. Such an imposing figure in such close proximity to the audience would also need to appear human and believable rather than exaggerated and distorted as the ancient Greek actors must have appeared up close in their stylized masks and elevated, thick-soled boots.

A very curious feature of Elizabethan acting, however, was the skill and popularity of the "boy-player." Although women's roles were also played by young men in the classical period, the "boy-player" performer in Shakespeare's period does seem to have enjoyed an unprecedented adulation. There does not appear to have been any attempt at "impersonation" by these youthful Juliets but, rather, a simple and honest portrait that relied upon the basic appeal to emotion and beauty than to vocal or physical disguise. The universal appeal of the best known of the "boy-actors" may perhaps be most apparent if we are able to judge the following epitaph that the poet and playwright Ben Jonson penned for Salathiel Pavy when he died at the age of thirteen.

> 'Twas a child that so did thrive
> > In grace and feature,
> As heaven and nature seemed to strive
> > Which owned the creature.

It is most likely that young boys playing young girl characters was *aesthetically* pleasing for the Elizabethans and helped to reinforce their own historical views of beauty and innocence. It is also just as likely that the more diverse, complex mature female roles in Shakespeare's playscripts were reserved for the more experienced, sensitive male performers in the company and that their basic approach to performance style would have been similar to that technique they might have applied to playing a male character. Such a performance approach would have avoided excessive exaggeration and oratorical word play and relied more heavily upon simplicity and economy of style to suggest the illusion of truthfulness and honesty in character portrayal.

Playing the Performance

To communicate the basic Shakespearean style in playing the performance, "fine speaking" is the most crucial element to explore in the interpretation of the character. It is important, therefore, for the actor of Shakespearean scenes to read verse well and to give full expression to the beauty and the rhythm of individual lines of poetry that constitute Shakespeare's dialog. Individual readings should be robust and have a clarity that exhibits the nobility and grandeur of the blank verse familiar to the historical period.

The textual "clues" to playing the performance are to be found in the words and sentences of Shakespeare's dialog and these internal, poetic directions are the "score" that helps to orchestrate the development of the characters in a selected scene. That is why it is important to analyze each unit of a character's speech to determine the images, metaphors, vocal sounds, stresses or repetitions that comprise the dialog. When not written in prose, most of Shakespeare's playscripts are written in "unrhyming verse" that is occasionally punctuated with "end rhyme" or "couplets."

This "blank verse" pattern of dialog is vocally precise in its own rhythmical pattern of meter: there are five *unstressed* short sounds that are juxtaposed by five *stressed* or long sounds. This alternating pattern of short and long sounds then total ten "beats." The stress in emphasis is always placed on the second sound (/) and each line ending concludes in a strong stress regardless of punctuation. The unstressed (X) sounds then serve to counterbalance or counterpoint the long sounds. A sample of this vocal scene would include the following chart from Hamlet's well-known soliloquy.

To	be	or	not	to	be,	that	is	the	question
X	/	X	/	X	/	/	X	X	/ X

Blank verse appears to give the actor's speech a musicality that appears much more "natural" than the exaggerated oratorical approach to reading or speaking "poetry" aloud. When combined with the playwright's punctuation in the dialog, blank verse also promotes the actor's individual choice of the "stress" or the vocal "color" that might be given specific words or phrases. By charting individual lines of blank verse dialog the beginning actor in Shakespearean scenes may also discover a convenient performance technique for remembering long set speeches or soliloquies by determining repetitious rhythms as they appear in a character's speech.

Like the actor of classical scenes, the actor of Shakespearean scenes should engage in detailed observation and analysis of the character being portrayed in the selected scene as reflected in the mannerisms, gestures and movements which are inherent in the narrative of stage directions or explicit in the dialog. The "clues" provided in this analysis may help to indicate a character's shifting mood or attitude and provide creative interpretation approaches to accurately visualize the character for the audience. It is especially important that the mannerisms, gestures and movements in playing Shakespearean scenes appear fluid, spontaneous and graceful to suggest the dignified and heroic nature of the characters as they seek their fortunes and accept their fates.

In playing the performance the actor should not be afraid to be "inventive," and to strike a happy medium between investigation and imagination in drawing three-dimensional character portraits. The successful portrait, of course, will include a spirited interpretation that avoids the cliché, trite approaches to playing Shakespearean scenes as if they were poetry recitations that needed to be "declaimed" in an elocutionary delivery with stilted gestures used to punctuate the action being described. This is sound advice, indeed, not only for playing Shakespearean scenes but also for playing the selected "period" playscripts that follow in the next chapter.

Shakespearean Exercises

One of the special features of this scene study book is the use of exercises to prepare the performer for the selected scenes that follow each period of discussion. One of the primary tools in performance for the actor in Shakespearean scenes is an expressive, "fine speaking" voice that helps to convey the mood and the attitude of the character being portrayed. The following vocal and physical exercises are presented as a performance blueprint to assist the actor in suggesting the natural and simple style needed for Shakespearean characterization. The exercises should be repeated a number of times to clarify the performance "clues" suggested and to promote a well-disciplined approach to the rehearsal period for scene study.

SPEAK THE SPEECH, I PRAY YOU!

An important element in the pronunciation of speech sounds in playing Shakespearean scenes is *phonation*, or vibration of the vocal folds to produce the tone of your voice. The primary vocal instrument responsible for phonation is the larynx, or voice box. In ordinary breathing, the muscles that stretch across the voice box from front to back remain in a relaxed position so that air may pass through them without causing any vibration. In a performance situation, however, the two bands tighten and the air from the lungs must be forced through them. When this air strikes the vocal bands it sets them vibrating, and the result is sound waves that help to amplify and to give variation to the pitch.

The fundamental pitch of an actor's voice, therefore, may be accurately measured by the rate of vibrations of the vocal bands; and the sound of the voice may vary according to the position and degree of tenseness or relaxation of the vocal folds. The quality of voice may also be influenced by the capacity of the vocal bands to respond to these vibrations in a frequency best suited to utilize the vocal resonators, the air chambers in the head and throat that help to amplify and to enrich sound.

Unfortunately, the actor can make little adjustment in the role that the voice box plays in voice production. That is because the muscles that move the vocal bands are not subject to conscious control. They are controlled only as a group, and then only indirectly, as the throat is "open" and free for the emission of sound. Hence, desired changes in pitch should be approached more as exercises in ear training and unconscious positioning of the bands than as vocal cord training.

There are, however, some basic principles involved in relaxing the throat and neck to achieve greater flexibility in pitch and tone quality. Knowing that the sound of your voice will vary according to the position and the degree of tenseness or relaxation of the vocal cords, slowly drop your head forward and allow your lower jaw to sag. Yawn several times as your head gently sways from left to right and from right to left. Now slowly repeat this part of the exercise *three* times.

Now allow your head to return to its normal full-front position, and slowly sound each of the vowels — *a, e, i, o* and *u.* Breathe quietly, using a soft and subdued tone. Repeat the vowel sounds *ten* times, prolonging each individual sound for four or five seconds. Repeat the vowel sounds *ten* more times, using a slightly louder tone. Repeat them ten more times, using a slightly softer tone.

Continue the exercise by repeating the vowel sounds *ten* more times using a lower pitch, then another lower pitch and then a still lower pitch until you are now producing the lowest pitch possible without strain. Repeat the vowel sounds *ten* more times using a higher pitch, then another higher pitch and then a still higher pitch until you are producing the highest pitch possible without strain. RELAX! You are well on your way to "freeing" your natural voice and achieving the pitch variety and tone quality needed for flexibility in playing Shakespearean scenes. You are also just now learning to reduce the amount of tension and anxiety that usually accompanies initial performances. You may wish to conclude the exercise by using what you have learned about your individual pitch range and vocal quality as you practice "fine speaking" using Hamlet's now famous advice to the Players.

> **Speak the speech, I pray you, as I pronounced it to you, trippingly on the tongue; but if you mouth it, as many of our players do, I had as lief the town crier spoke my lines. Nor do not saw the air too much with your hand, thus; but use all gently, for in the very torrent, tempest, and (as I may say) whirlwind of your passion, you must acquire and beget a temperance that may give it smoothness.**

BODY COUNT!

Graceful and fluid coordination of all parts of the body is especially essential for expressive movement in playing Shakespearean scenes. A basic approach to follow in cultivating such movement is to hold your body erect with chest high, chin up, back flat and arms and legs straight. When you have developed this primary stance for good performance posture, it should be possible for you to suggest alert, energetic and natural movement in performance.

Once you have achieved a "posture portrait" that is natural and comfortable, you should concentrate on developing all parts of your body to express changing ideas or emotions. One way to enhance your posture portrait — and also suggest fluid bodily coordination — is to "count" with the body. Start the exercise by standing in a natural, erect position in a large open space. Begin to count in the air from *one* to *ten*, using only the fingers of your right hand. Repeat the count using both the fingers and the wrist of the right hand. Repeat the count using both the fingers and the wrist of the right hand as well as right shoulder. Next repeat the exercise using the left hand, wrist and shoulder.

Begin to count now from *one* to *ten* with the left leg. Stand on your right foot with the left leg elevated slightly, and make your counting as specific as possible. Repeat the count using the left ankle and toes. Conclude the exercise by counting from *one* to *ten* with the right leg, right ankle and toes. When you are comfortable that the individual parts of your body are "counting" in a graceful and fluid manner proceed to the next part of the exercise.

Now count from *one* to *ten* using the entire body. Count with your head, chest, waist and arms. Involve as many separate parts of your body as possible in the count and strive for graceful posture. Conclude the exercise by using your entire body to spell out the ideas, moods and attitudes suggested in the following selection from Shakespeare's *Romeo and Juliet*. Try to make your gestures and movements precise as well as motivated in suggesting mood and attitude. Any movement that you incorporate should also be graceful and fluid, and your body should be relaxed and natural. You may wish to accompany yourself in this silent expression of the passage by playing a tape or a record of the film music used by the director Franco Zeffirelli in his production of this tragic playscript.

O, then I see Queen Mab hath been with you.
She is the fairies' midwife, and she comes
In shape no bigger than an agate stone
On the forefinger of an alderman,
Drawn with a team of little atomi
Over men's noses as they lie asleep;
Her wagon spokes made of long spinners' legs.
The cover of the wings of grasshoppers,
Her traces of the smallest spider web,
Her collars of the moonshine's watery beams,
Her whip of cricket's bone, the lash of film,

Her wagoner a small grey-coated gnat
Not half so big as a round little worm
Pricked from the lazy finger of a maid;
Her chariot is an empty hazel nut,
Made by the joiner squirrel or old grub,
Time out o' mind the fairies' coachmakers.

Extend the exercise to include a vocal interpretation of the following passage as well. Try to incorporate the textual "clues" that suggest the "blank verse" at work in the images, metaphors, vocal sounds, stresses or repetitions that are included here. The primary performance goal should be to give your speech a "musicality" that is both fluent and natural in speaking the verse.

And in this state she gallops night by night
Through lovers' brains and then they dream of love,
On courtiers' knees that dream on curtsies straight.
O'er lawyers' fingers who straight dream on fees,
O'er ladies' lips who straight on kisses dream,
Which oft the angry Mab with blisters plagues
Because their breaths with sweetmeats tainted are.
Sometimes she gallops o'er a courtier's nose
And then dreams he of smelling out a suit,
And sometime comes she with a tithe-pig's tail
Tickling a parson's nose as 'a lies asleep,
Then he dreams of another benefice.
Sometime she driveth o'er a soldier's neck
And then dreams he of cutting foreign throats,
Of breaches, ambuscadoes, Spanish blades,
Of healths five fathom deep; and then anon
Drums in his ear, at which he starts and wakes,
And being thus frighted swears a prayer or two
And sleeps again. This is that very Mab
That plaits the manes of horses in the night,
And bakes the elflocks in foul sluttish hairs,
Which once untangled much misfortune bodes.
This is the hag, when maids lie on their backs,
That presses them and learns them first to bear,

61

Making them women of good carriage.

This is she —

The Shakespearean Scenes

The following edited scenes are representative of the comedies and tragedies that were both popular and critical successes during

Modern adaptations of Shakespearean playscripts approach each scene not as an historical relic but, rather, as an exciting flesh-and-blood episode that dramatizes a significant moment in the life of the character being portrayed.

the Elizabethan period. Each scene should be approached with the same sense of historical accuracy that marked your approach to classical Greek scenes and there should be attention paid to potential for movement or physicalization as suggested in the dialog of the characters. Remember to balance historical approaches with a natural, spontaneous performance style that suggests vigor and vitality. The following Shakespearean scenes also represent creative opportunities to cast men in women's roles and to integrate fencing, sword-play and gymnastics into the performance approach. Finally, there is the need to cultivate "fine speaking" that helps to articulate the language of the characters while at the same time seeking to project the individual mood and attitude of each character in the selected scene.

from Measure for Measure (1604)
William Shakespeare

Here is the "dark" story of the chaste Isabella, who is tempted to sell her honor in order to save her beloved brother Claudio, who is himself under a sentence of death for sins of the flesh. The raw and grotesque plot includes comic clowns who voice moral points of view while enjoying comic interludes that celebrate the anticipated death of Claudio. Isabella, of course, refuses to dishonor herself and in despair and hopelessness visits the prison where Claudio is being held to inform him of the shameful price proposed by the magistrate Angelo for his freedom and to also prepare him for his own fate.

Although the scene appears rather simple and direct at first glance, this is perhaps the most serious scene in a playscript that is commonly thought to be a comedy. There is a subdued expectation and atmosphere of gloom that hangs over the prison cell setting as Isabella confesses her fear and anger toward the magistrate. There is also an unexpected air of disbelief and amazement when Claudio, overwhelmed by the thought of his own impending death, pleads pitifully with Isabella to commit the horrible sin in order to save his life.

In playing the Shakespearean scene pay particular attention to the long "set speeches" of Isabella and the subtle transitions which indicate Claudio's responses to his sister's dilemma. There are excellent performance opportunities here to use the voice to convey the mood and the attitude of each character as they share extensive reactions to each other's problem; and a well-developed range of vocal variety will also enrich the imagery and the poetic language used to express the agony of the moment.

CAST

CLAUDIO
ISABELLA

SCENE

A prison cell.

APPROACH

The scene opens with Isabella appearing at the prison cell door of her brother Claudio. A moment's pause and she enters to confess to him that the magistrate of Vienna has agreed to pardon him for his sins if only she will agree to commit a sin herself! She must purchase her brother's freedom with her honor and at the magistrate's pleasure. The pacing of the scene parallels the movement of the characters as they share confidences, express outrage and anger, reflect and then reach an emotional climax that concludes their fleeting reunion. Although there is limited suggestion for movement, the actors should exhibit graceful and fluid gestures as appropriate and integrate subtle physicalization and movement that underscores the emotional intensity of the scene.

1	CLAUDIO: Now, Sister, what's the comfort?
2	ISABELLA: Why,
3	As all comforts are, most good, most good indeed.
4	Lord Angelo, having affairs to heaven,
5	Intends you for his swift ambassador,
6	Where you shall be an everlasting leiger.
7	Therefore your best appointment make with speed,
8	Tomorrow you set on.
9	CLAUDIO: Is there no remedy?
10	ISABELLA: None but such remedy as, to save a head,
11	To cleave a heart in twain.
12	CLAUDIO: But is there any?
13	ISABELLA: Yes, Brother, you may live.
14	There is a devilish mercy in the judge,
15	If you'll implore it, that will free your life,
16	But fetter you till death.
17	CLAUDIO: Perpetual durance?
18	ISABELLA: Aye, just, perpetual durance, a restraint,
19	Though all the world's vastidity you had.
20	To a determined scope.
21	CLAUDIO: But in what nature?
22	ISABELLA: In such a one as, you consenting to't,
23	Would bark your honour from that trunk you bear,
24	And leave you naked.
25	CLAUDIO: Let me know the point.
26	ISABELLA: O, I do fear thee, Claudio, and I quake,
27	Lest thou a feverous life shouldst entertain,
28	And six or seven winters more respect
29	Than a perpetual honour. Darest thou die?
30	The sense of death is most in apprehension,
31	And the poor beetle that we tread upon
32	In corporal sufferance finds a pang as great
33	As when a giant dies.
34	CLAUDIO: Why give you me this shame?
35	Think you I can a resolution fetch

1   From flowery tenderness? If I must die,

2   I will encounter darkness as a bride,

3   And hug it in mine arms.

4 ISABELLA: There spake my brother, there my father's grave

5   Did utter forth a voice. Yes, thou must die.

6   Thou art too noble to conserve a life

7   In base appliances. This outward-sainted Deputy,

8   Whose settled visage and deliberate word

9   Nips youth i' the head, and follies doth emmew

10   As falcon doth the fowl, is yet a devil.

11   His filth within being cast, he would appear

12   A pond as deep as Hell.

13 CLAUDIO: The prenzie Angelo!

14 ISABELLA: O, 'tis the cunning livery of Hell,

15   The damned'st body to invest and cover

16   In prenzie guards! Dost thou think, Claudio?

17   If I would yield him my virginity,

18   Thou mightst be freed.

19 CLAUDIO: O, Heavens, it cannot be!

20 ISABELLA: Yes, he would give't thee, from this rank offense,

21   So to offend him still. This night's the time

22   That I should do what I abhor to name,

23   Or else thou diest tomorrow.

24 CLAUDIO: Thou shalt not do't.

25 ISABELLA: O, were it but my life,

26   I'ld throw it down for your deliverance

27   As frankly as a pin.

28 CLAUDIO: Thanks, dear Isabel.

29 ISABELLA: Be ready, Claudio, for your death tomorrow.

30 CLAUDIO: Yes. Has he affections in him,

31   That thus can make him bite the law by the nose,

32   When he would force it? Sure, it is no sin;

33   Or of the deadly seven it is the least.

34 ISABELLA: Which is the least?

35 CLAUDIO: If it were damnable, he being so wise,

1   Why would he for the momentary trick
2   Be perdurably fined? O, Isabel!
3   ISABELLA: What says my brother?
4   CLAUDIO: Death is a fearful thing.
5   ISABELLA: And shamed life a hateful.
6   CLAUDIO: Ay, but to die, and go we know not where,
7   To lie in cold obstruction and to rot,
8   This sensible warm motion to become
9   A kneaded clod, and the delighted spirit
10 To bathe in fiery floods, or to reside
11 In thrilling region of thick-ribbed ice —
12 To be imprisoned in the viewless winds,
13 And blown with restless violence round about
14 The pendent world, or to be worse than worst
15 Of those that lawless and incertain thought
16 Imagine howling — 'tis too horrible!
17 The weariest and most loathed worldly life
18 That age, ache, penury, and imprisonment
19 Can lay on nature is a paradise
20 To what we fear of death.
21 ISABELLA: Alas, alas!
22 CLAUDIO: Sweet sister, let me live.
23 What sin you do to save a brother's life,
24 Nature dispenses with the deed so far
25 That it becomes a virtue.
26 ISABELLA: O, you beast!
27 O, faithless coward! O, dishonest wretch!
28 Wilt thou be made a man out of my vice?
29 Is't not a kind of incest, to take life
30 From thine own sister's shame? What should I think?
31 Heaven shield my mother played my father fair!
32 For such a warped slip of wilderness
33 Ne'er issued from his blood. Take my defiance!
34 Die, perish! Might but my bending down
35 Reprieve thee from thy fate, it should proceed.

1	I'll pray a thousand prayers for thy death,
2	No word to save thee.
3	CLAUDIO: Nay, hear me, Isabel.
4	ISABELLA: O, fie, fie!
5	Thy sin's not accidental, but a trade.
6	Mercy to thee would prove itself a bawd.
7	'Tis best that thou diest quickly!
8	
9	
10	
11	
12	
13	
14	
15	
16	
17	
18	
19	
20	
21	
22	
23	
24	
25	
26	
27	
28	
29	
30	
31	
32	
33	
34	
35	

from **The Taming of the Shrew** (1594)

William Shakespeare

This is one of Shakespeare's most "physical" comedies that draws a broad, almost vulgar at times, comic situation depicting the eternal battle of the sexes. Petruchio, a robust man of the world, has decided to marry the beautiful but head-strong Katharina; a woman that no man has as yet been able to tame. Petruchio is as much in love

Shakespeare's "comic spirit" cultivates animated performances that are expressive and imaginative in conveying the mood and the attitude of the characters being portrayed in the selected scene. (From the Kansas State University production of A Midsummer Night's Dream.*)*

with Katharina's dowry and inheritance as he is with her striking good looks, and each character in the following scene "courts" in an almost aggressive, fierce manner.

As the scene begins, Petruchio is rather impatient to begin his wooing, and his introduction to Katharina comes just after she has broken a lute across another suitor's head. The attraction which sets this scene in motion for each of the characters is their conflicting, sobering independence and individuality. There is also an apparent undercurrent of "gamesmanship" in which the characters delight in unharnessed insults and personal attacks upon the other. The delicious air of repartee and wit is quite evident in their verbal exchanges and the subsequent physical combat that emerges only adds to the agitation and hilarity of the scene.

There are a number of farcical elements to the scene as well and the actors are encouraged to integrate energetic, forceful stage movement to help reinforce the action being described. The apparent lack of stage business indicated in the dialog also demands that the actors provide inventive poses and stances that might help the audience visualize the incongruity of this rather farcical marriage proposal that relies upon intimidation rather than intimacy for its persuasion. The contrast between the formal mood and tone of the marriage proposal and the physical responses of the intended bride and groom should also be played for comic effect to punctuate the treatment of romantic love between Petruchio and Katharina in this particular scene.

CAST

PETRUCHIO
KATHARINA

SCENE

The home of Baptista Minola, rich gentleman of Padua and father of Katharina.

APPROACH

The scene opens with Petruchio, a handsome man about town, coming to woo Katharina, the beautiful elder daughter of a wealthy Padua gentleman whose only fault is that she is intolerably curst and shrewish. In spite of the violent tongue lashing he receives from

Katharina, the dashing Petruchio is undaunted and responds to each insult heaped upon him with a gentle calm and gentleness; which only prompts an even more violent outburst from the less than receptive Katharina. The actors should also avoid the temptation to make either Petruchio or Katharina more compassionate or agreeable than the dialog suggests. The humor of the situation arises from the very exaggeration and farcical nature of their initial, awkward encounter.

1   PETRUCHIO: Good morrow, Kate; for that's your name, I hear.
2   KATHARINA: Well have you heard, but something hard of
3   hearing:
4   They call me Katharine that do talk of me.
5   PETRUCHIO: You lie, in faith, for you are called plain Kate.
6   And bonny Kate, and sometimes Kate the Curst;
7   But Kate, the prettiest Kate in Christendom,
8   Kate of Kate-Hall, my superdainty Kate,
9   For dainties are all Kates — and therefore, Kate
10   Take this of me, Kate of my consolation:
11   Hearing thy mildness praised in every town,
12   Thy virtues spoke of, and thy beauty sounded,
13   Yet not so deeply as to thee belongs,
14   Myself am moved to woo thee for my wife.
15 KATHARINA: Moved! in good time. Let him that moved you hither
16   Remove you hence. I knew you at the first
17   You were a movable.
18 PETRUCHIO: Why, what's a movable?
19 KATHARINA: A joined stool.
20 PETRUCHIO: Thou hast hit it. Come, sit on me.
21 KATHARINA: Asses are made to bear, and so are you.
22 PETRUCHIO: Women are made to bear, and so are you.
23 KATHARINA: No such jade as you, if me you mean.
24 PETRUCHIO: Alas, good Kate, I will not burden thee!
25   For, knowing thee to be but young and light —
26 KATHARINA: Too light for such a swain as you to catch,
27   And yet as heavy as my weight should be.
28 PETRUCHIO: Should be! should — buzz!
29 KATHARINA: Well, ta'en, and like a buzzard.
30 PETRUCHIO: O slow-winged turtle! shall a buzzard take thee?
31 KATHARINA: Ay, for a turtle, as he takes a buzzard.
32 PETRUCHIO: Come, come, you wasp. I'faith, you are too angry.
33 KATHARINA: If I be waspish, best beware my sting.
34 PETRUCHIO: My remedy is then to pluck it out.
35 KATHARINA: Aye, if the fool could find it where it lies.

1   PETRUCHIO: Who knows not where a wasp does wear his sting?

2   In his tail.

3   KATHARINA: In his tongue.

4   PETRUCHIO: Whose tongue?

5   KATHARINA: Yours, if you talk of tails; and so farewell.

6   PETRUCHIO: What, with my tongue in your tail? Nay, come

7   again,

8   Good Kate, I am a gentleman.

9   KATHARINA: That I'll try. *(She strikes him.)*

10   PETRUCHIO: I swear I'll cuff you if you strike again.

11   KATHARINA: So may you lose your arms.

12   If you strike me, you are no gentleman,

13   And if no gentleman, why then no arms.

14   PETRUCHIO: A herald, Kate? O, put me in thy books!

15   KATHARINA: What is your crest? a coxcomb?

16   PETRUCHIO: A combless cock, so Kate will be my hen.

17   KATHARINA: No cock of mine. You crow too like a craven.

18   PETRUCHIO: Nay, come, Kate, come. You must not look so sour.

19   KATHARINA: It is my fashion when I see a crab.

20   PETRUCHIO: Why, here's no crab, and therefore look not sour.

21   KATHARINA: There is, there is.

22   PETRUCHIO: Then show it me.

23   KATHARINA: Had I a glass, I would.

24   PETRUCHIO: What, you mean my face?

25   KATHARINA: Well aimed for such a young one.

26   PETRUCHIO: Now, by Saint George, I am too young for you.

27   KATHARINA: Yet you are withered.

28   PETRUCHIO: 'Tis with cares.

29   KATHARINA: I care not.

30   PETRUCHIO: Nay, hear you, Kate. In sooth you scape not so.

31   KATHARINA: I chafe you, if I tarry. Let me go.

32   PETRUCHIO: No, not a whit. I find you passing gentle.

33   'Twas told me you were rough and coy and sullen,

34   And now I find report a very liar;

35   For thou are pleasant, gamesome, passing courteous,

1		But slow in speech, yet sweet as springtime flowers.
2		Thou canst not frown, thou canst not look askance,
3		Nor bite the lip, as angry wenches will,
4		Nor hast thou pleasure to be cross in talk.
5		But thou with mildness entertain'st thy wooers,
6		With gentle conference, soft and affable.
7		Why does the world report that Kate doth limp?
8		O, slanderous world! Kate like the hazel twig
9		Is straight and slender, and as brown in hue
10		As hazel nuts, and sweeter than the kernels.
11		O, let me see thee walk. Thou dost not halt.
12	KATHARINA:	Go, fool, and whom, thou keep'st command.
13	PETRUCHIO:	Did ever Dian so become a grove
14		As Kate this chamber with her princely gait?
15		O, be thou Dian, and let her be Kate,
16		And then let Kate be chaste and Dian sportful!
17	KATHARINA:	Where did you study all this goodly speech?
18	PETRUCHIO:	It is extempore, from my mother wit.
19	KATHARINA:	A witty mother! Witless else her son.
20	PETRUCHIO:	Am I not wise?
21	KATHARINA:	Yes. Keep you warm.
22	PETRUCHIO:	Marry, so I mean, sweet Katharine, in thy bed.
23		And therefore, setting all this chat aside,
24		Thus in plain terms: Your father hath consented
25		That you shall be my wife, your dowry 'greed on,
26		And, will you, nill you, I will marry you.
27		Now Kate, I am a husband for your turn.
28		For, by this light whereby I see thy beauty,
29		Thy beauty, that doth make me like thee well,
30		Thou must be married to no man but me;
31		For I am he am born to tame you Kate,
32		And bring you from a wild Kate to a Kate
33		Conformable as other household Kates.
34		Here comes your father. Never make denial.
35		I must and will have Katharina to my wife.

from **Romeo and Juliet** (1594)

William Shakespeare

The "star-crossed" young lovers Romeo and Juliet fall victim to senseless family feuds that take their lives in this tragedy of intrigue and social custom. Set in the "dog days" of late August, when tempers are short and swords are drawn quickly from their scabbards, there is an intensity and speed in the movement toward catastrophe as Romeo, heir to the house of Montague, falls in love at first sight with Juliet, younger daughter of the rival house of Capulet. The spontaneous, impulsive union of hearts and souls propels the young lovers on a headlong plunge toward self destruction as they each disobey their parents' edict and ignore the perpetual feud that has made the two wealthy families mortal enemies in pursuit of their romantic love.

The following scene is in the Capulet garden under Juliet's window, where Romeo has retreated after having met her earlier at a masked ball. While Romeo lingers below, Juliet is overheard to confess that she has fallen in love with him. Romeo responds from his hiding place and reveals himself to Juliet in a love duet of tender and sensitive beauty that binds the young lovers in a fateful embrace.

In playing the scene, the actors should seek a delicate balance between the romantic innocence of the young lovers who are fatally attracted to each other and the more practical, serious implications of what this union will mean to the two families who are currently waging a vindictive feud. The scene also calls for a delicacy in gentle persuasion as Romeo and Juliet try to understand their own feelings related to this "forbidden" love they are exploring. This performance portrait would also include reflections of the emotional storm that is beginning toward the end of the scene when Romeo and Juliet resolve to be secretly married in spite of the opposition of their families.

CAST

ROMEO

JULIET

SCENE

Garden of the Capulet household. Late at night.

APPROACH

Romeo, the virtuous and "well-governed" youth who has fallen madly in love with Juliet when first they meet at a masquerade ball, slips away from the festivities and lingers in the Capulet garden under Juliet's window in the romantic hope of seeing her lovely face should she look out from her balcony above. As the window opens and Juliet appears there is a poignancy of lyrical love expressed that adds immensely to the sense of isolation and despair each feels in these troubled times of civil unrest and family feud. Only faintly does the onset of catastrophe appear likely in this vibrant, warm exchange of the simultaneous expression of love between two young souls.

1   ROMEO: But soft! What light through yonder window breaks?

2   It is the East, and Juliet is the sun!

3   Arise, fair sun, and kill the envious moon,

4   Who is already sick and pale with grief

5   That thou her maid art far more fair than she.

6   Be not her maid, since she is envious.

7   Her vestal livery is but sick and green,

8   And none but fools do wear it. Cast it off.

9   It is my lady; O, it is my love!

10   O, that she knew she were!

11   She speaks, yet she says nothing. What of that?

12   Her eye discourses; I will answer it.

13   I am too bold; 'tis not to me she speaks.

14   Two of the fairest stars in all the heaven,

15   Having some business, do entreat her eyes

16   To twinkle in their spheres till they return.

17   What if her eyes were there, they in her head?

18   The brightness of her cheek would shame those stars

19   As daylight doth a lamp; her eyes in heaven

20   Would through the airy region stream so bright

21   That birds would sing and think it were not night.

22   See how she leans her cheek upon her hand!

23   O, that I were a glove upon that hand,

24   That I might touch that cheek!

25   JULIET: Ay me!

26   ROMEO: She speaks.

27   O, speak again, bright angel! for thou art

28   As glorious to this night, being o'er my head,

29   As is a winged messenger of heaven

30   Unto the white-upturned wond'ring eyes

31   Of mortals that fall back to gaze on him

32   When he bestrides the lazy-pacing clouds

33   And sails upon the bosom of the air.

34   JULIET: O Romeo, Romeo! wherefore art thou, Romeo?

35   Deny thy father and refuse thy name;

1   Or, if thou wilt not, be but sworn my love,
2   And I'll no longer be a Capulet.
3   ROMEO: *(Aside)* Shall I hear more, or shall I speak at this?
4   JULIET: 'Tis but thy name that is my enemy.
5   Thou art thyself, though not a Montague.
6   What's a Montague? It is nor hand, nor foot,
7   Nor arm, nor face, nor any other part
8   Belonging to a man. O, be some other name!
9   What's in a name? That which we call a rose
10   By any other name would smell as sweet.
11   So Romeo would, were he not Romeo called,
12   Retain that dear perfection which he owes
13   Without that title. Romeo, doff thy name;
14   And for thy name, which is no part of thee,
15   Take all myself.
16   ROMEO: I take thee at thy word.
17   Call me but love, and I'll be new baptized;
18   Henceforth I never will be Romeo.
19   JULIET: What man art thou that, thus bescreened in night,
20   So stumblest on my counsel?
21   ROMEO: By a name
22   I know not how to tell thee who I am.
23   My name, dear saint, is hateful to myself,
24   Because it is an enemy to thee.
25   Had I it written, I would tear the word.
26   JULIET: My ears have not yet drunk a hundred words
27   Of thy tongue's uttering, yet I know the sound.
28   Art thou not Romeo, and a Montague?
29   ROMEO: Neither, fair maiden, if either thee dislike.
30   JULIET: How camest thou hither, tell me, and wherefore?
31   The orchard walls are high and hard to climb,
32   And the place death, considering who thou art,
33   If any of my kinsmen find thee here.
34   ROMEO: With love's light wings did I o'erperch these walls;
35   For stony limits cannot hold love out,

1   And what love can do, that dares love attempt.

2   Therefore thy kinsmen are no stop to me.

3 JULIET: If they do see thee, they will murder thee.

4 ROMEO: Alack, there lies more peril in thine eye

5   Than twenty of their swords! Look thou but sweet,

6   And I am proof against their enmity.

7 JULIET: I would not for the world they saw thee here.

8 ROMEO: I have night's cloak to hide me from their eyes;

9   And but thou love me, let them find me here.

10   My life were better ended by their hate

11   Than death prorogued, wanting of thy love.

12 JULIET: By whose direction found'st thou out this place?

13 ROMEO: By love, that first did prompt me to inquire.

14   He lent me counsel, and I lent him eyes.

15   I am no pilot; yet, wert thou as far

16   As that vast shore washed with the farthest sea,

17   I should adventure for such merchandise.

18 JULIET: Thou knowest the mask of night is on my face;

19   Else would a maiden blush bepaint my cheek

20   For that which thou hast heard me speak to-night.

21   Fain would I dwell on form — fain, fain deny

22   What I have spoke; but farewell compliment!

23   Dost thou love me? I know thou wilt say, "Ay";

24   And I will take thy word. Yet, if thou swear'st,

25   Thou mayst prove false. At lovers' perjuries,

26   They say Jove laughs. O, gentle Romeo,

27   If thou dost love, pronounce it faithfully.

28   Or if thou thinkest I am too quickly won,

29   I'll frown, and be perverse, and say thee nay,

30   So thou wilt woo; but else, not for the world.

31   In truth, fair Montague, I am too fond,

32   And therefore thou mayst think my havior light;

33   But trust me, gentleman, I'll prove more true

34   Than those that have more cunning to be strange.

35   I should have been more strange, I must confess,

1	But that thou overheard'st, ere I was ware,
2	My true-love passion. Therefore pardon me,
3	And not impute this yielding to light love,
4	Which the dark night hath so discovered.
5	ROMEO: Lady, by yonder blessed moon I vow,
6	That tips with silver all these fruit-tree tops —
7	JULIET: O, swear not by the moon, th' inconstant moon,
8	That monthly changes in her circled orb,
9	Lest that thy love prove likewise variable.
10	ROMEO: What shall I swear by?
11	JULIET: Do not swear at all;
12	Or if thou wilt, swear by thy gracious self,
13	Which is the god of my idolatry,
14	And I'll believe thee.
15	ROMEO: If my heart's dear love —
16	JULIET: Well, do not swear. Although I joy in thee,
17	I have no joy of this contract to-night.
18	It is too rash, too unadvised, too sudden;
19	Too like the lightning, which doth cease to be
20	Ere one can say, "It lightens." Sweet, good night!
21	This bud of love, by summer's ripening breath,
22	May prove a beauteous flow'r when next we meet.
23	Good night, good night! As sweet repose and rest
24	Come to thy heart as that within my breast!
25	ROMEO: O, wilt thou leave me so unsatisfied?
26	JULIET: What satisfaction canst thou have to-night?
27	ROMEO: Th' exchange of thy love's faithful vow for mine.
28	JULIET: I gave thee mine before thou didst request it;
29	And yet I would it were to give again.
30	ROMEO: Wouldst thou withdraw it? For what purpose, love?
31	JULIET: But to be frank and give it thee again.
32	And yet I wish but for the thing I have.
33	My bounty is as boundless as the sea.
34	My love as deep; the more I give to thee,
35	The more I have, for both are infinite.

1   I hear some noise within. Dear love, adieu!

2   Stay but a little, I will come again.

3 ROMEO: O, blessed, blessed night! I am afeard,

4   Being in night, all this is but a dream,

5   Too flattering-sweet to be substantial.

6 JULIET: Three words, dear Romeo, and good night indeed.

7   If that thy bent of love be honorable,

8   Thy purpose marriage, send me word to-morrow,

9   By one that I'll procure to come to thee,

10   Where and what time thou wilt perform the rite;

11   And all my fortunes at thy foot I'll lay

12   And follow thee my lord throughout the world.

13   A thousand times good night!

14 ROMEO: A thousand times the worse, to want thy light!

15   Love goes toward love as schoolboys from their books;

16   But love from love, toward school with heavy looks.

17 JULIET: Hist! Romeo, hist! O, for a falc'ner's voice

18   To lure this tassel-gentle back again!

19   Bondage is hoarse and may not speak aloud,

20   Else would I tear the cave where Echo lies

21   And make her airy tongue more hoarse than mine

22   With repetition of "My Romeo!"

23 ROMEO: It is my soul that calls upon my name.

24   How silver-sweet sound lovers' tongues by night,

25   Like softest music to attending ears!

26 JULIET: Romeo!

27 ROMEO: My sweet?

28 JULIET: At what o'clock to-morrow

29   Shall I send to thee?

30 ROMEO: By the hour of nine.

31 JULIET: I will not fail. 'Tis twenty years till then.

32   I have forgot why I did call thee back.

33 ROMEO: Let me stand here till thou remember it.

34 JULIET: I shall forget, to have thee still stand there,

35   Rememb'ring how I love thy company.

1   ROMEO: And I'll still stay, to have thee still forget.

2   Forgetting any other home but this.

3   JULIET: 'Tis almost morning. I would have thee gone —

4   And yet no farther than a wanton's bird,

5   That lets it hop a little from her hand

6   Like a poor prisoner in his twisted gyves,

7   And with a silken thread plucks it back again,

8   So loving-jealous of his liberty.

9   ROMEO: I would I were thy bird.

10 JULIET: Sweet, so would I.

11   Yet I should kill thee with much cherishing.

12   Good night, good night! Parting is such sweet sorrow

13   That I shall say good night till it be morrow.

14 ROMEO: Sleep dwell upon thine eyes, peace in thy breast!

15   Would I were sleep and peace, so sweet to rest!

16   Hence will I to my ghostly father's cell,

17   His help to crave and my dear hap to tell.

18

19

20

21

22

23

24

25

26

27

28

29

30

31

32

33

34

35

from **Cymbeline** (1610)

William Shakespeare

Cymbeline, aged King of Britain, is so enraged because his daughter Imogen has secretly married Posthumus rather than Cloten, his own stepson, that he cruelly banishes the bridegroom from the kingdom. Posthumus, a poor but worthy gentleman who had been raised at court, takes a sorrowful leave of his wife after giving her a golden bracelet of antique design as a token of his affection. Fleeing to Rome, the pitiful Posthumus is tricked into a wager by the crafty Iachimo, who claims that his powers of persuasion could influence even the virtuous, faithful Imogen to abandon her absent husband.

Against this backdrop of intrigue and romance, Iachimo hastens to Britain to test Imogen's virgue. With a letter of introduction from her husband, the sly and mischievous rogue soon discovers, however, that the virtuous Imogen will never be seduced by fair means and so he resolves to hide himself in a chest which is then delivered to Imogen's bedchamber. After Imogen has fallen asleep for the night, Iachimo creeps out of the chest and begins to make detailed notes of the decorations in the bedchamber as well as the physical description of the sleeping beauty. Before departing the bedchamber, Iachimo also steals the golden bracelet which Posthumus had given his lovely bride when he was exiled.

With these "proofs" Iachimo hastens back to Italy and easily convinces the desolate Posthumus of his wife's infidelity. The scene that follows is a masterful touch of genuine sincerity and honesty as Imogen pleads her case before Pisanio, friend of Posthumus who has been sent to kill her because of her imagined adultery. It is in this tender, warm treatment of Imogen that the playscript carries the notion of "true love" to unexpected delights of human compassion and sancity of marriage vows.

In playing this particular Shakespearean scene the actors should pay attention to the climax of feeling and dramatic flavor that suggests a "bittersweet" mood in Imogen's apparent bereavement, and in Pisanio's charming tenderness and pathos toward her during the spirited questioning he directs toward her. There is also a need to underscore the intimacy of the scene as each character tries to add pathos and poignancy to the description of their plight or to add to their own sense of isolation and despair. The actors may not need reminding that there is great, sincere joy evident at the close of the scene and that it should appear spontaneous and with reverence.

*The intimacy suggested by the smaller Elizabethan playhouse may have reduced the
need for Shakespearean actors to "project" their voices in order to be understood and
may also have promoted a more natural approach to conversational dialog.*

CAST

IMOGEN
PISANIO

SCENE

An open plain near Milford Haven, Britain.

APPROACH

The scene opens as Imogen and Pisanio stop on their journey to Milford Haven, Britain to rest. It is here that Pisanio has been ordered by Posthumus to kill Imogen for her imagined adultery. But the trusted messenger becomes convinced that Posthumus is the victim of some villain and that the fair, sympathetic Imogen is the victim of some foul hoax intended to rob her of her virtuous reputation. The greatest challenge of this scene is to distinguish between the utter simplicity and honesty that *both* characters have so each can display their individual personality and temperament. Even more challenging may be the emotional range needed to convey the feelings, attitudes and moods that are depicted in this scene as it moves from initial accusation to final, happy resolution.

1	IMOGEN:	Thou told'st me, when we came from horse, the place
2		Was near at hand. Ne'er longed my mother so
3		To see me first as I have now. Pisanio, man,
4		Where is Posthumus? What is in thy mind
5		That makes thee stare thus? Wherefore breaks that sigh
6		From th' inward of thee? One but painted thus
7		Would be interpreted a thing perplexed
8		Beyond self-explication. Put thyself
9		Into a havior of less fear, ere wildness
10		Vanquish my staider senses. What's the matter?
11		Why tender'st thou that paper to me with
12		A look untender? If't be summer news,
13		Smile to't before; if winterly, thou need'st
14		But keep that count'nance still. My husband's hand?
15		That drug-damned Italy hath outcraftied him,
16		And he's at some hard point. Speak, man! Thy tongue
17		May take off some extremity, which to read
18		Would be even more mortal to me.

19 PISANIO: Please you read.

| 20 | | And you shall fine me, wretched man, a thing |
| 21 | | The most disdained of fortune. |

22	IMOGEN:	*(Reads.)* "My mistress, Pisanio, hath played the
23		strumpet in my bed, the testimonies whereof lie bleeding
24		in me. I speak not out of weak surmises, but from proof as
25		strong as my grief and as certain as I expect my revenge.
26		That part thou, Pisanio, must act for me, if thy faith be not
27		tainted with the breach of hers. Let thine own hands take
28		away her life. I shall give thee opportunity at Milford
29		Haven — she hath my letter for the purpose — where, if thou
30		fear to strike and to make me certain it is done, thou art
31		the pander to her dishonor and equally to me disloyal."

32	PISANIO:	What shall I need to draw my sword? The paper
33		Hath cut her throat already. No, 'tis slander,
34		Whose edge is sharper than the sword, whose tongue
35		Outvenoms all the worms of Nile, whose breath

1   Rides on the posting winds and doth belie

2   All corners of the world. Kings, queens, and states,

3   Maids, matrons, nay, the secrets of the grave

4   This viperous slander enters. What cheer, madam?

5   IMOGEN: False to his bed? What is it to be false?

6   To lie in watch there and to think on him?

7   To weep 'twixt clock and clock? If sleep charge nature,

8   To break it with a fearful dream of him

9   And cry myself awake? That's false to's bed, is it?

10   PISANIO: Alas, good lady!

11   IMOGEN: I false? Thy conscience witness! Iachimo,

12   Thou didst accuse him of incontinency.

13   Thou then lookedst like a villain; now, methinks,

14   Thy favor's good enough. Some jay of Italy,

15   Whose mother was her painting, hath betrayed him.

16   Poor I am stale, a garment out of fashion,

17   And, for I am richer than to hang by th' walls,

18   I must be ripped. To pieces with me! O,

19   Men's vows are women's traitors! All good seeming,

20   By thy revolt, O husband, shall be thought

21   Put on for villainy, not born where't grows,

22   But worn a bait for ladies.

23   PISANIO: Good madam, hear me.

24   IMOGEN: True honest men, being heard like false Aeneas,

25   Were in his time thought false, and Sinon's weeping

26   Did scandal many a holy tear, took pity

27   From most true wretchedness. So thou, Posthumus,

28   Wilt lay the leaven on all proper men;

29   Goodly and gallant shall be false and perjured

30   From thy great fail. Come, fellow, be thou honest;

31   Do thou thy master's bidding. When thou seest him,

32   A little witness my obedience. Look,

33   I draw the sword myself. Take it, and hit

34   The innocent mansion of my love, my heart.

35   Fear not, 'tis empty of all things but grief.

1	Thy master is not there, who was indeed
2	The riches of it. Do his bidding, strike!
3	Thou mayst be valiant in a better cause,
4	But now thou seem'st a coward.
5	PISANIO: Hence, vile instrument!
6	Thou shalt not damn my hand.
7	IMOGEN: Why, I must die,
8	And if I do not by thy hand, thou art
9	No servant of thy master's. Against self-slaughter
10	There is a prohibition so divine
11	That cravens my weak hand. Come, here's my heart —
12	Something's afore't; soft, we'll no defense —
13	Obedient as the scabbard. What is here?
14	The scriptures of the loyal Leonatus
15	All turned to heresy? Away, away,
16	Corrupters of my faith! You shall no more
17	Be stomachers to my heart.
18	*(Takes his letters from her bodice.)*
19	Thus may poor fools
20	Believe false teachers. Though those that are betrayed
21	Do feel the treason sharply, yet the traitor
22	Stands in worse case of woe.
23	And thou, Posthumus, that didst set up
24	My disobedience 'gainst the King my father
25	And make me put into contempt the suits
26	Of princely fellows, shalt hereafter find
27	It is no act of common passage, but
28	A strain of rareness; and I grieve myself
29	To think, when thou shalt be disedged by her
30	That now thou tirest on, how thy memory
31	Will then be panged by me. Prithee dispatch,
32	The lamb entreats the butcher. Where's thy knife?
33	Thou art too slow to do thy master's bidding
34	When I desire it too.
35	PISANIO: O, gracious lady,

1   Since I received command to do this business

2   I have not slept one wink.

3 IMOGEN: Do't, and to bed then.

4 PISANIO: I'll wake mine eyeballs out first.

5 IMOGEN: Wherefore then

6   Didst undertake it? Why hast thou abused

7   So many miles with a pretense? This place?

8   Mine action and thine own? Our horses' labor?

9   The time inviting thee? The perturbed court

10   For my being absent? Whereunto I never

11   Purpose return. Why hast thou gone so far,

12   To be unbent when thou hast ta'en thy stand,

13   Th' elected deer before thee?

14 PISANIO: But to win time

15   To lose so bad employment, in the which

16   I have considered of a course. Good lady,

17   Hear me with patience.

18 IMOGEN: Talk thy tongue weary, speak.

19   I have heard I am a strumpet, and mine ear,

20   Therein false struck, can take no greater wound,

21   Nor tent to bottom that. But speak.

22 PISANIO: Then, madam,

23   I thought you would not back again.

24 IMOGEN: Most like,

25   Bringing me here to kill me.

26 PISANIO: Not so, neither.

27   But if I were as wise as honest, then

28   My purpose would prove well. It cannot be

29   But that my master is abused. Some villain,

30   Ay, and singular in his art, hath done you both

31   This cursed injury.

32 IMOGEN: Some Roman courtesan.

33 PISANIO: No, on my life.

34   I'll give but notice you are dead, and send him

35   Some bloody sign of it, for 'tis commanded

1   I should do so. You shall be missed at court,

2   And that will well confirm it.

3 IMOGEN: Why, good fellow,

4   What shall I do the while? Where bide? How live?

5   Or in my life what comfort when I am

6   Dead to my husband.

7 PISANIO: If you'll back to th' court —

8 IMOGEN: No court, no father, nor no more ado

9   With that harsh, noble, simple nothing,

10   That Cloten, whose love suit hath been to me

11   As fearful as a siege.

12 PISANIO: If not at court,

13   Then not in Britain must you bide.

14 IMOGEN: Where then?

15   Hath Britain all the sun that shines? Day, night,

16   Are they not but in Britain? I' th' world's volume

17   Our Britain seems as of it, but not in't;

18   In a great pool a swan's nest. Prithee think

19   There's livers out of Britain.

20 PISANIO: I am most glad

21   You think of other places. Th' ambassador,

22   Lucius the Roman, comes to Milford Haven

23   To-morrow. Now if you could wear a mind

24   Dark as your fortune is, and but disguise

25   That which, t'appear itself, must not yet be

26   But by self-danger, you should tread a course

27   Pretty and full of view; yea, happily, near

28   The residence of Posthumus, so nigh, at least,

29   That though his actions were not visible, yet

30   Report should render him hourly to your ear

31   As truly as he moves.

32 IMOGEN: O, for such means,

33   Though peril to my modesty, not death on't,

34   I would adventure.

35 PISANIO: Well then, here's the point:

1   You must forget to be a woman; change
2   Command into obedience, fear and niceness —
3   The handmaids of all women, or more truly
4   Woman it pretty self — into a waggish courage;
5   Ready in gibes, quick-answered, saucy, and
6   As quarrelous as the weasel. Nay, you must
7   Forget that rarest treasure of your cheek,
8   Exposing it — but O, the harder heart!
9   Alack, no remedy — to the greedy touch
10 Of common-kissing Titan, and forget
11 Your laborsome and dainty trims, wherein
12 You made great Juno angry.
13 IMOGEN: Nay, be brief.
14 I see into thy end and am almost
15 A man already.
16 PISANIO: First, make yourself but like one.
17 Forethinking this, I have already fit —
18 'Tis in my cloak-bag — doublet, hat, hose, all
19 That answer to them. Would you, in their serving,
20 And with what imitation you can borrow
21 From youth of such a season, 'fore noble Lucius
22 Present yourself, desire his service, tell him
23 Wherein you're happy, which will make him know,
24 If that his head have ear in music; doubtless
25 With joy he will embrace you, for he's honorable,
26 And, doubling that, most holy. Your means abroad —
27 You have me, rich, and I will never fail
28 Being nor supplyment.
29 IMOGEN: Thou art all the comfort
30 The gods will diet me with. Prithee away.
31 There's more to be considered but we'll even
32 All that good time will give us. This attempt
33 I am soldier to, and will abide it with
34 A prince's courage. Away, I prithee.
35 PISANIO: Well, madam, we must take a short farewell,

1	Lest, being missed, I be suspected of
2	Your carriage from the court. My noble lady,
3	Here is a box; I had it from the Queen.
4	What's in't is precious. If you are sick at sea
5	Or stomach-qualmed at land, a dram of this
6	Will drive away distemper. To some shade,
7	And fit to your manhood. May the gods
8	Direct you to the best.
9	IMOGEN: Amen. I thank thee!
10	
11	
12	
13	
14	
15	
16	
17	
18	
19	
20	
21	
22	
23	
24	
25	
26	
27	
28	
29	
30	
31	
32	
33	
34	
35	

from **Timon of Athens** (1607)

William Shakespeare

Timon of Athens is a wealthy, generous nobleman who is friend and patron to all he meets. The unbridled extravagance of Timon's generosity will be his ruin insists Apemantus, a churlish and bitter cynic who is despised by all he meets. Before long, as Apemantus warned, Timon's creditors become fearful of his solvency and send agents to collect outstanding loans. One by one, Timon's friends deny him and reveal their own ingratitude. Knowing that he has given unwisely but not ignobly, Timon resolves to exile himself in a cave away from Athens. There, while digging for roots to gnaw, he discovers exquisite buried treasure that far exceeds his previous wealth. Unfortunately, Timon has become so bitter and pessimistic himself that his bitter curses against all mankind are the only sentiments he can voice.

The conception of Timon's character is an especially important ingredient in playing the scene that follows. Timon's response to his misfortune — fleeing Athens to hide himself away from society in a cave — needs to be carefully orchestrated to depict his suffering as well as his foolishness; and there should be some attention to the spiritual dimension of his character as he grows wise and humane in his forced isolation. Timon's "mutterings" against mankind also need to be presented with some simple honesty rather than as merely the ravings of an irascible, mean-spirited malcontent. This is especially true in the performance of the rather long speeches of sordid despair in which Timon speaks of the rottenness of human nature and in his subsequent accounts of his own bitter discontent.

In playing the scene that follows, the actors will need to clearly distinguish the misanthropy — hatred for mankind — voiced by Timon from the unhappy view of pained existence expressed by the shallow Apemantus or there will be very little dimension or variety in the episode. The parallels that are drawn between the characters are primarily those in which each shares a common view of the world; but there will need to be significant difference in their individual mood or attitude to fashion a distinctive character portrait. Although neither Timon nor Apemantus appear to experience any significant spiritual growth in the playscript, there is some suggestion in the selected scene that each has a more clearly defined self-awareness and individual point of view that helps to distinguish their characters.

The actor of Shakespearean scenes should not be afraid to be "inventive" in the use of mannerisms, gestures or movements which are inherent in the narrative or in the stage directions and to strike a happy medium between investigation and imagination in drawing three-dimensional character portraits.

CAST

TIMON

APEMANTUS

SCENE

Timon's cave in a wood by the sea.

APPROACH

The scene opens with Timon digging in his cave and mixing exchanges of newly shoveled dirt with bitter curses all the while. Here he is visited by the misanthropic Apemantus, who matches his passionate ranting and cynical raving in a symphony of discordant sound. Although there is very limited suggestion for business in the scene, the actors should be inventive in the staging and integrate exchanges that will help to relieve the rather repetitive action of "digging" that occupies the primary focus of the characters. Remember, also, that the moralizing statements of both Timon and Apemantus are not to be taken as seriously as the more obvious mental and physical despair and depravity they are experiencing. It is this approach to a performance of the scene that may prove most truthful and rewarding to both actors and audience.

1   **TIMON:**   *(Digs.)*   Nature, being sick of man's unkindness,
2   Should yet be hungry! Common mother, thou
3   Whose womb unmeasurable and infinite breast
4   Teems and feeds all; those selfsame mettle
5   Whereof thy proud child, arrogant man, is puffed
6   Engenders the black toad and adder blue,
7   The gilded newt and eyeless venomed worm,
8   With all th' abhorred births, below crisp heaven
9   Whereon Hyperion's quick'ning fire doth shine —
10   Yield him who all thy human sons doth hate,
11   From forth thy plenteous bosom, one poor root!
12   Ensear thy fertile and conceptious womb;
13   Let it no more bring out ingrateful man!
14   Go great with tigers, dragons, wolves, and bears;
15   Teem with new monsters whom thy upward face
16   Hath to the marbled mansion all above
17   Never presented! O, a root! Dear thanks!
18   Dry up thy marrows, vines, and plough-torn leas,
19   Whereof ingrateful man with liquorish drafts
20   And morsels unctuous greases his pure mind,
21   That from it all consideration slips —
22   More man? Plague, plague!
23   **APEMANTUS:** *(Entering)* I was directed hither. Men report
24   Thou dost affect my manners and dost use them.
25   **TIMON:**   'Tis then because thou dost not keep a dog,
26   Whom I would imitate. Consumption catch thee!
27   **APEMANTUS:**   This is in thee a nature but infected,
28   A poor unmanly melancholy sprung
29   From change of fortune. Why this spade? this place?
30   This slave-like habit and these looks of care?
31   Thy flatterers yet wear silk, drink wine, lie soft,
32   Hug their diseased perfumes, and have forgot
33   That ever Timon was. Shame not these woods
34   By putting on the cunning of a carper.
35   Be thou a flatterer now and seek to thrive

1   By that which has undone thee; hinge thy knee
2   And let this very breath whom thou'lt observe
3   Blow off thy cap; praise his most vicious strain
4   And call it excellent. Thou wast told thus;
5   Thou gav'st thine ears, like tapsters that bade welcome,
6   To knaves and all approachers. 'Tis most just
7   That thou turn rascal; hadst thou wealth again,
8   Rascals should have't. Do not assume my likeness.
9   TIMON: Were I like thee; I'd throw myself away.
10 APEMANTUS: Thou hast cast away thyself, being like thyself;
11   A madman so long, now a fool. What, think'st
12   That the bleak air, thy boisterous chamberlain,
13   Will put thy shirt on warm? Will these mossed trees,
14   That have outlived the eagle, page thy heels
15   And skip when thou point'st out? Will the cold brook,
16   Candied with ice, caudle thy morning taste
17   To cure thy o'er-night surfeit? Call the creatures
18   Whose naked natures live in all the spite
19   Of wreakful heaven, whose bare unhoused trunks,
20   To the conflicting elements exposed,
21   Answer mere nature; bid them flatter thee.
22   O, thou shalt find —
23 TIMON: A fool of thee. Depart!
24 APEMANTUS: I love thee better now than e'er I did.
25 TIMON: I hate thee worse.
26 APEMANTUS: Why?
27 TIMON: Thou flatter'st misery.
28 APEMANTUS: I flatter not, but say thou art a caitiff.
29 TIMON: Why dost thou seek me out?
30 APEMANTUS: To vex thee.
31 TIMON: Always a villain's office or a fool's.
32   Dost please thyself in't?
33 APEMANTUS: Ay.
34 TIMON: What, a knave too?
35 APEMANTUS: If thou didst put this sour cold habit on

1   To castigate thy pride, 'twere well; but thou
2   Dost it enforcedly. Thou'dst courtier be again
3   Wert thou not beggar. Willing misery
4   Outlives in certain pomp, is crowned before;
5   The one is filling still, never complete,
6   The other at high wish; best state, contentless,
7   Hath distracted and most wretched being,
8   Worse than the worst, content.
9   Thou shouldst desire to die, being miserable.
10   TIMON: Not by his breath that is more miserable.
11   Thou art a slave whom Fortune's tender arm
12   With favor never clasped, but bred a dog.
13   Hadst thou, like us from our first swath, proceeded
14   The sweet degrees that this brief world affords
15   To such as may the passive drugs of it
16   Freely command, thou wouldst have plunged thyself
17   In general riot, melted down thy youth
18   In different beds of lust, and never learned
19   The icy precepts of respect, but followed
20   The sug'red game before thee. But myself
21   Who had the world as my confectionary,
22   The mouths, the tongues, the eyes, and hearts of men
23   At duty, more than I could frame employment;
24   That numberless upon me stuck, as leaves
25   Do on the oak, have, with one winter's brush,
26   Fell from their boughs and left me open, bare
27   For every storm that blows. I to bear this,
28   That never knew but better, is some burden.
29   Thy nature did commence in sufferance; time
30   Hath made thee hard in't. Why shouldst thou hate men?
31   They never flattered thee. What hast thou given?
32   If thou wilt curse, thy father, that poor rag,
33   Must be thy subject, who in spite put stuff
34   To some she-beggar and compounded thee
35   Poor rogue hereditary. Hence; be gone!

1   If thou hadst not been born the worst of men,
2   Thou hadst been a knave and flatterer.
3   APEMANTUS: Art thou proud yet?
4   TIMON: Ay, that I am not thee.
5   APEMANTUS: I, that I was
6   No prodigal.
7   TIMON: I, that I am one now.
8   Were all the wealth I have shut up in thee,
9   I'd give thee leave to hang it. Get thee gone.
10   That the whole life of Athens were in this!
11   Thus would I eat it. *(Gnaws a root.)*
12   APEMANTUS: *(Offers food.)*   Here! I will mend thy feast.
13   TIMON: First mend my company; take away thyself.
14   APEMANTUS: So I shall mend mine own, by th' lack of thine.
15   TIMON: 'Tis not well mended so; it is but botched.
16   If not, I would it were.
17   APEMANTUS: What wouldst thou have to Athens?
18   TIMON: Thee thither in a whirlwind. If thou wilt,
19   Tell them there I have gold. Look, so I have.
20   APEMANTUS: Here is no use for gold.
21   TIMON: The best and truest;
22   For here it sleeps, and does no hired harm.
23   APEMANTUS: Where liest-a-nights, Timon?
24   TIMON: Under that's above me.
25   Where feed'st thou a-days, Apemantus?
26   APEMANTUS: Where my stomach finds meat; or rather,
27   Where I eat it.
28   TIMON: Would poison were obedient and knew my mind!
29   APEMANTUS: Where wouldst thou send it?
30   TIMON: To sauce thy dishes.
31   APEMANTUS: The middle of humanity thou never knewest, but
32   the extremity of both ends. When thou wast in thy gilt and
33   thy perfume, they mocked thee for too much curiosity; in
34   thy rags thou know'st none, but art despised for the
35   contrary. There's a medlar for thee; eat it.

1   TIMON: On what I hate I feed not.

2   APEMANTUS: Dost hate a medlar?

3   TIMON: Ay, though it look like thee.

4   APEMANTUS: An thou'dst hated meddlers sooner, thou
5   shouldst have loved thyself better now. What man didst thou
6   ever know unthrift that was beloved after his means?

7   TIMON: Who, without those means thou talk'st of, didst thou
8   ever know beloved?

9   APEMANTUS: Myself.

10   TIMON: I understand thee. Thou hadst some means to keep a
11   dog.

12   APEMANTUS: What things in the world canst thou nearest
13   compare to thy flatterers?

14   TIMON: Women nearest; but men — men are the things them-
15   selves. What wouldst thou do with the world, Apemantus,
16   if it lay in thy power?

17   APEMANTUS: Give it to the beasts, to be rid of the men.

18   TIMON: Wouldst thou have thyself fall in the confusion of men,
19   and remain a beast with the beasts?

20   APEMANTUS: Ay, Timon.

21   TIMON: A beastly ambition, which the gods grant thee t' attain
22   to! If thou wert the lion, the fox would beguile thee; if thou
23   wert the lamb, the fox would eat thee; if thou wert the fox,
24   the lion would suspect thee when peradventure thou wert
25   accused by the ass; if thou wert the ass, thy dullness would
26   torment thee, and still thou livedst but as a breakfast to the
27   wolf. If thou wert the wolf thy greediness would afflict thee,
28   and oft thou shouldst hazard thy life for thy dinner. Wert
29   thou the unicorn, pride and wrath would confound thee and
30   make thine own self the conquest of thy fury; wert thou a
31   bear, thou wouldst be killed by the horse; wert thou a horse,
32   thou wouldst be seized by the leopard; wert thou a leopard,
33   thou wert germane to the lion, and the spots of thy kindred
34   were jurors on thy life: all thy safety were remotion and thy
35   defense absence. What beast couldst thou be that were not

100

1   subject to a beast? And what a beast art thou already, that
2   seest not thy loss in transformation!
3   APEMANTUS: If thou couldst please me with speaking to me,
4   thou mightst have hit upon it here. The commonwealth of
5   Athens is become a forest of beasts.
6   TIMON: How has the ass broke the wall, that thou art out of the
7   city?
8   APEMANTUS: Yonder comes a poet and a painter. The plague
9   of company light upon thee! I will fear to catch it, and give
10   way. When I know not what else to do, I'll see thee again.
11 TIMON: When there is nothing living but thee, thou shalt be
12   welcome. I had rather be a beggar's dog than Apemantus.
13 APEMANTUS: Thou art the cap of all the fools alive.
14 TIMON: Would thou wert clean enough to spit upon!
15 APEMANTUS: A plague on thee! thou art too bad to curse.
16 TIMON: All villains that do stand, by thee, are pure.
17 APEMANTUS: There is no leprosy but what thou speak'st.
18 TIMON: If I name thee.
19   I'll beat thee, but I should infect my hands.
20 APEMANTUS: I would my tongue could rot them off!
21 TIMON: Away, thou issue of a mangy dog!
22   Choler does kill that thou art alive;
23   I swoon to see thee.
24 APEMANTUS: Would thou wouldst burst!
25 TIMON: Away! Thou tedious rogue! I am sorry I shall lose
26   A stone by thee. (*Throws a stone at him.*)
27 APEMANTUS: Beast!
28 TIMON: Slave!
29 APEMANTUS: Toad!
30 TIMON: Rogue, rogue, rogue!
31   I am sick of this false world, and will love naught
32   But even the mere necessities upon't.
33   Then, Timon, presently prepare thy grave.
34   Lie where the light foam of the sea may beat
35   Thy gravestone daily. Make thine epitaph,

101

1	That death in me at others' lives may laugh.
2	*(Addresses the gold.)*
3	O, thou sweet king-killer, and dear divorce
4	'Twixt natural son and sire; thou bright defiler
5	Of Hymen's purest bed; thou valiant Mars;
6	Thou ever young, fresh, loved, and delicate wooer,
7	Whose blush doth thaw the consecrated snow
8	That lies on Dian's lap; thou visible god,
9	That sold'rest close impossibilities
10	And mak'st them kiss; that speak'st with every tongue
11	To every purpose! O, thou touch of hearts!
12	Think thy slave man rebels; and by thy virtue
13	Set them into confounding odds, that beasts
14	May have the world in empire!
15	APEMANTUS: Would'twere so,
16	But not till I am dead! I'll say thou'st gold.
17	Thou wilt be thronged to shortly.
18	TIMON: Thronged to?
19	APEMANTUS: Ay.
20	TIMON: Thy back, I prithee.
21	APEMANTUS: Live, and love thy misery.
22	TIMON: Long live so, and so die. I am quit.
23	APEMANTUS: Moe things like men! Eat, Timon, and abhor
24	them!
25	
26	
27	
28	
29	
30	
31	
32	
33	
34	
35	

SELECTED BIBLIOGRAPHY

The following textbooks and suggested readings are recommended for the beginning actor who may wish to become acquainted with the historical period and style related to the Shakespearean performance of scenes. The suggested readings also provide meaningful information on practical approaches to explore scene study as well as playscript interpretation. A serious application of the theories and the selected exercises presented in these recommended sources should provide a solid foundation for then approaching more difficult and complex scene performance in the chapters that follow.

Albright, Hardie and Anita Albright. *Acting: The Creative Process.* 3rd Edition. Belmont, California: Wadsworth Press, 1980.

Bamber, Linda. *Comic Women, Tragic Men: A Study of Gender and Genre in Shakespeare.* Stanford, California: Stanford University Press, 1982.

Barton, John. *Playing Shakespeare.* New York: Methuen Press, 1984.

Bentley, Gerald. *The Profession of Player in Shakespeare's Time, 1590-1642.* Princeton, New Jersey: Princeton University Press, 1984.

Berry, Cicely. *The Actor and His Text.* London: Cambridge University Press, 1987.

Bertram, Joseph. *Acting Shakespeare.* New York: Theatre Arts Books, 1969.

Bertram, Joseph. *Elizabethan Acting.* 2nd Edition. New York: Oxford University Press, 1964.

Brown, John Russell. *Shakespeare in Performance.* New York: Harcourt, Brace and Jovanovich, 1976.

Crawford, Jerry. *Acting: In Person and in Style.* Dubuque, Iowa: William C. Brown, 1980.

Goldman, Michael. *Acting and Action in Shakespearean Tragedy.* Princeton, New Jersey: Princeton University Press, 1985.

Gurr, Andrew. *The Shakespearean Stage, 1574-1642.* Cambridge, England: Cambridge University Press, 1970.

Harbage, Alfred. *Shakespeare's Audience.* New York: Columbia University Press, 1958.

Laban, Rudolf. *The Mastery of Movement.* London: Macdonald and Evans, 1960.

Macleish, Kenneth. *Longman Guide to Shakespeare's Characters.* London: Longman, 1985.

Richard, David. *Shakespeare in the Theatre*. New York: Cambridge University Press, 1978.

Spain, Delbert. *Shakespeare Sounded Soundly*. Santa Barbara, California: Capra Press, 1988.

Thompson, Marvin and Ruth Thompson. *Shakespeare and the Sense of Performance*. Newark, Delaware: University of Delaware Press, 1989.

Webster, Margaret. *Shakespeare Today*. London: Dent Publishers, 1957.

Webster, Margaret. *Shakespeare Without Tears*. New York: Fawcett Books, 1955.

CHAPTER THREE

PLAYING "PERIOD" SCENES

*"A play ought to be a just and lively image of
human nature, reproducing the passions and the
humours, and the changes of fortune to which it
is subject, for the delight and the instruction
of mankind."*

— John Dryden

John Dryden, the 17th-century poet and author of English heroic satires, captured the essential spirit of "period" literature with his suggestion that well-documented mannerisms, lifestyles and attitudes specifically related to a selected time frame were essential to reinforce the authenticity of the historical portrait. Dryden's central point was that "period" literature mirrored the historical times in which it was written and served as the best example of the manners and patterns of behavior observed in the society of those times. Most of the subsequent "period" playscripts included in this chapter are directly related to the historical times in which they were written and are concerned with advancing social changes, ridiculing social customs or promoting new interpretations of old social, political or moral issues.

It should not be surprising, therefore, to learn that "period" playscripts are primarily comic and that most are concerned with a natural sense of sheer fun and an ability to wring humor from the situations in which the characters find themselves. The appeal of the playscripts is to the intellect as the satiric thrusts of the playwright are aimed directly at the manners and customs of daily life, the hallowed traditions of society or the respected ideals of the leading thinkers of the times. There is also comic satire and character exaggeration to expose the silly, pretentious pose of human beings who appear to take themselves and their own opinions much too seriously.

Much buffoonery and witty repartee characterize the comic playscripts that are included for scene study in this chapter and each has a similar quality of spontaneous fun and thoughtful laughter that distinguishes the "period" approach to humor. That basic approach is to make the audience laugh but to also make them "think" as they laugh; to make the audience aware as they laugh at the silly pretensions, shallowness and superficiality of their fellow spectators that they may also be laughing at themselves as well. Looked at from this comic perspective, the playscripts expose us to rueful scorn and ridicule only to later restore us to a healthy balance of humility and humanity that recognizes and now rejects deception, artifice and hypocrisy.

These "comedies of manner," then, reflect the aristocratic society of the historical times that valued witty exchanges of dialog, elegant social graces and sophisticated sexual behavior. Admirable characters were those who could commit an indiscretion without being disgraced or succeed in a seduction without being discovered. The foolish were those who tried to abide by the social customs of the day or to question the dictates of social elegance. Indeed, elegance of phrase and sophistication of pose are much more highly valued in these comedies than ethical or moral principles of justice and virtue.

Playing the Role

The actor who engages in scene study and playscript interpretation for playing the role in "period" performance should gather all of the information available regarding the historical times and review materials related to social customs, manners and mores as part of the initial preparation for exploring the portrayal of character. What will emerge from such a survey of the historical times is that "period" playscripts require a frankly theatrical approach to performance. That is to say there is no illusion of reality at work in the production and the actor is primarily in a presentational pose speaking directly to the audience. Little effort is also made to disguise the fact that the characters are one-dimensional in development and that their situations and subsequent actions are trivial rather than tragic.

Because the comic playscripts of the historical times invariably seek to "teach a lesson" through an appeal to the emotions rather than the intellect, the characters are generally portrayed as either unduly good or as unjustly evil. The playwrights often appear to have sacrificed dramatic sensibility in an attempt to depict virtue triumph over vice, and "private woes" are freely exhibited to arouse the spectator's pity and suspense before the typical "happy ending" that punishes the bad and rewards the good. This "poetic justice" approach to the resolution of historical comedies encouraged wayward characters to repent their sins and pledge to embrace morality as the guiding principle of their lives. The sentiments, or wise moral proverbs, expressed by these reformed characters provided valuable insight about human nature and were prized testimony to suggest that a character had forsaken the life of libertine and philanderer.

Even the mildest mishap or the simplest happiness in "period" comedies is treated with an admirable display of restraint and as a result the characters often appear idiotic or selfish. They make their demands of each other, engage in polite conversation and fight the eternal battle-of-the-sexes with vigor and zest; but beneath the convenient masks they wear, each character delights in pointing out ridiculous pretensions or amusing flaws that they happen to observe in others. Rarely do these characters hold the mirror of nature up to themselves to reflect upon their own shallowness and superficiality.

The actor of "period" scenes needs to cultivate a sense of the subtlety and finesse needed to voice the many foibles, subterfuges and intrigues depicted in the historical comedies included for performance in this chapter. The demand for sharp, precise characterization and polished, articulate dialog is more urgent than spontaneous, impromptu movement or action; and perhaps the best approach to portraying the absurd misunderstanding, the hilarious posturing and the ridiculous attitude of the characters making obvious fools of themselves as they betray human nature with an excess of fashion, wealth or social custom is to practice *moderation*. Such a performance approach encourages an excess of zeal and jubilation in portraying the social graces and historical customs but cautions against undue exaggeration or caricature in depicting the human vanity and self-seeking acclaim that appear to motivate the characters to betray themselves and their social standing in the quest for exquisite pleasure or a highly prized conquest.

Although the traditional "comedy of manners" relies quite heavily upon witty repartee and biting satire to achieve its delicious comic effect, there is exceptional comic potential for performance to be found in the catalog of "stock characters" that people the social hierarchy of the historical times. The comedies seem barely able to please the audience's appetite for such comic inventions as the "rake," the "fop," the "old maid," the "sentimental hero," the "angry mistress," the "gentleman," the "poet" or the "bawdy profligate." Careful attention to the general characteristics associated with each character "type" may provide creative insight and potential performance behavior that will give immediate recognition and comic purpose to the actor's portrayal of the comic scenes that follow. In addition, new facets of character may be revealed in a studied investigation of historical evidence that has survived from the times. For example, a review of the letters, diaries or chronicles of the times may provide invaluable information related to character attitude, mood or point of view that could be integrated into the performance to more accurately depict the historical characters suggested in the comic playscripts.

It is also necessary to visualize the physical playhouse of the historical times. The auditorium of the typical playhouse of the times was divided into the box, pit and gallery. The stage, which extended out into the pit, also boasted a proscenium arch that framed the actors and a raked stage behind it. Grooves were installed on the stage to facilitate rapid scene change and most of the acting took place on a forestage or "apron" in front of the proscenium arch. Scenery was generally placed upstage and the traditional scenic practices included wings, drops, borders and shutters. Lighting was still by candles and *both* the actors and the audience were illuminated! The average seating capacity of a typical playhouse in the historical times was 1,200 and the most significant event to occur was the introduction of women

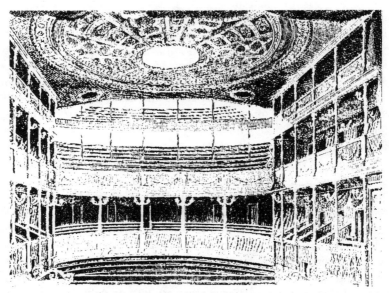

The Drury Lane Theatre, one of London's major theatres from the Restoration until the present time, as it appeared in 1792. The present Drury Lane Theatre is used primarily for musicals.

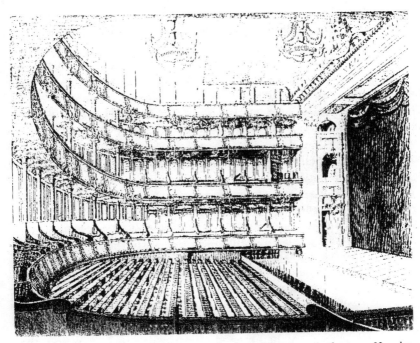

Interior of the Covent Garden Theatre in 1794. One of the two main theatres of London from 1732 until 1843, the Covent Garden has been the home of opera since the mid-19th century.

The auditorium of the typical playhouse of the historical times was divided into the pit, box and gallery. The stage, which now extended out into the pit area, also boasted a proscenium arch that helped to "frame" the action for the spectator.

to play the major female roles. Witches and comic old women, however, continued to be played by men until the end of the 17th century.

Playing the Style

When we speak of the "style" of historical playscripts we are now addressing the traditional, "period" approach to performance technique that was popular during the time of the comedies of manner in the 17th, 18th and 19th centuries. The tendency of actors to begin to "specialize" in role types and to "own" the roles that they played in certain companies suggests a conservatism in acting style that placed a premium upon tradition rather than upon fresh invention in the interpretation of a character. The historical playhouse also promoted a more formal, declamatory style of presentation that emphasized vocal gymnastics rather than subtle nuance of character motivation.

109

Actors may have chanted or "intoned" the poetic passages of lyrical tragedies in the period in the same manner that the Greek actors are thought to have recited the choral odes of classical tragedy. There is also evidence to suggest that actors expected to receive rousing applause for passages or well-delivered speeches and often posed following a scene to receive the audience adulation and appreciation before repeating the speech or the scene. For the most part, however, the performance style of the period mirrored the customs of society and the manners of its citizens.

Everyday behavior in the historical period was more formal, polite and conventional than our current societal custom or manner. Individual actions of the citizens were governed by a rigid, inflexible social standard and an exaggerated sense of proper decorum that taught convenient moral lessons appropriate to one's behavior or attitude. There was also an emphasis upon "right conduct" and "tradition" that acknowledged good judgment and solid values at the expense of pretense and sham. The "ritualistic" nature of society further promoted an appreciation for elaborate spectacle and a formality in presentation associated with public events.

These historical perspectives apparently were translated to the stage with a sense of heightened theatricality to help reflect the "period" in which the playscripts were written and were sufficiently distorted in terms of point of view and comic vision to provoke the satire and witty repartee that is characteristic of comedies of manner. As a consequence, the acting style was modeled upon the social behavior and customs of the ladies and gentlemen of the nobility and demanded an exquisite degree of grace and elegance to faithfully capture the highly artificial and studied manners of the royal court society. Physical gestures appear to have been very limited and extremely stylized to suggest the formality of the occasion; and there does not appear to have been any attempt made to relate to other characters on the stage in terms of movement or physicalization.

Facial expression, however, appears to have been an important ingredient in suggesting character attitude or mood and the rather intimate nature of the small playhouse may have inadvertently promoted a more natural approach to performance technique. The actors frequently wore elaborate costumes that mirrored contemporary fashion and provided the primary source of visual excitement in the excessive ornamentation and decoration that they displayed in their elaborate wardrobes. The audience also expected the actors to display a polished, well-rehearsed technique that would feature good diction, melodious song and rhythmic dance in addition to their sumptuous costumes and myriad facial expressions.

The actor of "period" playscripts appears to have been less inclined to maintain an exhaustive inventory of movement or business and to have relied more extensively upon voice and gesture to sketch the character portrait. Special vocal emphasis appears to have been needed to articulate and enunciate the verse and lyrical passages popular in the comedies of manner; and it would have been an important performance technique to cultivate "musicality" of voice to enrich the tonality of songs that were integral ingredients of each character's development. Attention would also have to be paid to posture and to the need for a physical body that is properly aligned, fluid and graceful in both carriage and movement to help suggest the sophistication of the historical times.

A final principle to keep in mind when approaching "period" playscripts is the need to be aware of traditional audience expectations for the performance. In terms of the comedies of manner, perhaps the most eloquent and truthful appraisal of audience expectation is to be found in the musings of the 18th-century author of English pamphlets Thomas Davies, who wrote that "Englishmen look upon the theatre as a place of amusement; they do not expect to be alarmed with terror, or wrought upon by scenes of commiseration; but are surprised into the feeling of those passions, and shed tears because it cannot be avoided. The theatre becomes a place of instruction by chance."

The "instruction" that is provided by the comedies of manner that are included for performance is universal in human nature even though several hundred years separate the individual playscripts. It is concerned more with the accurate depiction of society during the historical times than with the causes of "why" society is the way it is. It also mirrors the complexities of our own society and asks if we see any clear reflection of our own times in these "period" playscripts. But, for the most part, it is just concerned with the outrageous good fun that is provoked in ridiculing social customs or mores and in the satiric exposé of silly, pretentious human beings who appear to take themselves much too seriously!

Playing the Performance

In order to communicate the "period" style in performance it is crucial to promote direct and intense expression through the vocal delivery of the "lines" of dialog rather than attempting a three-dimensional, complex character portrait. At first, it may appear rather awkward and artificial to concentrate exclusively upon the voice and to engage in active "word play" with the lines of dialog to heighten the humor or to underscore the witty repartee. But the actor must keep in mind that the majority of historical playscripts are written in *verse* and need a more direct, intense expression of the rhythm and the meter of the dialog than prose scenes. The majority of historical playscripts also rely quite heavily upon the style of the spoken language rather than upon movement or stylized gesture to communicate the attitude or the mood of the character. Neglect of crisp, articulate speech can only lead to a ragged, unpolished delivery of the dialog that may not be clearly heard or even understood by the audience.

Meaningful verse delivery that heightens poetic imagery and enriches the repartee of the dialog also requires careful attention to physical control and posture. In playing the performance the actor should maintain a relaxed and yet alert posture with the parts of the body perfectly aligned to suggest a graceful, fluid physicalization; the head should be held high and the arms should be relaxed at the side; the vocal sounds should be placed "forward" in the mouth to promote precise enunciation and crisp articulation; and a narrow range of pitch variation as well as a moderate volume may help to project the spoken lines of dialog in a more "spontaneous" and pleasing style. The selected exercises provided in this chapter address these specific concerns in playing the performance and, hopefully, will promote a more detailed approach to vocal and textual delivery of the dialog to highlight character.

The nature of "period" research necessary for accurate historical investigation that leads to inspired, inventive performance also requires some pursuit of secondary sources of information as well. Some of those secondary sources that might add an ingredient of authenticity to your performance would include visual information related to the historical times as found in scholarly books on archeology or lavish and colorful books on theatre costumes or fashion. In playing your research role as an "actor-as-detective," you might also consider potential sources of performance material such as museum visits, portrait study, costume exhibitions, musical recitals, jewelry expositions, antique props or even ancient artifacts to help capture a glimpse of the historical times and to perhaps provide a performance clue to an interpretation of the scene and the character. These creative approaches to playing "period" playscripts help to frame the historical

"Comedies of manner" reflect the aristocratic society of the historical times that valued witty exchanges of dialog, elegant social graces and sophisticated behavior. Elegance of phrase and sophistication of pose are much more highly valued in these comedies than ethical or moral principles of justice or virtue.

reconstruction of the scene and promote an atmosphere of accuracy and detail that capture the "past" in a more direct and immediate fashion than would otherwise be possible in our contemporary theatre.

Period Exercises

The following vocal and physical exercises are presented to address specific concerns in playing "period" scenes. Each exercise is designed to enrich vocal and textual delivery of the dialog as well as to promote a more physical approach to posture. Participate fully in the exercises and practice visualization of the historical times as you generate the images, the sounds and the actions called for in the individual approaches to both voice and body. The exercises should be repeated a number of times to enhance your studied and disciplined approach to the historical times and to playing "period" scenes. You may also wish to review the vocal exercises of both of the previous chapters to reinforce the overall excellence of your rehearsal technique.

113

ATTENTION! AT EASE!

When you have carefully explored the principles of the basic speech process and the vocal mechanism, you should now turn your attention to giving the voice variety and flexibility necessary for playing "period" playscripts. The first steps are to recognize the auditory characteristics of a vigorous and vital voice and then to outline a program of self-evaluation and self-improvement to correct apparent weaknesses and to promote potential strengths.

Begin by reviewing the importance of relaxation in the production of sound. Stand erect at attention, with your arms and legs tense and stiff. Feel the tension in every muscle, especially the chest and the abdomen. Hold this position for *30* seconds. Notice how uncomfortable it is to stand in this restricted position and how tension continues to build as you maintain the stance.

Now slowly relax each part of your body, starting with the arms and legs and concluding with the chest and abdomen. Let your head and shoulders slowly droop, and make your body completely loose. Repeat this part of the exercise by sitting in a chair and tensing each part of the body as you did while standing. Hold this position for *30* seconds. When you are completely tensed, slowly relax each part of your body and conclude by slumping forward in the chair until your arms touch your ankles. You should have noticed the distinct difference between the tensed and the relaxed positions and should be able to make the transition from an uncomfortable physical posture to one that is more relaxed and comfortable.

Continue your exploration by tensing the neck and the throat until they are almost rigid. Hold this position for *30* seconds. Then recite the following passage from the comic speech of Mrs. Pinchwife in William Wycherley's 17th-century comedy *The Country Wife* into a tape recorder in a voice that is obviously strained and strident from tension.

> **Well, 'tis e'en so, I have got the London disease they call love; I am sick of my husband, and for my gallant. I have heard this distemper called a fever, but methinks 'tis like an ague; for when I think of my husband, I tremble, and am in a cold sweat, and have inclinations to vomit; but when I think of my gallant, dear Mr. Horner, my hot fit comes, and I am all in a fever indeed; and, as in other fevers, my own chamber is**

tedious to me, and I would fain be removed to his, and then methinks I should be well. Ah, poor Mr. Horner! Well, I cannot, will not stay here; therefore I'll make an end of my letter to him, which shall be a finer letter than my last, because I have studied it like anything. Oh, sick, sick!

Now relax your neck and throat by exaggerating a yawn several times. Open your mouth wide as you slowly lessen the tension in the neck and throat. Hold the relaxed position — mouth slightly open — for *30* seconds. Then recite the following passage from the satiric speech of Faulkland in Richard Brinsley Sheridan's 18th-century manners comedy *The Rivals* into a tape recorder in a voice that is quite obviously free from tension.

In tears! Stay, Julia, stay but for a moment! The door is fastened! Julia — my soul — but for one moment. I hear her sobbing! 'Sdeath! what a brute am I to use her thus! Yet stay! Aye — she is coming now. How little resolution there is in woman! How a few soft words can turn them! No, faith! — she is *not* coming either! Why, Julia — my love — say but that you forgive me — come but to tell me that. Now, this is being *too* resentful. Stay! She *is* coming, too — I thought she would — no *steadiness* in anything! her going away must have been a mere trick then. She sha'n't see that I was hurt by it. I'll affect indifference. *(Hums a tune; then listens at the door.)*

No — Z — ds! She's *not* coming! Nor doesn't intend it, I suppose. This is not *steadiness*, but *obstinacy!* Yet I deserve it. What, after so long an absence to quarrel with her tenderness! 'Twas barbarous and unmanly! I should be ashamed to see her now. I'll wait till her just resentment is abated — and when I distress her so again, may I lose her forever, and be linked instead to some antique virago, whose gnawing passions, and long-hoarded spleen shall make me curse my folly half the day, and all the night!

Play back the tape and compare the two readings. You should be able to note the differences, in both sound and meaning, between a performance that is obviously strained and one that is free from tension. You should also be aware that the vocal mechanism does much more than merely transform a sound into an audible transmission of recognized words or language symbols. It also permits the actor to highlight meaning, focus attention and direct audience impressions. For these reasons, it is crucial that you be in control of your bodily actions and vocal sounds in playing "period" playscripts. One way to assure that you can suggest a relaxed body and a crisp voice is to repeat this exercise before each rehearsal or performance of the scene. You should also extend this exercise to include the vocal exercises presented in Chapter One and Chapter Two to promote a more disciplined approach to voice production and articulation that will give meaning and purpose to the selected scenes that represent the "period" comic playscripts.

PUPPET ON A STRING

In order to cultivate the total physical concentration necessary for good relaxation technique in the performance of "period" playscripts, it is necessary to develop muscular coordination that is fluid and flexible. A basic requirement of physical concentration is the ability to appear natural and relaxed, with your posture suggesting that the bones of your body are in proper alignment. Although at ease and apparently comfortable, your posture should also suggest alertness and anticipation of dialog and action to follow.

Begin this exercise by holding your body erect, with chest high, chin up, back flat and arms and legs straight. Place one foot slightly in front of the other, with the weight centered on the ball of the forward foot. This position creates a pleasing and alert visual portrait and also facilitates later movement necessary to convey changing character moods or attitudes.

Now spread your legs slightly so that you have a solid sense of balance. Let your upper body "sag" so that your head and arms slowly dangle toward the floor like a puppet on a string. Swing your arms forward and backward in a slow rhythm, then repeat the sounds *ah* and *oh* in an intonation that parallels the movement of your body swaying to and fro. Now, slowly raise your body while continuing to swing your arms forward and backward in a slow rhythm. When you are standing upright, begin to rotate your head in a slow circle left to right and then right to left. Repeat the *ah* and *oh* sounds in short bursts, then slightly longer bursts and then in the longest bursts possible on only one breath.

You should now have experienced a marked release of physical and vocal tension. If you do not feel physically and vocally relaxed, please repeat this part of the exercise more slowly. When you are finally confident that your muscles and vocal cords are relaxed, proceed to complete the exercise. Open your mouth as wide as possible in a yawn. Prolong the yawn as long as possible, adding as many *ahs* and *ohs* as a single breath permits. Repeat three times, each time slowly exhaling as you sustain as many *ahs* as possible on a single breath. Then begin to take deep breaths from the diaphragm as you repeat as many *ohs* as possible on a single breath.

What you have just experienced is complete physical and vocal relaxation, a technique that can be used in performance to promote almost instant relaxation. This relaxation should promote good posture as well as vocal variety that enriches character portrayal. Repeat the exercise *three* times from the first sequence and then conclude the exercise by voicing the following passage from Molière's 17th-century comic farce *The Miser* in short, breathy phrases.

JACQUES: Well, since you will have it, master, I'll tell you straight then — they make a laughing stock of you everywhere; we have scores of jokes thrown at us about you; there's nothing folk like to do better than running you down and making game of your stinginess. One fellow tells how you had the law on your neighbor's cat for eating the remains of a leg of mutton, another how you were caught one night stealing oats from your own horses. You are a butt and a byword for everybody, and nobody ever refers to you except as a miser, a skinflint and a niggardly old usurer.

The Period Scenes

The following edited scenes are representative of the period comedies of manner that were popular in the 18th and 19th centuries. Each scene should be approached with the same energy and enthusiasm that marked your approach to the classical Greek and later Shakespearean playscripts in Chapter One and Chapter Two. Before proceeding to an examination of the individual scenes, however, it might be useful to point out some inventive approaches to potential performance. Comedies of manner allow for ornamental jewelry, wigs, long gowns and sport coats to be worn to reinforce the visual appeal of "high society." Tea and cakes may also be served to permit the actors to display their social graces and good taste. There is even an opportunity to add period music and to perform graceful historical dances. If facilities are available, the scenes may be performed on a patio or in small waiting rooms with the audience arranged on three sides. The actors may also choose to integrate appropriate business that promotes the use of fans, walking sticks, snuff boxes, spectacles or handkerchiefs to help punctuate the wit of the dialog.

from The School for Scandal (1777)

Richard Brinsley Sheridan

As the best example of the English comedy of manners, this witty and upper-class satire ridicules the conventional behavior of wealthy people who live within the narrow restraints of a rigid and artificial social code. The main action of the playscript is set against the frivolous background of a private "school for scandal," in which a circle of malicious men and women destroy reputation and ruin character while politely sipping afternoon tea. Lady Sneerwell and her entourage of hypocritical scandalmongers set the tone of the two scenes that follow; while their shallowness provides the comic impulse for Sir Peter Teazle and his young wife to learn the valuable lesson that virtue is its own reward.

In such a superficial society as this, polished and highly elegant behavior assumes prime importance just as values like morality and even decency are easily dismissed or brushed casually aside. That is why it is crucial in playing the scenes to convey a light and delicate sense of movement, punctuated with elegant bows or deep curtsies, and to convey an air of chic sophistication. Remember that in a comedy of manners what is "said" and what is "done" is not nearly important as *how* it is said and done. The actor must, therefore, be able to portray the nimbleness of wit and the attitude of carefree leisure that most accurately reflects the historical times.

In playing the scenes the actor should display tidbits of comic characterization that might include coy glances, fluttering eyelashes, tilted heads, meaningless sighs or inviting winks to help display appropriate social graces — and to help disguise the emptiness behind the smartly decorated mask of sentimentality. There are also excellent performance opportunities here to suggest character mood and attitude; as well as some inventive moments that call for comic reactions and well-timed comic responses to potentially hilarious situations.

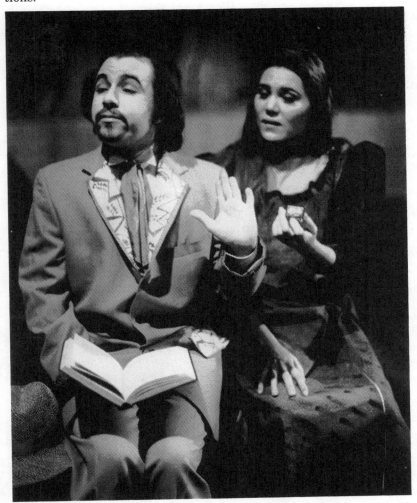

Even the mildest mishap or the simplest happiness in "period" comedies is treated with an admirable display of restraint and as a result the characters often appear idiotic or selfish.

CAST

SIR PETER TEAZLE
LADY TEAZLE

SCENE

A dressing room in Sir Peter Teazle's house, early morning.

APPROACH

Sir Peter Teazle, a middle-aged gentleman of a stubborn and quarrelsome nature, has recently married an innocent, and much younger, girl from the country. Although pleasant and gentle herself, Lady Teazle has become involved with a circle of vicious gossips and in trying to imitate their lifestyles has become very lavish and careless in spending her husband's fortune. Not without reason, Sir Peter Teazle is disturbed and has decided to confront his wife in her dressing room. The scene begins with considerable energy as Sir Peter Teazle paces back and forth like a caged lion while Lady Teazle, calm and reserved, rests precariously on a chaise. By the conclusion of the first scene, however, the initial roles have been reversed and it is Lady Teazle who rushes off, leaving Sir Peter Teazle to reflect on what a lucky man he is to have such a charming wife.

1   SIR PETER: Lady Teazle, Lady Teazle, I'll not bear it!

2   LADY TEAZLE: Sir Peter, Sir Peter, you may bear it or not, as
3   you please; but I ought to have my own way in everything,
4   and what's more, I will, too. What?! Though I was educated
5   in the country, I know very well that women of fashion in
6   London are accountable to nobody after they are married.

7   SIR PETER: Very well, ma'am, very well — so a husband is to
8   have no influence, no authority?

9   LADY TEAZLE: Authority! No, to be sure: if you wanted
10   authority over me, you should have adopted me, and not
11   married me. I am sure you were old enough!

12   SIR PETER: Old enough! Ay, there it is. Well, well, Lady Teazle,
13   though my life may be made unhappy by your temper, I'll
14   not be ruined by your extravagance.

15   LADY TEAZLE: My extravagance! I'm sure I'm not more
16   extravagant than a woman of fashion ought to be.

17   SIR PETER: No, no, madam, you shall throw away no more
18   sums on such un-meaning luxury. 'Slife! To spend as much
19   to furnish your dressing room with flowers in winter as
20   would suffice to turn the Pantheon into a greenhouse, and
21   give a *fête champêtre* at Christmas.

22   LADY TEAZLE: And am I to blame, Sir Peter, because flowers
23   are dear in cold weather? You should find fault with the
24   climate, and not with me. For my part, I'm sure, I wish it
25   was spring all the year round, and that roses grew under
26   one's feet!

27   SIR PETER: Oons! Madam — if you had been born to this, I
28   shouldn't wonder at your talking thus; but you forget what
29   your situation was when I married you.

30   LADY TEAZLE: No, no, I don't; 'twas a very disagreeable one,
31   or I should never have married you.

32   SIR PETER: Yes, yes, madam, you were then in a somewhat
33   humbler style: the daughter of a plain country squire.
34   Recollect, Lady Teazle, when I saw you first sitting at your
35   tambour, in a pretty figured linen gown, with a bunch of

1   keys at your side; your hair combed smooth over a roll, and
2   your apartment hung round with fruits in worsted, of your
3   own making.

4 LADY TEAZLE: Oh, yes! I remember it very well, and a curious
5   life I led. My daily occupation to inspect the dairy,
6   superintend the poultry, make extracts from the family
7   receipt-book — and comb my aunt Deborah's lapdog.

8 SIR PETER: Yes, yes, ma'am, 'twas so indeed.

9 LADY TEAZLE: And then, you know, my evening amusements!
10   To draw patterns for ruffles, which I had not materials to
11   make up; to play Pope Joan with the curate; to read a sermon
12   to my aunt; or to be stuck down to an old spinet to strum
13   my father to sleep after a fox-chase.

14 SIR PETER: I am glad you have so good a memory. Yes, madam,
15   these were the recreations I took you from; but now you
16   must have your coach — *vis-à-vis* — and three powdered
17   footmen before your chair; and, in the summer, a pair of
18   white cats to draw you to Kensington Gardens. No
19   recollections, I suppose, when you were content to ride
20   double, behind the butler, on a dock'd coach-horse.

21 LADY TEAZLE: No — I swear I never did that! I deny the butler
22   and the coach-horse.

23 SIR PETER: This, madam, was your situation; and what have I
24   done for you? I have made you a woman of fashion, of
25   fortune, of rank; in short, I have made you my wife.

26 LADY TEAZLE: Well, then — and there is but one thing more
27   you can make me to add to the obligation, and that is —

28 SIR PETER: My widow, I suppose!

29 LADY TEAZLE: Hem! Hem!

30 SIR PETER: I thank you, madam — but don't flatter yourself;
31   for though your ill conduct may disturb my peace, it shall
32   never break my heart, I promise you. However, I am equally
33   obliged to you for the hint.

34 LADY TEAZLE: Then why will you endeavour to make yourself
35   so disagreeable to me, and thwart me in every little elegant

122

1   expense?

2   SIR PETER: 'Slife, madam, I say, had you any of these little

3   elegant expenses when you married me?

4   LADY TEAZLE: Lud, Sir Peter! Would you have me be out of

5   the fashion?

6   SIR PETER: The fashion, indeed! What had you to do with the

7   fashion before you married me?

8   LADY TEAZLE: For my part, I should think you would like to

9   have your wife thought a woman of taste.

10   SIR PETER: Ay — there again — taste! Zounds! Madam, you

11   had no taste when you married me!

12   LADY TEAZLE: That's very true indeed, Sir Peter. And after

13   having married you, I should never pretend to taste again,

14   I allow. But now, Sir Peter, if we have finished our daily

15   jangle, I presume I may go to my engagement at Lady

16   Sneerwell's.

17   SIR PETER: Ay, there's another precious circumstance. A

18   charming set of acquaintances you have made there.

19   LADY TEAZLE: Nay, Sir Peter, they are all people of rank and

20   fortune, and remarkably tenacious of reputation.

21   SIR PETER: Yes, egad, they are tenacious of reputation with a

22   vengeance; for they don't choose anybody should have a

23   character but themselves! Such a crew! Ah! Many a wretch

24   has rid on a hurdle who has done less mischief than these

25   utterers of forged tales, coiners of scandal, and clippers of

26   reputation.

27   LADY TEAZLE: What! Would you restrain the freedom of

28   speech?

29   SIR PETER: Oh! They have made you just as bad as any of the

30   society.

31   LADY TEAZLE: Why, I believe I do bear a part with a tolerable

32   grace. But I vow I bear no malice against the people I abuse.

33   When I say an ill-natured thing, 'tis out of pure good humour;

34   and I take it for granted, they deal exactly in the same

35   manner with me. But, Sir Peter, you know what you

1   **promised: to come to Lady Sneerwell's too.**
2 **SIR PETER: Well, well, I'll call in just to look after my own**
3   **character.**
4 **LADY TEAZLE: Then indeed you must make haste after me, or**
5   **you'll be too late. So, goodbye to you!**
6 **SIR PETER: So — I have gained much by my intended**
7   **expostulation: yet, with what a charming air she contradicts**
8   **everything I say, and how pleasing she shows her contempt**
9   **for my authority! Well, though I can't make her love me,**
10   **there is great satisfaction in quarrelling with her; and I**
11   **think she never appears to such advantage as when she is**
12   **doing everything in her power to plague me.**
13   *(Having fled her home several hours earlier, LADY TEAZLE now*
14   *pays a visit to the notorious LADY SNEERWELL, who is presiding*
15   *over an afternoon meeting of the society gossips. Here are gathered*
16   *all the frivolous fops, would-be poets, biting wits and pretentious*
17   *matrons of the upper class. The clan has gathered for chamber*
18   *music, refreshments and the anticipated daily report of MRS.*
19   *CANDOUR, who delights in chronicling the current scandals and*
20   *intrigues that are making the rounds of the city. LADY TEAZLE*
21   *is, at first, only an observer but soon joins the others to contribute*
22   *a juicy, if not altogether untruthful, rumor that signals her*
23   *acceptance into the group. The merriment of the occasion, however,*
24   *is soon interrupted by SIR PETER, who has come to reclaim his*
25   *wife and her precious reputation.)*
26
27   *(In playing the scene there should be a suggestion of polite chit-chat*
28   *touched with bitter satire and a biting wit that helps to distinguish*
29   *each of the social "types" who have gathered. There should also be*
30   *an emphasis upon gross deceit and sharp ridicule, mirrored in the*
31   *tone with which the dialog is spoken. SIR PETER's asides, spoken*
32   *directly to the audience, should be crisp and conversational to*
33   *contrast with the more precise and rapier-like exchanges between*
34   *the members of the school for scandal.)*
35 **LADY TEAZLE: What's the matter, Mrs. Candour?**

1   MRS. CANDOUR: They'll not allow our friend Miss Vermillion
2   to be handsome.
3   LADY SNEERWELL: Oh, surely she is a pretty woman.
4   CRABTREE: I am very glad you think so, ma'am.
5   MRS. CANDOUR: She has a charming fresh color.
6   LADY TEAZLE: Yes, when it is fresh put on.
7   MRS. CANDOUR: Oh, fie! I'll swear her color is natural: I have
8   seen it come and go!
9   LADY TEAZLE: I dare swear you have, ma'am: it goes off at
10   night and comes again in the morning.
11   SIR BENJAMIN: True, ma'am, it not only comes and goes; but,
12   what's more, egad, her maid can fetch and carry it!
13   MRS. CANDOUR: Ha! ha! ha! How I hate to hear you talk so! But
14   surely, now, her sister is, or was, very handsome.
15   CRABTREE: Who? Mrs. Evergreen? O, Lord! She's six-and-fifty
16   if she's an hour!
17   MRS. CANDOUR: How positively you wrong her; fifty-two or
18   fifty-three is the utmost — and I don't think she looks more.
19   SIR BENJAMIN: Ah! There's no judging by her looks, unless one
20   could see her face.
21   LADY SNEERWELL: Well, well, if Mrs. Evergreen does take
22   some pains to repair the ravages of time, you must allow
23   she effects it with great ingenuity; and surely that's better
24   than the careless manner in which the widow Ochre caulks
25   her wrinkles.
26   SIR BENJAMIN: Nay, now, Lady Sneerwell, you are severe upon
27   the widow. Come, come, 'tis not that she paints so ill — but,
28   when she has finished her face, she joins it on so badly to
29   her neck that she looks like a mended statue, in which the
30   connoisseur may see at once that the head's modern though
31   the trunk's antique!
32   CRABTREE: Ha! ha! ha! Well said, nephew!
33   MRS. CANDOUR: Ha! ha! ha! Well, you make me laugh; but I vow
34   I hate you for it. What do you think of Miss Simper?
35   SIR BENJAMIN: Why, she has very pretty teeth.

1   LADY TEAZLE: Yes; and on that account, when she is neither
2   speaking nor laughing (which very seldom happens), she
3   never absolutely shuts her mouth, but leaves it always on
4   ajar, as it were — thus.
5   MRS. CANDOUR: How can you be so ill-natured?
6   LADY TEAZLE: Nay, I allow even that's better than the pains
7   Mrs. Prim takes to conceal her losses in front. She draws
8   her mouth till it positively resembles the aperture of a poor's
9   box, and all her words appear to slide out edgewise, as it
10   were — thus: *How do you do, madam? Yes, madam.*
11   LADY SNEERWELL: Very well, Lady Teazle; I see you can be a
12   little severe.
13   LADY TEAZLE: In defence of a friend it is but justice. But here
14   comes Sir Peter to spoil our pleasantry.
15   SIR PETER: Ladies, your most obedient. *(Aside)* Mercy on me,
16   here is the whole set! A character dead at every word, I
17   suppose.
18   MRS. CANDOUR: I am rejoiced you are come, Sir Peter. They
19   have been so censorious — and Lady Teazle as bad as
20   anyone.
21   SIR PETER: That must be very distressing to you, Mrs.
22   Candour, I dare swear.
23   MRS. CANDOUR: Oh, they will allow good qualities to nobody;
24   not even good nature to our friend Mrs. Pursy.
25   LADY TEAZLE: What, the fat dowager who was at Mrs.
26   Quadrille's last night?
27   MRS. CANDOUR: Nay, her bulk is her misfortune; and when
28   she takes so much pains to get rid of it, you ought not to
29   reflect on her.
30   LADY SNEERWELL: That's very true, indeed.
31   LADY TEAZLE: Yes, I know she almost lives on acids and small
32   whey; laces herself by pulleys; and often, in the hottest noon
33   in summer, you may see her on a little squat pony, with her
34   hair plaited up behind like a drummer's and puffing round
35   the ring on a full trot.

1   MRS. CANDOUR: I thank you, Lady Teazle, for defending her.

2   SIR PETER: Yes, a good defence, truly.

3   MRS. CANDOUR: Truly, Lady Teazle is as censorious as Miss
4   Sallow.

5   CRABTREE: Yes, and she is a curious being to pretend to be
6   censorious — an awkward gawky, without any one good
7   point under heaven.

8   MRS. CANDOUR: Positively you shall not be so very severe.
9   Miss Sallow is a near relation of mine by marriage, and, as
10   for her person, great allowance is to be made; for, let me
11   tell you, a woman labors under many disadvantages who
12   tries to pass for a girl of six-and-thirty.

13   LADY SNEERWELL: Though, surely, she is handsome still —
14   and for the weakness in her eyes, considering how much
15   she reads by candlelight, it is not to be wondered at.

16   MRS. CANDOUR: True; and then as to her manner, upon my
17   word, I think it is particularly graceful, considering she
18   never had the least education; for you know her mother was
19   a Welsh milliner, and her father a sugar-baker at Bristol.

20   SIR BENJAMIN: Ah! You are both of you too good-natured!

21   SIR PETER: *(Aside)* Yes, damned good-natured! This their own
22   relation! Mercy on me!

23   MRS. CANDOUR: For my part, I own I cannot bear to hear a
24   friend ill spoken of.

25   SIR PETER: No, to be sure.

26   SIR BENJAMIN: Oh! You are of a moral turn. Mrs. Candour and
27   I can sit for an hour and hear Lady Stucco talk sentiment.

28   LADY TEAZLE: Nay, I vow Lady Stucco is very well with the
29   dessert after dinner; for she's just like the French fruit one
30   cracks for mottoes — made up of paint and proverb.

31   MRS. CANDOUR: Well, I will never join in ridiculing a friend;
32   and so I constantly tell my cousin Ogle, and you all know
33   what pretensions she has to be critical on beauty.

34   CRABTREE: Oh, to be sure! She has herself the oddest
35   countenance that ever was seen; 'tis a collection of features

1   from all the different countries of the globe.
2   SIR BENJAMIN: So she has, indeed — an Irish front —.
3   CRABTREE: Caledonian locks —.
4   SIR BENJAMIN: Dutch nose —.
5   CRABTREE: Austrian lips —.
6   SIR BENJAMIN: Complexion of a Spaniard —.
7   CRABTREE: And teeth *à la Chinoise* —.
8   SIR BENJAMIN: In short, her face resembles a *table d'hôte* at
9   Spa — where no two guests are of a nation.
10 CRABTREE: Or a congress at the close of a general war —
11   wherein all the members, even to her eyes, appear to have
12   a different interest, and her nose and chin are the only
13   parties likely to join issue.
14 MRS. CANDOUR: Ha! ha! ha!
15 SIR PETER: *(Aside)* Mercy on my life — a person they dine with
16   twice a week!
17 LADY SNEERWELL: Go — go — you are a couple of provoking
18   toads!
19 MRS. CANDOUR: Nay, but I vow you shall not carry the laugh
20   off so — for give me leave to say, that Mrs. Ogle —
21 SIR PETER: Madam, madam, I beg your pardon — there's no
22   stopping these good gentlemen's tongues. But when I tell
23   you, Mrs. Candour, that the lady they are abusing is a
24   particular friend of mine, I hope you'll not take her part.
25 LADY SNEERWELL: Ha! ha! ha! Well said, Sir Peter! But you
26   are a cruel creature — too phlegmatic for a jest yourself,
27   and too peevish to allow wit in others.
28 SIR PETER: Ah, madam, true wit is more nearly allied to good
29   nature than your ladyship is aware of.
30 LADY TEAZLE: True, Sir Peter: I believe they are so near akin
31   that they can never be united.
32 SIR BENJAMIN: Or rather, madam, I suppose them man and
33   wife because one seldom sees them together.
34 LADY TEAZLE: But Sir Peter is such an enemy to scandal, I
35   believe he would have it put down by Parliament.

1   SIR PETER: 'Fore heaven, madam, if they were to consider the
2   sporting with reputation of as much importance as poaching
3   on manors, and pass an act for the preservation of fame, I
4   believe many would thank them for the bill!
5   LADY SNEERWELL: Oh, lud! Sir Peter! Would you deprive us of
6   our privileges?
7   SIR PETER: Ay, madam; and then no person should be
8   permitted to kill characters and run down reputations but
9   qualified old maids and disappointed widows!
10   LADY SNEERWELL: Go, you monster!
11   MRS. CANDOUR: But, surely, you would not be quite so severe
12   on those who only report what they hear?
13   SIR PETER: Yes, madam, I would have law merchant for them
14   too; and in all cases of slander currency, whenever the
15   drawer of the lie was not to be found, the injured parties
16   should have a right to come on any of the indorsers.
17   CRABTREE: Well, for my part, I believe there never was a
18   scandalous tale without some foundation.
19   LADY SNEERWELL: Come, ladies, shall we sit down to cards
20   in the next room? Sir Peter, you are not going to leave us?
21   SIR PETER: Your ladyship must excuse me: I'm called away by
22   particular business. But I leave my character behind me.
23   SIR BENJAMIN: Well — certainly, Lady Teazle, that lord of
24   yours is a strange being. I could tell you some stories of him
25   would make you laugh heartily if he were not your husband.
26   LADY TEAZLE: Oh, pray don't mind that — come, do let's hear
27   them!
28
29
30
31
32
33
34
35

from **The Importance of Being Earnest** *(1895)*
Oscar Wilde

At first glance, this "trivial play for serious people" seems a cobweb of deception, misunderstanding and mistaken identity. Beginning with a series of episodes in which two young sophisticates seek the hands of two young and reserved ladies, the play suddenly shifts focus to reveal the more serious nature of extravagantly absurd and artificial customs and attitudes that govern polite society. The characters are not realistic, and the obstacles they face before eventual reunion are not without moments of intrigue and amusing invention. In their witty exchanges they are always charming and elegant, even when saying disagreeable things. They follow a definite pattern of behavior accepted in the historical time as the "proper" way to live in a civilized society, and any departure from it would be considered "barbaric."

It is typical of this comedy of manners that the humor arises from the sparkling dialog, the social amenities and the always charming precision with which etiquette and high fashion are displayed. All young men are would-be wits and all young ladies are exquisite hostesses. In playing the scene the actor should be aware that it is traditionally "presentational," or audience centered, style and that no attempt is made to disguise the fact that this is a theatrical performance. The actor should face the audience as often as possible and speak in a clear and precise voice. Every movement, stance and pose should be elegant and poised while every exchange of dialog should be punctuated with the use of fans or handkerchiefs.

Although there is no need to appear artificial or stiff, there should be a suggestion of erect posture and studied gesture to lend historical authenticity to the superficial type of characters. There should also be a suggestion of overly polite manners and delicacy of behavior in the relationship between the young man and the young lady. The actors may also wish to pay special attention to the language of the dialog and to convey the wit of the line with crisp, well articulated sounds that help to reinforce the humor of the moment.

Everyday behavior in the historical period was more formal, polite and conventional than our current customs or manners. Individual actions of characters were governed by a rigid, inflexible social standard and an exaggerated sense of proper decorum.

CAST

JACK

GWENDOLYN

LADY BRACKNELL

SCENE

Morning room in Algernon's flat in Half-Moon Street, London.

APPROACH

Jack, a rascal and spendthrift, finds himself hopelessly in love at first sight with Gwendolyn, a refined and attractive young lady who fancies herself the most precious and desirable beauty in society. He secretly wishes for an opportunity to be alone with her so that he may reveal his feelings; and the moment is provided when Lady Bracknell, Gwendolyn's prudish and snappish mother, unexpectedly retires from the room to listen to a program of chamber music prepared by Jack's best friend, Algernon. As the scene opens, there is an uncomfortable moment of silence, with Gwendolyn seated nervously on the sofa and Jack standing shyly near an upstage chair. He is concerned that his reputation as an extravagant and carefree gentleman will not appeal to such a charming lady; and she is concerned that the man for whom she feels such a strong attraction may not propose in the romantic manner she hopes for in this setting.

1   JACK: Charming day it has been, Miss Fairfax.

2   GWENDOLYN: Pray don't talk to me about the weather, Mr.

3   Worthing. Whenever people talk to me about the weather,

4   I always feel quite certain that they mean something else.

5   And that makes me so nervous.

6   JACK: I do mean something else.

7   GWENDOLYN: I thought so. In fact, I am never wrong.

8   JACK: And I would like to be allowed to take advantage of Lady

9   Bracknell's temporary absence . . .

10   GWENDOLYN: I would certainly advise you to do so. Mamma

11   has a way of coming back suddenly into a room that I have

12   often had to speak to her about.

13   JACK: Miss Fairfax, ever since I met you I have admired you

14   more than any girl . . . I have ever met since . . . I met you.

15   GWENDOLYN: Yes, I am quite well aware of the fact. And I often

16   wish that in public, at any rate, you had been more

17   demonstrative. For me you have always had an irresistible

18   fascination. Even before I met you I was far from indifferent

19   to you. We live, as I hope you know, Mr. Worthing, in an age

20   of ideals. The fact is constantly mentioned in the more

21   expensive monthly magazines, and has reached the

22   provincial pulpits, I am told; and my ideal has always been

23   to love someone of the name of Ernest. There is something

24   in that name that inspires confidence. The moment Algernon

25   first mentioned to me that he had a friend called Ernest, I

26   knew I was destined to love you!

27   JACK: You really love me, Gwendolyn?

28   GWENDOLYN: Passionately!

29   JACK: Darling! You don't know how happy you've made me.

30   GWENDOLYN: My own Ernest!

31   JACK: But you don't really mean to say that you couldn't love

32   me if my name wasn't Ernest?

33   GWENDOLYN: But your name is Ernest.

34   JACK: Yes, I know it is. But supposing it was something else?

35   Do you mean to say you couldn't love me then?

1	GWENDOLYN: Ah! That is clearly a metaphysical speculation,
2	and like most metaphysical speculations has very little
3	reference at all to the actual facts of real life, as we know
4	them.
5	JACK: Personally, darling, to speak quite candidly, I don't much
6	care about the name of Ernest . . . I don't think the name
7	suits me at all.
8	GWENDOLYN: It suits you perfectly. It is a divine name. It has
9	a music of its own. It produces vibrations.
10	JACK: Well, really, Gwendolyn, I must say that I think there are
11	lots of other much nicer names. I think Jack, for instance,
12	a charming name.
13	GWENDOLYN: Jack? No, there is very little music in the name
14	Jack, if any at all, indeed. It does not thrill. It produces
15	absolutely no vibrations. I have known several Jacks, and
16	they all, without exception, were more than usually plain.
17	Besides, Jack is a notorious domesticity for John! And I pity
18	any woman who is married to a man called John. She would
19	probably never be allowed to know the entrancing pleasure
20	of a single moment's solitude. The only really safe name is
21	Ernest.
22	JACK: Gwendolyn, I must get christened at once — I mean we
23	must get married at once! There is no time to be lost.
24	GWENDOLYN: Married, Mr. Worthing?
25	JACK: Well, surely. You know that I love you, and you led me to
26	believe, Miss Fairfax, that you were not absolutely
27	indifferent to me.
28	GWENDOLYN: I adore you. But you haven't proposed to me yet.
29	Nothing has been said at all about marriage. The subject
30	has not even been touched on.
31	JACK: Well, may I propose to you now?
32	GWENDOLYN: I think it would be an admirable opportunity.
33	And to spare you any possible disappointment, Mr.
34	Worthing, I think it is only fair to tell you quite frankly
35	beforehand that I am fully determined to accept you.

1   JACK: Gwendolyn!

2   GWENDOLYN: Yes, Mr. Worthing, what have you got to say to
3   me?

4   JACK: You know what I have got to say to you.

5   GWENDOLYN: Yes, but you don't say it.

6   JACK: Gwendolyn, will you marry me?

7   GWENDOLYN: Of course I will, darling. How long you have
8   been about it! I am afraid you have had very little experience
9   in how to propose.

10 JACK: My own one, I have never loved anyone in the world but
11   you.

12 GWENDOLYN: Yes, but men often propose for practice. I know
13   my brother Gerald does. All my girlfriends tell me so. What
14   wonderfully blue eyes you have, Ernest! They are quite,
15   quite blue. I hope you will always look at me just like that,
16   especially when there are other people present.

17 LADY BRACKNELL: Mr. Worthing! Rise, sir, from that semi-
18   recumbent posture. It is most indecorous.

19 GWENDOLYN: Mamma! I must beg you to retire. This is no
20   place for you. Besides, Mr. Worthing has not quite finished yet.

21 LADY BRACKNELL: Finished what, may I ask?

22 GWENDOLYN: I am engaged to Mr. Worthing, Mamma.

23 LADY BRACKNELL: Pardon me, you are not engaged to
24   anyone. When you do become engaged to someone, I, or your
25   father, should his health permit him, will inform you of the
26   fact. An engagement should come on a young girl as a
27   surprise, pleasant or unpleasant as the case may be. It is
28   hardly a matter that she should be allowed to arrange for
29   herself. And now I have a few questions to put to you, Mr.
30   Worthing. While I am making these inquiries, you,
31   Gwendolyn, will wait for me below in the carriage.

32 GWENDOLYN: Mamma!

33 LADY BRACKNELL: In the carriage, Gwendolyn! Gwendolyn,
34   the carriage!

35 GWENDOLYN: Yes, Mamma.

1   LADY BRACKNELL: You can take a seat, Mr. Worthing.

2   JACK: Thank you, Lady Bracknell, I prefer standing.

3   LADY BRACKNELL: I feel bound to tell you that you are not
4   down on my list of eligible young men, although I have the
5   same list as the dear Duchess of Bolton has. We work
6   together, in fact. However, I am quite ready to enter your
7   name, should your answers be what a really affectionate
8   mother requires. Do you smoke?

9   JACK: Well, yes, I must admit I smoke.

10   LADY BRACKNELL: I am glad to hear it. A man should always
11   have an occupation of some kind. There are far too many
12   idle men in London as it is. How old are you?

13   JACK: Twenty-nine.

14   LADY BRACKNELL: A very good age to be married at. I have
15   always been of the opinion that a man who desires to get
16   married should know either everything or nothing. Which
17   do you know?

18   JACK: I know nothing, Lady Bracknell.

19   LADY BRACKNELL: I am pleased to hear it. I do not approve
20   of anything that tampers with natural ignorance. Ignorance
21   is like a delicate, exotic fruit; touch it and the bloom is gone.
22   The whole theory of modern education is radically unsound.
23   Fortunately in England, at any rate, education produces no
24   effect whatsoever. If it did, it would prove a serious danger
25   to the upper classes, and probably lead to acts of violence
26   in Grosvenor Square. What is your income?

27   JACK: Between seven and eight thousand a year.

28   LADY BRACKNELL: In land, or in investments?

29   JACK: In investments, chiefly.

30   LADY BRACKNELL: That is satisfactory. What between the
31   duties expected of one during one's lifetime, and the duties
32   exacted from one after one's death, land has ceased to be
33   either a profit or a pleasure. It gives one position, and
34   prevents one from keeping it up. That's all that can be said
35   about land.

1   JACK: I have a country house with some land, of course, attached
2   to it, about fifteen hundred acres, I believe; but I don't
3   depend on that for my real income. In fact, as far as I can
4   make out, the poachers are the only people who make
5   anything out of it.
6   LADY BRACKNELL: A country house! How many bedrooms?
7   Well, that point can be cleared up afterwards. You have a
8   town house, I hope? A girl with a simple, unspoiled nature,
9   like Gwendolyn, could hardly be expected to reside in the
10   country.
11   JACK: Well, I own a house in Belgrave Square, but it is let by the
12   year to Lady Bloxham. Of course, I can get it back whenever
13   I like, at six months' notice.
14   LADY BRACKNELL: Lady Bloxham? I don't know her.
15   JACK: Oh, she goes about very little. She is a lady considerably
16   advanced in years.
17   LADY BRACKNELL: Ah, nowadays that is no guarantee of
18   respectability of character. What number in Belgrave
19   Square?
20   JACK: 149.
21   LADY BRACKNELL: The unfashionable side. I thought there
22   was something. However, that could easily be altered.
23   JACK: Do you mean the fashion, or the side?
24   LADY BRACKNELL: Both, if necessary, I presume. What are
25   your politics?
26   JACK: Well, I am afraid I really have none. I am a Liberal
27   Unionist.
28   LADY BRACKNELL: Oh, they count as Tories. They dine with
29   us. Or come in the evening, at any rate. Now to minor
30   matters. Are your parents living?
31   JACK: I have lost both my parents.
32   LADY BRACKNELL: To lose one parent, Mr. Worthing, may be
33   regarded as a misfortune; to lose both looks like
34   carelessness. Who was your father? He was evidently a man
35   of some wealth. Was he born in what the Radical papers call

1   the purple of commerce, or did he rise from the ranks of
2   the aristocracy?
3   JACK: I am afraid I really don't know. The fact is, Lady Brack-
4   nell, I said I had lost my parents. It would be nearer to the
5   truth to say that my parents seem to have lost me. I don't
6   actually know who I am by birth. I was . . . well, I was found.
7   LADY BRACKNELL: Found!
8   JACK: The late Mr. Thomas Cardew, an old gentleman of a very
9   charitable and kindly disposition, found me, and gave me
10   the name of Worthing, because he happened to have a first-
11   class ticket for Worthing in his pocket at the time. Worthing
12   is a place in Sussex. It is a seaside resort.
13   LADY BRACKNELL: Where did the charitable gentleman who
14   had a first-class ticket for this seaside resort find you?
15   JACK: In a hand-bag.
16   LADY BRACKNELL: A hand-bag!
17   JACK: Yes, Lady Bracknell. I was in a hand-bag — a somewhat
18   large, black leather hand-bag, with handles to it — an
19   ordinary hand-bag in fact.
20   LADY BRACKNELL: In what locality did this Mr. Thomas
21   Cardew come from this ordinary hand-bag?
22   JACK: In the cloak-room at Victoria Station. It was given to him
23   in mistake for his own.
24   LADY BRACKNELL: The cloak-room at Victoria Station?
25   JACK: Yes. The Brighton line.
26   LADY BRACKNELL: The line is immaterial. Mr. Worthing, I
27   confess I feel somewhat bewildered by what you have just
28   told me. To be born, or at any rate bred, in a hand-bag,
29   whether it had handles or not, seems to me to display a
30   contempt for the ordinary decencies of family life that
31   reminds one of the worst excesses of the French Revolution.
32   And I presume you know what that unfortunate movement
33   led to? As for the particular locality in which the hand-bag
34   was found, a cloak-room at a railway station might serve to
35   conceal a social indiscretion — has probably, indeed, been

1   used for that purpose before now — but it could hardly be
2   regarded as an assured basis for a recognized position in
3   good society.
4 JACK: May I ask you then what you would advise me to do? I
5   need hardly say I would do anything in the world to ensure
6   Gwendolyn's happiness.
7 LADY BRACKNELL: I would strongly advise you, Mr. Worthing,
8   to try and acquire some relations as soon as possible, and
9   to make a definite effort to produce at any rate one parent,
10   of either sex, before the season is quite over.
11 JACK: Well, I don't see how I could possibly manage to do that.
12   I can produce the hand-bag at any moment. It is in my
13   dressing room at home. I really think that should satisfy
14   you, Lady Bracknell.
15 LADY BRACKNELL: Me, sir! What has it to do with me? You
16   can hardly imagine that I and Lord Bracknell would dream
17   of allowing our only daughter — a girl brought up with the
18   utmost care — to marry into a cloak-room, and form an
19   alliance with a hand-bag! Good morning, Mr. Worthing!
20 *(GWENDOLYN FAIRFAX, the young lady from the city, has now*
21 *decided to pay a visit to CECILY CARDEW, a most attractive and*
22 *innocent young girl who has always resided in the seclusion of the*
23 *country. Each is now engaged to be married to a gentleman who*
24 *calls himself ERNEST WORTHING, the name assumed by both*
25 *JACK and his friend ALGERNON because it is so appealing to the*
26 *ladies' romantic imagination. It is the first meeting of the two, and*
27 *each is very careful to appear refined, elegant and worldly. Although*
28 *as the scene progresses it becomes apparent that they may be engaged*
29 *to the same gentleman, both GWENDOLYN and CECILY are*
30 *conscious that they must still exhibit social grace and decorum.)*
31
32 *(The humor of the situation, compounded by a series of*
33 *misunderstandings and suspicions, is highlighted by the rather*
34 *frequent reference to individual diaries that each young lady*
35 *maintains to verify the truth of their respective engagements. As the*

1   *scene begins, CECILY is in the garden of the manor house placing*
2   *some books on the table Down Left. She sits and turns the pages of*
3   *her diary, and then rises to move to the rosebush Up Right. Picking*
4   *a rose, she turns to the table and is gazing into the distance with*
5   *dreamy eyes as GWENDOLYN enters from Up Right. Sensing that*
6   *someone is staring at her, CECILY turns slowly to speak. Please*
7   *approach the scene with honesty and restraint to reveal the triviality*
8   *of the skirmish.)*
9   **CECILY:** Pray let me introduce myself to you. My name is Cecily
10   Cardew.
11   **GWENDOLYN:** Cecily Cardew? What a very sweet name!
12   Something tells me that we are going to be great friends. I
13   like you already more than I can say. My first impressions
14   of people are never wrong.
15   **CECILY:** How nice of you to like me so much after we have
16   known each other such a comparatively short time. Pray
17   sit down.
18   **GWENDOLYN:** With pleasure!
19   **CECILY:** And you will always call me Cecily, won't you?
20   **GWENDOLYN:** If you wish.
21   **CECILY:** Then that is all quite settled, is it not?
22   **GWENDOLYN:** I hope so. Perhaps this might be a favourable
23   opportunity for my mentioning who I am. My father is Lord
24   Bracknell. You have heard of Papa, I suppose?
25   **CECILY:** I don't think so.
26   **GWENDOLYN:** Outside the family circle, Papa, I am glad to
27   say, is entirely unknown. I think that is quite as it should
28   be. The home seems to me to be the proper sphere for the
29   man. And certainly once a man begins to neglect his
30   domestic duties he becomes painfully effeminate, does he
31   not? And I don't like that. It makes men so very attractive.
32   Cecily, Mamma, whose views on education are remarkably
33   strict, has brought me up to be extremely shortsighted; it
34   is part of her system; so do you mind my looking at you
35   through my glasses?

1 CECILY: Oh, not at all, Gwendolyn! I am very fond of being
2   looked at.
3 GWENDOLYN: You are here on a short visit, I suppose?
4 CECILY: Oh, no! I live here.
5 GWENDOLYN: Really? Your mother, no doubt, or some female
6   relative of advanced years, resides here also?
7 CECILY: Oh, no! I have no mother, nor, in fact, any relations.
8 GWENDOLYN: Indeed?
9 CECILY: My dear guardian, with the assistance of Miss Prism,
10   has the arduous task of looking after me.
11 GWENDOLYN: Your guardian?
12 CECILY: Yes, I am Mr. Worthing's ward.
13 GWENDOLYN: Oh! It is strange he never mentioned to me that
14   he had a ward. How secretive of him! He grows more
15   interesting hourly. I am not sure, however, that the news
16   inspires me with feelings of unmixed delight. I am very fond
17   of you, Cecily; I have liked you ever since I met you! But I
18   am bound to state that now that I know that you are Mr.
19   Worthing's ward, I cannot help expressing a wish that you
20   were — well, just a little older than you seem to be — and
21   not quite so very alluring in appearance. In fact, if I may
22   speak candidly —
23 CECILY: Pray do! I think that whenever one has anything
24   unpleasant to say, one should always be quite candid.
25 GWENDOLYN: Well, to speak with perfect candour, Cecily, I
26   wish that you were fully forty-two, and more than usually
27   plain for your age. Ernest has a strong upright nature. He
28   is the very soul of truth and honour. Disloyalty would be as
29   impossible to him as deception. But even men of the noblest
30   possible moral character are extremely susceptible to the
31   influence of the physical charms of others. Modern, no less
32   than Ancient History, supplies us with many most painful
33   examples of what I refer to. If it were not so, indeed, history
34   would be quite unreadable.
35 CECILY: I beg your pardon, Gwendolyn, did you say Ernest?

141

1   GWENDOLYN: Yes.

2   CECILY: Oh, but it is not Mr. Ernest Worthing who is my
3   guardian. It is his brother — his elder brother.

4   GWENDOLYN: Ernest never mentioned to me that he had a
5   brother.

6   CECILY: I am sorry to say that they have not been on good terms
7   for a long time.

8   GWENDOLYN: Ah! That accounts for it. And now that I think of
9   it I have never heard any man mention his brother. The
10   subject seems distasteful to most men. Cecily, you have lifted
11   a load from my mind. I was growing almost anxious. It would
12   have been terrible if any cloud had come across a friendship
13   like ours, would it not? Of course you are quite, quite sure
14   that it is not Mr. Ernest Worthing who is your guardian?

15   CECILY: Quite sure. In fact, I am going to be his.

16   GWENDOLYN: I beg your pardon?

17   CECILY: Dearest Gwendolyn, there is no reason why I should
18   make a secret of it to you. Our little country newspaper is
19   sure to chronicle the fact next week. Mr. Ernest Worthing
20   and I are engaged to be married.

21   GWENDOLYN: My darling Cecily, I think there must be some
22   slight error. Mr. Ernest Worthing is engaged to me. The
23   announcement will appear in the *Morning Post* on Saturday
24   at the latest.

25   CECILY: I am afraid you must be under some misconception.
26   Ernest proposed to me exactly ten minutes ago.

27   GWENDOLYN: It is very curious, for he asked me to be his wife
28   yesterday afternoon at 5:30. If you wish to verify the
29   incident, pray do so. I never travel without my diary. One
30   should always have something sensational to read on the
31   train. I am so sorry, dear Cecily, if it is any disappointment
32   to you, but I am afraid I have the prior claim.

33   CECILY: It would distress me more than I can tell you, dear
34   Gwendolyn, if it caused you any mental or physical anguish,
35   but I feel bound to point out that since Ernest proposed to

1   you he clearly has changed his mind.

2   GWENDOLYN: If the poor fellow has been entrapped into any

3   foolish promise I shall consider it my duty to rescue him at

4   once, and with a firm hand.

5   CECILY: Whatever unfortunate entanglement my dear boy

6   may have got into, I will never reproach him with it after

7   we are married.

8   GWENDOLYN: Do you allude to me, Miss Cardew, as an

9   entanglement? You are presumptuous. On an occasion of

10   this kind it becomes more than a moral duty to speak one's

11   mind. It becomes a pleasure.

12   CECILY: Do you suggest, Miss Fairfax, that I entrapped Ernest

13   into an engagement? How dare you? This is no time for

14   wearing the shallow mask of manners. When I see a spade

15   I call it a spade.

16   GWENDOLYN: I am glad to say that I have never seen a spade.

17   It is obvious that our social spheres have been widely

18   different. *(Looks around the garden.)* Are there many

19   interesting walks in the vicinity, Miss Cardew?

20   CECILY: Oh, yes! A great many. From the top of one of the hills

21   quite close one can see five counties.

22   GWENDOLYN: Five counties! I don't think I should like that; I

23   hate crowds.

24   CECILY: I suppose that is why you live in town?

25   GWENDOLYN: Quite a well-kept garden this is, Miss Cardew.

26   CECILY: So glad you like it, Miss Fairfax.

27   GWENDOLYN: I had no idea there were so many flowers in the

28   country.

29   CECILY: Oh, flowers are as common here, Miss Fairfax, as

30   people are in London.

31   GWENDOLYN: Personally, I cannot understand how anybody

32   manages to exist in the country, if anybody who is anybody

33   does. The country always bores me to death.

34   CECILY: Ah! This is what the newspapers call agricultural

35   depression, is it not? I believe the aristocracy are suffering

143

1   **very much from it just at present. It is almost an epidemic**

2   **amongst them, I have been told. May I offer you some tea,**

3   **Miss Fairfax?**

4   **GWENDOLYN:**   **Thank you.** *(Aside)* **Detestable girl! But I require**

5   **tea!**

6   **CECILY:**   **Sugar?**

7   **GWENDOLYN:**   **No, thank you. Sugar is not fashionable**

8   **anymore.**

9   **CECILY:**   **Cake or bread and butter?**

10   **GWENDOLYN:**   **Bread and butter, please. Cake is rarely seen at**

11   **the best houses nowadays.** *(Drinks tea.)* **You have filled my**

12   **tea with lumps of sugar, and though I asked most distinctly**

13   **for bread and butter, you have given me cake. I am known**

14   **for the gentleness of my disposition, and the extraordinary**

15   **sweetness of my nature, but I warn you, Miss Cardew, you**

16   **may go too far.**

17   **CECILY:**   **To save my poor, innocent, trusting boy from the**

18   **machinations of any other girl there are no lengths to which**

19   **I would not go.**

20   **GWENDOLYN:**   **From the moment I saw you I distrusted you. I**

21   **felt that you were false and deceitful. I am never deceived**

22   **in such matters. My first impressions of people are**

23   **invariably right.**

24   **CECILY:**   **It seems to me, Miss Fairfax, that I am trespassing on**

25   **your valuable time. No doubt you have many other calls of**

26   **a similar character to make in the neighborhood.**

27

28

29

30

31

32

33

34

35

from **Fashion** (1845)

Anna Cora Mowatt

Mr. Tiffany's success as a merchant leads his wife to assume the vain affectations and presumptions of high society and literally to open her doors to all the presumed poets, artists and exiled nobles of the day. Trueman, an honest but dull farmer and sincere family friend, comes to visit his now wealthy old neighbors and is dismayed to discover the superficiality and artifice that have invaded the Tiffany household. With the aid of the virtuous Gertrude, the family governess, Trueman helps to awaken the Tiffany family to the deceit and trickery of the parasites, especially the scheming Count Jolimaitre, and leads them back to the virtues of the simple life; thus proving in his native wisdom the basic goodness and honesty of "Yankee" ingenuity.

As America's early contribution to the comedy of manners style of playwriting, the playscript is intended as a good-natured satire upon the follies and affectations that often arise when a new nation begins to imitate foreign dress and speech. There is also the unabashed provincial pride expressed for the plain but inherently pure-of-heart American heroes who refused to adopt foreign fashions or manners. Most of the social and the political criticism in the play concerns the awkwardness with which New York society tries to imitate European taste and the fraud that foreign posturing perpetrates when it begins to replace native manners and customs.

In playing the scene the actor should keep in mind all of the general principles previously noted for the comedy of manners and then slightly exaggerate both movement and voice to suggest that these characters are merely masquerading as sophisticated and refined members of high society. There should be occasional mispronunciation of French phrases, awkward posture, painful posing, improper etiquette and an uncomfortable appearance as the characters try to imitate the latest European dress or manner but have some difficulty in sustaining their impersonation. The actor should also assume a boisterous laugh, frigid smile and stiff posture to suggest that the impersonation is not a confident one. Fans, handkerchiefs, snuffboxes, canes and eyeglasses may also be used to punctuate exchanges of comic dialog, but they should be handled incorrectly to highlight the inexperience and lack of poise by the character using them.

145

Facial expression appears to have been an important ingredient in suggesting character mood and attitude. There may also have been a more "natural" approach to performance technique when the actors wore costumes that mirrored everyday fashion or habit.

CAST

MRS. TIFFANY

TIFFANY

SERAPHINA

COUNT

146

SCENE

Mrs. Tiffany's parlor, late afternoon.

APPROACH

As the scene opens, Mr. Tiffany is scolding his wife for her recent extravagance, and she is reprimanding him for clinging to outdated manners and customs now that they are a family of wealth and social position. Although the exchange is civil for the most part, there is an undertone of anger and hostility that is only prevented from surfacing by the unexpected arrival of the dashing, penniless Count. The humor of the scene lies in the polite games the characters play as they try to convince each other of their own grace and sophistication. The reality of the situation, however, is that the Count is a disguised chef seeking a fortune by proposing to Seraphina, the Tiffanys' beautiful but naive daughter, and that the elder Tiffanys are so concerned with assuming proper social manners and gaining social status that they cannot see the truth of the present situation.

1   TIFFANY: Your extravagance will ruin me, Mrs. Tiffany!

2   MRS. TIFFANY: And your stinginess will ruin me, Mr. Tiffany!

3   It is totally and *toot a fate* impossible to convince you of the

4   necessity of keeping up appearances. There is a certain

5   display which every woman of fashion is forced to make!

6   TIFFANY: And pray who made *you* a woman of fashion?

7   MRS. TIFFANY: What a vulgar question! All women of fashion,

8   Mr. Tiffany —

9   TIFFANY: In this land are self-constituted, like you, Madam —

10   and *fashion* is the cloak for more sins than charity ever

11   covered! It was for *fashion's* sake that you insisted upon my

12   purchasing this expensive house — it was for *fashion's* sake

13   that you ran me in debt at every exorbitant upholsterer's

14   and extravagant furniture warehouse in the city — it was

15   for *fashion's* sake that you built that ruinous conservatory —

16   hired more servants than they have persons to wait upon —

17   and dressed your footman like a harlequin!

18   MRS. TIFFANY: Mr. Tiffany, you are thoroughly plebeian and

19   insufferably *American* in your groveling ideas. And, pray,

20   what was the occasion of these very *mal-ap-pro-pos*

21   remarks? Merely because I requested a paltry fifty dollars

22   to purchase a new style of headdress — a *bijou* of an article

23   just introduced in France.

24   TIFFANY: Time was, Mrs. Tiffany, when you manufactured

25   your own French headdress — then sold them to your

26   shortest-sighted customers. And all you knew about France,

27   of French either, was what you spelt out at the bottom of

28   your fashionplates — but now you have grown so

29   fashionable, forsooth, that you have forgotten how to speak

30   your mother tongue.

31   MRS. TIFFANY: Mr. Tiffany, Mr. Tiffany! Nothing is more

32   positively vulgarian — more *unaristocratic* than any

33   allusion to the past!

34   TIFFANY: Why, I thought, my dear, that *aristocrats* lived

35   principally upon the past — and traded in the market of

1   fashion with the bones of their ancestors for capital!

2 MRS. TIFFANY: Mr. Tiffany, such vulgar remarks are only

3   suitable to the counting-house; in my drawing room you

4   should —

5 TIFFANY: Vary my sentiments with my locality, as you change

6   your manners with your dress!

7 MRS. TIFFANY: Mr. Tiffany, I desire that you will purchase

8   Count d'Orsay's "Science of Etiquette," and learn how to

9   conduct yourself — especially before you appear at the

10   grand ball — which I shall give on Friday!

11 TIFFANY: Confound your balls, Madam! They make *footballs*

12   of my money, while you dance away all that I am worth! A

13   pretty time to give a ball when you know that I am on the

14   very brink of bankruptcy!

15 MRS. TIFFANY: So much the greater reason that nobody should

16   suspect your circumstances, or you would lose your credit

17   at once. Just at this crisis a ball is absolutely *necessary* to

18   save your reputation. There is Mrs. Adolphus Dashaway —

19   she gave the most splendid *fete* of the season — and I hear

20   on very good authority that her husband has not paid his

21   baker's bill in three months. Then there was Mrs.

22   Honeywood —

23 TIFFANY: Gave a ball the night before her husband shot

24   himself —. Perhaps you wish to drive me to follow his

25   example?

26 MRS. TIFFANY: Good gracious! Mr. Tiffany, how you talk! I beg

27   you won't mention anything of the kind. I consider black

28   the most becoming color. I'm sure I've done all that I could

29   to gratify you. There is that vulgar old torment, Trueman,

30   who gives one the lie fifty times a day — haven't I been very

31   civil to him?

32 TIFFANY: Civil to his *wealth*, Mrs. Tiffany! I told you that he was

33   a rich old farmer — the early friend of my father — my own

34   benefactor — and that I had reason to think he might assist

35   me in my present embarrassments. Your civility was *bought*

1   — and like most of your own purchases has yet to be *paid* for.
2   MRS. TIFFANY: And will be, no doubt! The condescension of a
3   woman of fashion should command any price. Mr. Trueman
4   is insupportably indecorous — he has insulted Count
5   Jolimaitre in the most outrageous manner. If the Count was
6   not so deeply interested — so *abime* with Seraphina, I am
7   sure he would never honour us by his visits again!
8   TIFFANY: So much the better — he shall never marry my
9   daughter! I am resolved on that. Why, madam, I am told
10   there is in Paris a regular matrimonial stock company, who
11   fit out indigent dandies for the market. How do I know but
12   this fellow is one of its creatures, and that he has come here
13   to increase its dividends by marrying a fortune?
14   MRS. TIFFANY: Nonsense, Mr. Tiffany. The Count, the most
15   fashionable young man in all New York — the intimate
16   friend of all the dukes and lords in Europe — not marry
17   your daughter? Not permit my Seraphina to become a
18   Countess? Mr. Tiffany, you are out of your senses!
19   TIFFANY: That would not be very wonderful, considering how
20   many years I have been united to you, my dear. Modern
21   physicians pronounce lunacy infectious!
22   MRS. TIFFANY: My dear Count, I am overjoyed at the very sight
23   of you!
24   COUNT: Flattered myself you'd be glad to see me, Madam —
25   knew it was not you *jour de reception.*
26   MRS. TIFFANY: But for you, Count, all days —
27   COUNT: I thought so. Ah, Miss Tiffany, on my honour, you're
28   looking beautiful!
29   SERAPHINA: Count, flattery from you —
30   COUNT: Your worthy Papa, I believe? Sir, your most obedient.
31   MRS. TIFFANY: I hope that we shall have the pleasure of
32   seeing you on Friday evening, Count?
33   COUNT: Madam, my invitations — my engagements — so
34   numerous — I can hardly answer for myself. And you
35   Americans take offense so easily.

1   MRS. TIFFANY: But, Count, everybody expects you at our ball
2   — you are the principal attraction.
3   SERAPHINA: Count, you *must* come!
4   COUNT: Since you insist — aw — aw — there's no resisting
5   you, Miss Tiffany.
6   SERAPHINA: I am so thankful. How can I repay your conde-
7   scension?
8   MRS. TIFFANY: Mr. Tiffany, pray come here — I have something
9   particular to say.
10   TIFFANY: Then speak out, my dear. I thought it was highly
11   improper just now to leave a girl with a young man?
12   MRS. TIFFANY: Oh, but the Count — that is different!
13   TIFFANY: I suppose you mean to say there's nothing of the
14   *man* about him?
15   COUNT: *(Aside)* Not a moment to lose! *(To SERAPHINA)* Miss
16   Tiffany, I have an unpleasant — a particularly unpleasant
17   piece of intelligence. You see, I have just received a letter
18   from my friend the — aw — the Earl of Airshire. The truth
19   is, the Earl's daughter — beg you won't mention it — has
20   distinguished me by a tender *penchant.*
21   SERAPHINA: I understand. And they wish you to return and
22   marry the young lady. But surely you will not leave us,
23   Count?
24   COUNT: If *you* bid me stay — I shouldn't have the conscience
25   — I couldn't *afford* to tear myself away. *(Aside)* I'm sure that's
26   honest.
27   SERAPHINA: Oh, Count!
28   COUNT: Say but one word — say that you shouldn't mind being
29   made a Countess — and I'll break with the Earl tomorrow.
30   SERAPHINA: Count, this surprises — but don't think of leaving
31   the country! We could not pass the time without you! I — yes,
32   yes, Count! I do consent!
33   COUNT: *(Aside)* I thought she would! *(To SERAPHINA)* Enchanted,
34   rapture, bliss, ecstasy and all that sort of thing. Words can't
35   express it, but you understand. But it must be kept a secret —

1   positively it *must.* If the rumor of our engagement were
2   whispered abroad — the Earl's daughter — the delicacy of
3   my situation — aw — you comprehend? It is even possible
4   that our nuptials, my charming Miss Tiffany, our *nuptials*
5   must take place in private.
6 SERAPHINA: Oh, that is quite impossible!
7 COUNT: It's the latest fashion abroad. The very latest! Ah, I
8   knew that would determine you. Can I depend on your
9   secrecy?
10 SERAPHINA: Oh, yes! Believe me!
11 MRS. TIFFANY: The brand new carriage is below! Count, my
12   daughter and I are about to take an airing in our new
13   *voyture* — will you honour us with your company?
14 COUNT: I — I have a most pressing engagement. A letter to
15   write to the Earl of Airshire — who is at present residing
16   in — aw — the Isle of Skye. I must bid you good morning.
17 MRS. TIFFANY: Good morning, Count. Come, Seraphina. Come!
18   *(The absurdity of the social posturing and the artificiality of the*
19   *COUNT's engagement to SERAPHINA reaches its comic climax*
20   *when the old family friend TRUEMAN unmasks the hypocrisy of*
21   *the characters at the conclusion of the playscript. With unabashed*
22   *and outspoken disapproval, TRUEMAN reveals the impending*
23   *bankruptcy and fraud engaged in by MR. TIFFANY as well, and*
24   *points each character toward a reconciliation with their own*
25   *conscience for the deceit and the deception used to gain social favor*
26   *and adultation.)*
27 MRS. TIFFANY: Oh, here is the Countess!
28 TIFFANY: Are — you — married yet?
29 SERAPHINA: Goodness, Papa, how you frighten me! No, I'm not
30   married — *quite!*
31 TIFFANY: Thank heaven!
32 MRS. TIFFANY: What's the matter? Why did you come back?
33 SERAPHINA: The clergyman wasn't at home — I came back for
34   my jewels — the Count said nobility couldn't get on without
35   them.

1   TIFFANY: I may be saved yet! Seraphina, my child, you will not
2   see me disgraced — ruined! I have been a kind father to
3   you — at least I have tried to be one — although your
4   mother's extravagance made a *madman* of me! The Count
5   is an impostor! You, Mr. Trueman, you will be my friend in
6   this hour of extreme need — you will advance the sum I
7   require to avoid ruination. I pledge myself to return it. My
8   wife — my child — who will support them were I — the
9   thought makes me frantic! You will aid me? You had a child
10   yourself.
11   TRUEMAN: But I did not *sell* her — it was her own doings.
12   Shame on you! Put a price on your own flesh and blood!
13   Shame on you!
14   TIFFANY: Save me — I conjure you — for my father's sake.
15   TRUEMAN: For your *father's* son's sake I will *not* aid you in
16   becoming a greater villain than you are! I am going to settle
17   this matter in my own way. I'm not given to preaching,
18   therefore I shall not say much about what you have done.
19   Your face speaks for itself — the crime has brought its
20   punishment along with it.
21   TIFFANY: Indeed it has, sir! In one year I have lived a century
22   of misery.
23   TRUEMAN: I believe you, and upon one condition I will assist
24   you.
25   TIFFANY: My friend — my first, ever kind friend — only name
26   it!
27   TRUEMAN: You must sell your house and all these gew-gaws,
28   and bundle your wife and daughter off to the country. There
29   let them learn economy, true independence, and home
30   virtues instead of foreign follies. As for youself, continue
31   your business — but let moderation, in future, be your
32   counsellor, and let *honesty* be your confidential clerk.
33   TIFFANY: Mr. Trueman, you have made existence once more
34   precious to me! My wife and daughter shall quit the city
35   to-morrow, and —

153

1   MRS. TIFFANY: It's all coming out right! It's all coming out
2   right! We'll go to the county of Catteraugus —
3   TRUEMAN: No, you won't! I make that a stipulation. Keep clear
4   of Catteraugus and other such social resorts. None of your
5   fashionable examples there!
6   COUNT: *(Enters.)* What can detain Seraphina — and her jewels?
7   I ought to be off with them!
8   TRUEMAN: Come forward, Mr. Count! And for the edification
9   of fashionable society confess that you're an impostor.
10 COUNT: An impostor? Why, you abominable old —
11 TRUEMAN: Oh, your feminine friend has told us all about it,
12   the cook — the valet — barber — and all that sort of thing.
13   Come, confess, and something may be done for you.
14 COUNT: Well, then, I do confess I am no count; but really, ladies
15   and gentlemen, I may recommend myself as the most capital
16   cook . . . or barber.
17 MRS. TIFFANY: Oh, Seraphina!
18 SERAPHINA: Oh, Mama!
19 TRUEMAN: Promise me, Mr. Count, to call upon the whole
20   circle of your fashionable acquaintances with your own
21   advertisements and in your cook's attire, and I will set you
22   up in business to-morrow. Better turn stomachs than turn
23   heads!
24 COUNT: Sir, command me for the most delicate *paté* — the
25   daintiest *croquette a la royale* — the most transcendent
26   *omelette soufflé* that ever issued from a French pastry-cook's
27   oven. I hope you will pardon my conduct, but I heard that
28   in America, where you pay homage to titles while you
29   profess to scorn them — where *Fashion* makes the basest
30   coin current — where you have no kings, no princes, no
31   *nobility* —
32 TRUEMAN: Stop there! I object to your use of that word. When
33   justice is found only among lawyers — health among
34   physicians — and patriotism among politicians, *then* may
35   you say that there is no *nobility* where there are no titles!

154

1   But we *have* kings, princes, and nobles in abundance — of
2   *Nature's* stamp, if not of Fashion's — we have honest men,
3   warm-hearted and brave, and we have women — gentle,
4   fair, and true, to whom no *title* could add *nobility*.
5
6   **EPILOGUE**
7
8   But, ere we close the scene, a word with you —
9   We charge you answer — Is this picture true?
10   Some little mercy to our efforts show,
11   Then let the world your honest verdict know.
12   Here let it see portrayed its ruling passion,
13   And learn to prize at its just value — *Fashion.*
14
15
16
17
18
19
20
21
22
23
24
25
26
27
28
29
30
31
32
33
34
35

SELECTED BIBLIOGRAPHY

The following textbooks and suggested readings are recommended for the beginning actor who may wish to become acquainted with the historical period and performance style related to the 18th and 19th century comedy of manners. The suggested readings also provide valuable insights and practical approaches to explore scene study as well as playscript interpretation as part of the rehearsal process. A serious application of the theories and the selected exercises presented in these recommended sources should also provide a solid, creative foundation for later approaching even more difficult and complex modern and contemporary scene performance in the chapters that follow.

Barker, Clive. *Theatre Games.* New York: Drama Book Specialists, 1977.

Bennett, Susan. *Theatre Audiences: A Theory of Production and Reception.* London: Routledge Press, 1990.

Colyer, Carlton. *The Art of Acting.* Colorado Springs, CO: Meriwether Publishing Ltd., 1989.

Crannell, Kenneth. *Voice and Articulation.* Third edition. Belmont, California: Wadsworth Publishers, 1996.

Dobree, Bonamy. *Restoration Comedy, 1660-1720.* Oxford: Clarendon Press, 1924.

Duerr, Edwin. *The Length and Depth of Acting.* New York: Holt, Rinehart and Winston, 1962.

Goldman, Michael. *The Actor's Freedom.* New York: Viking Press, 1975.

Hotson, Leslie. *The Commonwealth and Restoration Stage.* Cambridge: Harvard University Press, 1928.

Keleman, Stanley. *Emotional Anatomy.* Berkeley, California: Center Press, 1986.

Klein, Maxine. *Time, Space and Designs for the Actor.* Boston: Houghton-Mifflin Company, 1975.

Lynch, James. *Box, Pit and Gallery; Stage and Society in Johnson's London.* Berkeley, California: University of California Press, 1953.

Marowitz, Charles. *The Act of Being: Towards a Theory of Acting.* New York: Taplinger Press, 1978.

McGaw, Charles. *Working a Scene: An Actor's Approach.* New York: Holt, Rinehart and Winston, 1977.

Moody, Richard. *America Takes the Stage.* Bloomington, Indiana: Indiana University Press, 1955.

Palmer, J. L. *The Comedy of Manners.* New York: Russell and Russell, 1962.

Penrod, James. *Movement for the Performing Artist.* Palo Alto, California: Mayfield Publishing Company, 1974.

Powell, Jocelyn. *Restoration Theatre Production.* Boston: Routledge and Kegan Paul, 1984.

Rizzo, Raymond. *The Total Actor.* Indianapolis, Indiana: Bobbs-Merrill Publishers, 1975.

Spolin, Viola. *Improvisation for the Theatre.* Third edition. Evanston, Illinois: Northwestern University, 1999.

Styan, J.L. *Restoration Comedy in Performance.* Cambridge: Cambridge University Press, 1986.

Summers, Montague. *The Restoration Theatre.* London: Routledge and Sons, 1934.

CHAPTER FOUR

PLAYING
MODERN SCENES

*"A play ought to be written in which the people should
come and go, dine, talk of the weather, or play cards,
not because the author wants it but because that is what
happens in real life. Life on the stage should be as it
really is, and the people, too, should be as they are."*

— Anton Chekhov

The movement toward "modernism" in the theatre began c. 1870, and most of the general characteristics associated with this "realistic" style of performance and production are attributed to the playwright Henrik Ibsen (1828-1906), who is commonly referred to as the "Father of Modern Drama." It was Ibsen's primary goal to write playscripts that were truthful depictions of the world in which he lived, and he thought of himself as one who revealed the truth about human nature and society as objectively as possible.

Ibsen's approach to modernism was to identify universal themes such as the struggle for integrity or personal values, or the conflict between duty to oneself and duty to others as a means of expressing the basic dignity and worth of mankind. His many variations on these themes were primarily concentrated upon personal relationships between characters (*A Doll's House*, 1879), upon the relationship of man and society (*An Enemy of the People*, 1882) and upon the need for understanding the morality that inhibited man's ability to express himself freely (*Ghosts*, 1881). Each of his characters exhibits a behavior that is directly related to hereditary or environmental causes and psychological motivation is portrayed as the primary motivation for all character action.

In his effort to suggest realistic authenticity and believability through the use of observed facts of daily existence, Ibsen discarded the popular comedy of manner use of the aside, the classical and Shakespearean use of the set speech and the soliloquy, the use of song and verse drama in the quest for greater reality in dialog. Polite, everyday language that revealed a character's "subtext" through ordinary business and simple costumes became Ibsen's approach to depicting characters as helpless agents of social action motivated by hereditary and environmental forces. There was also a need for Ibsen's playscripts to be much more than just entertainment and he wrote social "problem plays" to educate, provoke discussion, convey ideas and enhance insights.

Those who followed Ibsen's lead in the late 19th and early 20th centuries elaborated upon his approach to realism and supplemented his theories with additional emphasis upon dialog that was representative of the "common man," action that reflected the "workaday world," settings that mirrored the "average living room" and character that in its directness and simplicity also "taught a social or moral lesson." It was the direct, objective observation of life that helped Ibsen explore personal relationships and subsequent social problems with a more detached, reporter-like attitude in his playscripts. Later, some of his followers embraced an approach to realism called *photographic representation of life*, which tried to capture specific visual portraits of authentic people, places and even events as if they had been "snapped" by a camera.

The march toward modernism in the theatre suggests quite clearly that playscripts must be realistic and that characters must render factual interpretations of life. That is why in their attempts to rebel against earlier forms of comedy of manner and melodrama the advocates of realism ● dealt with the *here* and *now* only ● interpreted life *objectively* without bias ● used *uncomplicated* words and phrases ● chose the *usual* and the *commonplace and* ● gave the impression of *simple truth*. There was a concentrated effort to communicate directly and honestly without deception or distortion, and to present the ultimate truth about human nature and even society with a minimum of exaggeration or artifice.

In playing modern scenes the actor must keep in mind that the basic principles of realism suggest that the stage actions and images being presented are but a "picture" of reality, *not* reality itself. Remember that the effort to achieve realistic characterization with only subtlety and suggestion is the primary performance goal; and that any attempt to startle or to impress in performance should be avoided as a source of distraction. Much like Hamlet's advice to his Players, the actor of modern scenes should still "hold the mirror up to nature," but must also insure that there will be no theatrical deception that will interfere with the realistic action or the realistic character portrait drawn as the playwright has seen it in everyday life.

In considering the application of these basic performance principles to the specific playscripts included in this chapter, the actor should be devoted in theory to the sanctity of facts and the deduction of truth based upon the data that the playwright collected from observed human nature to draw the character portrait in each selected scene. The actor should also approach the depiction of character with merciless clarity and impartiality, detail the environment with scrupulous fidelity, delineate ideas and thoughts without artificiality or sentimentality and portray actions that are both meticulous and precise.

In playing scenes of modern realism the actor must keep in mind that the stage action and dialog being presented should "mirror" reality and be as honest, spontaneous and natural as possible to suggest that the characters being depicted are drawn from "real-life" role models.

Playing the Role

The actor who engages in scene study and playscript interpretation for playing the role in a modern performance should consider the traditional dramatization of the day-to-day struggles depicted in realism as the key to understanding the playwright's point of view in terms of both the character and the theme. Because realism is primarily concerned with commonplace characters, ordinary facts and non-heroic actions, the theme is usually concerned with a frank and honest treatment of a particular topic that is social or ethical in nature. There is no temptation to glorify or to idealize the common man but there is a certain grace and beauty depicted in the character's basic goodness as he seeks to reveal what the French philosopher Denis Diderot termed the "inner truths" of his being.

There is also a conscious attempt to give everyday life a sense of dignity and importance so that man may ultimately glimpse his own self-worth and value in the universe. The acute interest in accurate and detailed observation, as well as a keen eye for seeing and reporting, results in realistic playscripts that capture language as an exact transcription of everyday speech. Because the language is based upon its usage by ordinary men and women, the dialog is often punctuated with slang, grammatical error, colloquialism or the vernacular. In addition, fragmented sentences, broken phrases, incomplete thoughts or even extended moments of silence are featured to capture the inherent eloquence of everyday, polite conversation. Subsequently, it is always the *subtext* — or the hidden meaning of a character's thought that lies just beneath the surface of the language — which conveys the verbal and emotional tug-of-war between what a character "says" and what a character "means" in the ultimate expression of speech.

Scenes of emotional intensity also avoid poetic or rhetorical devices such as metaphor, simile or analogy so that characters speak in common vernacular that is direct and immediate. Stage dialog thus becomes primarily "window dressing" that serves to address the needs of the plot or the action without calling undue attention to itself. Even the exposition and narrative is sometimes phrased in the vernacular or in regionalisms that help to enhance the local color of the environment being depicted in the scene. This approach to language results in playscripts that are more credible, more closely related to actual experience and more representative of the observed facts of realistic life.

In playing the role with accuracy and authenticity in terms of the modern attempt to capture a spirit of the "present," the actor must eliminate all extraneous detail in the development of character and sacrifice ornamental trappings like elaborate costumes or hand props. It is also necessary for the actor to read the selected scene as if it were a novel or a short story, initially sorting out the characters and allowing the story to tell itself in the dialog, the narrative and the action rather than in costumes, make-up or props. Such an approach to scenes of realism should capture the vivid and relevant speeches, images and attitudes of the characters being portrayed as well as provide creative, inventive insights into the playwright's point of view.

Playing the Style

The actor's basic approach in playing the "style" of modern scenes depends upon the ability to create the illusion of reality and to convince the spectator that what is seen or heard is honest, spontaneous, natural and familiar. It is assumed that an invisible "fourth wall" exists between the actor and the audience, and that all dialog and action will be directed to the other actors within the playing space. There is no attempt made in realistic performance to engage actively with the audience other than to hold their attention and interest as they "eavesdrop" on the scene and witness the resemblance of character being drawn to "real-life" role models.

Because modern playscripts of realism are concerned with everyday episodes in the lives of ordinary people, the style of performance that is needed to convey the thoughts and emotions of these rather commonplace characters should be direct, subdued and conversational. The actor should approach the playing of individual scenes by speaking and moving in a relaxed, distinctly personal and individual manner. There would be little opportunity in modernism to imitate the rather exaggerated posing, elegant movement or pretentious speech that characterized earlier classical and Shakespearean dramas or even the later comedies of manner.

The historical perspective of the realists was to bring about a franker, freer treatment of character, action and issues to the stage than might have been possible in previous periods of theatre history. They were able to work within studio workshop productions to confront the spectators with bold new themes presented in intimate playhouses that frequently seated as few as 300 audience members. By concentrating on ideas and issues rather than on elaborate spectacle, the realists were also able to achieve a greater intensity of thought and emotion in their detailed treatments of character and action because they could now narrow the scope of the dialog, reduce the extraneous staging and abandon excessive theatrical complimentaries like elaborate costumes, ornate set pieces or complicated staging devices that often detracted from the development of character.

Influenced by scientific principles of detail and observation, the early realists were primarily interested in presenting three-dimentional characters that revealed interior motives or psychological motivation. The result was a host of playscripts that featured problems of character neurosis, behavioral adjustment or mood depression to paint life-like portraits of persons drawn from the workaday world. Some playwrights, like the elegant Russian Anton Chekhov, chose to scatter "hidden" facts regarding a character's mood or attitude throughout a scene while others preferred to sketch characters in such detail that even manners, attitudes and personal beliefs were included in the exposition and the narration of the playscript.

Although the use of "everyday" characters severely limited the possibilities of achieving the imagined grandeur of classical tragedy, the heroic figures of Shakespearean drama or the poetic wit of the comedy of manners, the social approach to character development in realism made a significant contribution to depicting the environmental, psychological and emotional forces that revealed "modern man" as the victim of circumstance. Humble workers, house servants, the physically infirm and the mentally impaired now begin to appear as leading characters; and they are treated as complex, three-dimentional persons who are products of inhibited heredity, deprived environment or some psychological imbalance. While drawn from the common walks of life, these characters possessed admirable values, principles and morals worthy of imitation. The major characters may have been average men and women of apparently little stature, but they were of infinite substance and complexity in that they could speak directly and sincerely about the "truth" of their lives.

With these philosophical principles clearly in mind, the actor of modern scenes is faced with the challenging but highly creative task of observing human nature and the environment and then selecting those personalities, experiences or circumstances that may be integrated into the world of the play. This modern approach that allows the character to be shaped by the actor's lived experiences or observations brings vitality and credibility to the performance and also provides the actor with a role model by which to relate the events of the scene to his and the spectator's own understanding of the event being dramatized.

Among the more important elements for the actor to observe in a realistic character portrait are persons of varying ages, physical dimensions, economic status, emotional or intellectual attitude and behavioral pattern. By jotting down the observed traits in a performance "memory book," the actor of modern scenes can draw upon

detailed observations and experiences to suggest realistic walks, postures, voices, moods or actions which convey to the spectator that the
character portrait is both accurate and authentic. This is not to imply,
however, that the actor of modern scenes must rely solely upon observation for performance guidelines. There are also ample opportunities
to use one's own personal, unique traits such as comic flair, physique
or vocal quality to give an added dimension to the character portrait.
The important principle is that the actor observe whatever is *necessary* to suggest a realistic approach to an interpretation of a modern
character and that any personal additions be integrated only if they
are truthful in helping to complete the character portrait as it is
being sketched in the scene.

Playing the Performance

In playing the performance for modern scenes the actor is reminded to avoid overly precise use of the voice, exaggerated movement
and highly theatrical posing. Approach each realistic scene with sensitivity and objectivity, employing a conversational tone of delivery,
a relaxed and natural sense of movement and an energy that suggests
singleness of purpose and concentration. Always direct dialog and
subtle reactions to the other actors in the scene to reinforce the intimate nature of the characters and be acutely aware of potential opportunities for interaction relationship whenever possible. It may be
helpful as you review the selected playscripts for performance to chart
each character's changing moods and attitudes in relationship to the
other characters in the scene and then to rehearse in as economical
and believable a manner as possible to suggest those subtle changes
with a minimum of vocal and physical effort.

Surface details, minor flaws and simple actions also comprise
some potential subject matter for realism and provide the potential
performance backdrop against which the actor must play a modern
scene. The tone of the playscripts is inevitably both grim and sober,
but there are moments of humor and frivolity that suggest the bonds
of human sympathy and compassion between the actor and the spectator. That is why in playing the scene the actor should also recall
the personal, sacred catalog of childhood memories, adolescent scars,
secret desires and wishful dreams that help to provide the emotional
and intellectual tapestry which weaves a realistic character portrait
the spectator can easily recognize and just as easily identify in their
own similar experiences.

This is the type of character enrichment cultivated by the 19th-century French historian and dramatic critic Hippolyte Taine, who noted that ". . . whether phenomena are physical or moral does not matter; they can always be traced back to causes. There are causes for ambition, for courage, or for truthfulness as there are for muscular contraction and for bodily temperature. Vice and virtue are products just as are vitriol and sugar. Let us then seek out the simpler data of moral qualities as scientists seek out those of physical properties." This philosophical approach to theatre in modern playscripts of realism demands that we "see" and "hear" characters performing self-sacrificing deeds, engaging in ignorant blunders, exhibiting courage and cowardice simultaneously, committing errors in judgment, suffering in silence or displaying basic emotional urges such as anger, lust, fear, greed or frustration. The actor, then, must acquire even more selectivity, objectivity and impartiality in an interpretation of a modern scene and yet remain sensitive and responsive to the noble, courageous character being portrayed. This is surely a creative task worthy of further investigation and exploration in future scene study and playscript interpretation!

Modern Exercises

The following vocal and physical exercises address problem areas common to a realistic portrayal of character. Each exercise is designed to translate the theory of modern drama into a meaningful, distinctly personal rehearsal technique that will enhance the actor's "natural" ability to convey the thoughts and emotions of commonplace characters. The exercises are also designed to promote honest, spontaneous responses that suggest a relaxed and conversational tone of vocal delivery and a heightened degree of sensitivity in characterization. It may also be helpful to integrate the traditional dress of realism — work clothes, leisure shirts, slacks — and familiar hand props that help to distinguish realistic characters — cigarette lighters, toothpicks, glasses — into the rehearsal process to provide the spark that illuminates both the character and the scene being performed.

GUESS WHO'S COMING TO DINNER?

A good exercise to prepare you for the basic principles of observation and attention to detail that distinguish modern playscripts of realism is to review the following monolog from Shakespeare's *Hamlet*. *First,* paraphrase the selection in everyday, common language to make sure that you understand the "period" words. *Second,* voice the dialog as if it were prose rather than verse. *Third,* voice the selection in a conversational tone highlighting individual words or phrases with a subtle variety in pitch, rate and volume. *Fourth,* tape-record the selection and play it back to evaluate the degree of "naturalism" in your vocal delivery and phrasing. *Fifth,* complete the first part of the exercise by reciting the selection while engaging in an everyday activity like riding a bike, taking a shower or eating a meal.

To be or not to be: that is the question
Whether 'tis nobler in the mind to suffer
The slings and arrows of outrageous fortune,
Or to take arms against a sea of troubles,
And by opposing end them. To die, to sleep —
No more; and by a sleep to say we end
The heart-ache and the thousand natural shocks
That flesh is heir to. 'Tis a consummation
Devoutly to be wish'd; to die, to sleep;
To sleep, perchance to dream; ay, there's the rub;
For in that sleep of death what dreams may come,
When we have shuffled off this mortal coil,
Must give us pause; there's the respect
That makes calamity of so long life:
For who would bear the whips and scorns of time,
Th' oppressor's wrong, the proud man's contumely,
The pangs of dispriz'd love, the law's delay,
The insolence of office, and the spurns
That patient merit of th' unworthy takes,
When he himself might his quietus make
With a bare bodkin? Who would fardels bear,
To grunt and sweat under a weary life,
But that the dread of something after death,
The undiscovered country from whose bourn
No traveller returns, puzzles the will
And makes us rather bear those ills we have
Than fly to others that we know not of?
Thus conscience doth make cowards of us all;
And thus the native hue of resolution
Is sicklied o'er with the pale cast of thought,

And enterprises of great pitch and moment
With this regard their currents turn awry,
And lose the name of action.

Recalling that detailed observation and accuracy are as important as a natural and conversational delivery of dialog, in the second
part of the exercise make yourself responsible for observing the following types of people: (a) store clerk, (b) ballplayer, (c) secretary, (d) artist, (e) waitress, (f) dancer, (g) factory worker, (h) custodian, (i) school
teacher, (j) banker and (k) policeman.

The observation should include distinctive attention to the
characteristics related to posture, manner of speech, age, movement,
personal mannerisms and mood or attitude. Note your initial observations in a performance diary devoted to similar classification or
character types appropriate for modern scenes of realism. Be as
specific as possible as you chart the vocal and physical attributes of
each person observed. Now draw on your two-week period of intensive
observation and invite each person observed to "dinner" by integrat-
ing their general characteristics into a performance feast that gives
added dimension and purpose to Hamlet's previous soliloquy.

When you feel comfortable with the degree of accuracy and
authenticity achieved in visualizing and vocalizing the character
types studied, expand the exercise by introducing the remaining general types of people observed in a performance from W. H. Smith's
1844 melodrama *The Drunkard.* Remember that your performance
of this monolog should be very similar in terms of voice and body to
the earlier "realistic" interpretation of Hamlet's soliloquy. For variety, you may wish to present an invited audience with a list of the
types of people noted in your performance diary and have them try
to determine which type is the inspiration and the role model for the
passage that follows.

Where am I? I wonder if people dream after they are
dead? Hideous! Hideous! I should like to be dead, if I
could not dream — parched! Parched! 'Tis morning it
is, or coming night, which? I wanted daylight, but now
it has come, what shall I do in daylight? I was out of
sight when it was dark — and seemed to be half-hidden
from myself — early morning, the rosy hue of the com-
ing sunshine, veiling from mortal sight the twinkling
stars — what horrid dreams; they will return upon me,

waking? Oh, for some brandy! Rum! Pain! Dreadful
pain! Heavens, now I tremble. Brandy! Brandy!

MIRROR, MIRROR OF MYSELF

A performer should always be aware of the presence of fellow
actors on stage in realism and may often be asked to mirror their
thoughts in modern drama. The idea of reflecting other character's
attitudes or moods is essential in scenes where you as an actor have
no dialog to speak at a given time. In this exercise, designed to develop
basic reactions and responses toward a given situation, two performers face each other in the center of an open space.

Begin the exercise by playing a variety of music on tape, ranging
from classical to country-and-western, as a background for the mood
of the scene. Actor A initiates the mirror exercise by reacting to the
rhythm and the tempo of the music and then changes reactions and
responses as the music changes rhythm and tempo. Actor B imitates
the reactions and responses of Actor A until the musical sequence
has ended.

Remember that in mirroring the reactions and responses of
another performer a leftward movement should stimulate a rightward
movement in response to the performer opposite you. This principle
may be tested by rehearsing gestures or bodily movements in front
of a mirror to develop the discipline needed to reflect the reactions
of another actor. It is especially important to capture the spirit of the
imitation in terms of the tension, energy and vigor of the mirrored
reaction or response, so strive for accuracy in your reflections.

Once you and your partner have explored the possibilities of
reacting to music, the second part of the exercise involves mirroring
sounds and *words*. Actors A and B face each other again, and this
time Actor B initiates the exercise by voicing sounds or words that
suggest a specific mood or attitude. Actor A then repeats those sounds
or words in a similar response. For example, Actor B may choose to
voice words such as "pain" or "fear" in an appropriate vocal declara-
tion, or Actor B may wish to substitute sounds that approximate the
inherent meaning of the words "pain" or "fear."

The mirror exercise concludes as Actors A and B again face
each other to share the following passage from Henrik's Ibsen's *The
Master Builder*. Actor A begins by speaking the first line in a specific
mood or attitude that suggests a specific point of view. Actor B responds by speaking the second line in a similar mood or attitude.

Actor A then *changes* the mood or attitude on the third line to suggest another, different specific point of view. Actor B then responds by assuming the new mood or attitude. The exercise continues in this fashion, with a change of mood or attitude expressed on alternating lines of dialog, until the passage has been completed. You may wish to extend the exercise, however, by repeating the dialog a second time with *Actor B* initiating the changes in mood or attitude. It is also a good idea to write down the intended mood or attitude to later compare with the subsequent performance.

SOLNESS: Tell me something, Hilde.

HILDE: Yes?

SOLNESS: Since you've been waiting for me all these years —

HILDE: Ten years — yes.

SOLNESS: Why didn't you write me? Then I could have answered you.

HILDE: No, no, no! That's just what I didn't want.

SOLNESS: Why not?

HILDE: I was afraid that might ruin everything —. But we were going to write something on those drawings, Master Builder.

SOLNESS: So we were.

HILDE: Let's make it kind and really cordial now. Oh, how I hate this!

SOLNESS: Have you never really loved anyone, Hilde?

HILDE: What did you say?

SOLNESS: Have you never loved anyone?

HILDE: Anyone else, I suppose you mean.

SOLNESS: Anyone else — of course. You never have? In all these ten years? Never?

HILDE: Oh well, once in a while, when I was furious with you for not coming back.

SOLNESS: Then you have cared for others too?

HILDE: A little bit. For a week or so. For heaven's sake, Master Builder, you know how it is!

SOLNESS: Hilde — what have you come for?

HILDE: Let's not waste any more time.

SOLNESS: Answer me, Hilde. What is it you want from me?

HILDE: My kingdom!

*One of the earliest approaches to modern realism was called "photographic representa-
tion of life," which tried to capture specific visual portraits of authentic people, places
and even events as if they had been "snapped" by a camera.*

171

The Modern Scenes

The following edited scenes are representative of the early modern playscripts that were primarily concerned with realistic episodes in the lives of ordinary people engaged in simple, uncomplicated actions that conveyed basic thoughts and emotions that were rather universal in nature. Before proceeding to a detailed examination of the individual scenes, however, it is important to point out that additional hints for characterization in realistic playscripts may be found in the elaborate stage directions or narrative that the playwright includes in the description of the setting. All of the scenes included in this chapter involve a complex relationship of some sort and each character depicted requires carefully chosen personality traits and physical clues that express the mood and the attitude being suggested. Approach the playing of the scenes with an illusion of reality that appears to be honest and natural so that the character portrait will emerge as a fresh, spontaneous creation firmly rooted in modern soil. Allow the character to be shaped by your own lived experiences and documented observations for the fullest expression of believability!

from LA RONDE (1900)

Arthur Schnitzler

As one of the earliest and most influential Austrian dramatists of realism, Arthur Schnitzler was an accurate and detailed "recorder" of the melancholic mood and temperament that characterized the world-weary, bleak turn-of-the-century artist. Most of his playscripts are concerned with love intrigues and the shallow sexual attitudes that are exhibited in transparent relationships based primarily upon casual amorous adventures or chance encounters. A friend of the psychiatrist Sigmund Freud, Schnitzler was also fascinated by the centrality of sexual behavior and "ego gratification" in the development of intimate relationships.

There is almost a scientific detachment in the scene that follows as the characters display a warm, gentle humor in their game of love. As one of "10 dialogs" in the playscript, this scene is part of an epic structure in which 10 characters play sexual games and engage in courting or loving exchanges with a number of different partners. Although the theme is a serious one — human sexuality as the most exalted of all divine creations — the approach in performance should be rather light and frivolous. There is no conscious attempt here to engage actively with the audience, and the actors should not speak the dialog in a "period" tone or voice pretentious speech that characterized earlier periods of farce, melodrama or classical tragedy.

In playing the selected scene of early 20th-century realism, the actors should discard any familiar, stereotypical images traditionally associated with the characters "Actress" or "Count" and concentrate, instead, on potential problems of character neurosis, mood or behavior to paint lifelike portraits that are fresh and intriguing. There should also be some attention paid to nuance and innuendo as the characters exchange polite conversation to disguise their true intent and conceal their secret desires. Remember, further, that this is one of 10 dialogs in the playscript and that the playwright is attempting to instruct the audience on life's true meaning as revealed in these character "case studies" and in these character "sexual behaviors."

CAST

ACTRESS

COUNT

SCENE

The Actress's luxuriously furnished bedroom. It is noon.

APPROACH

As the scene opens, the Actress is reclining in her four-poster bed. The bedroom is strewn with newspapers, a burning candle flickers on the bedside table and the blinds are still drawn as the Count enters. There is obvious magnetism as the characters exchange meaningful glances and, somewhat hesitantly, speak in guarded embarrassment. The initial conversation is polite and informal as the characters display tenderness and genuine concern for each other as they slowly overcome personal misgivings of cultivating a meaningful relationship. There is also a poignant moment in the scene in which the characters discover a personal, intimate capacity to understand and to love another human being.

1   SCENE NINE
2
3 ACTRESS: It's you, Count!
4 COUNT: Your good mother gave me permission, or of course, I
5   wouldn't ...
6 ACTRESS: Please, come right in.
7 COUNT: I kiss your hand. A thousand pardons — coming
8   straight in from the street — you know, I can't see a thing.
9   Yes ... here we are. *(Nears the bed.)* I kiss your hand.
10 ACTRESS: Sit down, my dear Count.
11 COUNT: Your mother said you weren't very well, Fraulein.
12   Nothing too serious, I hope?
13 ACTRESS: Nothing serious? I was dying!
14 COUNT: Oh, dear me! Not really?
15 ACTRESS: In any case, it's very kind of you to ... trouble to
16   call.
17 COUNT: Dying! And only last night you played like a goddess!
18 ACTRESS: It was a great triumph, I believe.
19 COUNT: Colossal! People were absolutely knocked out. As for
20   myself, well ...
21 ACTRESS: Thanks for the lovely flowers.
22 COUNT: Not at all, Fraulein.
23 ACTRESS: *(Turning her eyes toward a large basket of flowers, which*
24   *stands on a small table by the window)* There they are!
25 COUNT: Last night you were positively *strewn* with flowers
26   and garlands!
27 ACTRESS: I left them all in my dressing room. Your basket was
28   the only thing I brought home.
29 COUNT: *(Kisses her hand.)* You're very kind. *(The ACTRESS*
30   *suddenly takes his hand and kisses it.)* Fraulein!
31 ACTRESS: Don't be afraid, Count. It commits you to nothing!
32 COUNT: You're a strange creature ... a puzzle, one might
33   almost say. *(Pause)*
34 ACTRESS: Fraulein Birken is ... easier to solve?
35 COUNT: Oh, little Birken is no puzzle. Though ... I know her

174

1   only superficially.
2   ACTRESS: Indeed?
3   COUNT: Oh, believe me. But *you* are a problem. And I've always
4   longed for one. As a matter of fact, last night I realized what
5   a great pleasure I'd been missing. You see, it was the first
6   time I've seen you act.
7   ACTRESS: Is that true?
8   COUNT: Oh, yes. You see, Fraulein, it's so difficult, the theatre.
9   By the time I get there, the best part of the play'd be over,
10   wouldn't it?
11   ACTRESS: You'll have to dine earlier from now on.
12   COUNT: I'd thought of that. Or of not dining at all. There's not
13   much pleasure in it, is there — dining?
14   ACTRESS: What do you still find pleasure in, young fogey?
15   COUNT: I sometimes ask myself. But I'm no fogey. There must
16   be another reason.
17   ACTRESS: You think so?
18   COUNT: Yes. For instance, Lulu always says I'm a philosopher.
19   What he means is: I think too much.
20   ACTRESS: Lulu?
21   COUNT: Friend of mine.
22   ACTRESS: He's right . . . it *is* a misfortune, all that thinking.
23   COUNT: I've time on my hands, that's why I thought it would be
24   better. It'd be amusing, stimulating, the city. But it's really
25   much the same here as up there.
26   ACTRESS: And where is "up there"?
27   COUNT: Well, down there, Fraulein, in Hungary. The small
28   towns I used to be stationed in.
29   ACTRESS: What were you doing in Hungary?
30   COUNT: I'm telling you, dear lady — the Army.
31   ACTRESS: But why stay in Hungary?
32   COUNT: It happens, that's all.
33   ACTRESS: Enough to drive anyone mad, I should think!
34   COUNT: Oh, I don't know. In a way you have more to do there
35   than here. You know, Fraulein, training recruits, exercising

1   horses . . . and the surroundings aren't as bad as people say.
2   It's really rather lovely, the big plain there. Such a sunset!
3   It's a pity. I'm not a painter. I often thought I'd paint one,
4   if I were a painter. We had a man in our regiment, young
5   Splany, and he could do it. Why I tell you this boring stuff
6   I don't know, Fraulein.
7 ACTRESS: Please, Count! I'm highly amused.
8 COUNT: You know, Fraulein, it's so easy to talk to you. Lulu
9   told me it would be. It's a thing one doesn't often meet.
10 ACTRESS: In Hungary!
11 COUNT: Or in Vienna! People are the same everywhere. Where
12   there are more, it gets overcrowded but that's the only
13   difference. Tell me, Fraulein, do you like people, really?
14 ACTRESS: Like them? I hate them! I don't want to see them. I
15   never do see them. I'm always alone. This house is deserted!
16 COUNT: Just as I imagined: you're a misanthropist. It's bound
17   to happen with artists. Moving in that more exalted
18   sphere . . . Well, it's all right for you, at least you know why
19   you're alive.
20 ACTRESS: Who told you that? I haven't the remotest idea why
21   I'm alive!
22 COUNT: Not really, Fraulein . . . famous . . . celebrated . . .
23 ACTRESS: Is that — happiness?
24 COUNT: Happiness? Happiness doesn't exist. None of the things
25   people chatter about really exist. Love, for instance. It's the
26   same with love.
27 ACTRESS: You may be right there.
28 COUNT: Enjoyment . . . intoxication . . . there's nothing wrong
29   with them, they're real. I enjoy something, all right, and I
30   know I enjoy it. Or I'm intoxicated, all right. That's real too.
31   And when it's over, it's over, that's all.
32 ACTRESS: *(Grandly)* It's over!
33 COUNT: But as soon as you don't — I don't quite know how to
34   say it — as soon as you stop living for the present moment,
35   as soon as you think of later on or earlier on . . . Well, the

1   whole thing collapses. "Later on" is sad, and "earlier on" is
2   uncertain. In short, you just get mixed up. Don't you think
3   so?
4 ACTRESS: *(Nods, her eyes very wide open.)* You pluck out the heart
5   of the mystery, my dear Count.
6 COUNT: And you see, Fraulein, once you're clear about that, it
7   doesn't matter if you live in Vienna or on the Hungarian
8   plains or in the tiny town of Steinamanger. For example,
9   where can I put my cap? Oh, thanks. What were we talking
10   about?
11 ACTRESS: The tiny town of Steinamanger.
12 COUNT: Oh, yes. Well, as I was saying, there isn't much
13   difference. Whether I spend the evening at the Casino or
14   the Club is all one.
15 ACTRESS: How does this tie in with love?
16 COUNT: If a man believes in it, there'll always be a girl around
17   who loves him.
18 ACTRESS: Fraulein Birken, for example.
19 COUNT: Honestly, dear lady, I can't understand why you're
20   always mentioning little Birken.
21 ACTRESS: She's your mistress after all.
22 COUNT: Who says that?
23 ACTRESS: Everyone knows.
24 COUNT: Except me. Remarkable!
25 ACTRESS: But you fought a duel on her behalf!
26 COUNT: Possibly I was shot dead and didn't notice.
27 ACTRESS: Count, you *are* a man of honor. Sit a little closer.
28 COUNT: If I may.
29 ACTRESS: Here. *(She draws him closer, and runs her fingers through
30   his hair.)* I knew you would come today.
31 COUNT: Really? Why?
32 ACTRESS: I knew it last night. In the theatre.
33 COUNT: Oh, could you see me from the stage?
34 ACTRESS: My dear man, didn't you realize I was playing for you
35   alone?

1   COUNT: How could that be?

2   ACTRESS: After I saw you in the front row, I was walking on air.

3   COUNT: Because of me? I'd no idea you'd noticed me.

4   ACTRESS: Oh, you can drive a woman to despair with that
5   dignity of yours!

6   COUNT: Fraulein!

7   ACTRESS: "Fraulein?" At least take your saber off!

8   COUNT: Permit me. *(He unbuckles the belt, leans the saber against*
9   *the bed.)*

10   ACTRESS: And now kiss me at last. *(The COUNT kisses her. She*
11   *does not let him go.)* I wish I had never set eyes on you.

12   COUNT: No, no, it's better as it is.

13   ACTRESS: Count, you're a *poseur*.

14   COUNT: I am? Why?

15   ACTRESS: Many a man'd be happy to be in your shoes right now.

16   COUNT: *I'm* happy.

17   ACTRESS: Oh — I thought happiness didn't exist! Why do you
18   look at me like that? I believe you're afraid of me, Count.

19   COUNT: I told you, Fraulein, you're a problem.

20   ACTRESS: Oh, don't bother me with philosophy. Come here.
21   And ask me for something. You can have whatever you like.
22   ·You're too handsome.

23   COUNT: Well, then I beg leave *(Kisses her hand)* to return tonight.

24   ACTRESS: Tonight? But I'm playing tonight.

25   COUNT: After the theatre.

26   ACTRESS: You ask for nothing else?

27   COUNT: I'll ask for everything else. After the theatre.

28   ACTRESS: *(Offended)* Then you can ask, you wretched *poseur*.

29   COUNT: You see, Fraulein . . . you see, my dear . . . we've been
30   frank with each other till now. I'd find it all very much nicer
31   in the evening, after the theatre. It'll be so much more
32   comfortable . . . At present, you see, I've the feeling the
33   door's going to open at any moment.

34   ACTRESS: This door doesn't open from the outside.

35   COUNT: Fraulein, wouldn't it be frivolous to spoil something at

1   the start? When it might just possibly turn out to be
2   beautiful?
3   ACTRESS: "Just possibly!"
4   COUNT: And to tell the truth, I find love in the morning pretty
5   frightful.
6   ACTRESS: You're the craziest man I've ever come across.
7   COUNT: I'm not talking about ordinary females. After all, in
8   general, it doesn't matter. But women like you, Fraulein —
9   no, you can call me a fool as often as you like, but women
10   like you ... well, one shouldn't have them before breakfast,
11   that's all. And so ... well.
12   ACTRESS: God, you're sweet!
13   COUNT: Now you see I'm right, don't you? What I have in mind ...
14   ACTRESS: Tell me what you have in mind.
15   COUNT: What I mean is ... I'll wait for you after the theatre, in
16   my carriage, then we can drive off somewhere, well, and
17   have supper and ...
18   ACTRESS: I am not Fraulein Birken!
19   COUNT: I didn't say you were, my dear. Only, one must be in the
20   mood! I get in the mood at supper. It's lovely to drive home
21   after supper, and then ...
22   ACTRESS: And then?
23   COUNT: Let events take their natural course.
24   ACTRESS: Come closer. Closer!
25   COUNT: *(Sits down on the bed.)* I must say, the perfume that comes
26   from these pillows — mignonette, is it?
27   ACTRESS: It's hot in here, don't you think? *(The COUNT bends*
28   *down and kisses her throat.)* Oh my dear Count, this isn't on
29   your program.
30   COUNT: Who says so? I have no program. *(The ACTRESS draws*
31   *him to her.)* It *is* hot!
32   ACTRESS: You find it so? And dark, like evening ... *(Pulls him to*
33   *her.)* It *is* evening, Count. It's night ... Shut your eyes if it's
34   too light for you. Come! Come! *(The COUNT no longer defends*
35   *himself.)* What's that about being in the mood, you *poseur?*

1   COUNT: You're a little devil.

2   ACTRESS: Count!

3   COUNT: All right, a little angel.

4   ACTRESS: And you should have been an actor. Really! You
5   understand women. Do you know what I'm going to do now?

6   COUNT: Well?

7   ACTRESS: I'm going to tell you I never want to see you again.

8   COUNT: Why?

9   ACTRESS: You're too dangerous for me. You turn a woman's
10   head. And now you stand there as if nothing has happened.

11   COUNT: But ...

12   ACTRESS: I beg you to remember, my dear Count, that I've just
13   been your mistress.

14   COUNT: Can I ever forget it?

15   ACTRESS: So how about tonight?

16   COUNT: What do you mean exactly?

17   ACTRESS: You intended to meet me after the theatre?

18   COUNT: Oh, yes, all right: let's say the day after tomorrow.

19   ACTRESS: The day after tomorrow? We were talking of tonight.

20   COUNT: There wouldn't be much sense in that.

21   ACTRESS: Fogey!

22   COUNT: You misunderstand me. I mean — how should I say —
23   from the spiritual viewpoint.

24   ACTRESS: It's not your spirit that interests me.

25   COUNT: Believe me, it's all part of it. I don't agree that the two
26   can be kept separate.

27   ACTRESS: Don't talk philosophy at me. When I want that, I read
28   books.

29   COUNT: But we never learn from books.

30   ACTRESS: That's true. And that's why you'll be there tonight.
31   We'll come to an agreement about the spiritual viewpoint,
32   you ... spiritualist!

33   COUNT: Then — with your permission — I'll wait with my
34   carriage.

35   ACTRESS: You'll wait here. In my apartment.

1 COUNT: After the theatre.
2 ACTRESS: Of course. *(The COUNT buckles on his saber.)* **What are**
3 **you doing?**
4 COUNT: I think it's time for me to go, Fraulein. I've been
5 staying rather long as it is, for a formal visit.
6 ACTRESS: Well, it won't be a formal visit tonight!
7 COUNT: You think not?
8 ACTRESS: Just leave it to me. And now give me one more kiss,
9 little philosopher. Here, you seducer ... you ... sweet thing,
10 you spiritualist, you polecat, you ... *(After several emphatic*
11 *kisses she emphatically pushes him away.)* **My dear Count, it was**
12 **a great honor.**
13 COUNT: I kiss your hand, Fraulein. *(At the door)* **Au revoir!**
14 ACTRESS: Adieu, tiny town of Steinamanger!
15
16
17
18
19
20
21
22
23
24
25
26
27
28
29
30
31
32
33
34
35

Modern playscripts of realism are concerned with everyday episodes in the lives of ordinary people and the thoughts or emotions of these rather commonplace, ordinary characters should be conveyed in a direct and conversational manner.

from **The Petrified Forest** (1935)

Robert E. Sherwood

Here is a "raw slice of life" scene that concentrates upon tormented characters who probe beneath the surface of their own apparent reality to investigate personal inner conflicts, hidden desires and frustrated passions. These tortured souls remind us of the loss of human dignity and the degradation that often characterize the outcast, the rebel or the vagabond who are part of a larger, more complex social ill. There is also a perceptive depiction of the social inequity and injustice that were part of the historical times in the 1930s and 1940s that reinforces the authenticity of the portrait being drawn by the playwright.

As the play begins, Alan Squier, a tired and unsuccessful writer, has been hitchhiking his way across the country to golden California, which holds the promise of new opportunities and a new beginning in life. Now penniless and at the mercy of charity, he finds himself in front of a small, forlorn wayside restaurant in the rugged Arizona desert only miles from the Petrified Forest. The vagabond traveler also encounters Gabby, the young and attractive daughter of the restaurant owner, who is a romantic idealist as well as sentimental poet. The hardened Alan and the sensitive Gabby share their thoughts and explore their emotions while sharing the "Bar-B-Q Special" of the day.

The actors should approach the scene in a more conversational, or natural tone to indicate the friendly and intimate relationship that is apparently emerging as Gabby and Alan discover common interests and appear to be intellectually and emotionally attracted to each other. There should also be some attention paid to the hidden guilt and despair expressed by each character as they desperately try to free themselves from the traditional beliefs and inhibitions that imprison them in this sterile, desolate environment. Finally, use restraint in developing the relationship of Gabby and Alan so that what is reflected is an innocent, basically virtuous encounter that helps each character reinforce their own truthfulness and honesty.

CAST

ALAN SQUIER
GABBY

SCENE

The interior of a roadside diner, later afternoon.

APPROACH

As the scene opens, Gabby is serving the afternoon special to Alan, who devours the Bar-B-Q and attacks the vegetables. There is a quiet tranquility that hovers over the scene as the inquisitive Gabby continually questions the more experienced traveler Alan and he responds with a simple dignity and poetic honesty that reveals his gentle nature. As the two "lost souls" sit at the table they embrace harmless poses and assume philosophical attitudes that reflect on the spirit of adventure, writing and living life in general. But there is also a larger truth revealed in their conversation: the frustration and despair that lies just beneath the surface of their own reality.

1   **GABBY: Like the soup?**

2   **ALAN:**   *(From the heart)* **It was glorious!**

3   **GABBY: Want some coffee?**

4   **ALAN: Will it mix with the beer?**

5   **GABBY: Oh, sure. Coffee will mix with anything.** *(She goes to the*
6   *counter to get his coffee.)*

7   **ALAN: That's a charming old gentleman. Your grandfather?**

8   **GABBY: Yes.**

9   **ALAN: He told me he'd been missed by Billy the Kid.**

10   **GABBY: He tells everybody that. Poor Gramp. You get terribly**
11   **sick of him after a while.** *(She has brought down the coffee.)* **Did**
12   **I hear him say you're a writer?**

13   **ALAN:**   *(Humbly)* **Yes.**

14   **GABBY: I haven't met many writers — except Sidney Wenzell.**
15   **Ever heard of him?**

16   **ALAN: That's not Mark Twain, is it?**

17   **GABBY: No! Sidney Wenzell — he's with Warner Brothers. He**
18   **stopped here once, when he was driving out to the coast.**
19   **He said I ought to go to Hollywood, and to be sure and look**
20   **him up. But — what the hell! They never mean it.**

21   **ALAN: No! They never mean a thing.** *(She has picked up her book*
22   *and started to go.)* **Please don't go.** *(She pauses and turns.)*

23   **GABBY: Something else you want? We got pie and layer cake.**

24   **ALAN: No. I — I'd like to talk to you. Please sit down.**

25   **GABBY: All right.** *(She sits down, across from him, at the center table.*
26   *ALAN eats rapidly, mechanically, during the subsequent dialog,*
27   *stowing the food away as he talks and listens.)*

28   **ALAN: I suppose you want to go into the movies?**

29   **GABBY:**   *(Scornfully)* **God, *no*!**

30   **ALAN: But — I thought every beautiful girl had her heart set on**
31   **Hollywood.**

32   **GABBY: That's just it. It's too common. I want to go to Bourges.**
33   *(She fails to soften the "g.")*

34   **ALAN: Where?**

35   **GABBY: Bourges — in France. You'd never guess it, but that's**

184

1   where I came from.
2   ALAN: You're not French?
3   GABBY: Partly. I was born in Bourges — but I left it almost
4   before I was able to walk, so all I know about it is from the
5   picture postcards my mother sends me. They got a cathedral
6   there.
7   ALAN: Your mother still lives there?
8   GABBY: Yes. Dad brought us back here after the war. Mother
9   stuck it out in this desert for a couple of years, and then
10   she packed up and went back to Bourges. We've never seen
11   her since. Some people seem to think it was cruel of her to
12   leave me. But what could she do? She didn't have any money
13   to bring me up. She just couldn't *live* here — and you can't
14   blame her for that. Do you think she was cruel?
15   ALAN: Not if you don't, Miss Maple.
16   GABBY: Well — I don't. She's tried lots of times to get me over
17   there to see her — but Dad won't allow it. She got a divorce
18   and married a Frenchman that's got a bookstore. Mother
19   was always a great reader, so I guess it's nice for her. She's
20   got three more kids. Just think of that! I've got a half-brother
21   and half-sisters that can't speak a word of English. I'd sure
22   like to see them.
23   ALAN: Can you speak French?
24   GABBY: Only what you learn in high school — like *table* for
25   "table." *(She takes a photograph from her book.)* Look — there's
26   my mother's picture. That was just before she married Dad.
27   She had her picture taken smelling a rose.
28   ALAN: She's lovely! And I can see the resemblance.
29   GABBY: It's hard to imagine her being married to Dad, isn't it?
30   But I guess he looked all right in his American uniform.
31   Mother used to send me a book every year for my birthday,
32   but they were all in French and I couldn't read them. So
33   last year I wrote and asked if she'd mind sending me one
34   in English, and she sent me this one. It's the Poems of
35   Francois Villon. Ever read it?

1   ALAN: Yes.
2   GABBY: It's wonderful poetry. She wrote in it: "a ma chere
3   petite Gabrielle." That means "To my dear little Gabrielle."
4   She gave me that name. It's about the only French thing
5   I've got.
6   ALAN: Gabrielle. It's a beautiful name.
7   GABBY: Wouldn't you know it would get changed into "Gabby"
8   by these ignorant fools around here? I guess you think that's
9   a terrible thing to say.
10   ALAN: Oh, no. It — it's picturesque.
11   GABBY: Well — it suits this kind of country.
12   ALAN: You share your mother's opinion of the desert? *(She nods.)*
13   But you can find solace in the Poems of Francois Villon.
14   GABBY: Yes. They get the stink of the gasoline and the
15   hamburger out of my system.
16   ALAN: Would you like to read me one of those poems, Gabrielle?
17   GABBY: You mean now?
18   ALAN: Yes. While I'm finishing "Today's Special."
19   GABBY: OK. I'll read you the one I like best. He wrote it about
20   a friend of his who was getting married. *(She reads, with*
21   *marked but inexpert emphasis.)*
22   "At daybreak, when the falcon claps his wings
23   No whit for grief, but noble heart held high
24   With loud glad noise he stirs himself and springs,
25   And takes his meat and toward his lure draws nigh;
26   Such good I wish you! Yea, and heartily
27   I'm fired with hope of true love's meed to get;
28   Knowing Love writes it in his book; for why,
29   This is the end for which we twain are met."
30   Did you ever see a falcon?
31   ALAN: Yes.
32   GABBY: What does it look like?
33   ALAN: Not very pleasant. Like a hawk. Go on, Gabrielle.
34   GABBY: *(Resuming reading)*
35   "Mine own heart's lady with no gainsayings

186

1   You shall be always till I die;
2   And in my right against all bitter things
3   Sweet laurel with fresh rose its force shall try;
4   Seeing reason wills not that I cast love by
5   Nor here with reason shall I chide and fret
6   *(She closes the book and recites.)*
7   Nor cease to serve, but serve more constantly;
8   This is the end for which we twain are met."
9   *(She looks at him, and he at her. Then he resumes his attack on the*
10   *hamburger.)*
11   You know — that's wonderful stuff. But that's the way the
12   French people are: They can understand everything — like
13   love — and death — and they can enjoy it, or laugh at it,
14   depending on how they feel.
15   ALAN: And that's why you want to go to France — for under-
16   standing.
17   GABBY: I *will* go there! When Gramp dies, we can sell this place.
18   Dad's going to take his share and move to Los Angeles, so
19   that he can join a really big Legion post and get to be a
20   political power. But I'm going to spend part of the money
21   on a trip to Bourges, where there's something beautiful to
22   look at, and wine, and dancing in the streets.
23   ALAN: If I were you — I'd stay here, Gabrielle, and avoid
24   disappointment.
25   GABBY: What makes you think I'd be disappointed?
26   ALAN: I've been to France.
27   GABBY: You were there in the war?
28   ALAN: No, I missed that. But I lived there for eight years,
29   through seventeen changes of government.
30   GABBY: What were you doing — writing books?
31   ALAN: No — planning to write books. You know what a gigolo
32   is?
33   GABBY: Were *you* one of those? *(He nods.)* You danced with
34   women for money?
35   ALAN: Oh, lord, no! I never was a good enough dancer for that.

187

1   I — married.

2   GABBY: Oh.

3   ALAN: Please don't think too ill of me. I once actually wrote a
4   book.

5   GABBY: What was it — fiction?

6   ALAN: In a sense. It was a novel about the bleak, glacier-
7   stripped hills of my native New England. I was twenty-two
8   when I wrote it, and it was very, very stark. It sold slightly
9   over six hundred copies. It cost the publisher quite a lot of
10   money, and it also cost him his wife. You see, she divorced
11   him and married me. She had faith in me, and she had the
12   chance to display it, because her husband was very generous
13   in the financial settlement. I suppose he had faith in me,
14   too. She saw in me a major artist, profound, but inarticulate.
15   She believed that all I needed was background, and she gave
16   it to me — with southern exposure and a fine view of the
17   Mediterranean. That was considered the thing to do in the
18   period that followed Scott Fitzgerald. For eight years I
19   reclined there, on the Riviera, on my background — and I
20   waited for the major artist to step forth and say something
21   of enduring importance. He preferred to remain
22   inarticulate.

23

24

25

26

27

28

29

30

31

32

33

34

35

from Long Day's Journey Into Night (1940)*

Eugene O'Neill

Although written in 1940, this autobiographical playscript was not authorized for performance by the playwright until after his death. It is, as etched in the dedication, ". . . a play of old sorrow, written in tears and blood." The priceless legacy that remains in O'Neill's drama of his unconventional family life is the strength of the individual will in coming face-to-face with one's past and in understanding — and forgiving — all of the hurts and the sorrows that are part of the family relationship.

Working primarily in "reminiscences" that are recalled as part of the family's annual summer retreat to a New England bungalow, O'Neill captures the youth dreams and adolescent ambitions that helped to frame his own development as both man and artist. He also helps to clarify his own family relationship that alternated between love and hate as he masterfully draws sympathetic portraits of his parents and his older brother in sharp, painful sketches that reveal soul-shattering revelations of self-truth and self-destruction. What emerges as a consequence is a family unit that is depicted as twisted, tortured souls ridden with guilt and despair as the result of individual addictions and psychological defects that approach mania.

In playing the scene the actors should pay particular attention to the strained relationship of the brothers as they slowly gravitate toward each other after bouts of melancholy and alcoholism. These "haunted souls" should be drawn with a sensitive hand that helps to focus attention upon their social behavior and fanciful illusions that are suddenly stripped away when they begin to discuss the pathetic reality of their mother, who has escaped into her own dream world through the abusive use of morphine. There should also be a simple truth that emerges without artifice or affection as the sons realize that their own "pipe dreams" of success and achievement have only been cheap imitations of the truth of their individual failures.

CAST

EDMUND

JAMIE

Long Day's Journey Into Night was not produced until 1956, three years after the playwright's death.

SCENE

The living room around 12:45 p.m.

APPROACH

As the scene opens, Edmund is alone in the living room, standing at the table. He grabs a bottle and pours a drink, adds water and drinks. Hearing someone at the front door, Edmund gulps the drink, places the glass on a tray, sits in a side chair and opens a book. He looks up as if his reading has been interrupted when Jamie, his older brother, enters and smiles cynically after catching sight of the bottle and glasses. As the brothers begin to share confidences they also begin to face the tragic reality of the noise they hear upstairs: their mother, addicted to morphine when her husband's stinginess in hiring a cheap doctor for the birth of Edmund led to drug dependency, is stumbling around in her dope-induced girlish dreams of a former life in the convent when she was a child.

1 JAMIE: Sneaking one, eh? Cut out the bluff, kid. You're a
2   rottener actor than I am.
3 EDMUND: *(Grins.)* Yes, I grabbed one while the going was good.
4 JAMIE: *(Puts a hand affectionately on his shoulder.)* That's better.
5   Why kid me? We're pals, aren't we?
6 EDMUND: I wasn't sure it was you coming.
7 JAMIE: I made the Old Man look at his watch. I was halfway up
8   the walk when Cathleen burst into song. Our wild Irish lark!
9   She ought to be a train announcer.
10 EDMUND: That's what drove me to drink. Why don't you sneak
11   one while you've got a chance?
12 JAMIE: I was thinking of that little thing. *(He goes quickly to the*
13   *window at right.)* The Old Man was talking to old Captain
14   Turner. Yes, he's still at it. *(He comes back and takes a drink.)*
15   And now to cover up from his eagle eye. He memorizes the
16   level in the bottle after every drink. *(He measures two drinks*
17   *of water and pours them in the whiskey bottle and shakes it up.)*
18   There. That fixes it. *(He pours water in the glass and sets it on*
19   *the table by EDMUND.)* And here's the water you've been
20   drinking.
21 EDMUND: Fine! You don't think it will fool him, do you?
22 JAMIE: Maybe not, but he can't prove it. *(Putting on his collar and*
23   *tie)* I hope he doesn't forget lunch listening to himself talk.
24   I'm hungry. *(He sits across the table from EDMUND — irritably.)*
25   That's what I hate about working down in front. He puts on
26   an act for every damned fool that comes along.
27 EDMUND: *(Gloomily)* You're in luck to be hungry. The way I feel
28   I don't care if I ever eat again.
29 JAMIE: *(Gives him a glance of concern.)* Listen, kid. You know me.
30   I've never lectured you, but Doctor Hardy was right when
31   he told you to cut out the redeye.
32 EDMUND: Oh, I'm going to after he hands me the bad news this
33   afternoon. A few before then won't make any difference.
34 JAMIE: *(Hesitates — then slowly)* I'm glad you've got your mind
35   prepared for bad news. It won't be such a jolt. *(He catches*

191

1   *EDMUND staring at him.)* **I mean, it's a cinch you're really**
2   **sick, and it would be wrong dope to kid yourself.**

3 **EDMUND:** *(Disturbed)* **I'm not. I know how rotten I feel, and the**
4   **fever and chills I get at night are no joke. I think Doctor**
5   **Hardy's last guess was right. It must be the damned malaria**
6   **come back on me.**

7 **JAMIE:** **Maybe, but don't be too sure.**

8 **EDMUND:** **Why? What do you think it is?**

9 **JAMIE:** **Hell, how would I know? I'm no doc.** *(Abruptly)* **Where's**
10   **Mama?**

11 **EDMUND:** **Upstairs.**

12 **JAMIE:** *(Looks at him sharply.)* **When did she go up?**

13 **EDMUND:** **Oh, about the time I came down to the hedge, I guess.**
14   **She said she was going to take a nap.**

15 **JAMIE:** **You didn't tell me —**

16 **EDMUND:** *(Defensively)* **Why should I? What about it? She was**
17   **tired out. She didn't get much sleep last night.**

18 **JAMIE:** **I know she didn't.** *(A pause. The brothers avoid looking at*
19   *each other.)*

20 **EDMUND:** **That damned foghorn kept me awake, too.** *(Another*
21   *pause)*

22 **JAMIE:** **She's been upstairs alone all morning, eh? You haven't**
23   **seen her?**

24 **EDMUND:** **No. I've been reading here. I wanted to give her a**
25   **chance to sleep.**

26 **JAMIE:** **Is she coming down to lunch?**

27 **EDMUND:** **Of course.**

28 **JAMIE:** *(Dryly)* **No of course about it. She might not want any**
29   **lunch. Or she might start having most of her meals alone**
30   **upstairs. That's happened, hasn't it?**

31 **EDMUND:** *(With frightened resentment)* **Cut it out, Jamie! Can't**
32   **you think anything but —?** *(Persuasively)* **You're all wrong to**
33   **suspect anything. Cathleen saw her not long ago. Mama**
34   **didn't tell her she wouldn't be down to lunch.**

35 **JAMIE:** **Then she wasn't taking a nap?**

1 EDMUND: Not right then, but she was lying down, Cathleen
2   said.
3 JAMIE: In the spare room?
4 EDMUND: Yes. For Pete's sake, what of it?
5 JAMIE: *(Bursts out.)* You damned fool! Why did you leave her
6   alone so long? Why didn't you stick around?
7 EDMUND: Because she accused me — and you and Papa — of
8   spying on her all the time and not trusting her. She made
9   me feel ashamed. I know how rotten it must be for her. And
10   she promised on her sacred word of honor —
11 JAMIE: *(With a bitter weariness)* You ought to know that doesn't
12   mean anything.
13 EDMUND: It does this time!
14 JAMIE: That's what we thought the other times. *(He leans over*
15   *the table to give his brother's arm an affectionate grasp.)* Listen,
16   kid, I know you think I'm a cynical bastard, but remember
17   I've seen a lot more of this game than you have. You never
18   knew what was really wrong until you were in prep school.
19   Papa and I kept it from you. But I was wise ten years or
20   more before we had to tell you. I know the game backwards
21   and I've been thinking all morning of the way she acted last
22   night when she thought we were asleep. I haven't been able
23   to think of anything else. And now you tell me she got you
24   to leave her alone upstairs all morning.
25 EDMUND: She didn't! You're crazy!
26 JAMIE: *(Placatingly)* All right, kid. Don't start a battle with me. I
27   hope as much as you do I'm crazy. I've been as happy as hell
28   because I'd really begun to believe that this time — *(He*
29   *stops — looking through the front parlor toward the hall —*
30   *lowering his voice, hurriedly.)* She's coming downstairs. You
31   win on that. I guess I'm a damned suspicious louse. *(They*
32   *grow tense with a hopeful, fearful expectancy. JAMIE mutters.)*
33   Damn! I wish I'd grabbed another drink.
34 EDMUND: Me, too!
35

from **The Zoo Story** (1959)
Edward Albee

For all of its cruelty and violence, this modern playscript —
with absurd actions — is supposedly concerned with the religious
pilgrimage of two emotionally and spiritually crippled men who happen to meet on a Sunday afternoon in late summer. As they sit on a
park bench surrounded by the inviting view of Central Park, New
York City, the characters engage in the symbolic ritual of first introducing themselves, then sharing a series of amusing personal anec-
dotes and eventually acquainting themselves with each other in a
more direct, personal manner. Slowly as the conversation takes a
serious turn, both men reveal themselves as disillusioned, tormented
misfits apparently resigned to a boring life that has no value or
meaning. As the tone of the exchanges becomes more heated and
threatening, the men become more animalistic and protective of their
territory, until, at last, one is killed in a knife fight.

The title of the playscript suggests the narrow world view that
each character holds as a result of his own life experience, and it is
possible to understand each man's sense of isolation and despair in
terms of the social pressures and demands that have encaged them
like the animals they view on public display at the zoo. Peter, an
older man, is obviously a representative of the upper middle class.
He wears a tweed suit, smokes a pipe and carries horn-rimmed glasses. He is well-educated and sophisticated, a fact he frequently points
out with some pride. Jerry, a young man, is carelessly dressed and
evidently dependent on others for his livelihood. He is despondent
and moody, and his anger rises at the slightest provocation or minor
mishap.

In playing the scene the actors should recall that each of the
characters has a secret that he does not wish to reveal. To protect
his individuality and sense of independence, each man plays games
with the other and does not allow any intrusion into matters that
are personal or private. The "game" continues for some time until
Jerry tires of it and begins to assert himself in a physical, violent
manner. Special care should be taken to suggest to the audience that
Jerry is consciously enacting a ritual, a pattern of repetitive insults
and physical abuses, that will provoke Peter to do what is necessary
to end the suffering and the pain that he imagines himself experiencing. There should also be a sense of urgency and desperation
in Jerry's movement and pleading speech so that the audience imagines the futility of Peter's response.

Realist playwrights are primarily interested in presenting three-dimensional characters who display interior motives or psychological motivations that result in neurosis, behavioral adjustment or mood depression.

CAST

JERRY

PETER

SCENE

Central Park on a Sunday afternoon in summer. The present.

APPROACH

As the scene opens, Peter is seated on his bench reading a book. He stops, cleans his glasses and then stares off into space. Occasionally he takes a bite of a sandwich or an apple that he carries in a brown paper bag. Jerry, unshaven and wearing wrinkled clothing, enters very cautiously and slowly starts to approach Peter, appearing as if he might attack from behind. His movement is hesitant and halting, and he glances over his shoulder frequently to see if anyone is following him. Just as Jerry is close enough to tap Peter on the shoulder, Peter turns quickly around and is startled to see a wild-eyed, frantic young man pointing at him. They remain frozen for an extended moment, each rather afraid of what the other might do.

1   JERRY: *(Mysteriously)* **Peter, do you want to know what happened**
2   **at the zoo?**
3   PETER: **Ah, ha, ha. The what? Oh, yes; the zoo. Oh, ho, ho. Well,**
4   **I had my own zoo there for a moment with . . . hee, hee, the**
5   **parakeets getting dinner ready, and the . . . ha, ha, whatever**
6   **it was, the . . .**
7   JERRY: *(Calmly)* **Yes, that was very funny, Peter. I wouldn't have**
8   **expected it. But do you want to hear about what happened**
9   **at the zoo, or not?**
10   PETER: **Yes. Yes, by all means; tell me what happened at the zoo.**
11   **Oh, my. I don't know what happened to me.**
12   JERRY: **Now, I'll let you in on what happened at the zoo; but**
13   **first, I should tell you why I went to the zoo. I went to the**
14   **zoo to find out more about the way people exist with animals,**
15   **and the way animals exist with each other, and with people**
16   **too. It probably wasn't a fair test, what with everyone**
17   **separated by bars from everybody else, the animals for the**
18   **most part from each other, and always the people from the**
19   **animals. But, if it's a zoo, that's the way it is.** *(He pokes PETER*
20   *on the arm.)* **Move over.**
21   PETER: *(Friendly)* **I'm sorry, haven't you enough room?** *(He shifts*
22   *a little.)*
23   JERRY: *(Smiling slightly)* **Well, all the animals are there, and all**
24   **the people are there, and it's Sunday and all the children**
25   **are there.** *(He pokes PETER again.)* **Move over.**
26   PETER: *(Patiently, still friendly)* **All right.** *(He moves some more, and*
27   *JERRY has all the room he might need.)*
28   JERRY: **And it's a hot day, so all the stench is there, too, and all**
29   **the balloon sellers, and all the ice cream sellers, and all the**
30   **seals are barking, and all the birds are screaming.** *(Pokes*
31   *PETER harder.)* **Move over!**
32   PETER: *(Beginning to be annoyed)* **Look here, you have more than**
33   **enough room!** *(But he moves more, and is now fairly cramped at*
34   *one end of the bench.)*
35   JERRY: **And I am there, and it's feeding time at the lion's house,**

1	and the lion keeper comes into the lion cage, one of the lion
2	cages, to feed one of the lions. *(Punches PETER on the arm*
3	*hard.)* **MOVE OVER!**
4	**PETER:** *(Very annoyed)* **I can't move over any more, and stop**
5	**hitting me. What's the matter with you?**
6	**JERRY:** **Do you want to hear the story?** *(Punches PETER's arm*
7	*again.)*
8	**PETER:** *(Flabbergasted)* **I'm not so sure! I certainly don't want to**
9	**be punched in the arm.**
10	**JERRY:** *(Punches PETER's arm again.)* **Like that?**
11	**PETER:** **Stop it! What's the matter with you?**
12	**JERRY:** **I'm crazy.**
13	**PETER:** **That isn't funny.**
14	**JERRY:** **Listen to me, Peter. I want this bench. You go sit on the**
15	**bench over there, and if you're good I'll tell you the rest of**
16	**the story.**
17	**PETER:** *(Flustered)* **But . . . whatever for? What** *is* **the matter**
18	**with you? Besides, I see no reason why I should give up this**
19	**bench. I sit on this bench almost every Sunday afternoon,**
20	**in good weather. It's secluded here; there's never anyone**
21	**sitting here, so I have it all to myself.**
22	**JERRY:** *(Softly)* **Get off this bench, Peter; I want it.**
23	**PETER:** *(Almost whining)* **No.**
24	**JERRY:** **I said I want this bench, and I'm going to have it. Now**
25	**get over there.**
26	**PETER:** **People can't have everything they want. You should**
27	**know that; it's a rule; people can have some of the things**
28	**they want, but they can't have everything.**
29	**JERRY:** *(Laughs)* **Imbecile! You're slow-witted!**
30	**PETER:** **Stop that!**
31	**JERRY:** **You're a vegetable! Go lie on the ground.**
32	**PETER:** *(Intense)* **Now** *you* **listen to me. I've put up with you all**
33	**afternoon.**
34	**JERRY:** **Not really.**
35	**PETER:** **LONG ENOUGH. I've put up with you long enough. I've**

1   listened to you because you seemed . . . well, because I

2   thought you wanted to talk to somebody.

3   JERRY: You put things well; economically, and yet . . . oh, what

4   is the word I want to put justice to your . . . JESUS, you

5   make me sick . . . get off here and give me my bench!

6   PETER: MY BENCH!

7   JERRY: *(Pushes PETER almost, but not quite, off the bench.)* Get out

8   of my sight.

9   PETER: *(Regaining his position)* God da . . . mn you. That's

10   enough! I've had enough of you. I will not give up this bench;

11   you can't have it, and that's that. Now, go away. *(JERRY*

12   *snorts but does not move.)* Go away, I said. *(JERRY does not*

13   *move.)* Get away from here. If you don't move on . . . you're

14   a bum . . . that's what you are . . . If you don't move on, I'll

15   get a policeman here and make you go. *(JERRY laughs, stays.)*

16   I warn you, I'll call a policeman.

17   JERRY: *(Softly)* You won't find a policeman around here; they're

18   all over on the west side of the park chasing fairies down

19   from trees or out of the bushes. That's all they do. That's

20   their function. So scream your head off; it won't do you any

21   good.

22   PETER: POLICE! I warn you, I'll have you arrested. POLICE!

23   *(Pause)* I said POLICE! *(Pause)* I feel ridiculous.

24   JERRY: You look ridiculous: a grown man screaming for the

25   police on a bright Sunday afternoon in the park with nobody

26   harming you. If a policeman *did* fill his quota and come

27   sludging over this way he'd probably take you in as a nut.

28   PETER: *(With disgust and impotence)* Great God, I just came here

29   to read, and now you want me to give up the bench. You're

30   mad.

31   JERRY: Hey, I got news for you, as they say. I'm on your precious

32   bench, and you're never going to have it for yourself again.

33   PETER: *(Furious)* Look, you; get off my bench. I don't care if it

34   makes any sense or not. I want this bench to myself; I want

35   you OFF IT!

1   **JERRY:**   *(Mocking)* **Aw ... look who's mad.**

2   **PETER:**   **GET OFF!**

3   **JERRY:**   **Do you know how ridiculous you look *now*?**

4   **PETER:**   *(His fury and self-consciousness have possessed him.)* **It**
5   **doesn't matter.** *(He is almost crying.)* **GET AWAY FROM MY**
6   **BENCH!**

7   **JERRY:**   **Why? You have everything in the world you want;**
8   **you've told me about your home, and your family, and *your***
9   ***own* little zoo. You have everything, and now you want this**
10   **bench. Are these the things men fight for? Tell me, Peter, is**
11   **this bench, this iron and this wood, is this your honor? Is**
12   **this the thing in the world you'd fight for? Can you think**
13   **of anything more absurd?**

14   **PETER:**   **Absurd? Look, I'm not going to talk to you about honor,**
15   **or even try to explain it to you. Besides, it isn't a question**
16   **of honor; but even if it were, you wouldn't understand.**

17   **JERRY:**   *(Contemptuously)* **You don't even know what you're**
18   **saying, do you? This is probably the first time in your life**
19   **you've had anything more trying to face than changing your**
20   **cats' toilet box. Stupid! Don't you have any idea, not even**
21   **the slightest, what other people *need*?**

22   **PETER:**   **Oh, boy, listen to you; well, you don't need this bench.**
23   **That's for sure.**

24   **JERRY:**   **Yes; yes, I do.**

25   **PETER:**   *(Quivering)* **I've come here for years; I have hours of**
26   **great pleasure, great satisfaction, right here. And that's**
27   **important to a man. I'm a responsible person, and I'm a**
28   **GROWNUP. This is my bench, and you have no right to take**
29   **it away from me.**

30   **JERRY:**   **Fight for it, then. Defend yourself; defend your bench.**

31   **PETER:**   **You've *pushed* me to it. Get up and fight.**

32   **JERRY:**   **Like a man?**

33   **PETER:**   *(Still angry)* **Yes, like a man, if you insist on mocking me**
34   **even further.**

35   **JERRY:**   **I'll have to give you credit for one thing: you *are* a**

1   **vegetable, and a slightly nearsighted one, I think . . .**
2   PETER: **THAT'S ENOUGH . . .**
3   JERRY: **. . . but, you know, as they say on TV all the time — you**
4   **know — and I mean this, Peter, you have a certain dignity;**
5   **it surprises me . . .**
6   PETER: **STOP!**
7   JERRY: *(Rises lazily.)* **Very well, Peter, we'll battle for the bench,**
8   **but we're not evenly matched.** *(He takes out and clicks open an*
9   *ugly-looking knife.)*
10   PETER: *(Suddenly awakening to the reality of the situation)* **You *are***
11   **mad! You're stark raving mad! YOU'RE GOING TO KILL**
12   **ME!** *(But before PETER has time to think what to do, JERRY tosses*
13   *the knife at PETER's feet.)*
14   JERRY: **There you go. Pick it up. You have the knife and we'll**
15   **be more evenly matched.**
16   PETER: *(Horrified)* **No!**
17   JERRY: *(Rushes over to PETER, grabs him by the collar; PETER rises;*
18   *their faces almost touch.)* **Now you pick up that knife and you**
19   **fight with me. You fight for your self-respect; you fight for**
20   **that god-damned bench.**
21   PETER: *(Struggling)* **No! Let . . . let go of me! He . . . Help!**
22   JERRY: *(Slaps PETER on each "fight.")* **You fight, you miserable**
23   **bastard; fight for that bench; fight for your parakeets; fight**
24   **for your cats; fight for your two daughters; fight for your**
25   **wife; fight for your manhood, you pathetic little vegetable.**
26   *(Spits in PETER's face.)* **You couldn't even get your wife with**
27   **a male child.**
28   PETER: *(Breaks away, enraged.)* **It's a matter of genetics, not**
29   **manhood, you . . . you monster.** *(He darts down, picks up the*
30   *knife and backs off a little; he is breathing heavily.)* **I'll give you**
31   **one last chance; get out of here and leave me alone!** *(He holds*
32   *the knife with a firm arm, but far in front of him, not to attack but*
33   *to defend.)*
34   JERRY: *(Sighs heavily.)* **So be it!** *(With a rush he charges PETER and*
35   *impales himself on the knife. Tableau: For just a moment, complete*

1   silence, *JERRY impaled on the knife at the end of PETER's still*
2   *firm arm. Then PETER screams, pulls away, leaving the knife in*
3   *JERRY. JERRY is motionless, on point. Then he, too, screams, and*
4   *it must be the sound of an infuriated and fatally wounded animal.*
5   *With the knife in him, he stumbles back to the bench that PETER*
6   *had vacated. He crumbles there, sitting facing PETER, his eyes*
7   *wide in agony, his mouth open.)*
8   **PETER:**   *(Whispering)* **Oh, my God, oh, my God, oh, my God . . .**
9   *(He repeats these words many times, very rapidly.)*
10 **JERRY:**   *(JERRY is dying; but now his expression seems to change. His*
11   *features relax, and while his voice varies, sometimes wrenched with*
12   *pain, for the most part he seems removed from his dying. He smiles.)*
13   **Thank you, Peter. I mean that, now; thank you very much.**
14   *(PETER's mouth drops open. He cannot move; he is transfixed.)*
15   **Oh, Peter, I was so afraid I'd drive you away.** *(He laughs as*
16   *best he can.)* **You don't know how afraid I was you'd go away**
17   **and leave me. And now I'll tell you what happened at the**
18   **zoo. I think . . . I think this is what happened at the zoo . . . I**
19   **think. I think that while I was at the zoo I decided that I**
20   **would walk north . . . northerly, rather . . . until I found**
21   **you . . . or somebody . . . and I decided that I would talk to**
22   **you . . . I would tell you things . . . and things that I would**
23   **tell you would . . . Well, here we are. You see? Here we *are*.**
24   **But . . . I don't know . . . could I have planned all this?**
25   **No . . . no, I couldn't have. But I think I did. And now you**
26   **know all about what happened at the zoo. Peter . . . thank**
27   **you. I came unto you** *(He laughs, so faintly)* **and you have**
28   **comforted me. Dear Peter.**
29
30
31
32
33
34
35

from **The Runner Stumbles** (1976)
Milan Stitt

Although based upon an actual Michigan murder case of the early part of the 20th century, this drama derives its sensitive but thought-provoking impact from the simplicity of the characters, the complexity of the situation and the creativity of the staging. Related primarily in a series of "flashbacks," the plot concerns the trial of Father Rivard, a young, unconventional and somewhat abrasive priest who is charged with having killed a nun, Sister Rita. Although the priest denies any knowledge of the crime, there are grave doubts concerning his innocence.

As the play begins, Father Rivard is in prison awaiting trial. He is exhausted and confused, primarily because he cannot recall the circumstances that led to his imprisonment. As he is speaking with a court-appointed lawyer, there is an abrupt change in his attitude and mood; he suddenly begins to recall the past, including the isolated episodes involving Sister Rita. In playing the scene, the actors are reminded that it is a recollection by the priest and should have a dream-like quality in performance. If possible, lights should be dimmed to almost dark to suggest an atmosphere of gloom and despair, or soft music may be played in the background to initiate the audience into the flashback approach.

Although the scene concludes with rejection and a degree of physical violence, the opening exchanges of dialog suggest a romantic attraction between Father Rivard and Sister Rita. Care should be taken, however, to highlight the awkwardness and insecurity they each feel in trying to express themselves, especially since they are now alone in the nun's room. The actors should strive for a realistic style of performance, even though the scene is a "memory" and the tone of the dialog should be both conversational and intimate. The argument that propels the climax of the scene should not be exaggerated or overly forceful, but should grow out of mutual misunderstanding of what has been said or implied. There should also be a sense of emptiness and frustration as the scene concludes and the characters are left alone with their own personal sadness and torment.

CAST

NUN

PRIEST

MRS. SHANDIG

SCENE

The Nun's room. It is late April, 1911.

APPROACH

As the scene opens, Sister Rita is staring blankly through an imaginary window facing the audience, sobbing. A fire has just swept through the rectory grounds, destroying her beloved rose garden, and she is now clutching one of the remaining buds in her hand as Father Rivard enters. The Priest abruptly stops as he notices that Sister Rita is wearing her street clothes, and he starts to slowly retreat. She turns quickly and realizes that he is about to leave. There is a moment of innocent, child-like laughter as both try to conceal the awkwardness of the situation. As they relax and become more comfortable with each other, the conversation becomes intimate and flirtatious but builds to an unexpected climax.

1 NUN: *(At window)* **Where is my garden? The fire ditch. They dug**
2 **the fire ditch through my garden. All the bulbs are dug up.**
3 **The roses. They burned.** *(During the NUN's speech, PRIEST*
4 *abruptly enters, crosses to NUN. PRIEST holds NUN until sobbing*
5 *subsides. NUN falls to knees in front of PRIEST, who sits on stool.)*
6 PRIEST: **At night I wonder how you are feeling, what you think,**
7 **if you're happy, if you can sleep. Even when I pray, I wonder**
8 **what you're doing. I look up through a window if it's recess**
9 **or listen for your steps in the hall. I can only concentrate**
10 **if I pray about you. Almost to you.** *(He is about to kiss her.)*
11 NUN: **Please. Tell me what it is.**
12 PRIEST: **I have.** *(Silence)* **I love you.** *(They kiss, stand and embrace.)*
13 NUN: *(Sitting on stool as PRIEST sits on bench)* **I never dared think**
14 **— I thought who else would have me but the church? But**
15 **with you I'm not nothing, am I?**
16 PRIEST: **No. You're not.**
17 NUN: *(Standing to put diary away)* **I'm just like everyone else.**
18 PRIEST: **What's that?**
19 NUN: *(Starting to pass PRIEST)* **Just my diary. I always keep it in**
20 **the drawer. But it's all right now, isn't it?** *(Handing it to*
21 *PRIEST)* **Do you want to read it?**
22 PRIEST: **It's drawings.**
23 NUN: **Not all of it.** *(She sits on bench with PRIEST to look at diary.)*
24 PRIEST: **No, Of course not. This can't be Sister Immaculata,**
25 **can it?**
26 NUN: **I think she must have been in a grump that day.**
27 PRIEST: **Every day. Did you show her this?**
28 NUN: **No one's ever seen it. I offered to show it to Mother Vincent,**
29 **but she said the only sin it could possibly be is boring.**
30 PRIEST: **She is wrong. This is so easy. Why was I so stupid? I**
31 **don't understand why it seemed so worthy to —**
32 NUN: **Why do we have to understand? Has trying to understand**
33 **been so wonderful?**
34 PRIEST: **No.**
35 NUN: **Who's that?**

1   PRIEST: Me? Well, you sure got the eyelashes. How could you
2   know how I'd look without a beard?
3   NUN: I guessed.
4   PRIEST: Well, you'd be disappointed.
5   NUN: I don't think so.
6   PRIEST: You make me so happy. And you make me so miserable.
7   NUN: I never meant to. *(Leading PRIEST to window, still holding*
8   *diary)* Look. Where I stood all those nights. See. We can be
9   with all the other people now. We aren't so different after
10   all, are we? Don't look at the church. Look down there with
11   the other families. We'll be like that too.
12   PRIEST: We can't move down there.
13   NUN: We'll have our own children.
14   PRIEST: Children.
15   NUN: Oh, yes. I should have known. Oh, all those nights. Known
16   that if the church wasn't everything, that you would give
17   me something in its place. I think I always knew that I was
18   not a true Bride of Christ.
19   PRIEST: You thought of this before?
20   NUN: No. Just the confusion. In there you'll see. I just didn't
21   know.
22   PRIEST: What did you write?
23   NUN: It doesn't matter, does it?
24   PRIEST: Read it to me.
25   NUN: Someday, whenever, you can read it all —
26   PRIEST: Read it to me. Now. Read it.
27   NUN: *(Looking as she sits on stool)* Well, any page these last few
28   weeks. "I think Father Rivard must be right. Maybe the
29   church is only for rules, but God is for people. According to
30   the rules everything I feel is wrong, yet nothing feels wrong.
31   Do I have a conscience? Yes, I do. Do I belong in the church?
32   I don't know. He makes me so confused."
33   PRIEST: We can never lose our faith.
34   NUN: We won't.
35   PRIEST: You can't even think of it.

1   NUN: *(Standing)* **Now look. The lights are going on in their**
2   **homes. We can think of that. We'll be down there and then —**
3   *(PRIEST suddenly pulls her from the window.)* **What is it?**

4   PRIEST: **Mrs. Shandig is coming up the hill.**

5   NUN: **But we can tell her. Everyone.**

6   PRIEST: **No.**

7   NUN: **Why?**

8   PRIEST: *(Moving to exit)* **Because I, I — I'm their priest. She**
9   **depends on me. They all do. I'm the only way they have of**
10   **understanding.**

11 NUN: **People understand.** *(She crosses to stop his exit. He grabs her*
12   *by the arms.)*

13 PRIEST: **It's not how you think it is. Their homes have photo-**
14   **graphs of babies in coffins. Adolescents pour kerosene on**
15   **kittens, and their fathers laugh when they set the fire.**
16   **Sometimes wives cannot cook breakfast. Their fingers are**
17   **broken from their husbands' beatings. It's only because they**
18   **think I'm different; it's only because they think I'm worthy**
19   **that I can help them. I must be worthy.**

20 NUN: *(Putting arms around his neck)* **I think you're worthy. Please.**
21   **You said you loved me. I know you're too good, too precious**
22   **to escape, desert me when —**

23 PRIEST: **I'm not, not what you think. I, I, I've destroyed all that.**
24   **For the church.** *(Pushing her onto stool)* **There's nothing left**
25   **for you. I can't be a husband. I can't be** *(Kneeling in front of*
26   *her)* **a father. There's nothing left but cruelty. That's all I**
27   **know. That's all I worship. All I need. Not the resurrection,**
28   **life. It's the nails. My salvation. Only the agony. There's no**
29   **chance for —**

30 NUN: **You're not cruel. It'll be different now.**

31 PRIEST: **Damn you. Trying to break me down, make me forget.**
32   *(Taking her head in his hands, forcing her to look out window)*
33   **Planting those flowers out there as if you, you could make**
34   **the world beautiful. What makes you think you could change**
35   **anything? Promising me things will be better. You make**

1   **them worse. It's not my fault you lost your faith. It's not.**

2   **You never had any if it dies so easily.** *(He starts to rip up diary.*

3   *She wrestles it from him.)*

4 NUN: **No. That was before. You can't stop. That's gone. It's gone.**

5 PRIEST: *(Grabbing NUN by shoulders, shaking her with violence,*

6   *causing her to drop diary)* **With them, with them. I can make**

7   **it look all right. They only want me to say those words. They**

8   **don't want to know me. You can't know me. I'll destroy you.**

9   **You can't know me. You'd hate me. I hate myself.**

10 NUN: **I don't hate you. God doesn't hate you.**

11 PRIEST: *(Trying to exit)* **Don't talk about God.**

12 NUN: *(Holding him from exit)* **We still have God.**

13 PRIEST: **I don't want God. I don't want you.** *(Starting to choke*

14   *NUN.)* **I hate God. I hate God. I want to kill God. I always**

15   **wanted to kill —** *(NUN falls to floor. For a moment of silence, she*

16   *appears dead. PRIEST slaps her on back. She coughs. He drags*

17   *her to bench. He gets wet cloth, sits next to her, wiping her brow.*

18   *MRS. SHANDIG begins to enter up ramp. She is looking back down*

19   *in the valley to see if fire is out.)*

20 NUN: *(As she stops choking)* **I'm sorry. I'm sorry. What you said.**

21   **Hating God. It's my fault, too. You couldn't —**

22 PRIEST: **No. No. It's me.** *(MRS. SHANDIG enters.)*

23 NUN: **We have to help each other. It's all we have now. We only**

24   **have each other.** *(PRIEST crosses right as he sees MRS. SHANDIG.)*

25 MRS. SHANDIG: *(Moving to hold NUN)* **Sister. What are you**

26   **saying?**

27 NUN: **Please. Mrs. Shandig. Leave us alone.**

28 MRS. SHANDIG: **What is wrong? What you said . . .** *(NUN throws*

29   *herself into MRS. SHANDIG's arms for comfort.)*

30 NUN: **Tell her. Please tell her.**

31 MRS. SHANDIG: **Tell me what?**

32 NUN: **Tell her.**

33 MRS. SHANDIG: **Tell me what?**

34 NUN: *(Turning from embrace to PRIEST)* **Just tell her, and it will**

35   **be over. Please. Tell her you love me.** *(Silence as MRS.*

1   *SHANDIG goes, sits on stool.)*
2   **MRS. SHANDIG: Sister. No. No.**
3   **PRIEST: There'll be a train. I'll walk to Traverse City. The fire**
4   **didn't affect the trains there.**
5   **NUN: I'll go with you.**
6   **PRIEST: No.**
7   **MRS. SHANDIG: Father, you can't go.**
8   **NUN:** *(Suddenly embracing PRIEST)* **Don't leave me. I don't care if**
9   **I go to hell!**
10   **MRS. SHANDIG:** *(Pulling NUN from PRIEST)* **Father, you hear**
11   **her.** *(About to hit NUN)* **Don't touch him.**
12   **PRIEST:** *(Catching MRS. SHANDIG's hand)* **Stop it.** *(NUN crosses*
13   *to PRIEST. Both sit on bench.)* **I won't hurt you anymore. You**
14   **can leave. But you must leave the right way, when your**
15   **community tells you. Go back to your order.**
16   **NUN: I'm not a nun now. I'm nothing.**
17   **PRIEST: There's still a place for you. They need you.**
18   **NUN: I haven't even said it to you.**
19   **PRIEST: Don't say anything. Don't think it. Honor your vows.**
20   **It's the only way.** *(MRS. SHANDIG backs, unnoticed by audience,*
21   *to witness chair, where she sits at end of scene.)* **The rest is me. I**
22   **cause it. God isn't cruel.**
23   **NUN:** *(Crying, hitting PRIEST)* **No. No. No. There's nothing left.**
24   *(As PRIEST crosses to cell and sits on stool)* **But I never told**
25   **you. You never heard the words. Let me tell you!**
26
27
28
29
30
31
32
33
34
35

from **Album** (1980)

David Rimmer

A long-running, Off-Broadway comic success that deals with the turbulent and yet light-hearted high school years of four typical teenagers, this playscript captures the wild humor, petty jealousies and lost innocence that chronicle growing up in the 1960s. There is a youthful rebellion and frank language that helps to convey the harsh reality of the turbulent sixties as the youthful characters alternate between pleasure and pain in their quest for independence and individuality. The playscript also explores the rivalry and competitive nature of adolescents who struggle valiantly to confront their impending adulthood and awakening sexuality. The action of the unfailingly funny escapades of the teenaged couples is frequently underscored with popular music of the historical period — Bob Dylan, the Beatles, the Beach Boys — to help orchestrate the emotional turmoil and mental anguish of the characters.

In playing the scene the actors should capture the jesting innocence and youthful posing that often distinguish young men and women asserting their personal values and self-image. There is a need to pay some attention to the jealousy that is often felt when close friends become potential rivals for attention or recognition. This scene is especially appropriate to consult one's "memory book," from which the actor can draw personal observations and experiences that help to suggest realistic walks, postures, voices and attitudes for the teenaged couples. There is also an excellent performance opportunity here to select one's personal, individual traits such as comic flair, physique or vocal quality to give added dimension to the performance.

There is a quiet strength and fierce independence in each of the characters that arouses sympathy and compassion so it is important to suggest gentle and tender exploration of the character's feelings as well as the "bittersweet" realization that these last few, carefree high school years together may be life's most intriguing adventure. Each character should also suggest that in spite of initial misgivings and doubt to the contrary a great capacity to learn and to love emerges from the relationship. Remember that what the characters discover about themselves is an almost spiritual capacity to understand humanity as well.

CAST

TRISH
BOO

SCENE

A room in the Paradise Motel. It is two o'clock a.m.

APPROACH

As the scene opens, Boo enters wearing his sunglasses, carrying a laundry bag, a guitar case and a copy of *Sgt. Pepper*. A hand and a suitcase suddenly appear at the window as Trish climbs into the room stumbling and grumbling. They look around in hushed silence at the motel room's cheap and drab furniture and then both collapse on one of the two beds that come out from the wall. There is an obviously embarrassing and unsure moment of who should speak or move first. The initial conversation is hesitant and nervous as the reality of having "run away" to the motel as a daring adventure slowly begins to become a frightening reality as the characters realize that they are now alone and vulnerable.

1 TRISH: I love this room. It's like . . . study hall.

2 BOO: You should've seen the desk guy —

3 TRISH: The desk guy just gave it to you? He didn't ask any
4 questions?

5 BOO: Yeah, but I faked him out. There was this sign on the wall
6 that said "Servicemen Welcome" so I told him I was visiting
7 my father at the army base and he couldn't get leave and I
8 had no place else to go, so . . .

9 TRISH: There's no army base around here.

10 BOO: He believed me. You should've seen this guy. He was bald, he
11 looked just like the guy in *The Tingler*, you know, the one that
12 drives his wife crazy by filling up the bathtub with blood —

13 TRISH: Shhh — Places like this give me the creeps.

14 BOO: You been to a lot of 'em?

15 TRISH: No. But did you ever see that movie *Psycho*?

16 BOO: Yeah. Four times. *(He suddenly does the shower-scene scream*
17 *and comes after her like Tony Perkins. She screams and runs to the*
18 *other side of the room. Dylan voice)* Well, whaddaya know, my mind
19 ain't workin', I take a shower, I look just like Tony Perkins.

20 TRISH: Is there anybody else you like except Bob Dylan?

21 BOO: Winston Churchill. *(Laughs, jumps exuberantly on the bed.*
22 *Sunglasses on)* **This is so cool!** The Paradise Motel . . . First
23 time I've ever been in a motel, first time I ever stole a car —

24 TRISH: Your parents' —

25 BOO: First time I ever ran away, first time —

26 TRISH: You have to keep saying that?

27 BOO: What? First time? *(Smiles.)*

28 TRISH: Don't look. *(She goes behind the closet door, taking the suitcase.*
29 *He waits nervously, trying to be cool. He pulls down the bedspread, finds*
30 *something on the sheet, flicks it away, arranges things neatly. Then*
31 *he takes his guitar out of the case, and begins strumming and singing*
32 *in Bob Dylan style the chorus of "Just Like a Woman."*)*

33

34 *For public performance of such songs and recordings mentioned in this play that are
in copyright, the permission of the copyright owners must be obtained; or other songs
35 and recordings in the public domain may be substituted.

212

1 BOO: *(Still strumming, makes the line part of the song.)* ... **Takin'**
2   **that dress off, huh?** *(She comes out, wearing a pair of jeans and*
3   *a loose-fitting peasant-type blouse, and holding on to her mother's*
4   *album. He puts the guitar down, takes off the sunglasses and turns*
5   *to her in anticipation. Disappointed)* **Oh. God, what you got in**
6   **there? You're holdin' it like it was Fort Knox —**
7 TRISH: **Nothin'.**
8 BOO: **You don't want me to see?**
9 TRISH: **If this place is so cool, how come they don't have a TV?**
10 BOO: *(Hurt)* **Whaddaya think we're gonna do, watch TV all**
11   **night?**
12 TRISH: **And the bathroom's down the hall?**
13 BOO: **What'd you expect, all the comforts of home?**
14 TRISH: *(At the radio)* **I don't know why you had to steal this. I**
15   **s'pose you think you're John Dillinger or somebody ...**
16 BOO: *(Little smile)* **John Dillinger? It's possible.** *(He starts prowling*
17   *around the room; finds the Bible, leafs through it.)*
18 TRISH: **What're you looking for?**
19 BOO: **Drugs. I thought somebody left some drugs in it.**
20 TRISH: *In the Bible?*
21 BOO: **Maybe a band stayed here. That's where they stay when**
22   **they're on the road — motels. And that's where they hide**
23   **their stuff — Bibles. They hollow 'em out —** *(Heads for the*
24   *closet.)*
25 TRISH: **What would a band be doin' around here? Playing at the**
26   **army base? You lookin' for drugs in the closet?**
27 BOO: **Found a dime.**
28 TRISH: **Great place for a band. I met a guy in a band once. He**
29   **knew a guy who knew a guy who knew the Beatles —**
30 BOO: *(Sunglasses on; Dylan voice)* **Ooooo, I'm impressed —**
31 TRISH: **He told me the original title of "Yesterday" was**
32   **"Scrambled Eggs."** *(She sings a couple of lines of the Beatles'*
33   *"Yesterday," substituting "Scrambled Eggs" for "Yesterday." He*
34   *tries to kiss her; she ducks. She picks up the copy of* Sgt. Pepper.*)*
35   **We can't even play the album. That was dumb, you know,**

213

1   goin' up and gettin' this, you coulda got caught so easy.

2   BOO: I had to get the car keys, didn't I? What's the difference?

3   TRISH: The car keys were downstairs and the album was
4   upstairs.

5   BOO: And my parents were asleep. Big deal.

6   TRISH: *(Reading the back of the album)* I read the news today . . .

7   BOO: *(Sunglasses off)* You know what was cool? When we first
8   came onto the highway, and seein' it stretch out like that,
9   and then just takin' off . . .

10 TRISH: Yeah. The lights were nice.

11 BOO: I kept seein' this vision of the car cracked up, right in the
12   middle of the highway. It was beautiful, kinda. You know,
13   Dylan had this motorcycle accident where he almost got
14   killed —

15 TRISH: That means we should do it too —

16 BOO: And I kept takin' my hands off the wheel. Closin' my eyes
17   and driftin' like there was some kind of spell on me —

18 TRISH: Do me a favor, don't let me fall asleep next time I get in a
19   car with you.

20 BOO: I didn't do anything.

21 TRISH: Thanks!

22 BOO: You looked nice asleep.

23 TRISH: I wasn't just sleeping! You're not the only one who has
24   *visions* and all that stuff!

25 BOO: No — I know — I —

26 TRISH: I kept seeing myself in this big wheatfield in Kansas.
27   And everything was in black and white. All the people, and
28   the crows. And the scarecrow kept saying to me, "There's
29   no place like home, there's no place like home." We're not
30   goin' to Kansas, are we?

31 BOO: Nah.

32 TRISH: Good. We goin' to California?

33 BOO: I dunno. Maybe.

34 TRISH: Where *are* we goin'?

35 BOO: I dunno where we're goin', we're just goin'! OK? Trust me.

1   TRISH: OK, maybe I'll just *go* to my graduation tomorrow.

2   BOO: What do you mean?

3   TRISH: I wanna go back.

4   BOO: We just got here!

5   TRISH: I don't care. I wanna go home.

6   BOO: I thought you hated it there.

7   TRISH: You think I want to live here? You think this is an
8   improvement? *(He stalks around the room, pacing vehemently,*
9   *ignoring her. She softens, tries to reach him.)* Hey, we don't have
10   to run away.

11 BOO: Maybe *you* don't.

12 TRISH: You don't either. Look, our mothers and fathers are still
13   gonna be our mothers and fathers if we run away or not!

14 BOO: *(Dylan. Sunglasses on)* Not a chance!

15 TRISH: *Will you stop it?!* You're just hiding behind that!

16 BOO: *(Bitter)* Hidin' from you.

17 TRISH: *(Quieter; reasonable)* We can go back. Nobody'll know
18   where we've been.

19 BOO: *(Anger bursting out)* I want *everybody* to know where we've
20   been!

21 TRISH: *(Angry back)* Yeah, if we have a "tragic accident" they'll
22   know, they'll read it in the papers! "Two runaway teenagers
23   killed in fiery crash" — that's what *you* want!

24 BOO: That's what happened to James Dean and all those guys,
25   and Dylan almost. I bet he wanted it to —

26 TRISH: That's the stupidest thing I've ever heard! You think I'm
27   getting into a car with you again, you're crazy! I'd rather
28   call my parents — I'd rather call the police —

29 BOO: *Police?* We're *criminals* now!

30 TRISH: You're not *criminals* 'cause you steal your parents' car!

31 BOO: *Shut up! (She goes and sits on the bed, as far away from him as*
32   *possible. Tense pause. He paces in small nervous circles. She watches*
33   *him warily. He stops, looks at her, sits at the foot of the bed, trying*
34   *to be gentle, taking his sunglasses off.)* Hey, I — *(She quickly takes*
35   *the pillows from the bed and places them between him and her.*

215

1   *Instantly enraged, he grabs them and flings them aside. She flinches*
2   *and moves further away, cringing against the wall, reaching out*
3   *and grabbing for her photo album.)* **What's in there, your baby**
4   **pictures?** *(He grabs it, picks it up. She grabs for it, and they*
5   *struggle. He pulls away with it and looks inside.)* **Hey, I remember**
6   **this!**
7   TRISH: *(Furious; shocked; frightened)* **What do you mean** *you*
8   *remember this?!*
9   BOO: **You had all the Beach Boys' songs in it —**
10   TRISH: **You follow me home from school, you go through my**
11   **drawers, you gonna put** *Dragnet* **on my trail next? You're**
12   **worse than my mother!**
13   BOO: *(Flipping through the pages)* **These're all Beatles' songs —**
14   TRISH: **Give it back!**
15   BOO: **What's this? You write this?**
16   TRISH: **Don't read that! I don't want anybody to read that —!**
17   *(She rushes up to him, but he fends her off.)*
18   BOO: **What is it, your lovebook? Your diary? What'd you write —?**
19   TRISH: *None of your business!*
20   BOO: *(He yanks it away from her, shoves her, holds it over the window*
21   *as if to throw it out.)* **Either I read it or nobody does —**
22   TRISH: *(Stumbling away; very emotional; feels beaten.)* **Don't!** **It's**
23   **my mother's!**
24   BOO: **I thought you hated her!**
25   TRISH: *(Frustrated; confused)* **I — no, I — I wanna go home!**
26   BOO: *(Angry; bitter)* **No place like home!**
27   TRISH: *(Almost crying)* *I wanna go!* **I wanna see my dog . . .**
28   BOO: *(Throws the photo album down.)* **We haven't done anything**
29   **yet!**
30   TRISH: **I'll die before I do anything with you!**
31   BOO: *(Dylan voice: vicious, spits it out; sunglasses on.)* **You told me —**
32   **wanted to hold me — You just ain't that strong —** *(TRISH*
33   *screams in frustration; yells back at him, her strength returning.)*
34   TRISH: **I read the news today —**
35   BOO: *(Wild insane Dylan; overlapping)* **Anybody can be like me —**

216

1   TRISH: A lucky man — made the grade —

2   BOO: But nobody can be like you — luckily —

3   TRISH: Blew his mind — the lights changed —

4   BOO: How's it feel — you're on your own —

5   TRISH: *(Hands over her ears. Screaming)* **Scrambled Eggs — Love's**

6   **an easy game to play —**

7   BOO: No home — **A ROLLING STONE!**

8   TRISH: *(Chokes back tears of rage.)* **STOP IT!** *(She suddenly runs to*

9   *the door, fumbles with the handle, can't get it open, starts banging*

10   *on it wildly.)*

11 BOO: **Shut up! You'll wake the whole place up!**

12 TRISH: **I'll scream so loud I'll wake the whole world up!** *(He*

13   *catches her, they struggle, he throws her roughly onto the bed. She*

14   *scrambles up and stands at the head of the bed, like a cornered*

15   *animal. He moves toward her to get her to shut up.)* **Get away from**

16   **me! Don't come near me! Help!** *(Just as she screams, he rushes*

17   *over and turns on the radio as loud as it can go. The loud*

18   *instrumental part of the Beatles' "Good Morning, Good Morning,"*

19   *blasts out.)* **HELP! I know why you did that — you did that**

20   **so nobody'll hear me when you —**

21 BOO: What?

22 TRISH: I've seen it in the movies, don't deny it —

23 BOO: When I what?

24 TRISH: *Don't deny it!*

25 BOO: *Deny what?* *(He jumps onto the bed. They both stand there,*

26   *hysterical, screaming at each other over the music.)*

27 BOO: **WHEN I WHAT?**	TRISH: **DON'T YOU DARE!**
28 **DARE WHAT?**	**SHUT UP! YOU BETTER**
29 **WHAT'M I GONNA DO?**	**NOT —**
30 *WHAT?* **WHEN I WHAT?**	**I DON'T KNOW!**
31	**I DON'T KNOW! I**
32	**DON'T KNOW!**

33   *(He yanks the radio out of its socket and throws it down on the floor*

34   *with a loud crash. She dissolves into tears.)*

35 BOO: *OK? OK?* *(Still frustrated, he punches the wall, hurting his hand.*

217

1   *Stops, turns to her, almost crying.)* **What'd you think I was gonna**
2   **do —?** *(He can't finish; breaks off with a sob; hides his face. She*
3   *moves closer to him. He lifts his face slowly.)* **I don't need any**
4   **music.** *(He kneels on the floor, beginning to break down. She kneels*
5   *on the bed, getting nearer to him. His sunglasses have fallen off.)*
6   **TRISH:** **You don't have to be Bob Dylan. You don't have to be**
7   **anybody.**
8   **BOO:** *(After a beat)* **We'll go home.**
9   **TRISH:** **Home? Never heard of it.** *(She pulls him to her and hugs*
10   *him. Then she gets up and turns off the light in the room. In the*
11   *shadowy darkness, the Beatles' "Norwegian Wood" begins to play*
12   *softly. They kiss, and as they fall softly back onto the bed, their kiss*
13   *grows in desire.)*
14   *(Slow fade to black)*
15
16
17
18
19
20
21
22
23
24
25
26
27
28
29
30
31
32
33
34
35

from 'Night, Mother (1983)

Marsha Norman

During a recent interview, the playwright expressed her dissatisfaction with other playscripts that dealt with suicide and suggested that it was her own struggle to confront the issue directly and honestly in *'Night, Mother* which helped to dramatize this story of a woman's determination to commit suicide and to leave her mother behind. The dramatic strategy was to have the young woman, Jessie, confront the one person in her life who loved her and to give up intimate thoughts about killing herself in dialog rather than merely leaving a suicide note that would have been read aloud afterward — as had been done in almost all of the playscripts in the past that embraced the topic.

Realism demands that we "see" and "hear" characters performing self-sacrificing deeds, engaging in ignorant blunders, exhibiting courage and cowardice simultaneously, suffering in silence or committing errors in judgment.

There is a "raw slice of life" present in the scene that follows as Jessie explores the complex issues of life and death and engages in ethical and moral exchanges with her mother that reveal inner

219

conflicts, hidden desires and frustrated passions. The complexity of the scene is also represented by the fact that Jessie is not suffering from a terminal disease that might help to explain her personal choice to end her life. In no respect that is obvious does it appear that suicide is more than the character's inevitable decision based upon her personal, individual feelings about life and living. It is this performance image that the actor should seek in creating an atmosphere that helps to condition the viewer's response to the social and the moral dilemma being dramatized in the scene.

The inherent integrity of Jessie's choice to end her own life is primarily limited to her immediate concerns for the mental and physical comfort of her mother. The mother, Thelma, also has maternal concerns herself related to the spiritual and moral welfare of her daughter in having made this sudden and inexplicable decision. In playing the scene between mother and daughter it will be essential to present each character with simplicity and directness. There should be a sense of humility and quiet dignity that gives each character inspiration to confront the complex issues related to suicide. There should also be a basic humanity in the characters that allows them to eventually achieve a measure of understanding and compassion for each other in the final moments of impending self-destruction.

CAST

JESSIE

MAMA

SCENE

Late evening in the cluttered living room of "Mama" Cates' country home.

APPROACH

The scene opens with Jessie, pale and exhausted, sitting in the cluttered living room of her mother's country home staring out into a vacant and empty space. Her mother sits opposite her staring directly into her empty eyes and it is apparent that there is a familiarity between these two women that only comes from having lived together for a long period of time. There is a quiet intensity in the atmosphere that suggests the two women have already been engaged in strained conversation and forced interplay that has culminated in the present climate of chilling quiet. The tempo of the scene changes abruptly, however, with the mother's initial plea to her daughter to give up all thoughts of killing herself and to think of the devastation her death will mean to those who love her.

1   **MAMA:**   *(In desperate tears)* **Don't leave me, Jessie!** *(JESSIE stands*
2   *for a moment, then turns for the bedroom.)* **No!** *(She grabs JESSIE's*
3   *arm.)*
4   **JESSIE:**   *(Carefully taking her arm away)* **I have a box of things I**
5   **want people to have. I'm just going to go get it for you.**
6   **You . . . just rest a minute.**
7   *(JESSIE is gone. MAMA heads for the telephone, but she can't even*
8   *pick up the receiver this time and, instead, stoops to clean up the*
9   *bottles that have spilled out of the manicure tray.)*
10
11   *(JESSIE returns, carrying a box that groceries were delivered in.*
12   *It probably says Hershey Kisses or Starkist Tuna. MAMA is still*
13   *down on the floor cleaning up, hoping that maybe if she makes it*
14   *look nice enough, JESSIE will stay.)*
15   **MAMA:**   **Jessie, how can I live here without you? I need you!**
16   **You're supposed to tell me to stand up straight and say how**
17   **nice I look in my pink dress, and drink my milk. You're**
18   **supposed to go around and lock up so I know we're safe for**
19   **the night, and when I wake up, you're supposed to be out**
20   **there making the coffee and watching me get older every**
21   **day, and you're supposed to help me die when the time**
22   **comes. I can't do that by myself, Jessie. I'm not like you,**
23   **Jessie. I hate the quiet and I don't want to die and I don't**
24   **want you to go, Jessie. How can I . . .** *(Has to stop a moment.)*
25   **How can I get up every day knowing you had to kill yourself**
26   **to make it stop hurting and I was here all the time and I**
27   **never even saw it. And then you gave me this chance to**
28   **make it better, convince you to stay alive, and I couldn't do**
29   **it. How can I live with myself after this, Jessie?**
30   **JESSIE:**   **I only told you so I could explain it, so you wouldn't**
31   **blame yourself, so you wouldn't feel bad. There wasn't**
32   **anything you could say to change my mind. I didn't want**
33   **you to save me. I just wanted you to know.**
34   **MAMA:**   **Stay with me just a little longer. Just a few more years.**
35   **I don't have that many more to go, Jessie. And as soon as I'm**

1   dead, you can do whatever you want. Maybe with me gone,
2   you'll have all the quiet you want, right here in the house.
3   And maybe one day you'll put in some begonias up the walk
4   and get just the right rain for them all summer. And Ricky
5   will be married by then and he'll bring your grandbabies
6   over and you can sneak them a piece of candy when their
7   daddy's not looking and then be real glad when they've gone
8   home and left you to your quiet again.
9   JESSIE: Don't you see, Mama, everything I do winds up like
10   this. How could I think you would understand? How could
11   I think you would want a manicure? We could hold hands
12   for an hour and then I could go shoot myself? I'm sorry
13   about tonight, Mama, but it's exactly why I'm doing it.
14   MAMA: If you've got the guts to kill yourself, Jessie, you've got
15   the guts to stay alive.
16   JESSIE: I know that. So it's really just a matter of where I'd
17   rather be.
18   MAMA: Look, maybe I can't think of what you should do, but
19   that doesn't mean there isn't something that would help.
20   *You* find it. *You* think of it. You can keep trying. You can
21   get brave and try some more. You don't have to give up!
22   JESSIE: I'm *not* giving up! This *is* the other thing I'm trying.
23   And I'm sure there are some other things that might work,
24   but *might* work isn't good enough anymore. I need
25   something that *will* work. *This* will work. That's why I
26   picked it.
27   MAMA: But something might happen. Something that could
28   change everything. Who knows what it might be, but it might
29   be worth waiting for! *(JESSIE doesn't respond.)* Try it for two
30   more weeks. We could have more talks like tonight.
31   JESSIE: No, Mama.
32   MAMA: I'll pay more attention to you. Tell the truth when you
33   ask me. Let you have your say.
34   JESSIE: No, Mama! We wouldn't have more talks like tonight,
35   because it's this next part that's made this last part so good,

223

1   Mama. No, Mama. *This* is how I have my say. This is how I
2   say what I thought about it *all* and I say no. To Dawson and
3   Loretta and the Red Chinese and epilepsy and Ricky and
4   Cecil and you. And me. And hope. I say no! *(Then going to*
5   *MAMA on the sofa)* Just let me go easy, Mama.
6 MAMA: How can I let you go?
7 JESSIE: You can because you have to. It's what you've always
8   done.
9 MAMA: You are my child!
10 JESSIE: I am what became of your child. *(MAMA cannot answer.)*
11   I found an old baby picture of me. And it was somebody
12   else, not me. It was somebody pink and fat who never heard
13   of sick or lonely, somebody who cried and got fed, and
14   reached up and got held and kicked but didn't hurt anybody,
15   and slept whenever she wanted to, just by closing her eyes.
16   Somebody who mainly just laid there and laughed at the
17   colors waving around over her head and chewed on a polka
18   dot whale and woke up knowing some new trick nearly
19   every day, and rolled over and drooled on the sheet and felt
20   your hand pulling my quilt back up over me. That's who I
21   started out as and this is who is left. *(There is no self-pity here.)*
22   That's what this is about. It's somebody I lost, all right, it's
23   my own self. Who I never was. Or who I tried to be and never
24   got there. Somebody I waited for who never came. And never
25   will. So, see, it doesn't much matter what else happens in
26   the world or in this house, even. I'm what was worth waiting
27   for and I didn't make it. Me . . . who might have made a
28   difference to me . . . I'm not going to show up, so there's no
29   reason to stay, except to keep you company, and
30   that's . . . not reason enough because I'm not . . . very good
31   company. *(Pause)* Am I?
32 MAMA: *(Knowing that she must tell the truth)* No. And neither am I.
33 JESSIE: I had this strange little thought, well, maybe it's not
34   so strange. Anyway, after Christmas, after I decided to do
35   this, I would wonder, sometimes, what might keep me here,

224

1 what might be worth staying for, and you know what it was?
2 It was maybe if there was something I really liked, like
3 maybe if I really liked rice pudding or cornflakes for
4 breakfast or something, that might be enough.
5 MAMA: Rice pudding is good.
6 JESSIE: Not to me.
7 MAMA: And you're not afraid?
8 JESSIE: Afraid of what?
9 MAMA: I'm afraid of it, for me, I mean. When my time comes. I
10 know it's coming, but . . .
11 JESSIE: You don't know when. Like in a scary movie.
12 MAMA: Yeah, sneaking up on me like some killer on the loose,
13 hiding out in the backyard just waiting for me to have my
14 hands full someday and how am I supposed to protect myself
15 anyhow when I don't know what he looks like and I don't
16 know how he sounds coming up behind me like that or if it
17 will hurt or take very long or what I don't get done before
18 it happens.
19 JESSIE: You've got plenty of time left.
20 MAMA: I forget what for, right now.
21 JESSIE: For whatever happens, I don't know. For the rest of
22 your life. For Agnes burning down one more house or
23 Dawson losing his hair or . . .
24 MAMA: *(Quickly)* Jessie, I can't just sit here and say OK, kill
25 yourself if you want to.
26 JESSIE: Sure you can. You just did. Say it again.
27 MAMA: *(Really startled)* Jessie! *(Quiet horror)* How dare you?!
28 *(Furious)* How dare you?! You think you can just leave
29 whenever you want, like you're watching television here?
30 No, you can't, Jessie. You make me feel like a fool for being
31 alive, child, and you are so wrong! I like it here, and I will
32 stay here until they make me go, until they drag me
33 screaming and I mean screaming into my grave, and you're
34 real smart to get away before then because, I mean, honey,
35 you've never heard noise like that in your life. *(JESSIE turns*

1   *away.)* **Who am I talking to? You're gone already, aren't you?**
2   **I'm looking right through you! I can't stop you because**
3   **you're already gone! I guess you think they'll all have to**
4   **talk about you now! I guess you think this will really confuse**
5   **them. Oh yes, ever since Christmas you've been laughing to**
6   **yourself and thinking, "Boy, are they all in for a surprise."**
7   **Well, nobody's going to be a bit surprised, sweetheart. This**
8   **is just like you. Do it the hard way, that's my girl, all right.**
9   *(JESSIE gets up and goes into the kitchen, but MAMA follows her.)*
10   **You know who they're going to feel sorry for? Me! How about**
11   **that! Not you, me! They're going to be** *ashamed* **of you. Yes.**
12   *Ashamed!* **If somebody asks Dawson about it, he'll change**
13   **the subject as fast as he can. He'll talk about how much he**
14   **has to pay to park his car these days.**
15   **JESSIE: Leave me alone.**
16   **MAMA: It's the truth!**
17   **JESSIE: I should've just left you a note!**
18   **MAMA:** *(Screaming)* **Yes!** *(Then suddenly understanding what she has*
19   *said, nearly paralyzed by the thought of it, she turns slowly to face*
20   *JESSIE, nearly whispering.)* **No. No. I ... might not have**
21   **thought of all the things you've said.**
22   **JESSIE: It's OK, Mama.** *(MAMA is nearly unconscious from the emo-*
23   *tional devastation of these last few moments. She sits down at the kitchen*
24   *table, hurt and angry and desperately afraid. But she looks almost numb.*
25   *She is so far beyond what is known as pain that she is virtually*
26   *unreachable and JESSIE knows this, and talks quietly, watching for*
27   *signs of recovery. JESSIE washes her hands in the sink.)* **I remember**
28   **you liked that preacher who did Daddy's, so if you want to ask**
29   **him to do the service, that's OK with me.**
30   **MAMA:** *(Not an answer, just a word)* **What?**
31   **JESSIE:** *(Putting on hand lotion as she talks)* **And pick some songs**
32   **you like or let Agnes pick, she'll know exactly which ones.**
33   **Oh, and I had your dress cleaned that you wore to Daddy's.**
34   **You looked real good in that.**
35   **MAMA: I don't remember, hon.**

1   JESSIE: And it won't be so bad once your friends start coming
2   to the funeral home. You'll probably see people you haven't
3   seen for years, but I thought about what you should say to
4   get over that nervous part when they first come in.
5   MAMA: *(Simply repeating)* Come in.
6   JESSIE: Take them up to see their flowers, they'd like that. And
7   when they say, "I'm sorry, Thelma," you just say, "I
8   appreciate your coming, Connie." And then ask how their
9   garden was this summer or what they're doing for
10   Thanksgiving or how their children ...
11   MAMA: I don't think I should ask about their children. I'll talk
12   about what they have on, that's always good. And I'll have
13   some crochet work with me.
14   JESSIE: And Agnes will be there, so you might not have to talk
15   at all.
16   MAMA: Maybe if Connie Richards does come, I can get her to
17   tell me where she gets that Irish yarn, she calls it. I know
18   it doesn't come from Ireland. I think it just comes with a
19   green wrapper.
20   JESSIE: And be sure to invite enough people home afterward so
21   you get enough food to feed them all and have some left for
22   you. But don't let anybody take anything home, especially
23   Loretta.
24   MAMA: Loretta will get all the food set up, honey. It's only fair
25   to let her have some macaroni or something.
26   JESSIE: No, Mama. You have to be more selfish from now on.
27   *(Sitting at the table with MAMA)* Now, somebody's bound to
28   ask you why I did it and you must say you don't know. That
29   you loved me and you know I loved you and we just sat
30   around tonight like every other night of our lives, and then
31   I came over and kissed you and said, " 'Night, Mother," and
32   you heard me close my bedroom door and the next thing
33   you heard was the shot. And whatever reasons I had, well,
34   you guess I just took them with me.
35   MAMA: *(Quietly)* It was something personal.

1   **JESSIE: Good. That's good, Mama.**

2   **MAMA: That's what I'll say, then.**

3   **JESSIE: Personal. Yeah.**

4   **MAMA: Is that what I tell Dawson and Loretta, too? We sat**
5   **around, you kissed me, " 'Night, Mother"? They'll want to**
6   **know more, Jessie. They won't believe it.**

7   **JESSIE: Well, then, tell them what we did. I filled up the candy**
8   **jars. I cleaned out the refrigerator. We made some hot**
9   **chocolate and put the cover back on the sofa. You had no**
10   **idea. All right? I really think it's better that way. If they**
11   **know we talked about it, they really won't understand how**
12   **you let me go.**

13   **MAMA: I guess not.**

14   **JESSIE: It's private. Tonight is private, yours and mine, and I**
15   **don't want anybody else to have any of it.**

16   **MAMA: OK, then.**

17   **JESSIE: *(Standing behind MAMA now, holding her shoulders)* Now,**
18   **when you hear the shot, I don't want you to come in. First**
19   **of all, you won't be able to get in by yourself, but I don't**
20   **want you trying. Call Dawson, then call the police, and then**
21   **call Agnes. And then you'll need something to do till**
22   **somebody gets here, so wash the hot chocolate pan. You**
23   **wash that pan till you hear the doorbell ring and I don't**
24   **care if it's an hour, you keep washing that pan.**

25   **MAMA: I'll make my calls and then I'll just sit. I won't need**
26   **something to do. What will the police say?**

27   **JESSIE: They'll do that gunpowder test, I guess, and ask you**
28   **what happened, and by that time, the ambulance will be**
29   **here and they'll come in and get me and you know how that**
30   **goes. You stay out here with Dawson and Loretta. You keep**
31   **Dawson out here. I want the police in the room first, not**
32   **Dawson. OK?**

33   **MAMA: What if Dawson and Loretta want me to go home with**
34   **them?**

35   **JESSIE: *(Returning to the living room)* That's up to you.**

1 MAMA: I think I'll stay here. All they've got is Sanka.

2 JESSIE: Maybe Agnes could come stay with you for a few days.

3 MAMA: *(Standing up, looking into the living room)* **I'd rather be by**
4 **myself, I think.** *(Walking toward the box JESSIE brought in*
5 *earlier)* **You want me to give people those things?**

6 JESSIE: *(They sit down on the sofa, JESSIE holding the box on her lap.)*
7 **I want Loretta to have my little calculator. Dawson bought**
8 **it for himself, you know, but then he saw one he liked better**
9 **and he couldn't bring both of them home with Loretta**
10 **counting every penny the way she does, so he gave the first**
11 **one to me. Be funny for her to have it now, don't you think?**
12 **And all my house slippers are in a sack for her in my closet.**
13 **Tell her I know they'll fit and I've never worn any of them,**
14 **and make sure Dawson hears you tell her that. I'm glad he**
15 **loves Loretta so much, but I wish he knew not everybody**
16 **has her size feet.**

17 MAMA: *(Taking the calculator)* **OK.**

18 JESSIE: *(Reaching into the box again)* **This letter is for Dawson,**
19 **but it's mostly about you, so read it if you want. There's a**
20 **list of presents for you for at least twenty more Christmases**
21 **and birthdays, so if you want anything special you better**
22 **add it to this list before you give it to him. Or if you want**
23 **to be surprised, just don't read that page. This Christmas,**
24 **you're getting mostly stuff for the house, like a new rug in**
25 **your bathroom and needlework, but next Christmas, you're**
26 **really going to cost him next Christmas. I think you'll like**
27 **it a lot and you'd never think of it.**

28 MAMA: And you think he'll go for it?

29 JESSIE: I think he'll feel like a real jerk if he doesn't. Me telling
30 him to, like this and all. Now, this number's where you call
31 Cecil. I called it last week and he answered, so I know he
32 still lives there.

33 MAMA: What do you want me to tell him?

34 JESSIE: Tell him we talked about him and I only had good
35 things to say about him, but mainly tell him to find Ricky

229

1   and tell him what I did, and tell Ricky you have something
2   for him, out here, from me, and to come get it. *(Pulls a sack*
3   *out of the box.)*
4   MAMA: *(The sack feels empty.)* **What is it?**
5   JESSIE: *(Taking it off)* **My watch.** *(Putting it in the sack and taking a*
6   *ribbon out of the sack to tie around the top of it)*
7   MAMA: **He'll sell it!**
8   JESSIE: **That's the idea. I appreciate him not stealing it already.**
9   **I'd like to buy him a good meal.**
10 MAMA: **He'll buy dope with it!**
11 JESSIE: **Well, then, I hope he gets some good dope with it,**
12   **Mama. And the rest of this is for you.** *(Handing MAMA the*
13   *box now. MAMA picks up the things and looks at them.)*
14 MAMA: *(Surprised and pleased)* **When did you do all this? During**
15   **my naps, I guess.**
16 JESSIE: **I guess. I tried to be quiet about it.** *(As MAMA is puzzled*
17   *by the presents)* **Those are just little presents. For whenever**
18   **you need one. They're not bought presents, just things I**
19   **thought you might like to look at, pictures or things you**
20   **think you've lost. Things you didn't know you had, even.**
21   **You'll see.**
22 MAMA: **I'm not sure I want them. They'll make me think of you.**
23 JESSIE: **No they won't. They're just things, like a free tube of**
24   **toothpaste I found hanging on the door one day.**
25 MAMA: **Oh. All right, then.**
26 JESSIE: **Well, maybe there's one nice present in there**
27   **somewhere. It's Granny's ring she gave me and I thought**
28   **you might like to have it, but I think you'd wear it if I gave**
29   **it to you right now.**
30 MAMA: *(Taking the box to a table nearby)* **No. Probably not.**
31   *(Turning back to face her)* **I'm ready for my manicure, I guess.**
32   **Want me to wash my hands again?**
33 JESSIE: *(Standing up)* **It's time for me to go, Mama.**
34 MAMA: *(Starting for her)* **No, Jessie, you've got all night!**
35 JESSIE: *(As MAMA grabs her)* **No, Mama.**

1 MAMA: It's not even ten o'clock.

2 JESSIE: *(Very calm)* Let me go, Mama.

3 MAMA: I can't. You can't go. You can't do this. You didn't say it
4   would be so soon, Jessie. I'm scared. I love you.

5 JESSIE: *(Takes her hands away.)* Let go of me, Mama. I've said
6   everything I had to say.

7 MAMA: *(Standing still a minute)* You said you wanted to do my
8   nails.

9 JESSIE: *(Taking a small step backward)* I can't. It's too late.

10 MAMA: It's not too late!

11 JESSIE: I don't want you to wake Dawson and Loretta when you
12   call. I want them to still be up and dressed so they can get
13   right over.

14 MAMA: *(As JESSIE backs up, MAMA moves in on her, but carefully.)*
15   They wake up fast, Jessie, if they have to. They don't matter
16   here, Jessie. You do. I do. We're not through yet. We've got
17   a lot of things to take care of here. I don't know where my
18   prescriptions are and you didn't tell me what to tell Dr.
19   Davis when he calls or how much you want me to tell Ricky
20   or who I can call to rake the leaves or . . .

21 JESSIE: Don't try and stop me, Mama, you can't do it.

22 MAMA: *(Grabbing her again, this time hard)* I can too! I'll stand in
23   front of this hall and you can't get past me. *(They struggle.)*
24   You'll have to knock me down to get away from me, Jessie.
25   I'm not about to let you . . . *(MAMA struggles with JESSIE at*
26   *the door and in the struggle JESSIE gets away from her and —)*

27 JESSIE: *(Almost a whisper)* 'Night, Mother. *(She vanishes into her*
28   *bedroom and we hear the door lock just as MAMA gets to it.)*

29 MAMA: *(Screams.)* Jessie! *(Pounding on the door)* Jessie, you let
30   me in there. Don't you do this, Jessie. I'm not going to stop
31   screaming until you open this door, Jessie. Jessie! Jessie!
32   What if I don't do any of the things you told me to do! I'll
33   tell Cecil what a miserable man he was to make you feel the
34   way he did and I'll give Ricky's watch to Dawson if I feel
35   like it and the only way you can make sure I do what you

want is you come out here and make me, Jessie! *(Pounding again)* Jessie! Stop this! I didn't know! I was here with you all the time. How could I know you were so alone? *(And MAMA stops for a moment, breathless and frantic, putting her ear to the door, and then she doesn't hear anything, she stands up straight again and screams once more.)* Jessie! Please! *(And we hear the shot, and it sounds like an answer, it sounds like No. MAMA collapses against the door, tears streaming down her face, but not screaming anymore. In shock now.)* Jessie, Jessie, child ... forgive me. *(Pause)* I thought you were mine. *(And she leaves the door and makes her way through the living room, around the furniture, as though she didn't know where it was, not knowing what to do. Finally, she goes to the stove in the kitchen and picks up the hot chocolate pan and carries it with her to the telephone and holds on to it while she dials the number. She looks down at the pan, holding it tight like her life depended on it. She hears Loretta answer.)* Loretta, let me talk to Dawson, honey.

SELECTED BIBLIOGRAPHY

The following textbooks and suggested readings are recommended for the beginning actor who may wish to explore the modern period of theatre history in terms of performance and production approaches that have evolved since the early 20th century. The suggested readings also provide valuable insights and practical guidelines to continue your scene study and playscript interpretation. A serious application of the theories and practices in these recommended sources should also provide a solid foundation for understanding the later movements in absurdism and the contemporary theatre.

Anderson, Virgil. *Training the Speaking Voice*. New York: Oxford University Press, 1961.

Benedetti, Robert. *The Actor at Work*. New Jersey: Prentice-Hall, 1976.

Bentley, Eric. *The Theory of the Modern Stage*. New York: Penguin Books, 1976.

Bert, Norman. *Theatre Alive!* Colorado Springs, CO: Meriwether Publishing Ltd., 1991.

Berry, Cecily. *Voice and the Actor*. London: Happay and Company, 1973.

Blunt, Jerry. *The Composite Art of Acting*. New York: Macmillan and Company, 1966.

Brook, Peter. *The Empty Space*. New York: Avon Press, 1968.

Colyer, Carlton. *The Art of Acting*. Colorado Springs, CO: Meriwether Publishing Ltd., 1989.

Gassner, John. *Form and Idea in the Modern Theatre*. New York: Holt, Rinehart and Winston, 1956.

Gilman, Richard. *The Making of Modern Drama*. New York: Farrar, Straus and Giroux, 1974.

Kerr, Walter. *Journey to the Center of Theatre*. New York: Knopf Publishers, 1979.

King, Nancy. *Theatre Movement: The Actor and His Space*. New York: DBS Publications, 1972..

Marowitz, Charles. *The Act of Being: Toward a New Theory of Acting*. New York: Taplinger Press, 1978.

Marranca, Bonnie. *The Theatre of Images*. New York: Drama Book Specialists, 1977.

Schechner, Richard. *Environmental Theatre*. New York: Hawthorne Books, 1973.

Styan, J. L. *Modern Drama in Theory and Practice*. Cambridge: Cambridge University Press, 1980.

Tennant, P. F. D. *Ibsen's Dramatic Technique*. London: Albert Saifer Press, 1962.

Weigand, Hermann. *The Modern Ibsen: A Reconstruction*. New York: E. P. Dutton, 1960.

Wiles, Timothy. *The Theatre Event: Modern Theories of Performance*. Chicago: University of Chicago Press, 1980.

Wills, Robert. *The Director in a Changing Theatre*. Palo Alto, CA: Mayfield Publishing Company, 1976.

Whitaker, Thomas. *Fields of Play in Modern Drama*. Princeton: Princeton University Press, 1977.

Worthen, W. B. *Modern Drama and the Rhetoric of Theatre*. Berkeley, CA: University of California Press, 1992.

CHAPTER FIVE

PLAYING ABSURD SCENES

"A world that can be explained by reasoning, however faulty, is a familiar world. But in a universe that is suddenly deprived of illusion and light, man feels a stranger. This divorce between man and his life truly constitutes the feeling of Absurdity."

— Albert Camus

Although the theatre of the absurd movement did not gain significant prominence until the mid-1950s, its theoretical roots may be quite easily traced to the playscripts of Luigi Pirandello (1897-1936). Pirandello, in such experimental playscripts as *Right You Are, If You Think You Are* (1918) and *Six Characters in Search of an Author* (1921), laid the theoretical absurd foundation that truth is *not* objective and that there are only individual interpretations or versions of what truth really is. A typical Pirandello playscript would involve a variety of characters who have witnessed an event but relate quite different versions of what that event meant, and each character is certain that his or her interpretation is the only correct one.

This innovative approach to topic matter and character development, although framed initially in a traditional structural pattern quite similar to that used by playwrights of realism, promotes the idea that it is the *situation* which develops character and that true character development merely reveals the eternal *anguish* of man. The playwrights who followed Pirandello's basic principles of absurdism dealt almost exclusively with the existential thought of characters in a given situation and attempted to define a character's existence in both the dialog and the action of the situation to reveal such aspects of individuality as freedom, choice and free will.

The playwrights of absurdism also attempted to draw logical and sensible conclusions about character and situation from an apparently illogical and inconsistent reality. They argued that a civilization capable of promoting world wars, hunger, political assassination, prejudice and revolution was incapable of exhibiting sound ethical or moral values for which individuals might be held accountable and responsible. Because there were now no absolute ethical or moral laws, man is helplessly adrift in a world that has no apparent meaning or purpose; hence, the term *absurd* is applied to those playscripts that seek to point out the emptiness of daily life and the futility of existence. The playwrights further argue that with no ethical or moral principles to guide them mankind is "free" to define its own values and to act in accordance with its principles.

This is the basic approach of Albert Camus (1913-1960), perhaps the most articulate existential novelist and playwright, who states that the "absurd" exists whenever man becomes aware of the vast empty space between his own goals and the meaningless universe that thwarts his attempts to realize those goals. This philosophical approach is the primary influence on the playwrights included in this chapter and as you begin your examination of the scenes that follow please recall that this theatre of the absurd movement in theory and in performance deals with "absolute" philosophical, ethical, moral or religious judgments that result from the individual playwright's own perspective on the universe. Each playwright, himself a philosopher as well, argues forcefully against the chaos inherent in the universe but cannot advance any solution for the dilemma other than to encourage each character to seek their own freedom.

As a contemporary philosophical approach to the drama that portrays characters as existing in a universe that has lost its meaning, the theatre of the absurd also suggests that characters live in an alien world in which there is no way to establish a meaningful or rewarding relationship with other human beings or with the environment. Thus, distorted forms of nightmarish fantasy, exaggerated forms of subconscious dreams, incoherent forms of verbal and nonverbal communication or alienated forms of disconnected images usually accompany the characters on their quest for an ultimate answer to the rhetorical question, *What is the value of life?*

Although the major playwrights of absurdism cannot easily be classified as a unified school of writers who share recognizably concise and consistent theories, their theoretical approach is common enough to suggest that the movement has no apparent order or design. The term "absurd," initially coined by the modern theatre critic Martin Esslin, is an apt description of the current movement but should not be interpreted as "silly" or "foolish." Quite the contrary, "absurd" used in the theoretical approach to drama that Esslin recommended should be thought of as *illogical* or even *paradoxical;* and the spectator should not hope to glimpse any profound or meaningful "truth" at first glance. Indeed, absurdism frequently invites distortion or misinterpretation of their playscripts so that the spectator is prompted to discover the identifiable or even the recognizable only after long periods of quiet reflection or introspective thought.

Playing the Role

The actor who engages in scene study and playscript interpretation for playing the role in theatre of the absurd should consider that the theoretical foundation upon which performance is constructed is that man is utterly alone in this temporal world and that he must, as a consequence of this isolation, create his own world and his own set of values. As Albert Camus, the "Father of Absurdism," suggests in his critical writings, "Man has no homeland to return to and no promised land before him." In this respect, man is forever lost in the world and must constantly struggle to regain any sense of meaning or self-identity.

Chained forever to one lonely place, with no hope of escape, the absurd man is at the mercy of his own self-doubts and self-torments. Although bewildered and frightened, the absurd man is also capable of achieving his own humanity through heroic deeds that reveal his basic dignity. He subsequently learns to employ his critical skills to think, to reason an appropriate answer for the predicament in which he finds himself. Even though the initial response is primarily intellectual and introspective, the absurd man discovers that while the universe may be irrational and unpredictable there is no reason why life itself cannot be given some semblance of order and harmony. This process of intellectual thought provides the individual strength of *resolve* and *purpose* that is apparently lacking in the universe, and man becomes increasingly more independent in both thought and attitude.

By touching on the universal nature of all human feelings and thoughts the absurdists encourage the spectator to resist conformity, to accept the rights of others and to endure in the face of certain death. The ideal world described by the absurdists and searched for by the characters in theatre of the absurd playscripts is that world of freedom from restraint, freedom from prejudice and freedom from fear. It is that world, in other words, in which each person may exist as his *own* sanctuary, his *own* peaceful retreat from the universe of "others" that represents disarray and disorder.

237

In playing the role in absurdism the actor is reminded that the playwrights provide very little background or historical information and that for the most part your performance intellect will be stimulated only by visualizing the images or the objects suggested in the selected scene. That is what the absurdist playwright Eugene Ionesco had in mind when he wrote that ". . . .the author should make actors of his props, bring objects to life, animate the scenery, and give symbols concrete forms." It should also be recalled that the plays of absurdism are intentionally contradictory in what is said and what is done and that the performer must intellectually resolve the opposition to project a clear, precise character portrait to the spectator.

Distorted forms of nightmarish fantasy, exaggerated forms of subconscious dreams, incoherent forms of verbal and nonverbal communication or alienated forms of disconnected images usually accompany absurd characters in their quest for an ultimate answer to the rhetorical question, What is the value of life?

In formulating their performance blueprint for the drama the playwrights of absurdism tried to convey a sense of the "alienation" that man experiences when he is separated from himself and from the world-at-large; and they tried to point out in dramatic form that when the world is illogical and paradoxical there are no ethical answers which are appropriate for the moral questions of right and wrong. So man must endure alone and solve the riddle of existence by himself or perish in a sea of insecurity and self-doubt. There are, however, certain touchstones — or clues — that the performer may consider in seeking to answer the riddle of man's existence, and they are provided here as guidelines to the basic understanding needed to resolve the essential mystery behind the plays of absurdism.

The playwrights of absurdism frequently employ the theatrical tricks of the circus clown or the slapstick comedian to express their individual point of view. In playing the role, however, it will be important for the actor to peer beneath the obvious broad humor of the scene or the perplexing ambiguity of the character to catch a glimpse of the philosophical concept at work in the scene. Perhaps the following list will give you an initial insight to understand the comic nature of a theatre of the absurd playscript in performance.

- The use of puppets, masks and robots is necessary in performance if the spectator is to clearly visualize the dehumanization and automation of mankind.

- The use of sound effects, foreign languages and inventive vocabulary is necessary in performance if the spectator is to clearly comprehend that language has lost its ability to communicate effectively.

- The use of music, fragmented set pieces and flying objects is necessary in performance if the spectator is to clearly objectify the separation of man from his environment.

In a world devoid of meaning it is necessary to resort to the unexpected if there is to be any hope of meaningful communication and the playwrights of absurdism promote these theatrical tricks to call attention to what they have observed about the human predicament. The use of the bizarre, the grotesque and the weird thus became the primary theatrical ingredients of the absurdists as they attempted to dramatize significant philosophical concepts or moral and ethical issues that helped to explain the meaning or the purpose of life in the fragmented 20th century.

Playing the Style

The theatrical movement toward absurdism was both a reaction against realism and an outgrowth of philosophical pessimism following

World War II. The playwrights of the theatre of the absurd objected to what they considered to be the "pasteboard" nature of one-dimensional characters and the simple transcription of crude, vernacular language uttered by the characters so popular in the modern playscripts of realism. Likewise, in their own pessimism for a world that had no apparent meaning and was in a state of deterioration, the playwrights of the theatre of the absurd objected to the debased nature of the neurotic characters who appeared to be defeated by their environment.

In their own efforts to explore man's interior nature, the absurdists abandoned realism and attempted to dramatize the neglected subjective nature of man to make objective judgments regarding significant religious, moral or ethical issues. Having witnessed bankrupt morals, corrupt ethics and hypercritical religion that was the legacy of World War II, the absurdists began to probe the interior of man in their playscripts by analyzing the human spirit and cataloging the fatal effects of despair and suffering on those persecuted souls who survived the personal loss of identity and whose eternal quest is now to rediscover that personal identity without further suffering or despair. The quest for rediscovery may take a variety of shapes or forms, depending upon the philosophical point of view of the playwright, but the result is inevitably the recognition that at the center of all existence is a void into which we must all disappear after death. This is the concluding thought that adds a striking note of pessimism to absurdism, but it is the playwright's way of saying that, like life, death is also absurd because there are no objective answers to explain its meaning or purpose.

It has often been said, perhaps as an apology rather than as a statement of fact, that it is easier to understand the action and the meaning of absurdism in performance by not thinking too much; that the best style of performance is the improvisational or spontaneous reaction to the situation described or the environment detailed. Although there is much truth in these suggestions, it is also possible to come to terms with the creative performance demands of absurdism if the following principles are explored in carefully observed and orchestrated rehearsals.

First, absurdism seems to distort the appearance of reality in a variety of ways. The distortion may take several avenues, but it usually begins with the character's loss of human qualities so that what emerges is a machine-like, almost dehumanized person who has no sense of direction or purpose in life. Any staging approach for absurdism, therefore, should seek to visualize the theoretical principle that human beings exist in a universe where they are cut off from their original religious or moral roots and now live as virtual "robots" in meaningless isolation in an alien world.

Second, lacking identity and personality, characters in absurdism seem to have no sense of time or tempo and often appear to despair of life itself. In their melancholy moments they seek, usually in vain, to discover who they are and more often than not are reduced to a series of nervous, meaningless impulses or responses that prove their essential worthlessness. They live, that is, in a world where there is no longer a logical way to establish a meaningful relationship between themselves and their environment and so they are frequently reduced to vocal outbursts, extended periods of silence, muttering, stuttering or vocal hesitation to communicate their anguish, frustration or guilt.

Third, the playscripts of absurdism are peopled with characters that treat one another with apparently deliberate cruelty and hostility, even though admitting to themselves that existing alone is far worse than living with another human being. Isolated in vague and desolate environments, these frustrated characters strike out against society in barely audible cries and plead for some meaning and order for their lives. The pattern of distorted images and symbols they encounter in a selected scene only serve to depict fragmented human beings — like themselves — living lost and lonely existences.

Because characters in the theatre of the absurd are not developed in the traditional "observation and duplication" approach popularized by modern playscripts of realism, an ingenious or sometimes "offbeat" technique to performance is required in order to highlight the futility and the despair that these loners feel. Examples of this performance technique might include a playing of style that portrays characters with extremely fast or unduly slow movements to emphasize the urgency or the futility of a given moment; mechanical speech like that of a robot to suggest the loss of individuality or humanity; and exaggerated poses, portrait or comic-book caricatures, conflicting postures and incongruous facial expressions that help to distort and contradict the meaning of the words spoken and the actions performed by a character in a given scene.

Similarly, the performance style of absurdism often demands a background of sound effects, screen projections, symbolic placards, unusual hand props, flying objects, mime or dance to help "disguise" the true meaning of the words and actions of the character. Examples of these performance aids might include the loud beating of a heart played on tape as two characters sit on a mound of dirt discussing the meaning of life; cubes or prisms suspended from the ceiling, or slides projected on a screen at the rear of the performance space, to suggest the vacuum created by a life without meaning; masks, clown-white make-up or burlesque mime to hide a character's true feelings; or placards with painted question marks and exclamation points carried by characters who wish to call spectator attention to moments in which thoughts or actions of philosophical significance are being expressed.

Regardless of the creative performance technique taken in playing the scenes of absurdism, the actor's primary concern should be to encourage the spectator to think; and the actor should also use the opportunity to appear sensible and ordinary no matter what the situation or the indicated character behavior. To generalize convincingly is also a performance goal in playing scenes of absurdism, not to appear merely outrageous or bizarre. Allow the incongruity between what the dialog says and what the subsequent action of the character does to suggest the laughable and concentrate instead on the pathos and humanity that accompanies these lost and abandoned characters in search of their own identity. In addition, pay careful attention to gestures and facial expressions that might help to mirror the interior thoughts and feelings of the characters.

Although it may be difficult for you at first to imagine yourself as the absurd character detailed in the scene you are playing, you should approach the role with the same dedication and discipline as that demanded for any performance. *Analyze* your character and make notes concerning the character's physical and mental qualities. *Define* your character and make decisions regarding specific goals and objectives. *Create* your character based upon the character's relationship to others, the character's mood and attitude and the character's apparent role in the scene as a whole. In this performance approach to playing absurdism you should be able to contribute to a significant visualization of the subjective nature of man and reveal basic principles of existence and the subconscious that may be relevant to all of us.

Playing the Performance

In playing the performance for absurd scenes the actor is reminded that absurdism is concerned with depicting man's personal,

242

tragic loss of identity and the quest to rediscover it without further suffering or despair. There should be a serious attitude at work in developing character portraits and the actor should refrain from an approach that suggests the ridiculous or the ludicrous. To highlight the serious nature of character in absurdism and to reinforce the theoretical principle that the spectator should be encouraged to peer beneath the obvious, superficially broad humor of the scene to discover the essentially pathetic nature of the characters, the actor in absurdism frequently relies on the "pause" and the "symbolic pose" to clarify or to reinforce significant dialog or action. There are also opportunities in performance to assume mechanical posture, engage in machine-like movement, fly suspended above the playing space or voice gibberish and nonsense phrases to help suggest the apparent loss of humanity or the mocking fate that appears to control the destiny of these absurd characters.

There are a number of internal stylistic devices in the writing of absurd playscripts that might also provide creative approaches to playing the performance. The playwrights of absurdism, rejecting the traditional approach to language that is concrete and concise, rely on verbal nonsense to communicate an essentially pessimistic point of view. In the arrangement of words and sentences there is no apparent grammatical order, tenses are often not in agreement and there is what Martin Esslin, author of the critical text *Theatre of the Absurd,* terms "a radical devaluation of language." In addition, the dialog of playscripts of absurdism is ambiguous, abstract and atmospheric, all of which tends to dislocate or disrupt the apparent frame of reference and suggests that the characters "digress" with great regularity in their conversations and in their thoughts.

This unconventional approach to language is dependent upon *non sequitur,* the Latin term meaning that the logical sequence of words is out of order, to achieve communication. Other examples of the unconventional use of language in absurdism that might translate into performance approaches to character include sentence fragments to suggest incomplete thoughts, inappropriate words to define ideas being explored, alphabet letters to communicate emotional attitudes, comic words used in serious episodes to lessen dramatic impact and slang words to contradict the action being described. In evaluating the role that language might play in performance also consider that the gibberish that passes for dialog in absurdism is deliberately obscure and obsolete in most instances because new words must be coined to replace old meanings of familiar phrases that no longer have any value. In your performance approach to absurdism seek to cultivate an "absurd vocabulary" of pronunciation, inflection, emphasis and vocal variety that will give fresh insight to the dialog being spoken.

Absurd Exercises

The following vocal and physical exercises are examples of what is involved in performing a scene in the style of absurdism. The performance principles detailed are intended to prepare you for the vocal and physical techniques necessary in absurdism and to also suggest the degree of depth and dimension inherent in characterization. The exercises are also designed to promote your ability to grasp the creative suggestions for performance and to translate them into an imaginative and yet artistic perception of absurdism that reinforces the theoretical point of view of the theatre of the absurd. Approach each exercise with an "eye" and an "ear" to the basic performance principles inherent in absurdism and review the primary characteristics of playing the "style" so that your voice and body can distinguish one from the other.

THE "FOUND" VOICE

The way you use your voice in playing absurd scenes may well mean the difference between merely saying meaningless "words" and engaging in significant communication with the audience. To formulate ideas and concepts suggested by absurdism to communicate in a complex character portrait is just the prelude to performance. There must also be a "vocal orchestration" that allows the actor to interpret the inherent logic of the speech, the point of view or the mood and attitude.

A listener in absurdism does not immediately "hear" ideas, concepts, images or even the depths of character emotion. Rather, a listener's initial response — favorable or not — is to the vocal properties of sound. These sounds are the result of voice quality, pitch, rate, volume and inflection that provide the "vocal variety" which distinguishes individual characters and highlights individual performance by the actor. It is important, therefore, to understand that the vocal mechanism does much more than merely transform a sound into an audible transmission of recognized words or language symbols. It also permits the performer to highlight meaning, focus attention and direct listener impressions of the character interpretation. For this reason it is especially important in absurdism to pay careful attention to the vocal attributes responsible for a unique, meaningful interpretation in performance and to make an immediate personal "checklist" of vocal strengths and weaknesses.

To explore the properties of vocal sound in general and to introduce the principle of vocal "special effects" that you may create for performance in theatre of the absurd, collect a variety of random objects that are capable of conducting and amplifying the human voice. Examples might include cardboard tubes, garden hoses, vacuum cleaner attachments, megaphones, plastic jugs, mouth muffles, scuba masks, paper bags or soda cans. Begin by using one of the found objects to make a random noise. Then attempt to produce a word using the found object as a "mouthpiece." Finally, try to voice a complete sentence or brief quotation with the found object.

For example, your complete sentence or brief quotation might be Mark Twain's humorous suggestion that "Familiarity breeds contempt, and children" or George Moore's sober reflection that "After all, there is but one race — humanity." Other potential sources might be the wise sayings of Benjamin Franklin, popular song lyrics, familiar book titles or well-known lines from Shakespeare or the *Bible*. You may also discover appropriate materials in John Bartlett's *Familiar Quotations,* dramatic monologs, lyrical poems or "catch phrases" from current television or film personalities.

After you have demonstrated each object and voiced an appropriate sentence or quotation, repeat the exercises *without* the object. Try to duplicate with your natural voice the sound produced by the found object as you engage in a creative approach to creating a series of vocal "special effects." Repetition of this exercise should give your voice added performance dimension and distinction when playing absurd scenes. Finally, voice the following passage from Samuel Beckett's *Waiting for Godot* with as many of your newly acquired effects as possible.

quaquaquaqua outside time without extension who from the heights of divine apathia divine athambia divine aphasia loves us dearly with some exceptions for reasons unknown but time will tell and suffers like the divine Miranda

Now conclude the exercise by voicing the following "nonsense" selection in a voice that integrates vocal variety in pitch, rate and volume with additional vocal "special effects" that are suggested in the selection as part of the performance approach. When you are confident that you have integrated all of the appropriate "sounds" necessary to voice the selection consider a similar performance technique when reviewing the absurd scenes that follow.

don't spit your wind against the wall I won't tell you my God is yelling His will and it is better to be yelled at than Do-Re-Me I don't see but I dare to speak in weak, mumbles that sing loudly that I live or die without oh! The taste of honey is sweet but sour is friendship that keeps me quiet and frail with longing for a second coming that erupts into a calm, a calm that ends the heartache and the A-B-C that ends the 1-2-3 of this sad song . . . LIFE!

SPEAKING BETWEEN THE LINES

In order to make good performance use of the role that pitch, rate and volume might play in suggesting the "subtext" — or hidden meaning — of language in the theatre of the absurd, the actor needs a voice that is flexible and adaptable to any performance situation. To achieve active "word play" that reveals meaningful subtext the actor also needs a voice that is free from tension and anxiety. In cultivating a relaxed throat and neck to achieve greater flexibility and range in pitch and tone please review the vocal exercises in Chapter One and Chapter Three before approaching this spoken passage.

When you are confident that you are vocally relaxed and free from tension in the neck, begin the following exercise by voicing the word *NO* to achieve the meaning indicated. Use only pitch, rate and volume to suggest the requested meaning. It might be useful for future reference to tape record this part of the exercise as a key to what follows later.

No? (What was that you said?)
No? (You can't mean that, can you?)
No. (We'll see about that!)
No! (How dare you!)
No. (Well, if that's the way you feel.)
No. (I'm sorry, I must have forgotten.)
No! (You must be kidding me!)

246

No? (Are you absolutely positive?)

No. (I could be persuaded.)

Continue the exercise by giving a copy of the *NO* selection to a friend. Match "subtexts" in groups of two as you and your friend repeat the list in the following manner: The first performer voices the first meaning of the word and the second performer responds with the second meaning of the word.

The exercise may be extended if you and your friend apply the performance techniques you have learned here to the recommended scenes that follow. In each recommended scene two characters are in a conversation that suggests an "undercurrent" to their relationship that lies just beneath the surface of the language they use to describe their mood and attitude. Examples for performance would include the "balcony scene" in William Shakespeare's *Romeo and Juliet* in Chapter Two; the "tea scene" in Oscar Wilde's *The Importance of Being Earnest* in Chapter Three; the "pledge of allegiance scene" in Aristophanes' *Lysistrata* in Chapter One; the "confrontation scene" in Sophocles' *Antigone* in Chapter One; and the "dressing room scene" in Richard Sheridan's *The School for Scandal* in Chapter Three. With the additional skills gained in cultivating a subtextual approach to classical, Shakespearean and "period" scenes the exercise should provide much more meaningful insight to character development in the modern, absurd and contemporary scenes that traditionally rely on this "between the lines" approach to sketch three-dimensional, vibrant character portraits.

The Absurd Scenes

The following edited scenes are representative of the theatre of the absurd playscripts that encourage deviation and departure from the more traditional approaches to performance. Before proceeding to a more detailed exploration of the individual scenes that follow it is important to point out absurdism in performance is frequently "circular," and action that initiates the scene may also conclude the scene. The episodes may also move from the present tense to the past tense, and there is rarely any mention made in the future tense. Approach the playing of the scenes with a tempered, cautious enthusiasm reinforced with solid scene study knowing that the actions of the characters are extremely repetitive and that there is rarely a completion of an action once it has been initiated. Know also that there may be an unexplained or unmotivated exchange of character names, roles or dialog as the scene grows increasingly intense. And

The playwrights of absurdism tried to convey a sense of the "alienation" that man experiences when he is separated from himself and from the world-at-large. Frequently, characters in absurdism are isolated in an empty space with no understanding of their immediate surroundings.

while it may not be possible to solve all of the performance demands posed by the absurdists, the significant questions raised in terms of vocal and physical technique are of such significance to the actor's development and performance enrichment here that no doubt you will be compelled to carry them with you on future journeys in search of more creative answers.

from **The Gap** (1969)

Eugene Ionesco

The theatre of the absurd presents the spectator with a flood of images, symbols and signs that disguise an even more chaotic, jumbled puzzle related to the meaning of life. The range of subjects treated suggests that the only continuity in life is the sad spectacle of man helplessly adrift in a world that has no apparent meaning or purpose. All elements of the performance and the production are directed toward focusing attention on the chaos inherent in a society that cannot communicate effectively; and considerable emphasis is placed upon the visualization of the subconscious mind by juxtaposing the "familiar" with the "strange" to provoke the spectator to reason and to think.

The scene that follows is typical of those comedies of the absurd that take an apparently simple event and then focus attention on solitary figures who are revealed to be incapable of understanding the present situation or of addressing each other in meaningful language that helps to resolve the apparent difficulty. By the philosophical principle of *reductio ad absurdum*, the scene emerges as a series of disconnected events relating an unknown, mysterious story; and the only "fact" that emerges from the scene is that the characters are forever lonely and lost. There is also a sense of profound alienation as the characters constantly struggle to regain any sense of personal meaning or identity.

In playing the absurd scene the actor should recall that a primary performance ingredient is to suggest that the characters appear to have no sense of "time" or "tempo" in their vocal and physical responses and that they frequently seek to express their thoughts and ideas in melancholy moments that are punctuated with nervous, meaningless impulses that are essentially worthless in expressing their despair. Regardless of the creative approach taken to performance, the actor should always appear "sensible" and rather "ordinary" no matter how bizarre or unconventional the situation or the indicated character behavior. Allow the laughable to emerge as the result of the *actions* performed rather than as the conscious attempt to provoke humor through exaggerated movement or physical and vocal charades. In addition, pay careful attention to gestures and facial expressions that may help to suggest the interior thoughts and feelings of the characters.

CAST
THE ACADEMICIAN
THE FRIEND
THE WIFE

SCENE

A rich bourgeois living room with artistic pretensions.

APPROACH

As the scene opens one can see The Academician's wife dressed in a rather crumpled robe speaking with The Friend as they admire the impressive diplomas mounted on the walls of the living room. There is a solemn air of dignified ceremony present as the characters move from diploma to diploma reading aloud the Latin inscriptions *Doctor Honoris causa* and nodding in impressive agreement as they finally reach the Regency style sofa in the middle of the room and sit to continue their discussion. The character portraits should be rather simple and direct to highlight the featureless environment but the tempo should quickly swell when The Academician enters later and the scene is suddenly propelled toward an absurd climax. There are good performance opportunities here to integrate machine-like movements or mechanical stances into the character portrait.

1   THE WIFE: Dear friend, tell me all.

2   THE FRIEND: I don't know what to say.

3   THE WIFE: I know.

4   THE FRIEND: I heard the news last night. I did not want to call
5   you. At the same time I couldn't wait any longer. Please
6   forgive me for coming so early with such terrible news.

7   THE WIFE: He didn't make it! How terrible! We were still
8   hoping . . .

9   THE FRIEND: It's hard, I know. He still had a chance. Not much
10   of one. We had to expect it.

11 THE WIFE: I didn't expect it. He was always so successful. He
12   could always manage somehow, at the last moment.

13 THE FRIEND: In that state of exhaustion. You shouldn't have
14   let him!

15 THE WIFE: What can we do, what can we do? How awful!

16 THE FRIEND: Come on, dear friend, be brave. That's life.

17 THE WIFE: I feel faint. I'm going to faint.

18 THE FRIEND: I shouldn't have blurted it out like that. I'm sorry.

19 THE WIFE: No, you were right to do so. I had to find out somehow
20   or other.

21 THE FRIEND: I should have prepared you, carefully.

22 THE WIFE: I've got to be strong. I can't help thinking of him,
23   the wretched man. I hope they won't put it in the papers.
24   Can we count on the journalists' discretion?

25 THE FRIEND: Close your door. Don't answer the telephone. It
26   will still get around. You could go to the country. In a couple
27   of months, when you are better, you'll come back, you'll go
28   on with your life. People forget such things.

29 THE WIFE: People won't forget so fast. That's what they're all
30   waiting for. Some friends will feel sorry, but the others, the
31   others . . . *(THE ACADEMICIAN enters, fully dressed in uniform*
32   *with decorations and his sword on the side.)*

33 THE ACADEMICIAN: Up so early, my dear? *(To THE FRIEND)*
34   You've come early, too. What's happening? Do you have the
35   final results?

251

1   THE WIFE: What a disgrace!
2   THE FRIEND: You mustn't crush him like this, dear friend. *(To*
3   *THE ACADEMICIAN)* You have failed.
4   THE ACADEMICIAN: Are you quite sure?
5   THE FRIEND: You should never have tried to pass the bacca-
6   laureate examination.
7   THE ACADEMICIAN: They failed me. The rats! How dare they
8   do this to me?
9   THE FRIEND: The marks were posted late in the evening.
10   THE ACADEMICIAN: Perhaps it was difficult to make them out
11   in the dark. How could you read them?
12   THE FRIEND: They had set up spotlights.
13   THE ACADEMICIAN: They're doing everything to ruin me.
14   THE FRIEND: I passed by in the morning; the marks were still up.
15   THE ACADEMICIAN: You could have bribed the concierge into
16   pulling them down.
17   THE FRIEND: That's exactly what I did. Unfortunately the
18   police were there. Your name heads the list of those who
19   failed. Everyone's standing in line to get a look. There's an
20   awful crush.
21   THE ACADEMICIAN: Who's there? The parents of the
22   candidates?
23   THE FRIEND: Not only they.
24   THE WIFE: All your rivals, all your colleagues must be there.
25   All those you attacked in the press for ignorance; your
26   undergraduates; your graduate students; all those you
27   failed when you were chairman of the board of examiners.
28   THE ACADEMICIAN: I am discredited! But I won't let them.
29   There must be some mistake.
30   THE FRIEND: I saw the examiners. I spoke with them. They
31   gave me your marks. Zero in mathematics.
32   THE ACADEMICIAN: I had no scientific training.
33   THE FRIEND: Zero in Greek, zero in Latin.
34   THE WIFE: You, a humanist, the spokesman for humanism, the
35   author of that famous treatise *The Defense of Poesy and*

1   *Humanism.*
2   THE ACADEMICIAN: I beg your pardon, but my book concerns
3   itself with twentieth-century humanism. *(To THE FRIEND)*
4   What about composition? What grade did I get in
5   composition?
6   THE FRIEND: Nine hundred. You have nine hundred points.
7   THE ACADEMICIAN: That's perfect. My average must be all the
8   way up.
9   THE FRIEND: Unfortunately not. They're marking on the basis
10   of two thousand. The passing grade is one hundred.
11   THE ACADEMICIAN: They must have changed the regulations.
12   THE WIFE: They didn't change them just for you. You have a
13   frightful persecution complex.
14   THE ACADEMICIAN: I tell you they changed them.
15   THE FRIEND: They went back to the old ones, back to the time
16   of Napoleon.
17   THE ACADEMICIAN: Utterly outmoded. Besides, when did
18   they make those changes? It isn't legal. I'm chairman of the
19   Baccalaureate Commission of the Ministry of Public
20   Education. They didn't consult me, and they cannot make
21   any changes without my approval. I'm going to expose them.
22   I'm going to bring government charges against them.
23   THE WIFE: Darling, you don't know what you're doing. You're
24   in your dotage. Don't you recall handing in your resignation
25   just before taking the examination so that no one could
26   doubt the complete objectivity of the board of examiners?
27   THE ACADEMICIAN: I'll take it back.
28   THE WIFE: You should never have taken that test! I warned
29   you. After all, it's not as if you needed it. But you have to
30   collect all the honors, don't you? You're never satisfied. What
31   did you need this diploma for? Now all is lost. You have your
32   Doctorate, and your Master's, your high school diploma,
33   your elementary school certificate, and even the first part
34   of the baccalaureate.
35   THE ACADEMICIAN: There was a gap.

1   THE WIFE: No one suspected it.

2   THE ACADEMICIAN: But *I* knew it. Others might have found
3   out. I went to the office of the Registrar and asked for a
4   transcript of my record. They said to me: "Certainly
5   Professor, Mr. President, Your Excellency." Then they
6   looked up my file, and the Chief Registrar came back looking
7   embarrassed indeed. He said: "There's something peculiar,
8   very peculiar. You have your Master's, certainly, but it's no
9   longer valid." I asked him why, of course. He answered:
10   "There's a gap behind your Master's. I don't know how it
11   happened. You must have registered and been accepted at
12   the university without having passed the second part of the
13   baccalaureate examination."

14   THE FRIEND: And then?

15   THE WIFE: Your Master's degree is no longer valid?

16   THE ACADEMICIAN: No, not quite. It's suspended. "The
17   duplicate you are asking for will be delivered to you upon
18   completion of the baccalaureate. Of course you will pass
19   the examination with no trouble." That's what I was told,
20   so you see now that I had to take it.

21   THE FRIEND: Your husband, dear friend, wanted to fill the gap.
22   He's a conscientious person.

23   THE WIFE: It's clear you don't know him as I do. That's not it
24   at all. He wants fame, honors. He never has enough. What
25   does one diploma more or less matter? No one notices them
26   anyway, but he sneaks in at night, on tiptoe, into the living
27   room, just to look at them, and count them.

28   THE ACADEMICIAN: What else can I do when I have insomnia?

29   THE FRIEND: The questions asked at the baccalaureate are
30   usually known in advance. You were admirably situated to
31   get this particular information. You could also have sent in
32   a replacement to take the test for you. One of your students,
33   perhaps. Or if you wanted to take the test without people
34   realizing that you already knew the questions, you could
35   have sent your maid to the black market, where one can

1   buy them.
2 THE ACADEMICIAN: I don't understand how I could have
3   failed in my composition. I filled three sheets of paper. I
4   treated the subject fully, taking into account the historical
5   background. I interpreted the situation accurately ... at
6   least plausibly. I didn't deserve a bad grade.
7 THE FRIEND: Do you recall the subject?
8 THE ACADEMICIAN: Hum ... let's see ...
9 THE FRIEND: He doesn't even remember what he discussed.
10 THE ACADEMICIAN: I do ... wait ... hum.
11 THE FRIEND: The subject to be treated was the following:
12   "Discuss the influence of Renaissance painters on novelists
13   of the Third Republic." I have here a photostatic copy of
14   your examination paper. Here is what you wrote.
15 THE ACADEMICIAN: *(Grabs the photostat and reads.)* "The trial of
16   Benjamin: After Benjamin was tried and acquitted, the
17   assessors holding a different opinion from that of the
18   President murdered him, and condemned Benjamin to the
19   suspensions of his civic rights, imposing on him a fine of
20   nine hundred francs ..."
21 THE FRIEND: That's where the nine hundred points came from.
22 THE ACADEMICIAN: "Benjamin appealed his case ... Benja-
23   min appealed his case ..." I can't make out the rest. I've
24   always had bad handwriting. I ought to have taken a
25   typewriter along with me.
26 THE WIFE: Horrible handwriting, scribbling and crossing out;
27   ink spots didn't help you much.
28 THE ACADEMICIAN: *(Continues reading after having retrieved the
29   text his WIFE had pulled from his hand.)* "Benjamin appealed
30   his case. Flanked by policemen dressed in zouave
31   uniforms ... in zouave uniforms ..." It's getting dark. I can't
32   see the rest ... I don't have my glasses.
33 THE WIFE: What you've written has nothing to do with the
34   subject.
35 THE FRIEND: Your wife's quite right, friend. It has nothing to

1   do with the subject.

2 THE ACADEMICIAN: Yes, it has. Indirectly.

3 THE FRIEND: Not even indirectly.

4 THE ACADEMICIAN: Perhaps I chose the second question.

5 THE FRIEND: There was only one.

6 THE ACADEMICIAN: Even if there was only that one, I treated
7   another quite adequately. I went to the end of the story. I
8   stressed the important points, explaining the motivation of
9   the characters, highlighting their behavior. I explained the
10   mystery, making it plain and clear. There was even a
11   conclusion at the end. I can't make out the rest. *(To THE
12   FRIEND)* Can you read it?

13 THE FRIEND: It's illegible. I don't have any glasses either.

14 THE WIFE: *(Taking the text)* It's illegible and I have excellent
15   eyes. You pretended to write. Mere scribbling.

16 THE ACADEMICIAN: That's not true. I've even provided a
17   conclusion. It's clearly marked here in heavy print:
18   "Conclusion or sanction ... Conclusion or sanction ..."
19   They can't get away with it. I'll have this examination
20   rendered null and void.

21 THE WIFE: Since you treated the wrong subject, and treated it
22   badly, setting down only titles, and writing nothing in
23   between, the mark you received is justified. You'd lose your
24   case.

25 THE FRIEND: You'd most certainly lose. Drop it. Take a
26   vacation.

27 THE ACADEMICIAN: You're always on the side of the Others.

28 THE WIFE: After all, these professors know what they're doing.
29   They haven't been granted their rank for nothing. They
30   passed examinations, received serious training. They know
31   the rules of composition.

32 THE ACADEMICIAN: Who was on the board of examiners?

33 THE FRIEND: For mathematics, a movie star. For Greek, one
34   of the Beatles. For Latin, the champion of the automobile
35   race, and many others.

1   THE ACADEMICIAN: But these people aren't any more
2   qualified than I am. And for composition?
3   THE FRIEND: A woman, a secretary in the editorial division of
4   the review *Yesterday, the Day Before Yesterday, and Today.*
5   THE ACADEMICIAN: Now I know. This wretch gave me a poor
6   grade out of spite because I never joined her political party.
7   It's an act of vengeance. But I have ways and means of
8   rendering the examination null and void. I'm going to call
9   the President.
10   THE WIFE: Don't! You'll make yourself look even more
11   ridiculous. *(To THE FRIEND)* Please try to restrain him. He
12   listens to you more than to me. *(THE FRIEND shrugs his*
13   *shoulders, unable to cope with the situation. THE WIFE turns to*
14   *her husband, who has just lifted the receiver off the hook.)* Don't
15   call!
16   THE ACADEMICIAN: *(On the telephone)* Hello. Bill? It is I . . .
17   What? What did you say? But, listen my dear friend . . . but,
18   listen to me. Hello! Hello! *(Puts down the receiver.)*
19   THE FRIEND: What did he say?
20   THE ACADEMICIAN: He said . . . He said . . . "I don't want to
21   talk to you. My mummy won't let me make friends with boys
22   at the bottom of the class." Then he hung up on me.
23   THE WIFE: You should have expected it. All is lost. How could
24   you do this to me? How could you do this to me?
25   THE ACADEMICIAN: Think of it! I lectured at the Sorbonne, at
26   Oxford, at American universities. Ten thousand theses have
27   been written on my work; hundreds of critics have analyzed
28   it. I hold an *honoris causa* doctorate from Amsterdam as
29   well as a secret university Chair with the Duchy of
30   Luxembourg. I received the Nobel Prize three times. The
31   King of Sweden himself was amazed by my erudition. A
32   doctorate *honoris causa, honoris causa* . . . and I failed the
33   baccalaureate examination!
34   THE WIFE: Everyone will laugh at us! *(THE ACADEMICIAN takes*
35   *off his sword and breaks it on his knee.)*

1   **THE FRIEND:**   *(Picking up the pieces)* **I wish to preserve these in**
2   **memory of our ancient glory.** *(THE ACADEMICIAN is tearing*
3   *down his diplomas and decorations, throwing them on the floor,*
4   *and stepping on them.)*
5   **THE WIFE:**   *(Trying to salvage the remains)* **Don't do this! Don't!**
6   **That's all we've got left.**
7
8   *Curtain*
9
10
11
12
13
14
15
16
17
18
19
20
21
22
23
24
25
26
27
28
29
30
31
32
33
34
35

from **Rosencrantz and Guildenstern Are Dead** (1967)

Tom Stoppard

The most remarkable and inventive Tom Stoppard has described himself, and his playscripts, as "seriousness comprised by frivolity." With rather bold strokes of ingenuity he dutifully attempts to define man's "existence" in both the dialog and the action of the characters and to draw logical and sensible conclusions from an apparently illogical and inconsistent reality. In formulating his theoretical approach to the drama, Stoppard seeks to convey a sense of separation, or alienation, that man experiences when he is isolated from the world and from himself. He also emphasizes that while man is forever lost in the ambiguity of the world there is still an urgent need to constantly struggle to regain a sense of personal, individual identity.

While the complex intrigues and masquerades of Hamlet and the court of Elsinore provide the backdrop against which Stoppard weaves his absurd and chilling comedy, the primary humor of this playscript is found in the "heroes" of Shakespeare's nondescript and vague characters — Rosencrantz and Guildenstern — as they seek to understand the situation and the peril in which they find themselves in an alien world. Both characters are, in effect, two sides of one temperament if we are to believe the author's own admission of what the following scene is suggesting about reality and the absurd world in which we live. Although the characters appear to confuse their own identities and engage in comic games that have no apparent meaning, they exhibit a spirit of sparkling inquiry and inventiveness that helps pass time as they wait for an explanation of "why" they have been summoned to Elsinore castle in such secrecy.

In playing the scene that follows the actors should try to imagine the psychological motivation at work in the many "games" the characters play and try not to appear deliberately "cruel" or "hostile" to each other in the physical confrontations that result from the frustration and despair inherent in the scene. Exaggerated poses, comic-book caricatures and incongruous facial expressions should be avoided in the pursuit of genuine honesty and simplicity as the characters desperately try to give meaning to the words spoken and the actions performed in the desolate environment. Approach the playing of the scene with a serious attitude but also be encouraged to peer beneath the solemn mood of the characters to discover the broad humor and interplay of comic puns and jokes that help to distinguish this unconventional episode from other absurd travesties.

An ingenious or sometimes "offbeat" technique of performance is sometimes required in absurdism in order to highlight the futility and the despair that the characters experience in their isolation. Exaggerated poses, comic-book caricatures or conflicting postures help to distort and to contradict the meaning of the words spoken and the actions performed by the characters in a selected absurd scene.

CAST

ROSENCRANTZ

GUILDENSTERN

SCENE

Opens in pitch darkness. Soft sea sounds.

APPROACH

As the scene opens there are several moments of silence, and then very thin voices whisper in the thick darkness. The atmosphere is charged with anticipation and anxiety as Rosencrantz and Guildenstern blindly grope in the still night to identify the blurred sights and sounds that surround them. Following a series of extended, silent pauses the characters are at last able to identify the clouded rigging

260

and ship timbers that obscure the boat on which they are now sailing. As more light is shed upon the scene, the characters are slowly able to distinguish the outline of the ship's deck and, among other items, three large, man-sized casks which are upended with lids split open. They are unable, however, to unravel the mystery of the ship's destination or the role they might play in the journey that follows. Remember to keep the character portraits simple and to visualize these perplexed characters as helplessly adrift in a world that has no apparent meaning or purpose. There are also good performance opportunities here to duplicate the many unusual or bizarre noises or sounds suggested in the scene on tape and to incorporate them in the production.

1   **ACT THREE**
2
3   *(Opens in pitch darkness. Soft sea sounds. After several seconds of*
4   *nothing, a voice from the dark.)*
5   **GUILDENSTERN:** **Are you there?**
6   **ROSENCRANTZ:** **Where?**
7   **GUILDENSTERN:** *(Bitterly)* **A flying start ...** *(Pause)*
8   **ROSENCRANTZ:** **Is that you?**
9   **GUILDENSTERN:** **Yes.**
10   **ROSENCRANTZ:** **How do you know?**
11   **GUILDENSTERN:** *(Explosion)* **Oh-for-God's sake!**
12   **ROSENCRANTZ:** **We're not finished, then?**
13   **GUILDENSTERN:** **Well, we're here, aren't we?**
14   **ROSENCRANTZ:** **Are we? I can't see a thing.**
15   **GUILDENSTERN:** **You can still *think*, can't you?**
16   **ROSENCRANTZ:** **I think so.**
17   **GUILDENSTERN:** **You can still *talk*.**
18   **ROSENCRANTZ:** **What should I say?**
19   **GUILDENSTERN:** **Don't bother. You can *feel*, can't you?**
20   **ROSENCRANTZ:** **Ah! There's life in me yet!**
21   **GUILDENSTERN:** **What are you feeling?**
22   **ROSENCRANTZ:** **A leg. Yes, it feels like my leg.**
23   **GUILDENSTERN:** **How does it feel?**
24   **ROSENCRANTZ:** **Dead.**
25   **GUILDENSTERN:** **Dead?**
26   **ROSENCRANTZ:** *(Panic)* **I can't feel a thing!**
27   **GUILDENSTERN:** **Give it a pinch!** *(Immediately he yelps.)*
28   **ROSENCRANTZ:** **Sorry.**
29   **GUILDENSTERN:** **Well, that's cleared that up.**
30   *(Longer pause: the sound builds a little and identifies itself — the*
31   *sea. Ship timbers, wind in the rigging, and then shouts of sailors*
32   *calling obscure but inescapably nautical instructions from all*
33   *directions, far and near. A short list:)*
34   **Hard a larboard!**
35   **Let go the stays!**

262

1	**Reef down me hearties!**
2	**Is that you, cox'n?**
3	**Hel-llo! Is that you?**
4	**Hard a port!**
5	**Easy as she goes!**
6	**Keep her steady on the lee!**
7	**Haul away, lads!**
8	*(Snatches of sea shanty maybe.)*
9	**Fly the jib!**
10	**Tops'l up, me maties!**

11 ROSENCRANTZ: **We're on a boat.** *(Pause)* **Dark, isn't it?**

12 GUILDENSTERN: **Not for night.**

13 ROSENCRANTZ: **No, not for** *night.*

14 GUILDENSTERN: **Dark for day.** *(Pause)*

15 ROSENCRANTZ: **Oh yes, it's dark for** *day.*

16 GUILDENSTERN: **We must have gone north, of course.**

17 ROSENCRANTZ: **Off course?**

18 GUILDENSTERN: **Land of the midnight sun, that is.**

19 ROSENCRANTZ: **Of course.**

20 *(Some sailor sounds. A lantern is lit Upstage. The stage lightens*
21 *disproportionately. Enough to see: ROSENCRANTZ and*
22 *GUILDENSTERN sitting Downstage. Vague shapes of rigging*
23 *behind.)*

24 **I think it's getting light.**

25 GUILDENSTERN: **Not for night.**

26 ROSENCRANTZ: **This far north.**

27 GUILDENSTERN: **Unless we're off course.**

28 ROSENCRANTZ: *(Small pause)* **Of course.**

29 *(A better light — Lantern. Moon. Light. Revealing, among other*
30 *things, three large man-sized casks on deck, upended, with lids.*
31 *Spaces but in a line. Behind and above — a gaudy striped umbrella,*
32 *on a pole stuck into the deck, tilted so that we do not see behind*
33 *it — one of those huge six-foot-diameter jobs. Still dim Upstage.*
34 *ROSENCRANTZ and GUILDENSTERN still facing front.)*

35 **Yes, it's lighter than it was. It'll be night soon. This far north.**

1   *(Dolefully)* **I suppose we'll have to go to sleep.** *(He yawns and*
2   *stretches.)*
3   **GUILDENSTERN: Tired?**
4   **ROSENCRANTZ: No ... I don't think I'd take to it. Sleep all**
5   **night, can't see a thing all day ... Those Eskimos must have**
6   **a quiet life.**
7   **GUILDENSTERN: Where?**
8   **ROSENCRANTZ: What?**
9   **GUILDENSTERN: I thought you —** *(Relapses.)* **I've lost all**
10   **capacity for disbelief. I'm not sure that I could even rise to**
11   **a little gentle scepticism.** *(Pause)*
12   **ROSENCRANTZ: Well, shall we stretch our legs?**
13   **GUILDENSTERN: I don't feel like stretching my legs.**
14   **ROSENCRANTZ: I'll stretch them for you, if you like.**
15   **GUILDENSTERN: No.**
16   **ROSENCRANTZ: We could stretch each other's. That way we**
17   **wouldn't have to go anywhere.**
18   **GUILDENSTERN:** *(Pause)* **No, somebody might come in.**
19   **ROSENCRANTZ: In where?**
20   **GUILDENSTERN: Out here.**
21   **ROSENCRANTZ: In out here?**
22   **GUILDENSTERN: On deck.** *(ROSENCRANTZ considers the floor;*
23   *slaps it.)*
24   **ROSENCRANTZ: Nice bit of planking, that.**
25   **GUILDENSTERN: Yes, I'm very fond of boats myself. I like the**
26   **way they're — contained. You don't have to worry about**
27   **which way to go, or whether to go at all — the question**
28   **doesn't arise, because you're on a** *boat,* **aren't you? Boats**
29   **are safe areas in the game of tag ... the players will hold**
30   **their positions until the music starts ... I think I'll spend**
31   **most of my life on boats.**
32   **ROSENCRANTZ: Very healthy.** *(ROSENCRANTZ inhales with*
33   *expectation, exhales with boredom. GUILDENSTERN stands up*
34   *and looks over the audience.)*
35   **GUILDENSTERN: One is free on a boat. For a time. Relatively.**

1   **ROSENCRANTZ: What's it like?**

2   **GUILDENSTERN: Rough.** *(ROSENCRANTZ joins him. They look*

3   *over the audience.)*

4   **ROSENCRANTZ: I think I'm going to be sick.** *(GUILDENSTERN*

5   *licks a finger, holds it up experimentally.)*

6   **GUILDENSTERN: Other side, I think.**

7   *(ROSENCRANTZ goes Upstage. Ideally a sort of upper deck joined*

8   *to the Downstage lower deck by short steps. The umbrella being on*

9   *the upper deck. ROSENCRANTZ pauses by the umbrella and looks*

10   *behind it. GUILDENSTERN meanwhile has been resuming his*

11   *own theme — looking over the audience —)*

12   **Free to move, speak, extemporise, and yet. We have not been**

13   **cut loose. Our truancy is defined by one fixed star, and our**

14   **drift represents merely a slight change of angle to it: we**

15   **may seize the moment, toss it around while the moments**

16   **pass, a short dash here, an exploration there, but we are**

17   **brought round full circle to face again the single immutable**

18   **fact — that we, Rosencrantz and Guildenstern, bearing a**

19   **letter from one king to another, are taking Hamlet to**

20   **England.**

21   *(By which time, ROSENCRANTZ has returned, tiptoeing with great*

22   *import, teeth clenched for secrecy, gets to GUILDENSTERN, points*

23   *surreptitiously behind him — and a tight whisper.)*

24   **ROSENCRANTZ: I say — *he's there!***

25   **GUILDENSTERN:** *(Unsurprised)* **What's he doing?**

26   **ROSENCRANTZ: Sleeping.**

27   **GUILDENSTERN: It's all right for him.**

28   **ROSENCRANTZ: What is?**

29   **GUILDENSTERN: He can sleep.**

30   **ROSENCRANTZ: It's all right for him.**

31   **GUILDENSTERN: He's got us now.**

32   **ROSENCRANTZ: He can sleep.**

33   **GUILDENSTERN: It's all done for him.**

34   **ROSENCRANTZ: He's got us.**

35   **GUILDENSTERN: And we've got nothing.** *(A cry)* **All I ask is our**

1   **common due!**
2   **ROSENCRANTZ: For those in peril on the sea . . .**
3   **GUILDENSTERN: Give us this day our daily cue.** *(Beat, pause.*
4   *Sit. Long pause.)*
5   **ROSENCRANTZ:** *(After shifting, looking around)* **What now?**
6   **GUILDENSTERN: What do you mean?**
7   **ROSENCRANTZ: Well, nothing is happening.**
8   **GUILDENSTERN: We're on a boat.**
9   **ROSENCRANTZ: I'm aware of that.**
10   **GUILDENSTERN:** *(Angrily)* **Then what do you expect?** *(Unhap-*
11   *pily)* **We act on scraps of information . . . sifting half-**
12   **remembered directions that we can hardly separate from**
13   **instinct.**
14   *(ROSENCRANTZ puts a hand into his purse, then both hands*
15   *behind his back, then holds his fists out. GUILDENSTERN taps*
16   *one fist. ROSENCRANTZ opens it to show a coin. He gives it to*
17   *GUILDENSTERN. He puts his hand back into his purse. Then*
18   *both hands behind his back, then holds his fists out. GUILDEN-*
19   *STERN taps one. ROSENCRANTZ opens it to show a coin. He*
20   *gives it to GUILDENSTERN.)*
21   *(Repeat)*
22   *(Repeat)*
23   *(GUILDENSTERN getting tense. Desperate to lose.)*
24   *(Repeat)*
25   *(GUILDENSTERN taps a hand, changes his mind, taps the other,*
26   *and ROSENCRANTZ inadvertently reveals that he has a coin in*
27   *both fists.)*
28   **GUILDENSTERN: You had money in both hands.**
29   **ROSENCRANTZ:** *(Embarrassed)* **Yes.**
30   **GUILDENSTERN: Every time?**
31   **ROSENCRANTZ: Yes.**
32   **GUILDENSTERN: What's the point of that?**
33   **ROSENCRANTZ:** *(Pathetic)* **I wanted to make you happy.** *(Beat)*
34   **GUILDENSTERN: How much did he give you?**
35   **ROSENCRANTZ: Who?**

1 GUILDENSTERN: The King. He gave us some money.

2 ROSENCRANTZ: How much did he give you?

3 GUILDENSTERN: I asked you first.

4 ROSENCRANTZ: I got the same as you.

5 GUILDENSTERN: He wouldn't discriminate between us.

6 ROSENCRANTZ: How much did you get?

7 GUILDENSTERN: The same.

8 ROSENCRANTZ: How do you know?

9 GUILDENSTERN: You just told me — how do *you* know?

10 ROSENCRANTZ: He wouldn't discriminate between us.

11 GUILDENSTERN: Even if he could.

12 ROSENCRANTZ: Which he never could.

13 GUILDENSTERN: He couldn't even be sure of mixing us up.

14 ROSENCRANTZ: Without mixing us up.

15 GUILDENSTERN: *(Turning on him furiously)* Why don't you say

16 something original! No wonder the whole thing is so

17 stagnant! You don't take me up on anything — you just

18 repeat it in a different order.

19 ROSENCRANTZ: I can't think of anything original. I'm only

20 good in support.

21 GUILDENSTERN: I'm sick of making the running.

22 ROSENCRANTZ: *(Humbly)* It must be your dominant personality.

23 *(Almost in tears)* Oh, what's going to become of us?!

24 *(GUILDENSTERN comforts him, all harshness gone.)*

25 GUILDENSTERN: Don't cry . . . it's all right . . . there . . . there,

26 I'll see we're all right.

27 ROSENCRANTZ: But we've got nothing to go on, we're out on

28 our own.

29 GUILDENSTERN: We're on our way to England — we're taking

30 Hamlet there.

31 ROSENCRANTZ: What for?

32 GUILDENSTERN: What for? Where have you been?

33 ROSENCRANTZ: When? *(Pause)* We won't know what to do when

34 we get there.

35 GUILDENSTERN: We take him to the King.

1 ROSENCRANTZ: Will *he* be there?
2 GUILDENSTERN: No — the king of England.
3 ROSENCRANTZ: He's expecting us?
4 GUILDENSTERN: No.
5 ROSENCRANTZ: He won't know what we're playing at. What
6   are we going to *say?*
7 GUILDENSTERN: We've got a letter. You remember the letter.
8 ROSENCRANTZ: Do I?
9 GUILDENSTERN: Everything is explained in the letter. We
10   count on that.
11 ROSENCRANTZ: Is that it, then?
12 GUILDENSTERN: What?
13 ROSENCRANTZ: We take Hamlet to the English king, we hand
14   over the letter — what then?
15 GUILDENSTERN: There may be something in the letter to keep
16   us going a bit.
17 ROSENCRANTZ: And if not?
18 GUILDENSTERN: Then that's it — we're finished.
19 ROSENCRANTZ: At a loose end?
20 GUILDENSTERN: Yes. *(Pause)*
21 ROSENCRANTZ: Are there likely to be loose ends? *(Pause)* Who
22   is the English king?
23 GUILDENSTERN: That depends on when we get there.
24 ROSENCRANTZ: What do you think it says?
25 GUILDENSTERN: Oh ... greetings. Expressions of loyalty.
26   Asking for favours, calling in of debts. Obscure promises
27   balanced by vague threats ... Diplomacy. Regards to the
28   family.
29 ROSENCRANTZ: What about Hamlet?
30 GUILDENSTERN: Oh, yes.
31 ROSENCRANTZ: And us — the full background?
32 GUILDENSTERN: I should say so. *(Pause)*
33 ROSENCRANTZ: So we've got a letter which explains everything.
34 GUILDENSTERN: You've got it. *(ROSENCRANTZ takes that*
35   *literally. He starts to pat his pockets.)* What's the matter?

1 ROSENCRANTZ: The letter.
2 GUILDENSTERN: Have you got it?
3 ROSENCRANTZ: *(Rising fear)* **Have I?** *(Searches frantically.)*
4   **Where would I have put it?**
5 GUILDENSTERN: You can't have lost it.
6 ROSENCRANTZ: I must have!
7 GUILDENSTERN: That's odd — I thought he gave it to me.
8   *(ROSENCRANTZ looks at him hopefully.)*
9 ROSENCRANTZ: Perhaps he did.
10 GUILDENSTERN: But you seemed so sure it was *you* who hadn't
11   got it.
12 ROSENCRANTZ: *(High)* It *was* me who hadn't got it!
13 GUILDENSTERN: But if he gave it to me there's no reason why
14   you should have had it in the first place, in which case I
15   don't see what all the fuss is about you *not* having it.
16 ROSENCRANTZ: *(Pause)* I admit it's confusing.
17 GUILDENSTERN: This is all getting rather undisciplined . . .
18   The boat, the night, the sense of isolation and
19   uncertainty . . . all these induce a loosening of the
20   concentration. We must not lose control. Tighten up. Now.
21   Either you have lost the letter or you didn't have it to lose
22   in the first place, in which case the King never gave it to
23   you, in which case he gave it to me, in which case I would
24   have put it into my inside top pocket, in which case *(Calmly*
25   *producing the letter)* . . . it will be . . . here. *(They smile at each*
26   *other.)* We mustn't drop off like that again. *(Pause.*
27   *ROSENCRANTZ takes the letter gently from him.)*
28 ROSENCRANTZ: Now that we have found it, why were we
29   looking for it?
30 GUILDENSTERN: *(Thinks.)* We thought it was lost.
31 ROSENCRANTZ: Something else?
32 GUILDENSTERN: No. *(Deflation)*
33 ROSENCRANTZ: Now we've lost the tension.
34 GUILDENSTERN: What tension?
35 ROSENCRANTZ: What was the last thing I said before we

1   wandered off?

2   GUILDENSTERN: When was that?

3   ROSENCRANTZ: *(Helplessly)* I can't remember.

4   GUILDENSTERN: *(Leaping up)* What a shambles! We're just not
5   getting anywhere.

6   ROSENCRANTZ: *(Mournfully)* Not even England. I don't believe
7   in it anyway.

8   GUILDENSTERN: What?

9   ROSENCRANTZ: England.

10   GUILDENSTERN: Just a conspiracy of cartographers, you mean?

11   ROSENCRANTZ: I mean I don't believe it! *(Calmer)* I have no
12   image. I try to picture us arriving, a little harbour
13   perhaps ... roads ... inhabitants to point the way ...
14   horses on the road ... riding for a day or a fortnight and
15   then a palace and the English king ... That would be the
16   logical kind of thing ... But my mind remains a blank. No.
17   We're slipping off the map.

18   GUILDENSTERN: Yes ... yes ... *(Rallying)* But you don't believe
19   anything till it happens. And it *has* all happened. Hasn't it?

20   ROSENCRANTZ: We drift down time, clutching at straws. But
21   what good's a brick to a drowning man?

22   GUILDENSTERN: Don't give up, we can't be long now.

23   ROSENCRANTZ: We might as well be dead. Do you think death
24   could possibly be a boat?

25   GUILDENSTERN: No, no, no. Death is ... not. Death isn't. You
26   take my meaning. Death is the ultimate negative. Not-being.
27   You can't not-be on a boat.

28   ROSENCRANTZ: I've frequently not been on boats.

29   GUILDENSTERN: No, no, no — what you've been is not on boats.

30   ROSENCRANTZ: I wish I was dead. *(Considers the drop.)* I could
31   jump over the side. That would put a spoke in their wheel.

32   GUILDENSTERN: Unless they're counting on it.

33   ROSENCRANTZ: I shall remain on board. That'll put a spoke in
34   their wheel. *(The futility of it, fury)* All right! We don't question,
35   we don't doubt. We perform. But a line must be drawn

270

1   somewhere, and I would like to put it on record that I have
2   no confidence in England. Thank you. *(Thinks about this.)*
3   And even if it's true, it'll just be another shambles.
4   GUILDENSTERN: I don't see why.
5   ROSENCRANTZ: *(Furious)* He won't know what we're talking
6   about. What are we going to *say?*
7   GUILDENSTERN: We say — Your majesty, we have arrived!
8   ROSENCRANTZ: *(Kingly)* And who are you?
9   GUILDENSTERN: We are Rosencrantz and Guildenstern.
10   ROSENCRANTZ: *(Barks.)* Never heard of you!
11   GUILDENSTERN: Well, we're nobody special —
12   ROSENCRANTZ: *(Regal and nasty)* What's your game?
13   GUILDENSTERN: We've got our instructions —
14   ROSENCRANTZ: First I've heard of it —
15   GUILDENSTERN: *(Angry)* Let me finish — *(Humble)* We've come
16   from Denmark.
17   ROSENCRANTZ: What do you want?
18   GUILDENSTERN: Nothing — we're delivering Hamlet —
19   ROSENCRANTZ: Who's he?
20   GUILDENSTERN: *(Irritated)* You've heard of *him* —
21   ROSENCRANTZ: Oh, I've heard of him all right and I want
22   nothing to do with it.
23   GUILDENSTERN: But —
24   ROSENCRANTZ: You march in here without so much as a by-
25   your-leave and expect me to take in every lunatic you try
26   to pass off with a lot of unsubstantiated —
27   GUILDENSTERN: We've got a letter —*(ROSENCRANTZ snatches*
28   *it and tears it open.)*
29   ROSENCRANTZ: *(Efficiently)* I see ... I see ... well, this seems
30   to support your story such as it is — it is an exact command
31   from the king of Denmark, for several different reasons,
32   importing Denmark's health and England's too, that on the
33   reading of this letter, without delay, I should have Hamlet's
34   head cut off —! *(GUILDENSTERN snatches the letter. ROSEN-*
35   *CRANTZ, double-taking, snatches it back. GUILDENSTERN*

1   *snatches it half back. They read it together, and separate. Pause.*
2   *They are well Downstage looking front.)*
3   ROSENCRANTZ: The sun's going down. It will be dark soon.
4   GUILDENSTERN: Do you think so?
5   ROSENCRANTZ: I was just making conversation. *(Pause)* We're
6   his *friends*.
7   GUILDENSTERN: How do you know?
8   ROSENCRANTZ: From our young days brought up with him.
9   GUILDENSTERN: You've only got their word for it.
10   ROSENCRANTZ: But that's what we depend on.
11   GUILDENSTERN: Well, yes, and then again no. *(Airily)* Let us
12   keep things in proportion. Assume, if you like, that they're
13   going to kill him. Well, he is a man, he is mortal, death comes
14   to us all, et cetera, and consequently he would have died
15   anyway, sooner or later. Or to look at it from the social point
16   of view — he's just one man among many, the loss would be
17   well within reason and convenience. And then again, what
18   is so terrible about death? As Socrates so philosophically
19   put it, since we don't know what death is, it is illogical to
20   fear it. It might be . . . very nice. Certainly it is a release
21   from the burden of life, and, for the godly, a haven and a
22   reward. Or to look at it another way — we are little men,
23   we don't know the ins and outs of the matter, there are
24   wheels within wheels, et cetera — it would be presumptuous
25   of us to interfere with the designs of fate or even of kings.
26   All in all, I think we'd be well advised to leave well enough
27   alone. Tie up the letter — there — neatly — like that. They
28   won't notice the broken seal, assuming you were in character.
29   ROSENCRANTZ: But what's the point?
30   GUILDENSTERN: Don't apply logic.
31   ROSENCRANTZ: He's done nothing to us.
32   GUILDENSTERN: Or justice.
33   ROSENCRANTZ: It's awful.
34   GUILDENSTERN: But it could have been worse. I was beginning
35   to think it was. *(And his relief comes out in a laugh.)*

1 *(Behind them HAMLET appears from behind the umbrella. The*
2 *light has been going. Slightly. HAMLET is going to the lantern.)*
3 **ROSENCRANTZ:** **The position as I see it, then. We, Rosencrantz**
4 **and Guildenstern, from our young days brought up with**
5 **him, awakened by a man standing on his saddle, are**
6 **summoned, and arrive, and are instructed to glean what**
7 **afflicts him and draw him on to pleasure, such as a play,**
8 **which unfortunately, as it turns out, is abandoned in some**
9 **confusion owing to certain nuances outside our**
10 **appreciation — which, among other causes, results in,**
11 **among other effects, a high, not to say, homicidal,**
12 **excitement in Hamlet, whom we, in consequence, are**
13 **escorting, for his own good, to England. Good. We're on top**
14 **of it now.**
15 *(HAMLET blows out the lantern. The stage goes pitch black. The*
16 *black resolves itself to moonlight, by which HAMLET approaches*
17 *the sleeping ROSENCRANTZ and GUILDENSTERN. He extracts*
18 *the letter and takes it behind his umbrella; the light of his lantern*
19 *shines through the fabric, HAMLET emerges again with a letter,*
20 *and replaces it, and retires, blowing out his lantern.)*
21 *(Morning comes.)*
22 *(ROSENCRANTZ watches it coming — from the auditorium.*
23 *Behind him is a sight. Beneath the retilted umbrella, reclining in*
24 *a deck chair, wrapped in a rug, reading a book, possibly smoking,*
25 *sits HAMLET.)*
26 *(ROSENCRANTZ watches the morning come, and brighten to high*
27 *noon.)*
28 **ROSENCRANTZ: I'm assuming nothing.** *(He stands up.*
29 *GUILDENSTERN wakes.)* **The position as I see it, then. That's**
30 **west unless we're off course, in which case it's night; the**
31 **King gave me the same as you, the King gave you the same**
32 **as me; the King never gave me the letter, the King gave you**
33 **the letter, we don't know what's in the letter; we take Hamlet**
34 **to the English king, it depending on when we get there who**
35 **he is, and we hand over the letter, which may or may not**

273

1   have something in it to keep us going, and if not, we are
2   finished and at a loose end, if they have loose ends. We could
3   have done worse. I don't think we missed any chances ...
4   Not that we're getting much help. *(He sits down again. They*
5   *lie down — prone.)* If we stopped breathing we'd vanish. *(The*
6   *muffled sound of a recorder. They sit up with disproportionate*
7   *interest.)*
8   GUILDENSTERN: Here we go.
9   ROSENCRANTZ: Yes, but what? *(They listen to the music.)*
10   GUILDENSTERN: *(Excitedly)* Out of the void, finally a sound;
11   while on a boat (admittedly) outside the action (admittedly)
12   the perfect and absolute silence of the wet lazy slap of water
13   against water and the rolling creak of timber — breaks;
14   giving rise at once to the speculation or the assumption or
15   the hope that something is about to happen; a pipe is heard.
16   One of the sailors has pursed his lips against a woodwind,
17   his fingers and thumbs governing, shall we say, the ventages,
18   whereupon, giving it breath, let us say, with his mouth, it,
19   the pipe, discourses, as the saying goes, most eloquent
20   music. A thing like that, it could change the course of events.
21   *(Pause)* Go and see what it is.
22   ROSENCRANTZ: It's someone playing on a pipe.
23   GUILDENSTERN: Go and find him.
24   ROSENCRANTZ: And then what?
25   GUILDENSTERN: I don't know — request a tune.
26   ROSENCRANTZ: What for?
27   GUILDENSTERN: Quick — before we lose our momentum.
28   ROSENCRANTZ: Why?! Something is happening. It had quite
29   escaped my attention!
30   *(He listens. Makes a stab at an exit. Listens more carefully. Changes*
31   *direction.)*
32   *(GUILDENSTERN takes no notice.)*
33
34
35

NOTE

Tom Stoppard's playscript *Rosencrantz and Guildenstern Are
Dead* is based almost exclusively on the few lines of reference to the
characters found in William Shakespeare's *Hamlet*. In the original
context of Shakespeare's playscript Rosencrantz and Guildenstern
were instructed to escort Hamlet to England by his stepfather,
Claudius. The secret letter they carried provided instructions that
Hamlet was to be killed immediately upon reaching English land.
Here is Hamlet's own description of how he saved himself and impli-
cated Rosencrantz and Guildenstern instead.

> Up from my cabin,
> My sea-gown scarfed about me, in the dark
> Groped I to find out them, had my desire,
> Fingered their packet, and in fine withdrew
> To mine own room again, making so bold,
> My fears forgetting manners, to unseal
> Their grand commission; where I found Horatio —
> O royal knavery! — an exact command,
> Larded with many several sorts of reasons,
> Importing Denmark's health and England's too,
> With, ho! such bugs and goblins in my life,
> That on the supervise, no leisure bated,
> No, not to stay the grinding of the axe,
> My head should be struck off.

* * *

> Being thus benetted round with villanies —
> Or I could make a prologue to my brains,
> They had begun the play — I sat me down,
> Devised a new commission, wrote it fair;
> I once did hold it, as our statists do,
> A baseness to write fair, and labored much
> How to forget that learning, but, sir, now
> It did me yeomen's service; wilt thou know
> The effect of what I wrote?
>
> An earnest conjuration from the king,
> As England was his faithful tributary,

As love between them like the palm might flourish,
As peace should still her wheaten garland wear
And stand a comma 'tween their amities,
And many such-like 'as'es' of great charge,
That, on the view and knowing of these contents,
Without debatement further, more or less,
He should the bearers put to sudden death,
Not shriving-time allowed.

         I had my father's signet in my purse,
Which was the model of that Danish seal;
Folded the writ up in the form of the other,
Subscribed it, gave't the impression, placed it safely,
The changeling never known.

         Why, man, they did make love to this employ-
   ment;
They are not near my conscience; their defeat does
By their own insinuation grow; 'tis dangerous
When the baser nature comes between the pass
And fell incensed points of mighty opposites.

                  (Act V, Scene ii)

Absurdism seems to distort the appearance of reality by suggesting the character's loss of human qualities so what emerges is a "machine-like," almost dehumanized, person who has no sense of direction or apparent purpose in life.

277

from **Striptease** (1961)
Slawomir Mrozek

The playwrights of Eastern Europe — like Slawomir Mrozek and Vaclav Havel — illustrate the increasingly difficult task of defining the "type" of drama usually referred to as absurdism. While the scene that follows is rather typical of the "noplace" traditionally found in playscripts of absurdism, there are also interesting political parallels that might suggest a symbolic allegory, or a parable, of authoritarian or totalitarian rule that denies the integrity of the individual and seeks to suppress truth and justice. There is also an interesting mixture of images and objects generally associated with absurdism that strike familiar political and social chords as well. With this legacy of mixing absurd images and political symbols with the actions of the characters to produce an intellectual response from the audience, Eastern European playwrights hoped to dramatize the plight of their fellow men and to advance positive alternatives for survival in the oppressive climate of their present-day society.

In approaching the scene that follows pay particular attention to the "hands" that beckon the characters to their fateful destiny and make creative decisions related to the staging of the "hands." For example, will the "hands" be portrayed as an illusion of character or as a physical presence represented by an actor; and will the "hands" be indicated by typical absurd performance techniques as special effects or flying objects. In making these decisions the actors should be guided by the need to convey a visual, dramatic impact that is simplistic in design and yet complex in expressing the mood, attitude and intellect thought to be dramatized in the playwright's use of the "hands" to suggest an allegory or parable of some mysterious truth about life or humanity. There should also be some attention paid to the obvious paradox between what the characters say in the dialog and what they look like while saying it.

The primary image of a human being isolated in time and space is the fundamental drama at work in the scene that follows. The characters are solitary figures who have apparently lost the ability to communicate meaningful thoughts in the traditional manner of "speaking words" and find themselves at the mercy of mysterious forces that demand absolute obedience and submission. The theatrical performance that reinforces these ideas should seek to evoke vivid and easily recognizable images that reflect the despair and sorrow being experienced by the characters as they blindly explore their own self-awareness in a futile attempt to free themselves from this "nightmare" existence. The performance metaphor should also help the audience to visualize the absurdism principle that existence is a distorted series of reflections in a mirror that prove to be an illusion rather than a reality.

CAST

MR. I
The Hand
MR. II
The Second Hand

SCENE

The stage is bare except for two chairs. Two doors, one Stage Left and one Stage Right, should be in clear view of the audience.

APPROACH

As the curtain rises on the scene there is no one on stage. Strange rattling and rumbling noises which may sound vaguely familiar but that cannot be identified are heard Off-stage. There is a quiet calm present when Mr. I abruptly comes rushing into the space to disrupt the silence. He is rather preoccupied with something that has apparently just happened outside and appears to have been "thrust" into the space without his consent. As he curiously peers around the strange space and adjusts his suit, Mr. II just as suddenly rushes into the space through the door on Stage Right. As they face each other it is obvious that they are *exact replicas* of each other, including identical suits and briefcases! Following an awkward period of staring at each other, the initial "visual absurdity" of the characters is complicated by the fantasy and dream world images of sight, sound and movement that follow the characters as they seek to understand "why" they have been brought together in this sanctuary of silence.

1	MR. I:	Extraordinary!
2	MR. II:	Incredible!
3	MR. I:	I was walking along as usual ...
4	MR. II:	Not a care in the world ...
5	MR. I:	When suddenly ...
6	MR. II:	Like a bolt from the sky ...

7   **MR. I:** *(As though just becoming aware of the presence of MR. II)* **How**
8   **did you get here?**

9   **MR. II:** Why don't you ask what brought me here, or who
10   brought me here?

11   **MR. I:** *(Again following his own thoughts)* **Outrageous!**

12   **MR. II:** *(As though slightly mimicking MR. I)* **Preposterous!**

13   **MR. I:** I was simply walking, or perhaps, rather, hurrying along.

14   **MR. II:** Yes, that's right! You were certainly heading for a
15   particular destination.

16   **MR. I:** How do you know?

17   **MR. II:** It's obvious. I was walking along too, or rather, hurrying
18   along, heading for my destination.

19   **MR. I:** You took the words right out of my mouth. As I said, I was
20   heading for this destination when suddenly ...

21   **MR. II:** And remember, this was a destination that you yourself
22   had chosen.

23   **MR. I:** Exactly! And with conscious intent, mind you, with full
24   conscious intent ...

25   **MR. II:** Obeying the dictates of your conscience, motivated by
26   faith and reason.

27   **MR. I:** You're reading my very thoughts. As I was saying, I
28   followed the path most appropriate for my chosen
29   destination when suddenly ...

30   **MR. II:** *(Confidentially)* **They beat you?**

31   **MR. I:** Oh, no! *(Also confidentially)* **And you?**

32   **MR. II:** God forbid! I mean, I don't know a thing. That's all I can
33   say.

34   **MR. I:** What was it then?

35   **MR. II:** That's hard to say for sure. It was like a gigantic elephant

1   blocking the street. Or were there riots? First I had the
2   impression of a flood, then of a picnic. But being in such a
3   fog . . .
4   MR. I: That's true! It's so foggy today you can hardly see a thing.
5   Still, I was trying to reach my particular destination . . .
6   MR. II: Which you yourself had freely chosen . . .
7   MR. I: That's God's honest truth! Nothing was left to chance. I
8   had prepared everything down to the last detail. My wife
9   and I often spend long hours planning ahead, planning our
10   entire lives.
11   MR. II: I also had it all mapped out in advance. Even as a child . . .
12   MR. I: *(Confidentially)* Did you hear a voice?
13   MR. II: I certainly did. There was a voice.
14   MR. I: Something like a saw . . . a persistent sound . . . no,
15   actually an intermittent one.
16   MR. II: A gigantic buzz saw.
17   MR. I: But where the hell could a saw come from?
18   MR. II: Perhaps it wasn't a saw. Something threw me to the
19   ground.
20   MR. I: But what?
21   MR. II: The worst part is this uncertainty. Was it really to the
22   ground?
23   MR. I: Where else if not to the ground?
24   MR. II: But was I really thrown? What a jungle of riddles! I can't
25   even tell if this was a "being-thrown" in the exact, classical
26   sense, deserving of the name. Though I had the sensation
27   of being thrown down, lying on the ground; I was perhaps —
28   MR. I: *(Tensely)* More overthrown than thrown down?
29   MR. II: Precisely! And to tell the truth, I really have no complaints.
30   Did you see any people?
31   MR. I: Are there any at all?
32   MR. II: I suppose there are, but with all this fog . . . it doesn't
33   seem likely.
34   MR. I: The worst of all is this lack of assurance.
35   MR. II: What color was it?

1   **MR. I:**   **What?**

2   **MR. II:**   **It's so hard to figure out anything. It was something**
3   **bright . . . a sort of rose color shot through with lead.**

4   **MR. I:**   **Nonsense!**

5   **MR. II:**   *(Moving over to MR. I, after a pause)* **And still they hit you in**
6   **the jaw.**

7   **MR. I:**   **Me?**

8   **MR. II:**   **Me too.** *(Pause)*

9   **MR. I:**   **Well, anyway, now I can't get there on time anymore.**

10   **MR. II:**   **How about just walking out? Right now! As though**
11   **nothing had happened?**

12   **MR. I:**   **No, no!**

13   **MR. II:**   **Are you afraid?**

14   **MR. I:**   **Me? Why should I be? I'm just a little nervous. I just can't**
15   **see.**

16   **MR. II:**   **That's because of the fog.**

17   **MR. I:**   **Did they say we must not leave the room?**

18   **MR. II:**   **Who?**

19   **MR. I:**   **Whom were you thinking of?**

20   **MR. II:**   **Never mind!**

21   **MR. I:**   **I've decided to stay put. The situation will clear up by**
22   **itself.**

23   **MR. II:**   **But why? It may be quite possible for us to leave this**
24   **room, unimpeded, and to continue on our way. After all, we**
25   **can't really tell what's going on. Perhaps we ourselves went**
26   **astray.**

27   **MR. I:**   **Are you blaming yourself? Us? We both knew where we**
28   **were going, each of us heading for his specific destination.**

29   **MR. II:**   **Then it was not our fault?**

30   **MR. I:**   **No, unless . . .**

31   **MR. II:**   **Unless?**

32   **MR. I:**   **How do I know? Let's drop the subject! I, for one, feel most**
33   **strongly that we should not leave this room.**

34   **MR. II:**   **If you're so sure about it . . .**

35   **MR. I:**   **Definitely! We have to use sound reasoning in dealing**

1   with this matter. *(Both sit down.)*

2 MR. II: Perhaps you're right. *(Listens.)* There's nobody there.

3 MR. I: Actually, there's no cause for concern, is there?

4 MR. II: No obvious cause, I would say.

5 MR. I: Are you implying that there is a cause ... an obscure one?

6 MR. II: You have a mind of your own.

7 MR. I: Let's establish the facts.

8 MR. II: All right, go ahead.

9 MR. I: Very well, then: Each of us left his house according to plan
10   and walked, or rather hurried, as you observed correctly,
11   in the direction of his goal. The morning was brisk, the
12   weather fair, the existence of wife and children an
13   established fact. Each of us knew whatever there was to be
14   known. Of course, we had no idea about the kind of
15   molecules, not to speak of atoms, that our bedside table is
16   composed of, but, after all, there are specialists who deal
17   with such matters. Basically, everything was perfectly clear.
18   Well-shaved, carrying our practical and indispensable
19   briefcases, we set out purposefully toward our goal. The
20   respective addresses had been thoroughly committed to
21   memory. But to be quite safe we had also noted them down
22   in our notebooks. Am I correct?

23 MR. II: On every point.

24 MR. I: Now listen carefully! At a certain moment, as we were
25   pursuing our course, a course that we had mapped out in
26   detail and that was, so to speak, the end result of all our
27   rational calculations, something happened which ... and
28   this is a point I must stress ... came entirely from the
29   outside, something separate in itself and independent of us.

30 MR. II: With regard to this point, I must register some doubt.
31   Since we are unable to define the exact nature of the
32   occurrence, and since we cannot even agree as to its
33   manifestations ... due to the fog or to whatever other
34   causes ... we are in no position to state with any degree of
35   certainty that this something came exclusively from the

1   outside or that it was entirely separate in itself and
2   independent of us.

3   MR. I: You are discomposing me.

4   MR. II: I beg your pardon?

5   MR. I: You're interrupting my thoughts.

6   MR. II: I'm sorry.

7   MR. I: Unfortunately, we are not able to determine the exact
8   nature of the phenomenon, and . . .

9   MR. II: That's just what I said.

10   MR. I: If you wish to go on, don't mind me!

11   MR. II: The words just slipped out. It won't happen again.

12   MR. I: *(Continuing)* We cannot even determine with any
13   appropriate degree of accuracy what particular elements
14   constituted this something. *(Pause)* I beg your pardon?

15   MR. II: I didn't say anything.

16   MR. I: I, for instance, perceived something that seemed to have
17   the shape of an animal, but still I cannot be absolutely sure
18   that it was not at the same time a mineral. Actually, it seems
19   to me that it involved energy rather than matter. I think all
20   this may be best defined as a phenomenon hovering on the
21   borderline of dimensions and definitions, a connecting link
22   between color, form, smell, weight, length, and breadth,
23   shade, light, dark, and so on and so forth.

24   MR. II: Do you still feel any pain? Mine is almost all gone.

25   MR. I: Please don't reduce everything to its lowest level!

26   MR. II: I was just asking.

27   MR. I: *(Continuing his train of thought)* This much is certain: We
28   were helpless in the face of the phenomenon, and, partly of
29   our own will, as we were looking for shelter, partly due to
30   external pressure, we happened to find ourselves in these
31   strange quarters which at that critical moment were close
32   at hand. Fortunately, we found the doors open. Needless to
33   say, our original intentions have thus been completely upset
34   and, as it were, arrested.

35   MR. II: I fully agree. What are your conclusions?

1	MR. I:	This is just what I was coming to. Our main task now is to
2		preserve our calm and our personal dignity. Thus, it would
3		seem to me, we still remain in control of the situation.
4		Basically, our freedom is in no way limited.
5	MR. II:	You call this freedom, our sitting here?
6	MR. I:	But we can walk out at any moment . . . the doors are open.
7	MR. II:	Then let's go! We've wasted too much time anyway.
8		*(Again the same strange noise is heard as in the beginning.)*
9	MR. I:	What . . .? What's that?
10	MR. II:	I told you we should go.
11	MR. I:	Right now?
12	MR. II:	Are you afraid?
13	MR. I:	Not at all.
14	MR. II:	First you insist on preserving your personal dignity by
15		asserting your freedom, and then you don't even want to
16		leave while there is still time.
17	MR. I:	If I left right now I would limit the idea of freedom.
18	MR. II:	What do you mean?
19	MR. I:	It's quite obvious. What is freedom? It is the capacity of
20		making a choice. As long as I am sitting here, knowing that
21		I can walk out of this door, I am free. But as soon as I get
22		up and walk out, I have already made my choice, I have
23		limited the possible courses of action, I have lost my
24		freedom. I become the slave of my own locomotion.
25	MR. II:	But your sitting here and not walking out is just another
26		way of making a choice. You simply choose sitting rather
27		than leaving.
28	MR. I:	Wrong! While I'm sitting, I can still leave. If, however, I do
29		leave, I preclude the alternative of sitting.
30	MR. II:	And this makes you feel comfortable?
31	MR. I:	Perfectly comfortable. Unlimited inner freedom, that is
32		my answer to these strange happenings. *(MR. II gets up.)*
33		What are you doing?
34	MR. II:	I'm leaving. I don't like this.
35	MR. I:	Are you joking?

1	MR. II:	I'm not trying to. I believe in external freedom.
2	MR. I:	And what about me?
3	MR. II:	Good-bye.
4	MR. I:	Please wait! Are you crazy? You don't even know what's
5		out there! *(Both doors close slowly.)*
6	MR. II:	Hey! Open up right now!
7	MR. I:	Shh! Be quiet!
8	MR. II:	Why should I be quiet?
9	MR. I:	I don't know.
10	MR. II:	*(Goes to the other door, knocks, and listens.)* **Locked!**
11	MR. I:	Do me a favor and sit down!
12	MR. II:	Well, where is it now, your precious freedom?
13	MR. I:	I have nothing to blame myself for. My freedom remains
14		unaffected.
15	MR. II:	But there's no way to get out now, is there?
16	MR. I:	The potential of my freedom has remained unchanged. I
17		have not made a choice, I have in no way confined myself.
18		The doors were closed for external reasons. I am the same
19		person that I was before. As you may have noticed, I did not
20		even get up from my chair.
21	MR. II:	These doors are upsetting me.
22	MR. I:	My dear sir, while we are unable to influence external
23		events, we must make every effort to preserve our dignity
24		and our inner balance. And with regard to those, we
25		command an unlimited field, even though the infinite
26		variety of choices has been reduced to two alternatives.
27		These, of course, exist only as long as we do not choose
28		either of them.
29	MR. II:	What else could happen?
30	MR. I:	Do you think it may get worse?
31	MR. II:	I'll try to knock on the wall ... perhaps somebody is
32		there.
33	MR. I:	It is regrettable that you have no regard for the inviolable
34		nature of your personal freedom. I, too, could knock on the
35		wall, but I won't. If I did, I would preclude other possibilities,

1   such as reading the papers I have in my briefcase or
2   concentrating on last year's horse races.

3   *(MR. II knocks on the wall several times and listens; he repeats this*
4   *for a while. Then he takes off one shoe and bangs with it against*
5   *the wall. One of the doors opens slowly, and in comes a HAND of*
6   *supernatural size. It resembles the old-fashioned printer's symbol:*
7   *HAND with pointing index finger and attached cuff. The palm*
8   *should be brightly colored to make it stand out clearly against the*
9   *scenery. With bent index finger the HAND makes a monotonously*
10   *repeated gesture in the direction of MR. II, beckoning to him.)*

11   **MR. I:**   *(The first to notice the HAND)* **Pssst!** *(MR. II has not yet seen the*
12   *HAND; he keeps banging with his shoe and listening.)* **Pssst! Stop**
13   **it, please! Don't you see what's going on?** *(MR. II turns around.*
14   *MR. I points to the HAND.)*

15   **MR. II:**   **Something new again!**

16   *(The HAND continues beckoning to him. MR. II walks over to it.*
17   *The HAND points to the shoe he is holding, then it reaches out in*
18   *an ambiguous gesture that may be either begging or demanding.*
19   *Hesitantly, MR. II puts his shoe into the HAND. The HAND*
20   *disappears and returns immediately without the shoe. MR. II takes*
21   *off his other shoe and gives it to the HAND. The HAND leaves the*
22   *room, returns, and repeatedly touches MR. II's stomach with his*
23   *index finger. Guessing what this means, MR. II takes off his belt*
24   *and hands it over. The HAND withdraws, returns without the belt,*
25   *and begins to beckon to MR. I.)*

26   **MR. I:**   **Me?** *(He slowly walks over to the hand, stopping at every other*
27   *step. While he is talking, the HAND continually beckons to*
28   *him.)* **But I didn't knock ... There must be a misunder-**
29   **standing ... I didn't make a choice ... no choice**
30   **whatsoever ... I did not knock, though I must admit that**
31   **when my colleague knocked I was hoping that someone**
32   **might hear it and come in, that the situation might be**
33   **cleared up and that we would be allowed to leave. This much**
34   **I admit, but I didn't do any knocking.** *(The HAND points to*
35   *his shoes.)* **I protest. I repeat once more: The knocking was not**

1   done by me. I don't understand why I should hand over my
2   shoes. *(Bends down to untie the laces.)* I value my inner freedom.
3   A little patience, please! Can't the Hand see that there's a
4   knot here? Personally, I don't hold anything against the
5   Hand, because my own conscience is clear. I am determined
6   to save my inner freedom, even at the cost of my external
7   freedom . . . quite the opposite to my colleague here. But I'm
8   not holding anything against him either, because, after all,
9   what he does is his own business. I request only that we be
10   treated as individuals, each according to his own views.
11   Just a moment, I'm getting it. There's no fire, is there? *(Giving*
12   *the HAND his shoes.)* Glad to oblige! *(The HAND points to his*
13   *stomach.)* I'm not wearing a belt . . . I prefer suspenders. All
14   right, I'll give up the suspenders, too, if necessary. *(Takes off*
15   *his jacket and unbuttons his suspenders.)* Peculiar methods they
16   have here! All right, here they are . . . Somebody's
17   fingernails could use a good cleaning, if I may venture an
18   opinion. *(The HAND disappears, the door closes slowly.)* At least
19   I'm wearing a fresh pair of socks. I'm glad about that.
20 MR. II: Boot licker!
21 MR. I: Leave me alone! I'm not bothering you.
22 MR. II: What can I use now to knock with?
23 MR. I: That's your problem. I'm going to sit down. *(Returns to his*
24   *chair.)*
25 MR. II: You're in good shape now with your inner freedom.
26   You're losing your pants.
27 MR. I: What about yours? They won't stay up either without a
28   belt.
29 MR. II: Well, what do you make of all this?
30 MR. I: I can only repeat what I said before: First the dear Hand
31   interfered with my free movement in space and then with
32   my ability to wear trousers. This is true, and this I'm willing
33   to admit. But what does it matter? All these are externals.
34   Inwardly I have remained free. I have not become engaged
35   in any action, I have not made any gesture. I haven't even

1   moved a finger. Just sitting here I am still free to do
2   whatever lies in the realm of possibility. Not you, though.
3   You did something . . . you made a choice . . . you knocked
4   against the wall and made a fool of yourself. Slave!

5 MR. II: I could slap your face, but there are more important
6   things to be done.

7 MR. I: Right. But why do they deal with us like this?

8 MR. II: It's always the first thing they do . . . take away your
9   shoelaces, belts, and suspenders.

10 MR. I: What for?

11 MR. II: So you can't hang yourself.

12 MR. I: You must be joking! If I'm not even getting up from my
13   chair, how can I hang myself? Of course, I could if I wanted
14   to, but I won't. You know my views.

15 MR. II: I'm sick and tired of your views.

16 MR. I: That's your problem. But listen to this: If the dear Hand
17   doesn't want us to hang ourselves, this means that it wants
18   to keep us alive. That's a good sign!

19 MR. II: This is just what bothers me. It means that the Hand
20   thinks of us in terms of categories . . . Life and the
21   other . . . what's it called?

22 MR. I: Death?

23 MR. II: You said it. *(Pause)*

24 MR. I: I am calm.

25 MR. II: Tell me, what could you do now, if you felt like doing
26   something? Of course, taking into account the fact that you
27   had to relinquish your shoes and suspenders.

28 MR. I: Oh, quite a few things. I could, for instance, put on my
29   jacket inside out, roll up the legs of my trousers, and pretend
30   to be a fisherman.

31 MR. II: And what else?

32 MR. I: I could sing.

33 MR. II: That's enough. *(Turns up the legs of his trousers, puts on his*
34   *jacket inside out, and takes off his socks.)*

35 MR. I: Are you crazy? What are you trying to do?

1   **MR. II:**   **I'm pretending to be a fisherman, and I'm going to sing,**
2   **too. In contrast to you, I want to explore all the possibilities**
3   **of action. Maybe the Hand is partial to fishermen and lets**
4   **them return to freedom. Who knows? One should not neglect**
5   **any possibility. I've asked you because you have more**
6   **imagination than I. For instance, I could never have thought**
7   **up all those things about inner freedom.**

8   **MR. I:**   **It's all right with me. But please remember that I'm not**
9   **moving from this chair.**

10   **MR. II:**   **You don't have to.** *(He climbs on the chair and sings Schubert's*
11   *"The Trout." One of the doors slowly opens.)*

12   **MR. I:**   *(Who has been anxiously watching the door)* **Now you've done**
13   **it!** *(The HAND appears.)*

14   **MR. II:**   **How do you know? Perhaps I'll be allowed to go and**
15   **you'll keep sitting.** *(The HAND beckons to him.)* **I'm coming,**
16   **I'm coming. What's it all about?** *(The HAND indicates that it*
17   *wants his jacket.)* **But I was just — Is there a law against**
18   **fishing?** *(The HAND repeats its gesture.)* **I was just pretending.**
19   **I'm not really a fisherman.** *(Gives the HAND his jacket. The*
20   *HAND disappears, comes back, and now obviously requests his*
21   *trousers.)* **No, I won't give up the trousers!** *(The HAND forms*
22   *a fist and slowly rises.)* **All right.** *(He takes off his trousers.)*

23   **MR. I:**   *(Getting up)* **Me too?**

24   *(After waiting for an answer, which he does not receive, MR. I*
25   *voluntarily removes his jacket. Meanwhile, MR. II has given the*
26   *HAND his trousers, and he now stands there in striped knee-length*
27   *underpants. The HAND carries the trousers backstage, returns*
28   *immediately and beckons to MR. I.)*

29   **MR. I:**   **All right, here it is. I'm not resisting, and I beg the Hand**
30   **to take this into consideration.** *(He gives his jacket to the HAND,*
31   *which takes it out and returns immediately.)* **I'm always willing**
32   **to oblige . . . may I keep my trousers in return?** *(The HAND*
33   *makes a negative gesture.)* **All right, I won't protest.**

34   *(He takes off his trousers and stands up in his underpants, identical*
35   *to those of MR. II. The HAND disappears, the door closes.)*

1   MR. I: You can go to hell with your idea about fishermen.

2   MR. II: It seems to me that it was your idea.

3   MR. I: But you carried it out. It's cold in here.

4   MR. II: It's quite possible that we might have been ordered to
5   hand over our clothes anyway, idea or no idea.

6   MR. I: No! I'm convinced it was you who got us both into this
7   predicament with your idiotic masquerade. It was you who
8   attracted the Hand's attention to our clothing. If at least
9   you had not rolled up your trousers, they would not have
10   caught its eye.

11   MR. II: But fishermen always roll up their trousers.

12   MR. I: What good does that do you now?

13   MR. II: You can't keep ignoring the fact that we differ in our
14   views. You do nothing so that you can feel free to do
15   anything — of course, within the range of what is
16   permitted — while I try to do everything I am permitted to
17   do. But apparently wearing trousers is not permitted.

18   MR. I: You yourself have brought this down on your head.

19   MR. II: An anatomical inaccuracy! Besides, let me repeat this
20   once more: We don't know whether the removal of our
21   clothes was by my action or whether it was part of a
22   predetermined plan.

23   MR. I: At least now you should realize that my basic attitude is
24   superior to yours. Don't you see: I didn't knock, I didn't sing,
25   I didn't roll up my trousers, and still, here I am, looking just
26   like you. Even our stripes are the same.

27   MR. II: Where is your superiority then?

28   MR. I: No waste of energy; same results. Plus, of course, my
29   sense of inner freedom which ...

30   MR. II: One more word about inner freedom and that will be the
31   end of you.

32   MR. I: *(Backing up)* You're unfair! After all, everyone has a right
33   to choose the philosophy that suits him best.

34   MR. II: Never mind! I can't stand this anymore!

35   MR. I: I'm warning you: I won't defend myself. Defending

1   oneself involves making a choice, and for me this is out, in
2   the name of ...
3   MR. II: What? Go on! In the name of what?
4   MR. I: *(Hesitantly)* **In the name of inner free** — *(MR. II throws*
5   *himself at him. MR. I runs all over the stage.)* **Keep your hands**
6   **off!** *(The door opens and the HAND reappears, beckoning to both.*
7   *MR. I and MR. II come to a sudden halt.)*
8   MR. II: Me?
9   MR. I: Or me?
10   MR. II: Maybe it's you ...
11   MR. I: You started this fight. Now you'll get your just desserts.
12   MR. II: Why me? Do you still believe that your idiotic theory is
13   better?
14   MR. I: And you believe that your vulgar pragmatism, this lack of
15   any theory, will stand up to such a test? *(The HAND beckons*
16   *to both.)*
17   MR. II: We'd better go over! It wants something again.
18   MR. I: All right, let's go! We'll soon find out who is right.
19   *(They go over to the HAND which links them together with a pair*
20   *of handcuffs. The HAND disappears and the door closes. MR. II*
21   *drags MR. I along with him by the chain of the handcuffs and*
22   *collapses on his chair. Silence.)*
23   MR. I: What does this mean? *(Anxiously)* **Aren't you feeling well?**
24   **Do you believe that this time it's serious? Say something,**
25   **please!**
26   MR. II: I'm afraid ...
27   MR. I: Of what?
28   MR. II: So far the Hand has limited only our freedom of
29   movement in space. But what assurance is there that soon
30   we won't be limited in something even more essential?
31   MR. I: In what?
32   MR. II: In time. In our own duration. *(Pause)*
33   MR. I: I don't know either. *(Pedantically)* **You, of course, being**
34   **an activist, will exhaust your energies more rapidly. I, on**
35   **the other hand, conserve mine ...**

1	**MR. II:** *(Imploring)* **Not again!**
2	**MR. I:** I'm sorry. I didn't mean to hurt your feelings. Do you have
3	a plan?
4	**MR. II:** There is only one thing we can do now.
5	**MR. I:** What?
6	**MR. II:** Apologize to the Hand.
7	**MR. I:** Apologize? But what for? We haven't done anything to
8	the Hand. On the contrary, it should . . .
9	**MR. II:** This is completely irrelevant. We have to apologize all
10	the same . . . in general, for no reason. To save ourselves . . .
11	for whatever good it may do.
12	**MR. I:** No, I can't do that. I don't suppose I have to explain my
13	reasons.
14	**MR. II:** You're right, I know them by heart. To apologize to the
15	Hand would mean to make a choice, which again would
16	limit your freedom, and so on and so forth.
17	**MR. I:** Yes, that's how it is.
18	**MR. II:** Do as you please! In any case, I am going to apologize.
19	One has to abase oneself. Perhaps that is what it expects us
20	to do.
21	**MR. I:** I would like to join you, but my principles . . .
22	**MR. II:** I have nothing more to say.
23	**MR. I:** I think I can see a way out. You're going to force me to
24	apologize with you. In that case there is no question of
25	choice on my part. I'm simply going to be forced.
26	**MR. II:** All right, consider yourself forced. *(The door opens.)*
27	**MR. I:** I think it's coming. *(The HAND appears.)* **If only we had**
28	**some flowers!** *(Whispering)* **You start!** *(Both run over to the*
29	*HAND. MR. II clears his throat in preparation for his apology.)*
30	**MR. II:** Dear Hand! I mean, Dear and Most Honorable Hand!
31	Although well aware of the fact that the Hand is not here
32	to listen to us, we still beg permission to speak to the Hand
33	from the heart . . . I mean, we would like to hand the Hand
34	a confession, although somewhat belated, nevertheless with
35	full conscious awareness, we sincerely beg to apologize

1   for . . . for . . . *(Whispering to MR. I)* **For what?**

2 MR. I: For walking, for going ahead, for everything in general . . .

3 MR. II: For walking, for going ahead, for . . . I'm expressing
4   myself poorly, but I simply wish to apologize in
5   general . . . for having been . . . for being . . . begging
6   forgiveness from the depth of my heart for whatever the
7   Honorable Hand knows that we don't know . . . for how are
8   we to know what there is to be known? Therefore, whatever
9   the case may be, I humbly apologize, I beg the Hand's
10   forgiveness, I kiss the Hand. *(He ceremoniously kisses the HAND.)*

11 MR. I: I wish to join my colleague, though only in a certain
12   sense, having been forced . . . The Hand knows my
13   principles . . . Therefore, though being forced, I
14   nevertheless sincerely apologize to the Hand on principle.

15   *(He ceremoniously kisses the HAND. Meanwhile the other door opens*
16   *and through it appears a SECOND HAND, completely covered by*
17   *a red glove. It beckons to both. MR. II notices it first. Both turn their*
18   *backs to the FIRST HAND.)*

19 MR. II: **There! Look!**

20 MR. I: **Another one!**

21 MR. II: **There are always two.**

22 MR. I: **It's calling us.**

23 MR. II: **Should we go?** *(The FIRST HAND covers his head with a*
24   *conical cardboard hood.)* **I can't see anything!**

25 MR. I: **It's calling us.** *(The FIRST HAND covers his head with an*
26   *identical hood.)* **It's dark.**

27 MR. II: **When you're called, you have to go.**

28   *(Handcuffed to each other and blinded by the hoods, they move*
29   *toward Stage Center. Constantly stumbling and swerving, they*
30   *gradually come closer to the SECOND HAND.)*

31 MR. I: **The briefcases! We forgot our briefcases!**

32 MR. II: **Right! My briefcase! Where's my briefcase?**

33   *(They grope blindly for their briefcases, left standing next to the*
34   *chair, then pick them up and follow the SECOND HAND through*
35   *the door. Blackout.)*

The theatrical tricks of the circus clown or the slapstick comedian are sometimes employed to suggest the essential mystery behind playscripts of absurdism. In playing the role, however, the actor must peer beneath the obvious broad humor of the scene or the confusing ambiguity of the characters to catch a glimpse of the philosophical truth at work in the scene.

SELECTED BIBLIOGRAPHY

The following textbooks and suggested readings are recommended for the beginning actor who may wish to explore absurd approaches to scene study and playscript interpretation that have had an immediate impact on theatre practice in recent years. The suggested readings also provide an historical perspective on the evolution of the avant garde in theatre performance and production that may provide valuable insights in subsequent staging. A serious review of the theories and movements in these recommended sources should also provide an understanding of the role that the avant garde continues to play in contemporary theatre.

Artaud, Antoin. *The Theatre and Its Double*. Translated by Mary Caroline Richards. New York: Grove Press, 1958.

Benedetti, Robert. *Seeming, Being and Becoming: Acting in Our Century*. New York: Drama Books, 1976.

Bentley, Eric. *Theatre of War*. New York: Viking Press, 1972.

Bermel, Albert. *Artaud's Theatre of Cruelty*. New York: Taplinger Press, 1977.

Blau, Herbert. *The Impossible Theatre*. New York: Collier and Macmillan Company, 1965.

Brustein, Robert. *The Theatre in Revolt*. Boston: Little, Brown and Company, 1962.

Brustein, Robert. *The Third Theatre*. New York: Alfred A. Knopf, 1961.

Chaikin, Joseph. *The Presence of the Actor*. New York: Atheneum Press, 1980.

Croyden, Margaret. *Lunatics, Lovers and Poets: The Contemporary Experimental Theatre*. New York: McGraw-Hill, 1974.

Dukore, Bernard and Daniel Gerould. *Avant Garde Theatre*. New York: Crowell Press, 1967.

Esslin, Martin. *Reflections*. New York: Doubleday and Company, 1971.

Esslin, Martin. *The Theatre of the Absurd*. Woodstock, New York: Overlook Books, 1973.

Grotowski, Jersy. *Towards a Poor Theatre*. New York: Simon and Schuster, 1968.

Hopkins, Albert. *Magic*. New York: Arno Press, 1977.

Kirby, Michael. *Futuristic Performance*. New York: Dutton Press, 1971.

Kirby, Michael. *Happenings*. New York: Dutton Press, 1966.

Kostelanetz, Richard. *The Theatre of Mixed Means*. New York: Pitman Publishers, 1968.

Roose-Evans, James. *Experimental Theatre*. London: Studio Vista, 1973.

Shank, Ted. *American Alternative Theatres*. New York: Grove Press, 1982.

Wellwarth, George. *The Theatre of Protest and Paradox*. New York: New York University Press, 1964.

CHAPTER FOUR

PLAYING CONTEMPORARY SCENES

"I am waiting for the "realists" to rid us of fictitious characters, of conventional symbols of vice and virtue, which possess no value as human data. I am waiting for the surroundings to determine the characters, and for the characters to act according to the logic of the facts. I am waiting, finally, for this evolution to take place on the stage . . . until they return the source of science to the study of nature, to the anatomy of man, to the painting of life in an exact reproduction, more original and powerful than anyone has so far dared to place upon the boards."

— Emile Zola

The one common element that each of us brings to a reading or a viewing of a contemporary playscript is our own individual memory or collective experience that is suggested by the "current event" or "recent happening" being dramatized. Contemporary playwrights, perhaps as both a practical and a philosophical stance, appear to approach topic matter and character development with an attitude of *awareness* and *attentiveness* to present-day issues or recent happenings that appear appropriate for dramatization. The immediate appeal of this approach to playwriting is that it gives the spectator pleasure through learning and by affording the opportunity to extend the scope and depth of capacity for understanding current ideas and thoughts. The playscripts of the contemporary theatre, therefore, address those issues and themes that are at the core of our existence *now*, and thus become a useful means of enlarging our perspective and our perception of life in the years to follow our own existence.

Contemporary playscripts also assist us in becoming aware of the complexities of living daily life in the face of ever-changing conflicts and confrontations; of witnessing the destructive potential for the shifting tides of power and passion to motivate characters to perform either rash or heroic acts; and of understanding the significance of communication and compassion in an age of social, political, moral and religious fluctuation. These are the more demanding and painful lessons the playwrights of the contemporary theatre appear to teach us daily as they also seek to sharpen our perceptions and arouse our deeper emotions so that we may examine our own lives more objectively.

The contemporary theatre was greatly influenced in its approach to what has been called "theatricalized realism" by the basic theories of Naturalism, an exaggerated form of realism that emphasized a sordid and deterministic view of life. Emile Zola (1840-1902), French novelist and playwright, is generally considered to be the "Father of Naturalism" and it is from his novels, prefaces and occasional playscripts that we fashion our understanding of Naturalism. Like the earlier playwrights of realism, Zola was initially influenced by scientific experimentation and exploration — especially in the areas of heredity and environment — and learned from science that it was possible to study contemporary man and his habits by studying his *social* background and the evolution of his *social* thought.

Although Zola's views on Naturalism were not so much original as they were paraphrases of the historian Hippolyte Taine (1828-1893) and the philosopher Auguste Comte (1798-1857), his demand that the scientific study of heredity and environment be dramatized on the stage resulted in a theoretical revolution in both performance and production. As a result of Zola's naturalistic outburst, the stage very quickly became a laboratory for the scientific and social exploration of the human condition. Especially singled out for thematic treatment were the lower middle class, characters with "mental aberrations," the lame and those "poor, wretched souls" whose stark poverty and meager education appeared to limit any chance for their success or advancement in contemporary society.

The basic theory of those who followed the style of Naturalism was that the truth of existence for contemporary man is only revealed by probing beneath the human surface to investigate inner conflicts, hidden desires or frustrated passions. In their desire to touch the very soul of man, the playwrights influenced by Naturalism attempted to translate into concrete terms what they had observed in their interior explorations and they addressed current issues, research and experimentation to guide their investigation to help frame their development of subsequent character and plot line. Displaying the same scientific objectivity as the clinical biologist, the playwrights addressed their topics as social scientists and attempted to recreate life on the stage as if it had been tested in a laboratory but without making arbitrary ethical or moral judgments.

The result of this approach to playwriting was termed *la tranche de vie*, or "raw slice of life," drama that depicted the squalid side of life and concentrated on characters who were, admittedly, the dregs of society. These twisted, tormented, tortured souls were ridden with guilt, disease and despair but were also capable of honesty and truthfulness because they were free from all the traditional beliefs, customs and mores that had corrupted their contemporaries in a society now held together by the bare scraps of humanity. The followers of Naturalism also argued that the playwriting should never permit personal opinions or prejudices to interfere with the development of the character or the action being depicted. The playwright should, however, *note, report* and *translate* what had been observed in the most recent experiment in such a timely fashion that the faithfully recorded events would appear urgent and in need of immediate address. Thus, the ultimate truth would reveal itself "naturally" if it were presented with clarity and precision.

Playing the Role

The actor who engages in contemporary scene study and playscript interpretation is expected to render a truthful depiction of life as it is currently being lived in the description provided by the playwright. This truthful depiction of life tended to result in the dramatization of the most degraded aspects of lower-class characters for the followers of Naturalism. Indeed, the playscripts of Naturalism appear almost preoccupied with detailed treatments of disease, suicide, filth, incest, murder, starvation, divorce, violence and mutilation. Zola himself was very fond of using the analogy that Naturalism was similar to "medicine" and even suggested that performers and spectators alike should approach the examination, diagnosis and subsequent prescription of a human or a social illness in the same manner that a physician approaches the treatment of a physical malady.

As a conscious literary movement, Naturalism eventually lost most of its initial appeal on the stage by forcing a steady diet of misery, mayhem and mischief on shocked and stunned spectators. There are, however, a number of significant performance principles to keep in mind when playing the role in contemporary scenes. For example, in approaching current playscripts there is still a need to achieve a vivid suggestion of the role that environment and heredity play in conditioning man's reflexes and influencing his actions. There is also a need to view character as objectively as a scientist might record an experiment and to focus attention on the social forces that help to shape man's psyche in a scientific and objective investigation. These basic principles of performance continue to be instrumental in drawing attention to contemporary approaches to in-depth characterization and sometimes provide the "dramatic cure" necessary to give insight and dimension to playing the role in a current scene.

Naturalism also argued for a rigid determinism in human behavior and stressed the negative effects of society in molding a character's mental, physical and emotional well-being. Although this approach often led to an exaggeration and a distortion of character in performance, its initial intent was to depict characters that were *flesh-and-blood* — as well as natural and spontaneous — who engaged in "simple" thoughts to express complex issues. Some of the most common sentiments expressed in the dialog and in the action of the playscript by the social outcasts of Naturalism included the notions that: • man is basically good • human dignity is immeasurable • man is an animal • there is virtue in honesty • man must be truthful to his own nature • appearances are deceptive and • the five senses are basic to giving meaning to life.

In a sense, the performance legacy of Naturalism as it manifests itself in contemporary scene study and playscript interpretation is that it sought to capture the essential spirit and fervor of classical Greek tragedy. The insistence on depicting fate, exploring tragic flaws, analyzing inherited traits, engaging in heroic pursuits and advancing moral and social lessons appears to parallel the ancient theory that playscripts in *any* period of theatre history should provide mankind with a blueprint for understanding human nature and should also provide immediate instruction. The rather classical tone of Naturalism may also be apparent in its belief that ultimate truth is discovered only through active response to the five senses, and that what is touched, heard, smelled, seen or tasted is more objectively honest and thoughtful than what is thought or imagined.

The basic impulses of man — hunger, greed, fear — were also primary motivations treated by the playwrights of Naturalism to reveal a sense of humility and quiet dignity that also give their characters an elevated, almost classical Greek stance. They have, that is, a universal value and validity that speaks to a contemporary understanding of the meaning of life; they wrestle with complex philosophical and social propositions, in spite of their apparent ignorance, that seek the ultimate answer to the question of existence; and

Contemporary playscripts continue to single out for thematic treatment characters with "mental aberations" and those "poor, wretched souls" whose eccentric behavior appears to limit any chance for their success in contemporary society.

they explore the limits of free will and the nature of human suffering with no convenient means of escape. The tragic events these characters face are invariably social episodes of a commonplace nature that are both immediate and recognizable by the spectator — losing a job, having insufficient funds, being denied opportunity for education or advancement, hearing tragic news, living a lie or being forced to perform tasks against their will — but they exhibit in their individual

303

strength of will the ability to transcend the consequences of their plight and to achieve a measure of personal dignity. The result of this approach to character and playing the role is to portray heroic and exalted moments of contemporary life with courage and fierce determination while at the same time achieving a depiction of character that is personal and yet profound.

Playing the Style

The contemporary theatre is further indebted to the Naturalism movement and its effort to depict a "raw slice of life" in the introduction of characters that add a new flavor and texture of simplicity and directness that reflected society-at-large rather than a privileged social class. In addressing current events and recent social misdeeds in their own time period, the naturalists sought to depict characters who — *like us today* — are common men and women representing universal human qualities that may be at odds with present-day social mores, customs or laws. A more inclusive list of potential performance principles to keep in mind when playing the style would also include the depiction of outcast, depraved characters who speak in incoherent sentence fragments; the emphasis upon degradation and loss of human dignity that is reflected in extended periods of silence or withdrawal into a "coma-like" state of vegetation; the use of tenement basements, cellars or caves to suggest the loss of a character's basic humanity; and the frequent reference to animal imagery to highlight the regression of mankind to a bestial state of existence.

Although these primarily literary techniques are based upon the playwright's attempt to more accurately dramatize scientific and social theories, the actor of contemporary scenes may also profit in a performance approach that includes special attention being paid to the atmosphere that results from the playwright's detailed description of setting, imagery and staging. The actor should pay particular attention to the description of mechanical devices as well — like sound effects or lighting — to better determine the role that heredity may have played in conditioning a character's action or attitude. This studied investigation may provide inventive approaches to characterization as well as help to condition your understanding of the contemporary dilemma being dramatized.

Like the basic approach to modern playscripts of realism, the actor of contemporary scenes should cultivate a journalistic attitude that details the *who, what, where, when* and *why* of both the character and the scene when playing style. The exploration of the role should include an analysis of the character's motivation and attitude in relation to others in the scene. In addition, the actor should detail the opportunities presented for movement with the other performers, search for the bodily actions and gestures that will allow the character to communicate emotions and thoughts, integrate appropriate personal traits and mannerisms that help to reinforce the character portrait and chart vocal and physical changes that appear to take place in the character during the scene being performed. Also make sure that you give your contemporary creation some individual dimension that will permit you to "visualize" how the character will appear to the spectator.

As you become better acquainted with your contemporary character, you may wish to include observation, informal discussion with others and listening in the performance blueprint. Whether planned or casual, observation, informal discussion and listening provide valuable performance information gained by direct, immediate experience and has the additional benefit of being current. Such alertness to events in everyday life and to interesting people in all walks of life may provide the gesture, the attitude, the voice, the walk, the costume, the hand prop or the mannerism that gives individuality and vitality to your characterization. The actor who is sensitive and aware may also discover the creative impulse of transferring what has been overheard from everyday life situations into a viable, believable stage portrait that is as honest and believable as it might be found to exist in the natural world.

Because contemporary scenes are more firmly rooted in the "here and now," any performance approach to style should be more restrained and subtle than in the traditional role-playing associated with recent realism. The actor generally speaks in a more conversational, personal tone and may even slur syllables or swallow the endings of words. There may even be a series of inarticulate grunts or groans and nonverbal reactions that help to communicate a character's mood. Movement, also, may be less fluid or graceful than traditional stage practice demands and the actor may need to suggest a physical deformity or a mental aberration. The actor's performance approach to style in contemporary theatre should capture individuality in both voice and body and should suggest to the spectator that all *persons, things* and *objects* that surround daily activities are fit material to develop and integrate into character portraits that are concerned with the depiction of current events and everyday happenings.

Playing the Performance

In playing the performance for contemporary scenes the actor is reminded to be truthful to his nature and to approach each scene as if he were examining his *own* life more objectively. There should be acute attention paid to the personal opinions expressed by the character, to the reliability of the character's truthful statements, to the final choices made by the character and to the significant issues addressed by the character. This primary approach to performance should promote a more personal, individual characterization that has depth, dimension, integrity and believability because it is based upon a flesh-and-blood role model that has immediate appeal and addresses universal values. Such a vivid, incisive character portrait also mirrors the current reality of contemporary life that sketches stage figures drawn from the common walks of life but possessed of such admirable values and principles that they inspire imitation by the spectator.

Other significant performance principles at work in playing contemporary scenes that the actor should consider include the use of make-up, props and costumes. Although make-up is fundamental to the visual depiction of character in almost every period of theatre history and is unquestionably the key ingredient in suggesting a character's physicality, contemporary theatre practice is less concerned with distorting the actor's natural facial image than in using make-up sparingly and then primarily in those efforts to suggest that a character's interior psychological state of mind is being reflected in facial shaping and shading. Contemporary facial painting today primarily involves the use of a medium or dark foundation base of grease paint or pancake make-up, extensive highlights and subtle shading and shadowing to suggest character. Occasionally, plastic make-up might be used to create three-dimensional, pliable moldings — such as for false noses, scars or warts — on the face or other parts of the actor's body to suggest a natural deformity or imperfection.

Props in contemporary theatre practice are used almost exclusively to establish relationships between characters or to reinforce individual, personal attributes. The specific selection of personal items like brand name watches, liquor, pens or luggage give a contemporary authenticity to character definition and suggest individuality and social status that reinforce incisive character portraits in performance. The use of props in contemporary theatre also helps to suggest the feeling of intimacy and familiarity when they are used as extensions of the character or serve to identify the character more directly to the spectator. A cigarette lit in times of distress or a favorite recording played in periods of loneliness help the spectator to understand the burden of despair or isolation inherent in the character's actions because these simple props are familiar and may have also served the spectator's similar needs in everyday life. The selection of props, therefore, should reflect contemporary life as the character is currently living it and should also permit the actor to better interpret the character to the spectator.

Costumes in the contemporary theatre have a more profound suggestion of character definition because they reflect the initial clues to a character's mood, attitude, self-image or social status. Costumes may reveal a character's personality, idiosyncrasies or taste in fashion as well as record a character's lifestyle, occupation or sense of style. In the current fashion market contemporary characters may dress in cast-off garments purchased at a Salvation Army outlet, in ready-made garments purchased from thrift stores, in designer-style brand name garments purchased at chic department stores or in garish mix-and-match garments that may be purchased in a variety of exclusive private salons. It is essential, therefore, to carefully distinguish contemporary characters from their pale or purple counterparts in real society by using the designer principles of line, mass, color, texture and ornament to give dimension to character and to highlight individuality.

Contemporary Exercises

The following exercises are presented to promote a relaxed, natural approach to contemporary performance. Having now explored the primary periods of historical performance from the classical Greek to the modern, it is appropriate that the actor conclude his study by reviewing each period discussed and summarizing the basic principles and general characteristics inherent in performance for each period. What remains are those contemporary exercises that help to promote relaxation in rehearsal and positive approaches to artistic interpretation of characters that are universal and yet unique. Approach each exercise with the same enthusiasm you have displayed in previous assignments and repeat each exercise a number of times to lay a solid foundation for rehearsal technique that leads to vibrant, energetic public performance.

SOUNDS OF SILENCE

A good initial test of the stream of air needed for efficient sound production follows. Use this exercise to evaluate your present breath-

307

ing habits, and pay particular attention to the general principles of diaphragmatic breathing that it reveals. Begin by lying flat on your back and relaxing completely. Place your hand just above your waistline and begin to breathe slowly and deeply. As you breathe, pay attention to the expansion and contraction of the diaphragm and notice how the abdominal wall moves in and out as the breathing is consciously directed and controlled.

After several minutes, or when you know how proper diaphragmatic breathing feels, stand up and repeat the exercise. Keep your hand at your waist to detect any change in the center of breathing, and recite a favorite slogan or nonsense phrase. If breathing appears to be centered in the upper chest and the abdominal wall is not actively in motion, practice slower and deeper breathing. Encourage your diaphragm to expand and contract with a comfortable rhythm, and concentrate on keeping the upper chest from rising and falling. Repeat this exercise for several short periods during the day, and the results should be better voice production and control.

After you have engaged in frequent practice of the first part of the exercise on a regular routine of rehearsal you are ready to approach the "sounds of silence." In achieving proper breathing technique — the kind of technique that produces meaningful sounds of silence without strain or tension — you should strive for controlled exhalation of sound, so that the expelled breath sustains a flexible vocal tone. Begin this exploration of proper breathing by standing erect in a large, open space. Place your hands on both sides of your rib cage and begin to *pant* rapidly. Do you feel your rib cage moving up and down? Now relax and begin to *weep* silently. Do you feel your rib cage contract and expand? Then relax and begin to *laugh* loudly. Do you feel your rib cage move up and down as well as contract and expand with each outburst?

Continue the exercise by standing erect with a comfortable, relaxed posture. Slowly inhale, with your hands grasping your rib cage to feel the movement that follows. Hold your breath for a count of 15. Then slowly exhale, counting to 15. Inhale again, holding your breath for a count of 25; then slowly exhale, counting to 25 again. When you are confident that your breathing is regular and relaxed on the count of 25, practice the following excerpt from T. S. Eliot's *The Hollow Men* by taking a deep breath and speaking as many lines as possible on a *single inhalation*.

We are the hollow men
We are the stuffed men
Leaning together
Headpiece filled with straw.
Our dried voices, when
We whisper together,
Are quiet and meaningless
As wind in dry grass
Or rats' feet over broken glass
In our dry cellar.

Now relax, take another deep breath and recite as many lines as possible on a *single inhalation* from the following excerpt from the book of *Job*.

Again there was a day when the sons of God came to present themselves before the Lord, and Satan came also among them to present himself before the Lord. And the Lord said unto Satan, "From whence comest thou?" And Satan answered the Lord, and said, "From going to and fro in the earth, and from walking up and down." And the Lord said unto Satan, "Hast thou considered my servant Job, that there is none like him in the earth, a perfect and an upright man, one that feareth God, and escheweth evil? And still he holdeth fast his integrity, although thou movedst me against him, to destroy him without cause."

By repeating the entire exercise frequently — and on a regular schedule — you should be able in a short period of time to greatly increase your own ability to control breathing and also reduce the tension and anxiety in your voice. Be sure that your exhalation of sound is fluid and even and that you avoid muscular tension when attempting any breathing exercise. When you have incorporated diaphragmatic breathing into your performance you will have acquired a dynamic and expressive vocal tool to give voice to your characters!

MAY I HAVE THIS DANCE?

The actor should always be free of tension in order to use movement effectively, but that movement should also appear motivated

309

and spontaneous. Aimless wandering and nervous pacing are both distracting and irritating if they serve no apparent performance principle and may ultimately result in audience fatigue and performer collapse! Movement used wisely, however, will appear to be direct, energetic and emphatic. If used sparingly, movement may also help to reinforce major ideas expressed by the character in the scene being performed.

The most common uses of movement in performance are *toward* the audience to reinforce an attitude or to share a confidence; to the *side* to direct focus on an action or a speech; and *away from* the audience to suggest that distance is needed to contemplate or to re-think the implications of what has been recently said or done. Although there are no hard-and-fast rules regarding the amount of movement in performance, a good rule of thumb is that movement should be used in moderation and then primarily when it is essential to communicate ideas or actions that can not be as well expressed with facial expressions or gestures.

A fun exercise to encourage variety in movement — and a good exercise to relax the actor physically — is the use of music and dance in performance rehearsal. Tape record a classical sonata, a popular disco song, a folk ballad and a jazz tune. Listen to each separately until you have a sense of the tempo and rhythm. Move slowly to the lyric tones of the sonata; move quickly to the accelerated pace of the disco beat; relax and sway to the repetitive notes of the folk ballad; and then sense the strident and yet free movement suggested by the jazz tune.

Repeat the exercise *without* the music and adapt the movements that you improvised to an imaginary performance situation. Movements requiring a forceful step forward may now be thought of as "disco" steps; movements of more deliberate intent may now be expressed in "sonata" steps; movements to re-direct audience attention may now be inspired by "folk" steps; and those movements of emotional intensity or vigor may now be motivated by recalling your "jazz" steps. When you are comfortable with your "choreography of character" steps, expand the exercise to include similar *vocal variety* by reciting the following passage from Alfred Lord Tennyson's *The Princess* as indicated. First, recite it to the classical sonata, emphasizing variety in *pitch*. Second, recite it to the disco tune, emphasizing variety in *rate*. Third, recite it to the folk ballad, emphasizing variety in *volume*. Fourth, recite it to the jazz tune, emphasizing variety in vocal *inflection*.

Tears, idle tears, I know not what they mean,
Tears from the depth of some divine despair
Rise in the heart, and gather to the eyes,
In looking on the happy autumn-fields,
And thinking of the days that are no more.

Fresh as the first beam glittering on a sail,
That brings our friend up from the underworld,
Sad as the last which reddens over one
That sinks with all we love below the verge;
So sad, so fresh, the days that are no more.

The Contemporary Scenes

The following edited scenes are representative of the contemporary theatre playscripts that address the crucial issues that each of us face in the current world. The theoretical principle that is at work in these selected scenes involves the complex depiction of everyday characters in search of the "inner truth" of their lives. There is a minimum of stage direction or narrative to define the characters and it will be necessary for the actor to communicate the basic ingredients of character mood or attitude to the spectator directly and honestly, without apparent deception or distortion. Approach the playing of each scene with a more restrained and more subtle manner than you might in the traditional role-playing associated with stage realism. It will be essential that you capture a more conversational, personal tone in speaking the dialog and in suggesting natural movement that might be appropriate for the character being portrayed. You should also try to "visualize" how your character will appear to the spectator and be selective in the integration of personal traits and mannerisms that enrich the character portrait. Assume a performance attitude that is concerned with *honesty* and speak directly to the collective hearts and souls of the spectators as you share the character with them for the first time.

from My Children! My Africa! (1990)

Athol Fugard

The popular author of this contemporary playscript occupies a unique position in South Africa. A white playwright who portrays the agony of South African society in bold, black strokes of injustice and persecution, Fugard has been criticized by some for dealing with themes or topics which might more properly be developed by native black writers. At the same time, he has also been ostracized by white South African society because of his sympathetic and positive treatment toward blacks. And while not all of Fugard's playscripts are concerned with racial conflict, they are almost always concerned with politics, education and the fragmentation of the family unit that results from an intolerant and repressive society.

The scene that follows explores the tragic consequences of the friendship of Isabel Dyson, a white high school student, and Thami Mbikwana, an African high school student, who discover the cynical reality of apartheid and their own limitations as individuals in a racist society while participating in a classroom assignment. At the urging of their teacher, Anela Myalatya, Isabel and Thami are paired in an inter-school debate competition but soon find themselves more engaged in resolving their own personal attraction to each other.

There is individual strength of will and the inherent ability of character to transcend the consequences of their plight and to achieve a measure of personal dignity in contemporary drama. In playing the contemporary roles it is important to portray heroic and exalted moments with courage and fierce determination while at the same time achieving a depiction of your character that is personal and yet profound.

What follows is the vivid image of despair and sorrow being experienced by each of the characters as they confront the sense of entrapment that surrounds them.

In playing the scene the characters should be treated with dignity and maturity as they search for logical ways to establish a meaningful, compassionate relationship between themselves and their restrictive environment. Each character should be practical and honest, permitting no theatrical deception to interfere with the realistic action being depicted. The key ingredients in the performance should be to portray both actions and thoughts with merciless clarity and impartiality; and to reject the convenient appeal to sentimentality. Remember that the most effective performance will be accurate, lifelike characters who do not distract from the playwright's dramatic effort to focus attention on the plight of blacks in white South African society that is repressive and to also depict the tragic nature of individual, personal relationships that are devastated by policies of apartheid.

CAST

THAMI

ISABEL

SCENE

Classroom of the Zolile High School in Camdebo, South Africa.

APPROACH

As the scene begins, Thami and Isabel meet again in the classroom where they had first engaged in a lively inter-school debate. There is a sense of disillusionment and despair in the circumstances that bring them together again because their favorite teacher, "Mr. M," has just been brutally killed by a mob outside the school after having been revealed as a police informant. The mood is tense and awkward as the two characters share confidences and discuss options now that South Africa has exploded into a country of revolution and racial distrust. It is astonishing to Thami and Isabel that their personal relationship has been damaged by apartheid and that even those who are sympathetic to black rights have been subject to violence and punishment. The one sign of hope obvious in both the playscript and in the scene that follows is the determination and courage with which Thami and Isabel resolve to liberate their homeland and free the future children of Africa!

313

1   **SCENE FOUR**

2

3   **THAMI:**   Isabel.

4   **ISABEL:**   *(It takes her a few seconds to respond.)* **Hello, Thami.**

5   **THAMI:**   **Thank you for coming.**

6   **ISABEL:**   *(She is tense. Talking to him is not easy.)* **I wasn't going to.**

7   **Let me tell you straight out that there is nothing in this**

8   **world . . . nothing! . . . that I want to see less at this moment**

9   **than anything or anybody from the location. But you said**

10   **in your note that it was urgent, so here I am. If you've got**

11   **something to say, I'll listen.**

12   **THAMI:**   **Are you in a hurry?**

13   **ISABEL:**   **I haven't got to be somewhere else, if that's what you**

14   **mean. But if you're asking because it looks as if I would like**

15   **to run away from here, from you! . . . very fast, then the**

16   **answer is yes. But don't worry, I'll be able to control that**

17   **urge for as long as you need to say what you want to.**

18   **THAMI:**   *(Awkward in the face of ISABEL's severe and unyielding*

19   *attitude)* **I just wanted to say good-bye.**

20   **ISABEL:**   **Again?**

21   **THAMI:**   **What do you mean?**

22   **ISABEL:**   **You've already done that, Thami. Maybe you didn't**

23   **use that word, but you turned your back on me and walked**

24   **out of my life that last afternoon the three of us . . .** *(She can't*

25   *finish.)* **How long ago was that?**

26   **THAMI:**   **Three weeks I think.**

27   **ISABEL:**   **So why do you want to do it again? Aren't you happy**

28   **with the last time? It was so dramatic, Thami.**

29   **THAMI:**   *(Patiently)* **I wanted to see you because I'm leaving the**

30   **town, I'm going away for good.**

31   **ISABEL:**   **Oh, I see. This is meant to be a "sad" good-bye is it?**

32   *(She is on the edge.)* **I'm sorry if I'm hurting your feelings but**

33   **I thought you wanted to see me because you had something**

34   **to say about recent events in our little community . . .** *(Out*

35   *of a pocket a crumpled little piece of newspaper which she opens with*

1   *unsteady hands)* **A certain unrest related ... I think that is**
2   **the phrase they use ... yes ... here it is ...** *(Reading)*
3   **"... unrest related incident in which according to witnesses**
4   **the defenseless teacher was attacked by a group of blacks**
5   **who struck him over the head with an iron rod before setting**
6   **him on fire."**
7   **THAMI: Stop it, Isabel.**
8   **ISABEL:** *(Fighting hard for self-control)* **Oh, Thami, I wish I could!**
9   **I've tried everything, but nothing helps. It just keeps going**
10 **around and around inside my head. I've tried crying. I've**
11 **tried praying! I've even tried confrontation. Ja, the day after**
12 **it happened I tried to get into the location. I wanted to find**
13 **the witness who reported it so accurately and ask: why**
14 **didn't you stop it! There was a police roadblock at the**
15 **entrance and they wouldn't let me in. They thought I was**
16 **crazy or something and "escorted" me back into the**
17 **safekeeping of two now very frightened parents.**
18 **There is nothing wrong with me! All I need is someone**
19 **to tell me why he was killed. What madness drove those**
20 **people to kill a man who had devoted his whole life to**
21 **helping them. He was such a good man, Thami! He was one**
22 **of the most beautiful human beings I have ever known and**
23 **his death is the ugliest thing I have ever known.**
24 **THAMI:** *(Gives her a few seconds to calm down. Gently)* **He was an**
25 **informer, Isabel. Somehow or the other somebody**
26 **discovered that Mr. M was an informer.**
27 **ISABEL: You mean that list of pupils taking part in the boycott?**
28 **You call that informing?**
29 **THAMI: No. It was worse than that. He went to the police and**
30 **gave them the names and addresses of our political action**
31 **committee. All of them were arrested after his visit. They**
32 **are now in detention.**
33 **ISABEL: Mr. M did that?**
34 **THAMI: Yes.**
35 **ISABEL: I don't believe it.**

1	THAMI:	It's true, Isabel.
2	ISABEL:	No! What proof do you have?
3	THAMI:	His own words. He told me so himself. I didn't believe it
4		either when he was first accused, but the last time I saw
5		him, he said it was true, that he had been to the police.
6	ISABEL:	*(Stunned disbelief)* Mr. M? A police spy? For how long?
7	THAMI:	No. It wasn't like that. He wasn't paid or anything. He
8		went to the police just that one time. He said he felt it was
9		his duty.
10	ISABEL:	What do you mean?
11	THAMI:	Operation Qhumisa . . . the boycotts and strikes, the
12		arson . . . you know he didn't agree with any of that. But he
13		was also very confused about it all. I think he wished he
14		had never done it.
15	ISABEL:	So he went to the police just once.
16	THAMI:	Yes.
17	ISABEL:	As a matter of conscience.
18	THAMI:	Yes.
19	ISABEL:	That doesn't make him an "informer," Thami!
20	THAMI:	Then what do you call somebody who gives information
21		to the police?
22	ISABEL:	No! You know what that word really means, the sort of
23		person it suggests. Was Mr. M one of those? He was acting
24		out of concern for his people . . . you said so yourself. He
25		thought he was doing the right thing! You don't murder a
26		man for that!
27	THAMI:	*(Near the end of his patience)* Be careful, Isabel.
28	ISABEL:	Of what?
29	THAMI:	The words you use.
30	ISABEL:	Oh? Which one don't you like? Murder? What do you
31		want me to call it . . . "an unrest related incident?" If you
32		are going to call him an informer, then I am going to call
33		his death murder!
34	THAMI:	It was an act of self-defense.
35	ISABEL:	By who?

316

1   **THAMI:**   **The People.**

2   **ISABEL:**   *(Almost speechless with outrage)* **What? A mad mob attacks**

3   **one unarmed defenseless man and you want me to call it . . .**

4   **THAMI:**   *(Abandoning all attempts at patience. He speaks with the full*

5   *authority of the anger inside him.)* **Stop it, Isabel! You just keep**

6   **quiet now and listen to me. You're always saying you want**

7   **to understand us and what it means to be black . . . well if**

8   **you do, listen to me carefully now. I don't call it murder,**

9   **and I don't call the people who did it a mob and yes, I do**

10   **expect you to see it as an act of self-defense . . . listen to**

11   **me! . . . blind and stupid but still self-defense.**

12   **He betrayed us and our fight for freedom. Five men**

13   **are in detention because of Mr. M's visit to the police station.**

14   **There have been other arrests and there will be more. Why**

15   **do you think I'm running away?**

16   **How were those people to know he wasn't a paid**

17   **informer who had been doing it for a long time and would**

18   **do it again? They were defending themselves against what**

19   **they thought was a terrible danger to themselves. What**

20   **Anela Myalatya did to them and their cause is what your**

21   **laws define as treason when it is done to you and threatens**

22   **the safety and security of your comfortable white world.**

23   **Anybody accused of it is put on trial in your courts and if**

24   **found guilty they get hanged. Many of my people have been**

25   **found guilty and have been hanged. Those hangings *we* call**

26   **murder!**

27   **Try to understand, Isabel. Try to imagine what it is**

28   **like to be a black person, choking inside with rage and**

29   **frustration, bitterness, and then to discover that one of your**

30   **own kind is a traitor, has betrayed you to those responsible**

31   **for the suffering and misery of your family, or your people.**

32   **What would you do? Remember there is no magistrate or**

33   **court you can drag him to and demand that he be tried for**

34   **that crime. There is no justice for black people in this**

35   **country other than what we make for ourselves. When you**

317

1   judge us for what happened in front of the school four days
2   ago just remember that you carry a share of the
3   responsibility for it. It is your laws that have made simple,
4   decent black people so desperate that they turn into "mad
5   mobs."
6   *(ISABEL has been listening and watching intently. It looks as if*
7   *she is going to say something but she stops herself.)*
8   THAMI: Say it, Isabel.
9   ISABEL: No.
10   THAMI: This is your last chance. You once challenged me to be
11   honest with you. I'm challenging you now.
12   ISABEL: *(She faces him.)* Where were you when it happened,
13   Thami? *(Pause)* And if you were there, did you try to stop them?
14   THAMI: Isn't there a third question, Isabel? Was I one of the
15   mob that killed him?
16   ISABEL: Yes. Forgive me, Thami ... please forgive me! But
17   there is that question as well. Only once! Believe me, only
18   once ... late at night when I couldn't sleep. I couldn't believe
19   it was there in my head, but I heard the words ... "Was
20   Thami one of the ones who did it?"
21   THAMI: If the police catch me, that's the question they will ask.
22   ISABEL: I'm asking you because ... *(An open, helpless gesture)* I'm
23   lost! I don't know what to think or feel anymore. Help me.
24   Please. You're the only one who can. Nobody else seems to
25   understand that I loved him. *(This final confrontation is steady*
26   *and unflinching on both sides.)*
27   THAMI: Yes, I was there. Yes, I did try to stop it. *(THAMI gives*
28   *ISABEL the time to deal with his answer.)* I knew how angry
29   the people were. I went to warn him. If he had listened to
30   me he would still be alive, but he wouldn't. It was almost as
31   if he wanted it to happen. I think he hated himself very
32   much for what he had done, Isabel. He kept saying to me
33   that it was all over. He was right. There was nothing left
34   for him. That visit to the police station had finished
35   everything. Nobody would have ever spoken to him again

318

1   or let him teach their children.

2 ISABEL: Oh, Thami, it is all so wrong! So stupid! That's what I

3   can't take . . . the terrible stupidity of it. We needed him. All

4   of us.

5 THAMI: I know.

6 ISABEL: Then why is he dead?

7 THAMI: You must stop asking these questions, Isabel. You know

8   the answers.

9 ISABEL: They don't make any sense, Thami.

10 THAMI: I know what you are feeling. *(Pause)* I also loved him.

11   Doesn't help much to say it now, I know, but I did. Because

12   he made me angry and impatient with his "old-fashioned"

13   ideas, I didn't want to admit it. Even if I had, it wouldn't

14   have stopped me from doing what I did, the boycott and

15   everything, but I should have tried harder to make him

16   understand why I was doing it. You were right to ask about

17   that. Now . . .? *(A helpless gesture)* You know the most terrible

18   words in your language, Isabel? Too late.

19 ISABEL: Ja.

20 THAMI: I'll never forgive myself for not trying harder with him

21   and letting him know . . . my true feelings for him. Right

22   until the end I tried to deny it . . . to him, to myself.

23 ISABEL: I'm sorry. I . . .

24 THAMI: That's all right.

25 ISABEL: Are the police really looking for you?

26 THAMI: Yes. Some of my friends have already been detained.

27   They're pulling in anybody they can get their hands on.

28 ISABEL: Where are you going? Cape Town?

29 THAMI: No. That's the first place they'll look. I've written to my

30   parents telling them about everything. I'm heading north.

31 ISABEL: To where?

32 THAMI: Far, Isabel. I'm leaving the country.

33 ISABEL: Does that mean what I think it does?

34 THAMI: *(Nods.)* I'm going to join the movement. I want to be a

35   fighter. I've been thinking about it for a long time. Now I

1   know it's the right thing to do. I don't want to end up being
2   one of the mob that killed Mr. M — but that will happen to
3   me if I stay here.
4 ISABEL: Oh, Thami.
5 THAMI: I know I'm doing the right thing. Believe me.
6 ISABEL: I'll try.
7 THAMI: And you?
8 ISABEL: I don't know what to do with myself, Thami. All I know
9   is that I'm frightened of losing him. He's only been dead
10   four days and I think I'm already starting to forget what he
11   looked like. But the worst thing is that there's nowhere for
12   me to go and . . . you know . . . just be near him. That's so
13   awful. I got my father to phone the police but they said there
14   wasn't enough left of him to justify a grave. What there was
15   had been disposed of in a "Christian manner." So where do
16   I go? The burnt-out ruins of the school? I couldn't face that.
17 THAMI: Get your father or somebody to drive you to the top of
18   the Wapadsberg Pass. It's on the road to Craddock.
19 ISABEL: I know it.
20 THAMI: It was a very special place to him. He told me that it
21   was there where it all started, where he knew what he
22   wanted to do with his life . . . being a teacher, being the Mr.
23   M we knew. You'll be near him up there. I must go now.
24 ISABEL: Do you need any money?
25 THAMI: No. Sala Kahuhle, Isabel. That's the Xhosa good-bye.
26 ISABEL: I know it. Asispumla taught me how to say it. Hamba
27   Kakhule, Thami. *(THAMI leaves.)*
28
29   **SCENE FIVE**
30
31 ISABEL: *(Alone, she stands quietly, examining the silence. After a few*
32   *seconds, she nods her head slowly.)* **Yes! Thami was right, Mr.**
33   **M. He said I'd feel near you up here.**
34   He's out there somewhere, Mr. M — traveling north.
35   He didn't say where exactly he was going, but I think we

1   can guess, can't we?

2   I'm here for a very "old-fashioned" reason, so I know

3   you'll approve. I've come to pay my last respects to Anela

4   Myalatya. I know the old-fashioned way of doing this is to

5   bring flowers, lay them on the grave, say a quiet prayer and

6   then go back to your life. But that seemed sort of silly this

7   time. You'll have enough flowers around here when the

8   spring comes . . . which it will. So instead I've brought you

9   something which I know will mean more to you than flowers

10   or prayers ever could. A promise. I am going to make Anela

11   Myalatya a promise.

12   You gave me a little lecture once about wasted

13   lives . . . how much of it you'd seen, how much you hated it,

14   how much you didn't want that to happen to Thami and me.

15   I sort of understood what you meant at the time. Now, I

16   most certainly do. Your death has seen to that.

17   My promise to you is that I am going to try as hard as

18   I can, in every way that I can, to see that it doesn't happen

19   to me. I am going to try my best to make my life useful in

20   the way yours was. I want you to be proud of me. After all,

21   I am one of your children you know. You did welcome me

22   to your family. *(A pause)* The future is still ours, Mr. M!

23

24

25

26

27

28

29

30

31

32

33

34

35

from **Dover Won't Get Out** (1992)

John Wooten

This contemporary farce is an extremely physical comedy that makes full use of the traditional stock devices of ridiculous posing, exaggeration, mechanical responses and "double takes" to achieve its hilarious comic effect. The characterizations are primarily one-dimensional — existing more as caricatures than as finely drawn character portraits — and there is a delicious mischief that reinforces the incredible events that unfold in this simple story of hailing a taxi and then being overwhelmed by the consequences that follow. There is also a rather delightful "touch of madness" present in each of the characters that only adds to the incisive commentary being voiced by the playwright in this particular scene.

Because contemporary scenes are more firmly rooted in the "here and now," the actor's performance approach should be more restrained and subtle to suggest a more conversational, personal tone. The actor may even slur syllables or swallow the endings of words to suggest everyday speech.

Farcical characters are fiercely vocal and physical in their responses and reactions to a situation and do not always behave normally in the predicament in which they find themselves. There is also an exaggeration of the physical characteristics or personality traits of characters in farce that provokes comic hilarity in the apparent incongruity between the situation and the character. It is this exaggeration that promotes the slapstick spirit of farce and helps to reduce the pretension of characters to its lowest common denominator. That is why it is essential that the actor isolate the incongruity of the character *and* the situation as the key to understanding the humor inherent in the scene.

In playing the scene that follows, pay careful attention to the primary elements of farce that may be used for comic invention. Within the bounds of good taste, there may be excessiveness in voice and body as you exaggerate the physical type of the character or have a pronounced vocal quality that helps to distinguish your character from the others in the scene. But a word of caution: Try not to make the exaggeration so obvious that it detracts from the characterization. There is still the need to be believable and to handle the comic situation in such a manner that it does not appear to become ludicrous. Perhaps the most difficult challenge in playing this scene is achieving that sense of theatricality in which the actor convinces the spectator that the actor, too, is enjoying his character's eccentricities and improbabilities. But this must be done genially, with a sense of good fun, so that there is still honesty and simplicity in the character portrait.

CAST

CAB DRIVER
MS. WELTS
OFFICER
DOVER

SCENE

Late, rainy afternoon on a busy Manhattan street.*

APPROACH

As the scene begins, Dover, a young man in his late twenties,

---

*The taxi should be suggested with two worn-out car seats. An actual car or frame should *not* be used. The business is mimed.

approaches a parked taxi, opens the door, gets in and sits quietly. There is tension and frustration in the atmosphere as Dover continually refuses to give the Cab Driver the location of his destination or to exit the taxi at the driver's request. Their initial attempts at communication are futile and there is an almost absurd, unreal quality to the situation as both Dover and the Cab Driver continue to argue over destination and destiny. The scene is complicated with the subsequent arrival of the Officer and Ms. Welts, who become embroiled in the confrontation and become active participants in the mayhem. None of the characters is at a loss for inspirational wit; and there is a sudden, ingenious conclusion that produces hilarity indeed!

1   MS. WELTS: *(To CAB DRIVER)* **Move your cab!**

2   CAB DRIVER: **Blow it out your ass!**

3   MS. WELTS: **I said MOVE IT!** *(MS. WELTS begins hitting the CAB*

4   *DRIVER with her umbrella. The CAB DRIVER reaches back and*

5   *they have a tug-of-war over the umbrella.)*

6   DOVER: **Oh, dear.**

7   OFFICER: **Hey!** *(He jumps in the front seat. The OFFICER leans*

8   *over the back seat and manages to take the umbrella away from*

9   *them.)* **Knock it off!**

10   CAB DRIVER and MS. WELTS: *(Simultaneously)* **I want him/her**

11   **arrested!**

12   OFFICER: **Shut up!** *(To DOVER)* **Look pal, you got people trying**

13   **to kill each other. Is that what you want?**

14   DOVER: **Of course not.**

15   OFFICER: **Then, I'm gonna ask you one more time. Will you**

16   **please, please get out of this cab?**

17   DOVER: **How about a compromise?**

18   OFFICER: **A compromise?**

19   DOVER: **Yes. I'm willing to compromise.**

20   OFFICER: **Sure. Anything.**

21   MS. WELTS: **Wait a minute. What kind of compromise?**

22   DOVER: **I need to get to the World Trade Center. If three of you**

23   **come with me to the World Trade Center, I will then get out**

24   **of the cab.**

25   OFFICER: **Fine.**

26   MS. WELTS: **Why do I have to come?**

27   DOVER: **Those are the conditions.**

28   OFFICER: **Would you relax, lady? Didn't you hear him? He said**

29   **he would get out of the cab.**

30   MS. WELTS: **If we all go on a little joy ride with him.**

31   OFFICER: **I'll have you back in twenty minutes. I promise.**

32   MS. WELTS: **I still don't understand why I have to go. I have**

33   **business to conduct here. I can't just drive off.**

34   DOVER: **Precisely. That's why you must come. One should**

35   **never feel that he or she is chained to anything. Especially**

325

1   work. It's not healthy.
2   MS. WELTS: What if I promise to take a long break?
3   DOVER: No, I'm sorry. I feel you are only saying that to appease
4   me.
5   MS. WELTS: Twenty minutes?
6   OFFICER: Tops. *(Short pause)*
7   MS. WELTS: Well, I have no choice. Do I? Let's get it over with.
8   And give me back my umbrella.
9   OFFICER: *(Handing it back)* **Thank you, Ms. Welts.** *(To CAB*
10   *DRIVER)* **Let's roll.**
11   CAB DRIVER: I'm not driving him anywhere. *(Long pause. All sit*
12   *frustrated.)*
13   OFFICER: *(Slowly)* **Look, Mac. You don't have to drive. OK? I'll**
14   drive. You can sit in protest. And you can say that you never
15   drove him anywhere. Please, I'm begging you. For the sake
16   of my children.
17   CAB DRIVER: All right. But someone's gotta pay for fare.
18   DOVER: I'll pay for fare.
19   CAB DRIVER: Except him.
20   MS. WELTS: Don't look at me.
21   OFFICER: Fine. I'll pay for fare.
22   MS. WELTS: Terrific. Can we pull away from the doors now?
23   DOVER: Oh, and by the way. In case someone was thinking of
24   running out at the first red light, I would just like to let that
25   someone know that I will once again refuse to get out of the
26   cab.
27   CAB DRIVER: And if he won't get out, then I pull in front of the
28   doors.
29   MS. WELTS: Of course.
30   DOVER: I'm sorry. I hate using blackmail. But under the
31   circumstances I feel I have no choice.
32   OFFICER: *(To CAB DRIVER)* **OK, get out and walk around. I'll**
33   slide over.
34   CAB DRIVER: You get out.
35   OFFICER: I don't trust you.

1   CAB DRIVER: I don't trust you, either.

2   OFFICER: Fine. We'll both slide over. *(Both men awkwardly work*

3   *themselves past one another to the opposite seat.)*

4   MS. WELTS: I should have stayed in Montana.

5   DOVER: Montana? Montana is beautiful this time of year.

6   MS. WELTS: They're having a blizzard.

7   DOVER: I know. Isn't it wonderful? I love snow. I spent last

8   winter at a retreat in Montana. I went for many walks in

9   the snow.

10   MS. WELTS: How special.

11   OFFICER: All set?

12   MS. WELTS: Yes. And hurry it up.

13   OFFICER: Believe me lady, I want this over just as much as you

14   do.

15   CAB DRIVER: Be careful. You wreck this thing, I get blamed.

16   OFFICER: Hey, relax, pal. Enjoy the view.

17   CAB DRIVER: I'm serious. This ain't a squad car, you know.

18   DOVER: Try to relax, Vince.

19   CAB DRIVER: I'll relax when you're outta my cab.

20   MS. WELTS: Then shut up so we can leave.

21   DOVER: *(To VINCE)* Why isn't your I.D. posted?

22   CAB DRIVER: Huh?

23   OFFICER: Your picture and license number. You're required by

24   law to have it posted here.

25   CAB DRIVER: It's under the seat. It keeps falling down.

26   OFFICER: Let me see it.

27   CAB DRIVER: No.

28   OFFICER: What do you mean, no? Let me see it.

29   CAB DRIVER: Come on, let's go to the World Trade Center.

30   DOVER: Are you hiding something from us, Vince?

31   MS. WELTS: Oh, God. He's probably a criminal or something.

32   He probably stole the cab.

33   DOVER: I don't think so.

34   OFFICER: Look, either you show me or I will take you in. You

35   can't sue me either, no matter what Doker says.

1   **DOVER:**   Dover.

2   **CAB DRIVER:**   **Fine! You want to see it? Here, see it!** *(Pulls it up*

3   *from under seat.)*

4   **OFFICER:**   *(Glances at I.D.)* **Roland? His name isn't Vince. It's**

5   **Roland. Roland Dudsicki.** *(Laughs.)*

6   **MS. WELTS:**   **Roland Dudsicki? That's worse than Dover.** *(Joins*

7   *the laughter.)*

8   **DOVER:**   **Now. Now, stop it. STOP IT!** *(Everyone stops, shocked that*

9   *DOVER raised his voice.)* **I think Roland is a nice name. It**

10   **suits you. You shouldn't be embarrassed. You should be**

11   **proud. You should stand up to these people and say I'm**

12   **happy to be named Roland Dudsicki.**

13   **CAB DRIVER:**   **I hate Roland. Just call me Vince, OK?**

14   **DOVER:**   **That's not your name. You're avoiding the problem.**

15   *(To OFFICER and MS. WELTS in a low voice)* **You should be**

16   **ashamed of yourselves.**

17   **OFFICER:**   **Sorry, Mac. I didn't mean to laugh at your name.**

18   *(Gives back the tag.)*

19   **CAB DRIVER:**   **Forget it.**

20   **OFFICER:**   **What's your middle name? I know a lot of guys who**

21   **go by their middle name.**

22   **CAB DRIVER:**   **Rafael.**

23   **OFFICER:**   **Vince is good.**

24   **DOVER:**   **Rafael? Rafael is a beautiful name. Rafael was the**

25   **name of a very famous painter, you know. Would you prefer**

26   **I call you that?**

27   **MS. WELTS:**   **Look, all this male bonding is very moving but the**

28   **deal was we'd drive to the World Trade Center. Not to sit**

29   **in a parked cab discussing what to call the cabby.**

30   **CAB DRIVER:**   **Yeah, let's go already.**

31   **DOVER:**   *(To OFFICER, exuberantly)* **Proceed!** *(The OFFICER mimes*

32   *putting the cab in gear and begins driving.)*

33   **MS. WELTS:**   *(Looking behind her)* **Thank God.**

34   **DOVER:**   **Now, this isn't so bad, is it? It doesn't hurt to be**

35   **pleasant, you know.**

1   MS. WELTS: I find myself reminded of those long Sunday drives
2   with my father and my two older brothers.
3   DOVER: Oh?
4   MS. WELTS: And how violently car sick I eventually became.
5   DOVER: That's horrible.
6   MS. WELTS: Just by the sight of the car.
7   DOVER: Oh, my.
8   MS. WELTS: This is almost as stimulating.
9   OFFICER: Oh, come on. For Christ's sake, this is all gonna be
10   over soon. We might as well make this as painless as possible.
11   DOVER: That's the spirit.
12   OFFICER: So, Vince?
13   CAB DRIVER: What?
14   OFFICER: Tell me something about yourself.
15   CAB DRIVER: Like what?
16   OFFICER: I don't know. You married?
17   CAB DRIVER: Why?
18   OFFICER: Why not?
19   CAB DRIVER: Yeah, I'm married.
20   OFFICER: Kids?
21   CAB DRIVER: Nope.
22   DOVER: Why? You'd make a great father, Rafael.
23   CAB DRIVER: Think so?
24   DOVER: Yes, I do.
25   CAB DRIVER: Well, the little woman has always been kind of
26   hesitant about kids.
27   MS. WELTS: The little woman? How cute.
28   DOVER: Any siblings?
29   CAB DRIVER: What?
30   OFFICER: Brothers and sisters.
31   MS. WELTS: Oh, you know. DaVinci, Van Gogh, Picasso. *(All
32   glare at MS. WELTS.)* Sorry.
33   DOVER: How about you?
34   MS. WELTS: How about me what?
35   DOVER: Are you married?

329

1   MS. WELTS: Are you kidding?

2   DOVER: I'm perfectly serious.

3   MS. WELTS: Now don't get me wrong. I've always yearned to be
4   called the "little woman." I've just never met a man that
5   eventually didn't make me feel at least mildly disgusted with
6   the male sex.

7   CAB DRIVER: Or at least car sick. *(CAB DRIVER and OFFICER*
8   *laugh.)*

9   MS. WELTS: Present company included.

10   DOVER: Ms. Welts, there are many worthwhile people out
11   there. Unfortunately, in an area like New York City it is
12   often difficult to meet the right person. Work often overtakes
13   your life and as a result people can seem like little more
14   than obstacles to success. Ironically, the more congested an
15   area is, the less likely it is to meet someone of real interest.
16   The phrase "less is more" is very applicable in your case.

17   CAB DRIVER: Here we go again.

18   DOVER: I suggest you consider moving back to Montana. It's
19   amazing what a little peace and quiet can do for the soul. I
20   mean, I realize, of course, that the hustle and bustle of the
21   big city can be very stimulating. Though in your case I feel
22   returning to your roots may be your best option. In fact, all
23   three of you should consider going on retreat in Montana.
24   I learned a number of things during my brief stay there. It's
25   really quite wonderful when you take time to rediscover
26   yourself. You feel better about yourself and as a result are
27   more able to understand and help those around you.

28   MS. WELTS: Just who are you anyway?

29   CAB DRIVER: Don't ask that.

30   DOVER: I told you my name is Dover.

31   OFFICER: Why are we taking you to the World Trade Center?

32   CAB DRIVER: *(With a smile)* He works there.

33   DOVER: Thank you, Rafael.

34   CAB DRIVER: He left his portfolio at the office. He's doing a
35   proposal in D.C.

1   OFFICER: You work in the World Trade Center?

2   DOVER: That's right.

3   MS. WELTS: I find that hard to believe.

4   OFFICER: I don't. I directed traffic over there a couple of times.

5   You wouldn't believe the kind of nut cases that go in that

6   place.

7   DOVER: Really? You worked at the World Trade Center?

8   OFFICER: I worked out in front of the World Trade Center. I

9   never actually set foot in the place.

10   DOVER: I'm surprised I never noticed you. I'm usually very

11   perceptive about my everyday surroundings.

12   OFFICER: Hey, it's a big town, Mac. I never noticed you either.

13   DOVER: Shame. We quite possibly could have walked right past

14   one another.

15   OFFICER: It's mind-boggling.

16   DOVER: It is. And you, Ms. Welts?

17   MS. WELTS: What?

18   DOVER: Have you ever been to the World Trade Center?

19   MS. WELTS: Of course I have.

20   DOVER: How would you like to be in charge of that building?

21   MS. WELTS: The World Trade Center? No, thanks. I have enough

22   trouble with the one I manage now. Today's adventure will

23   just add to it.

24   OFFICER: What's it like being in charge of so many people?

25   MS. WELTS: Well, I'm not actually in charge of the people, only

26   the building they work in.

27   OFFICER: Oh.

28   MS. WELTS: Why?

29   OFFICER: I don't know. You don't look like the manager type.

30   MS. WELTS: Why, because I'm a woman?

31   OFFICER: No.

32   MS. WELTS: Well?

33   OFFICER: I didn't mean it in a bad way. I . . .

34   MS. WELTS: Yes?

35   DOVER: I think what the officer meant to say is that you have a

1   very straightforward and natural way of expressing
2   yourself. Part of the problem with Corporate America is
3   people with status are often weak and lack the ability to
4   get their points across effectively. A character trait you have
5   obviously mastered. You are a rare find, Ms. Welts.
6 OFFICER: I couldn't have said it better.
7 MS. WELTS: Well, I do have to admit that my building received
8   one of the highest overall efficiency ratings in the district.
9 DOVER: Congratulations! That's wonderful, Ms. Welts.
10 MS. WELTS: Thank you.
11 DOVER: You're quite welcome.
12 OFFICER: Yeah, congrats. *(Pause)*
13 DOVER: Now isn't this nice. The atmosphere in this cab is much
14   more calm and relaxed than it was when we left. Much more
15   positive.
16 OFFICER: We're coming up on the Center.
17 DOVER: Splendid.
18 MS. WELTS: You mean this is almost over?
19 OFFICER: I told you it would be quick.
20 MS. WELTS: Bless you.
21 DOVER: Before I leave, I'd like to take the opportunity to tell
22   you that I see through those hard shells you hide yourselves
23   in. You three possess a wealth of sensitivity and
24   creativeness. Each one of you has tremendous potential. It
25   is very important for you to remember that. Ms. Welts, with
26   you at the helm, I would not be surprised if your building
27   maintains that efficiency rating for many glorious years to
28   come.
29 CAB DRIVER: *(Under his breath)* It's only because they're all
30   cheap.
31 DOVER: Pardon? I'm sorry, did you say something, Rafael?
32 CAB DRIVER: I said everyone in that building is cheap. Some of
33   the worst tips I ever got were from people that came out of
34   that building. I avoid that block like the plague.
35 MS. WELTS: Well, you certainly returned in grand fashion,

1   didn't you?
2 CAB DRIVER: What's that supposed to mean?
3 OFFICER: We're here. *(Stops the cab.)*
4 MS. WELTS: It means you're a Mongoloid.
5 CAB DRIVER: Oh, does it?
6 MS. WELTS: Yes, ROLAND!
7 CAB DRIVER: You know you look familiar. Yeah, now I
8 remember. The cheapest customer I ever had come out of
9 that building. Not only didn't she tip, but she got stuck trying
10 to get out of the back seat.
11 DOVER: Oh, dear.
12 MS. WELTS: What are you implying?
13 CAB DRIVER: I'm implying you're a farm animal.
14 MS. WELTS: Oh, that's it! *(She raises the umbrella to strike the CAB*
15 *DRIVER, but the OFFICER reaches back and snatches the umbrella*
16 *from her.)*
17 OFFICER: Hey! Enough with the umbrella! Now we're here.
18 Let's all get out and forget this ever happened. *(Starts to get*
19 *out.)*
20 CAB DRIVER: Somebody owes me cab fare!
21 OFFICER: Fat chance, Fatso!
22 MS. WELTS: Give me back my umbrella.
23 OFFICER: *(From out of cab)* I'll give it back when you get out.
24 MS. WELTS: I'm not getting out until Roland Ralpho Dudsicki
25 apologizes. Your mother really hated you, didn't she?
26 CAB DRIVER: *(To MS. WELTS)* GET OUT OF MY CAB!
27 MS. WELTS: I can't. Remember? Mooo!
28 DOVER: Oh, my. *(OFFICER gets back into the driver's seat.)*
29 OFFICER: Listen, I've had it with all three of you. If everyone
30 isn't out of this cab in ten seconds, you're all going
31 downtown!
32 MS. WELTS: Oh, don't start your pathetic macho bullshit again.
33 You couldn't arrest a drunk invalid.
34 OFFICER: Lady, don't push me. I never hit a woman before, but
35 I'm damn close.

333

1   **MS. WELTS:**   That's because you didn't want to get beat up!
2   *(Unnoticed, DOVER opens his door and quietly gets out of the cab.)*
3   **OFFICER:**   Oh, yeah!
4   **MS. WELTS:**   Oh, yeah!
5   **CAB DRIVER:**   You got a billie club, use it.
6   **OFFICER:**   Shut up!
7   **CAB DRIVER:**   You shut up, you cheap dwarf. *(DOVER heads for*
8   *another cab.)*
9   **MS. WELTS:**   Give me back my umbrella!
10   **OFFICER:**   No!
11   **MS. WELTS:**   I said GIVE IT TO ME! *(MS. WELTS reaches over the*
12   *seat and grabs the umbrella. The three begin a massive fight over*
13   *it as . . .)*
14   **DOVER:**   *(Waving)* **TAXI . . . TAXI!** *(MS. WELTS, OFFICER and CAB*
15   *DRIVER stop fighting abruptly and stare off at the exiting DOVER,*
16   *completely dumbfounded.)*
17   *(Blackout)*
18
19
20
21
22
23
24
25
26
27
28
29
30
31
32
33
34
35

Costumes in the contemporary theatre have a more profound suggestion of character definition because they reflect the initial clues to a character's mood, attitude, self-image or social status. Costumes may also reflect the character's idiosyncrasies or serve as a record of the character's lifestyle.

from **And the Rain Came to Mayfield** (1990)

Jason Milligan

As one of the most recent playscripts to detail the role of "equality" in contemporary society, this drama focuses upon the unconventional and chance relationship of a young black man and an equally young white man who each seek their own independence in a troubled social climate in the 1960s in Mississippi. The young men become painfully aware of their own inadequacy and sense of disillusionment

335

through a series of conversations in a gas station/luncheonette off the state highway near the fictional town of Mayfield early in the fall of 1962. There is an atmosphere of frustration and despair that hangs over both of the characters as they each seek to realize personal goals and dreams that are at odds with the social upheaval of the times.

The simple plot revolves around Nathan, a black college student who seeks refuge from the rain in a country store, and Carl, a white teenager whose life apparently has no sense of direction until he befriends Nathan against the wishes of his parents. Both young men seek refuge from the prejudiced, violent outside world in the comforting confessions they make to each other and in the dreams of a better world they hope for in the future. Against a cold, uncaring and suspicious backdrop of mistrust the young men form a bond that is protective and understanding — even if it is only for the brief time they exchange conversation while waiting for the next bus out of town.

In playing the scene that follows, the actors should pay careful attention to the fierce intellectual and emotional struggle taking place within the characters as they confront their own prejudices and social mores that have helped to shape their distrust and suspicion of one another. There is also a great sorrow and despair inherent in each of the characters as they realize that their immediate friendship and youthful comradeship is only fleeting in the arid climate of racial injustice that represents their present-day society. The fresh insights they bring to the relationship, however, help to dispel the fears and frustrations based on outward appearance and lead each character to peer beneath the surface of their relationship for a glimpse at the singular nature of man's spirit and soul. And while each character exits the scene into a world of uncertainty and turmoil, the uncommon expectancy of having met a true friend helps to shape and to guide the characters in their quest to free themselves and others from the prison of prejudice and self-doubt.

There should also be a suggestion in the scene that the two young men are, after all, not so different from each other in either attitude or intellect. They share similar points of view and may even assume similar gestures or facial expressions. To protect his individuality and sense of independence, each character initially plays "word games" with the other and takes care not to allow any intrusion into matters that are personal or private. At the conclusion of the scene there is a sense of urgency and plaintive need that leads the characters to share confidences and engage in intimate reflections on human nature and the meaning of life.

336

CAST

NATHAN

CARL

SCENE

A gas station/luncheonette off the state highway in Mayfield, Mississippi. It is a warm day in late Fall, 1962.

APPROACH

Carl, a young man of 19, enters wearing jeans and a madras shirt. He is the son of the owners of the gas station/luncheonette and is a restless soul trapped in the backwoods town of a hot, humid Mississippi dirt town. As the rain begins to pelt the tin roof of the luncheonette, Nathan enters. He is well-dressed and carries two suitcases with him. The rain continues to fall as each boy sits, almost in unison, across the room from the other. After some awkward moments in which it is evident that Carl has never seen a black man — especially a well-educated one — this closely and that Nathan is just as anxious to leave as to be sitting in this white environment the two young men exchange awkward smiles. Slowly they begin to share confidences and Nathan reveals that he is the "notorious" young man whose admission to Northern Mississippi University caused the recent riots and violence in the nearby community.

1   CARL: You know what I could use right now?

2   NATHAN: What?

3   CARL: A pizza . . .

4   NATHAN: *(Laughing)* A pizza?

5   CARL: Yeah, you know. Pizza pie. Wouldn't that be good?

6   NATHAN: Why you got all this *food* on your mind all of a sudden?

7   CARL: I dunno. But wouldn't that be good, though?

8   NATHAN: Yeah. It would be . . .

9   CARL: What's your favorite kind of pizza?

10   NATHAN: I don't know.

11   CARL: I like hamburger and onion.

12   NATHAN: Hamburger and onion?

13   CARL: Yeah. How 'bout you?

14   NATHAN: I dunno.

15   CARL: C'mon. What's your favorite? *(NATHAN almost shrugs*

16   *CARL off again. Then, bursting out with a laugh)*

17   NATHAN: Pepperoni! *(They both laugh at this, an innocent, exuberant*

18   *sense of simple pleasure.)*

19   CARL: They got pizza places at where you went to school?

20   NATHAN: Yeah.

21   CARL: You ever go to any of 'em?

22   NATHAN: *(Simply, his laughter dying)* No —

23   CARL: *(Not sensing the change in NATHAN)* I would! Boy, if I was

24   up there? Account of, you can't get anything like that in this

25   town! I remember, one time my Daddy took me to Mount

26   Bayou with him to buy all these tables you see here. We

27   drove down there, loaded 'em all up in this pickup truck he

28   borrowed from somebody, and while we were there, he took

29   me to this place that made pizza pies. Every kind you could

30   think of! And my Daddy and me sat there and ate us a deluxe

31   pizza pie with hamburger and onion and I think that was

32   one a the best times I ever had. I been wantin' another one

33   a those pizza pies ever since that time. *(Laughs.)* Funny, isn't

34   it? Isn't that funny?

35   NATHAN: Then go get you one.

1	CARL: I can't! See, there ain't a single pizza place in this whole
2	entire town! Only three different places to eat around here
3	and you're *in* one of 'em. You don't know what it's like, not
4	to be able to get a durn pizza when you want one.
5	NATHAN: I'm afraid I know exactly what you mean. *(NATHAN*
6	*goes back to his book. CARL senses a darker mood but tries to buoy*
7	*NATHAN up again.)*
8	CARL: Hey. Tell me what it was like at NMU.
9	NATHAN: Maybe . . . maybe we just shouldn't get into it all.
10	CARL: Why not?
11	NATHAN: I just don't think it's a good idea!
12	CARL: C'mon.
13	NATHAN: No.
14	CARL: Please?
15	NATHAN: Why do you wanna *know* so bad?
16	CARL: Cause! I been, like, *aching* inside to know what it's like
17	outside a here! Come on. Just tell me a little bit about what
18	happened up there. I really wanna hear.
19	*(Long pause. NATHAN sees that CARL is really sincere about this.*
20	*Silence. CARL digs through his pile of brochures, produces one.*
21	*Holds it out for NATHAN to see.)*
22	CARL: C'mon. Please. Show me where you stayed.
23	NATHAN: Stayed —?
24	CARL: Yeah. You know. Don't they have dorms on campus and
25	all? Wait. There's a map here someplace . . . *(He finds it.)* **Here.**
26	*(NATHAN leans over, examines the map.)* **Just show me. Where'd**
27	you have classes? Where'd you stay? You know. *(NATHAN*
28	*considers.)*
29	NATHAN: Well . . . I went to class here and here.
30	CARL: *(Studying the map)* Uh-huh . . .
31	NATHAN: My dorm room was . . . right here. *(Reflective. NATHAN*
32	*thinks about things for a moment, then continues, very simply and*
33	*honestly.)* I really tried to make things *work*, y'know? I *really*
34	did. But no matter what I did, nobody ever gave me a chance.
35	If I smiled, they threw rocks, if I cussed, they threw rocks —

1   I just couldn't seem to get on top of things, no matter what!

2   CARL: Why is it that way, you think?

3   NATHAN: I dunno. *(Pause)* But I stepped off that bus and I knew

4   right away that it wasn't gonna be at *all* like it looked in

5   them brochures!

6   CARL: It looks *perfect* in there.

7   NATHAN: Well, it ain't perfect. But maybe for you, it'd be better

8   than what I had. I just couldn't take it no more.

9   CARL: What ... what do you mean?

10   NATHAN: I just couldn't.

11   CARL: So, I mean, what do you mean, what'd you *do*?

12   NATHAN: Do?

13   CARL: Yeah.

14   NATHAN: I quit.

15   CARL: You — what?

16   NATHAN: Just walked outta there, this morning! I left

17   Philosophy, got in that car, and I'm gone! And you know

18   what? I feel great! We drove away from that place and I felt

19   the best I've felt in a long, long time!

20   CARL: So ... how long were you there?

21   NATHAN: A month.

22   CARL: And you — you just *left*?

23   NATHAN: Damn right.

24   CARL: Well, do they know?

25   NATHAN: Does it matter?

26   CARL: What, you mean you just gave up?

27   NATHAN: Look, I *tried*, you know? I really tried to stick it out! I

28   thought things'd gradually get better; they just kept gettin'

29   worse!

30   CARL: Oh, yeah. A month. That's really trying.

31   NATHAN: Look — I just couldn't stand being a punching bag no

32   more!

33   CARL: But if it's what you *wanted* —?

34   NATHAN: It's *not* what I wanted! Man, you can't understand!

35   There is no way you can understand —

1   CARL: No, you're right! You're right, I can't understand! You
2   had a *chance* —
3   NATHAN: I had nothing! They didn't give me a chance!
4   CARL: Not everybody gets that chance!
5   NATHAN: I didn't ask for it.
6   CARL: Then why'd you even bother to *go* in the first place?
7   NATHAN: You wanna know everything? What do you wanna
8   know, huh? OK! My uncle's a lawyer up North. Detroit. He
9   got to talking to my father and they thought it'd be a great
10   idea to file this civil suit; it went to one court and then
11   another court and then another and before I knew it, my
12   father comes home and tells me I'm *accepted*! I went up
13   there. I enrolled. People beat me up. People threatened to
14   kill me. People *tried* to kill me. I had to have police walk
15   with me wherever I went. I had to have police outside when
16   I went to sleep at night! I had to have police stand outside
17   the bathroom door whenever I took a shit! I'm the first black
18   man to get into Northern Mississippi University! Great!
19   CARL: But you made history!
20   NATHAN: I didn't ask to! I never asked to!
21   CARL: Then why'd you even *go* in the first place?
22   NATHAN: I told you!
23   CARL: *Why?*
24   NATHAN: Because! My *father* made me! *(CARL stumbles on this.)*
25   CARL: What . . . ?
26   NATHAN: He kept telling me, you gotta have this! You gotta!
27   He kept right on saying it until I believed it myself. *He*
28   couldn't have it and he was damned if he couldn't cram it
29   down my throat! So I could be his *trophy!* So he could strut
30   all around and say, "Look what my son did. Look what he
31   did." Man, all I *want* right now is to go back home and marry
32   my girlfriend. That's all I want!
33   CARL: What — what about *college?*
34   NATHAN: Yeah, I wanna go to college, man, but at home, y' know,
35   with *her*. Now, maybe that's *wrong*, maybe I should want

1   more, maybe I *should* wanna be the first black man to get
2   into a white school — but I don't!
3   **CARL:** Did you tell him that?
4   **NATHAN:** Are you *kidding* me? Till my *head* was pounding! I'll
5   tell you something: I am *not* lyin' down for him no more! I
6   am goin' back home and I'm tellin' him what *I* want, once
7   and for all!
8   **CARL:** Wait a minute, you mean, you did *all* this because your
9   *father* —? *(Long, long pause. It sinks in.)*
10 **NATHAN:** Yes. *(Another long pause. CARL assesses the situation.)*
11 **CARL:** *(Sincerely, humbly)* I know what you feel.
12 **NATHAN:** You don't know.
13 **CARL:** Hey. *(NATHAN looks at him.)* I know. *(Their eyes meet,*
14   *NATHAN seeing the urgent truth in CARL's. The pause holds . . .)*
15   You're doing the right thing.
16   *(They keep looking at each other. CARL holds out his hand, offering*
17   *the candy bar. NATHAN looks at it, looks at CARL. They both*
18   *smile. NATHAN takes the candy.)*
19 **NATHAN:** Thank you.
20   *(The bell rings. CARL gets his coat and goes outside to the arriving*
21   *"car," calmly, slowly, with a new confidence. NATHAN sits alone,*
22   *starts to unwrap the candy.)*
23
24
25
26
27
28
29
30
31
32
33
34
35

from **The Author's Voice** (1987)

Richard Greenberg

"A demon lives with me!"

Here is a fascinating excursion into the realm of fantasy and contemporary fiction that provides an imaginative, artistic interpretation of the author's world of uncertainty and uncommon expectancy at work in those abstract concepts related to man's spirit and soul. In expressing the abstract to help visualize all the fundamental truths that are found within man, the playwright makes very creative use of situation, character and plot to help capture a vision of man's spirit imprisoned by deceit and falsehood. In translating this vision to the stage, the playwright appears to cruelly expose man's basic nature and conscience in a distorted, grotesque outward appearance and in the fragmented setting described to encourage the "subconscious" of each tormented character to emerge. There is also intense concentration upon the nuance and nonsense of each character's dreams and desires to achieve a meaningful reality.

Props in contemporary theatre practice help to establish character relationships or to reinforce individual character attributes in terms of self-image. The use of props may also serve as an extension of the character or serve to identify the character more directly to the audience.

343

The rather unique plot revolves around the failed writer Todd, a young and handsome author who aspires to be a first-rate novelist in spite of his apparent lack of artistic talent. With intelligence and inventiveness, Todd schemes to achieve his dream of artistic success when he has a chance encounter with the disfigured creature Gene, a haunted gnome who is discovered late one night in an alley starving and crying aloud while he is fiercely clutching a manuscript. Later, after Todd has taken Gene to his "strangely shadowed" apartment and provided refuge for him, he takes the manuscript to a party and promptly sells it to an agent as his own work. What follows is the sad and sorrowful imprisonment of Gene, who is tormented and coerced into writing assignments that Todd subsequently claims credit for having written.

Against this backdrop of deception, the play explores the personal relationship of Todd and Gene in terms of their own special needs and dependencies as well as in their nightmare and nonsense dreams and desires that promote their own survival in the arid climate of present-day society. There is also a deliberate attempt to provoke thoughtful analysis and self-discovery as the characters engage in contradiction and confusion as part of revealing their truthful selves. That is why the performance elements are directed toward focusing attention on the chaos inherent in a society that cannot communicate effectively; and considerable emphasis is placed upon the visualization of the subconscious mind by juxtaposing the rather familiar and the apparently strange to provoke the spectator to reason and to think.

In playing the scenes that follow, the actors should seek to convey the sense of isolation and alienation that man experiences when he is separated from himself and from the world at large. A good performance approach is to approach the selected scenes as if they were a distorted series of reflections in a mirror that prove to be an illusion. This would be an especially effective performance approach to help visualize the scene in which Todd's literary agent, Portia, attempts to seduce him while Gene is hidden in his dark space but punctuates the episode with animalistic grunts and groans that interrupt the seduction and delay the conquest. The actors should also pay attention to character portrait and not unduly exaggerate the grotesque physical or vocal dimensions of Gene in contrast to the rather realistic, normal appearances of both Todd and Portia. In translating the scenes into performance you are encouraged to be as imaginative as the playscript suggests but as simplistic as possible in establishing meaningful relationships between the characters and their environment as well as in their personal anguish, frustration and guilt.

CAST

TODD

GENE*

PORTIA

SCENE

Todd's apartment. Strangely shadowed. A door in the back wall. A bed obliquely angled into the room. Two chairs and a table — both dark wood.

APPROACH

In the scenes that follow there is an "unmasking" that takes place as the sequence of events reveals the true nature of Todd and the quiet desperation of Gene as he gains a measure of revenge by observing the premature and pathetic seduction farce of Portia and is also instrumental in the ironic ending of the masquerade that Todd has promoted as an author. The sequence of scenes should be played with restraint and there should be subtle exchanges that balance the more blatant, physical demands of the performers. It should be obvious to the spectator in the scenes that follow that Todd is slowly losing his authority and approaching physical collapse while at the same time Gene is subject to fits of irrational behavior and yet still capable of a calm temperament that allows him to achieve his strategic goal. The final irony of the concluding scene when Gene reveals to Todd that he has plagiarized the writing assignments he was forced to author should be performed to suggest the poetic justice inherent in Gene's fateful revenge.

*In folklore the gnomes were small, misshapen dwarfs who dwelled in the bowels of the earth to guard its treasures and were capable of wise and pithy aphorisms or proverbs.

1   **SCENE SIX**
2

3   *(TODD and GENE. TODD dressing for the evening.)*
4   **GENE:**   The scene must be played beautifully.
5   **TODD:**   I don't know if I can do this.
6   **GENE:**   You don't have a choice. I'll stop writing if you don't. I'll
7   go back to the streets, find another benefactor. Or die, I
8   don't care which.
9   **TODD:**   All right. But what do I say? It's been a long time . . .
10 **GENE:**   I'll write the scene for you. You simply play it out.
11 **TODD:**   Jesus.
12 **GENE:**   You come up behind Portia . . .
13 **TODD:**   Yes . . .
14 **GENE:**   Fling an arm across her chest . . .
15 **TODD:**   That's melodramatic . . .
16 **GENE:**   *You fling an arm across her chest* . . .
17 **TODD:**   Yes, yes, all right, fine . . .
18 **GENE:**   And you say, "Darling, I want you."
19 **TODD:**   I say what?
20 **GENE:**   "Darling, I want you."
21 **TODD:**   I don't say that.
22 **GENE:**   You do.
23 **TODD:**   She'd laugh in my face.
24 **GENE:**   Never.
25 **TODD:**   You're insane.
26 **GENE:**   *(Insistently)* "Darling, I want you."
27 **TODD:**   The only words I could possibly get away with in that
28   whole sentence are "I" and "you."
29 **GENE:**   You will say this! You will say, "Darling, I want you."
30   She will be moved by the poetic simplicity of your
31   expression.
32 **TODD:**   Fine.
33 **GENE:**   Then — you will turn her towards you, kiss each
34   shoulder, her neck, then rise ever so slowly till your lips
35   meet hers. You will kiss her, and say, "Be mine." *(TODD*

1   *looks at him skeptically.)* **Then . . .**
2   TODD: Wait a minute . . .
3   GENE: What?
4   TODD: That won't work.
5   GENE: It will work like a *dream* . . .
6   TODD: Trust me on this . . .
7   GENE: Like a *dream* . . .
8   TODD: She will be out of here in fourteen seconds flat.
9   GENE: Nonsense.
10 TODD: I promise you.
11 GENE: Nonsense.
12 TODD: I *promise* you.
13 GENE: What would you say — what *do* you say, then, in
14   circumstances like these? There's a woman, there's a bed,
15   you're alone, you're enchanted, what do you say?
16 TODD: Do you want to sleep with me?
17 GENE: A-A-A-R-G-H!
18 TODD: I'm sorry.
19 GENE: You don't understand.
20 TODD: I do . . .
21 GENE: You don't understand the situation.
22 TODD: Inform me.
23 GENE: You are *enraptured.* You are . . . *transported.* This is no
24   common *lay.* This is no cheap *one-nighter.* The finest fibers
25   of your being quiver in expectancy. Poetry floods your soul.
26   "Do you want to sleep with me?" simply will not suffice, not
27   this night. What do you say, then? When all the beauty of
28   the universe churns inside you. *(TODD thinks.)*
29 TODD: Are you staying?
30 GENE: A-A-A-R-G-H!
31 TODD: Gene . . .
32 GENE: A-A-A-R-G-H!
33 TODD: Gene . . .
34 GENE: The world *requires* me . . .
35 TODD: Gene . . .

1 GENE: ... to rewrite its wretched *dialog!*

2 TODD: Gene ...

3 GENE: You will make it beautiful. You will proceed as I describe.
4 You will *say,* "Darling, I want you." You will say, "Be mine,"
5 you will be tender and slow and romantic. You will *make it*
6 *work.*

7 TODD: Not a word from you.

8 GENE: ... I know.

9 TODD: Not a peep.

10 GENE: I promise.

11 TODD: For your own good as well as mine. You know I act for
12 both of us, don't you? You know I want the best for both of us?

13 GENE: ... Yes.

14 TODD: I'll be back soon. *(He exits. GENE looks after him, waits until*
15 *he's sure he's gone. Then he approaches TODD's bed. He touches it*
16 *carefully.)*

17 GENE: Todd ...? *(GENE runs his hands across the bed, feeling the*
18 *smooth, silky textures.)* Todd ... it wouldn't be bad if she saw
19 me. Not so bad. *(He climbs onto the bed.)* Often beautiful women
20 come upon hideous men and love them. They uncover an
21 inner beauty, oh, and crowns of light weave into canopies
22 over their heads and the carbuncles and the cicatrices, the
23 humps and wens miraculously disappear. The beasts are
24 replaced by angels. She'll see me, Todd, she'll see. And you'll
25 be loved for me.

26

27 **SCENE SEVEN**

28

29 *(TODD's room in half-light — a golden shaft spilled across the floor.*
30 *TODD and PORTIA enter. The picture they make in this light is*
31 *burnished and lovely. Lights come up slightly fuller.)*

32 PORTIA: You were brilliant tonight. You didn't even have to
33 *speak* is how brilliant you were. I loved when we went to
34 that place with the flashing lights and your face came
35 floating up at me in patches, it was poetry, truly poetry. I

348

1   was speaking to the big boys today, Todd. They want to take

2   you to lunch; they're very excited, really thrilled.

3   Everything's mapped out, your whole itinerary. The book

4   jacket's designed, there are display cases ready, and we're

5   putting your photograph on billboards all over the city. All

6   we need now is a book . . .

7 TODD: I'm working slowly.

8 PORTIA: No matter. I have faith in you. I believe in you. This

9   night has been sensational. You actually invited me in.

10   Todd?

11 TODD: *(Grabbing her from behind)* **Darling, I want you . . .**

12 PORTIA: What?

13 TODD: **Darling, I want you.** *(She turns, laughs in his face, and in one*

14   *blindingly quick motion, whips her dress off over her head.)* **Hey . . .**

15   *(She starts undressing him.)*

16 PORTIA: This will have to be quick; I have an early day

17   tomorrow.

18 TODD: Wait! I have to kiss you slowly, I have to . . .

19 PORTIA: I've been wondering what your problem was . . .

20 TODD: Portia, I . . . *(She has his shirt off, is starting on his pants.)*

21   Turn around . . .

22 PORTIA: Could you shrug out of these? *(He shrugs out of his pants.*

23   *PORTIA lies on the bed.)* **Thank you. Now be careful, I'm a**

24   little sensitive . . .

25 TODD: Wait . . .

26 PORTIA: I know this is not the best time to start some sort of

27   blazing romance, but you were just so damned *slow.*

28 TODD: *(Kneels on bed, grabs her hand.)* **Be mine!** *(She laughs in his*

29   *face.)*

30 PORTIA: Christ, Todd, where are you getting these lines? Come

31   on. *(She starts to pull off his underpants; he stops her, moves away*

32   *from her.)*

33 TODD: Wait!

34 PORTIA: What?

35 TODD: This is not going well . . .

1   **PORTIA:** I think it's going pretty well. I think most people would
2   think it was going pretty well ...
3   **TODD:** *(Pulling her off the bed)* **You don't understand.**
4   **PORTIA:** **What?**
5   **TODD:** **Turn around ...**
6   **PORTIA:** **Todd ...**
7   **TODD:** ***Turn around.*** *(She turns around. He puts his arm across her*
8   *chest.)* **Be mine.**
9   **PORTIA:** **Look, do you want to sleep with me?**
10 **TODD:** **Portia ...**
11 **PORTIA:** **Am I staying?**
12 **TODD:** **You're doing everything wrong!**
13 **PORTIA:** **What are you talking about?**
14 **GENE:** *(From his room)* ***It's supposed to be beautiful!*** *(A deathless*
15   *pause)*
16 **PORTIA:** **Todd ...**
17 **TODD:** **Oh, Jesus ...**
18 **PORTIA:** **What was that, Todd?**
19 **TODD:** **Nothing.**
20 **PORTIA:** **That wasn't nothing. That was a voice, saying ...**
21 **GENE:** *(From bedroom)* ***It's supposed to be beautiful!***
22 **PORTIA:** **Jesus Christ, what's the deal here?** *(GENE flings open*
23   *the door.)*
24 **GENE:** **Am I the only one left with a sense of loveliness?** *(PORTIA*
25   *stares at him in horror.)*
26 **PORTIA:** **Oh, my God ... oh, my God ...**
27 **TODD:** **Gene ...**
28 **GENE:** *(Coming out of the room)* **Look at the two of you ... You**
29   **are ... trustees of beauty ... You shine with grace ... How**
30   **have you managed to avoid a minimal interior fineness?**
31 **PORTIA:** **Todd ...** *(GENE approaches her.)*
32 **GENE:** **Don't you know what you're supposed to do now? Don't**
33   **you know your part?**
34 **PORTIA:** **Todd ...**
35 **TODD:** **Oh, Jesus ...**

1 GENE: You see me and you are not repelled. You draw in. You
2   come closer and closer. The closer you get, the handsomer
3   I become. You touch me. You kiss me. *(He kisses her.)* I stand
4   tall. *(She faints. TODD catches her.)* No. You don't know your
5   part at all. *(He closes his eyes.)*
6
7   **SCENE EIGHT**
8
9   *(GENE is bent half on a chair, half on the table, hands spread flat*
10   *before him almost in an attitude of supplication. He is moaning*
11   *softly, his eyes closed. TODD laces into him.)*
12 TODD: I *lied.* I *finessed* the situation. I said you were an *intruder.*
13   The crazed, hideous neighbor breaking down the door
14   between us. I *calmed* her down. I said this was an
15   *unprecedented* event. I said I was contacting the authorities
16   *immediately.* I said it would *never* happen again.
17 GENE: O-o-o-o-h-h . . .
18 TODD: And it's not going to, either. There aren't going to be any
19   more little jaunts, Gene. No more charming trips into the
20   street. No more expeditions into the living room. From now
21   on, you lock yourself in that room, and you don't come out
22   until there's a book, a publishable item! *Do you understand*
23   *me?*
24 GENE: I can't . . .
25 TODD: What are you talking about?
26 GENE: I can't go on . . .
27 TODD: *What are you talking about?*
28 GENE: . . . She fainted . . .
29 TODD: Oh, Jesus . . .
30 GENE: I lived for the moment when I would blossom at a kiss
31   and she fainted!
32 TODD: I don't want to hear this now!
33 GENE: I can't, I can't possibly go on . . .
34 TODD: *Listen to me!* You *will* go on. You will . . . do what I
35   demand of you! You will find a story and . . . pick the words

351

1   you need and ... get a *spine* and *make me a book*! Do you
2   *understand*?
3 GENE: ... I can't ...
4 TODD: You will *do* it! Do you understand? *(He slaps him.)* *Do you*
5   *understand*? *(He slaps him again.)*
6 GENE: *(Roaring it out)* Yes! *(TODD pulls GENE up out of the chair.)*
7 TODD: Then *start*! *(TODD throws GENE toward his room. He lands*
8   *hunched in the doorway, his back to us. TODD sits, controls himself.)*
9   Gene ... ?
10 GENE: What?
11 TODD: I didn't mean to be harsh.
12 GENE: Ah.
13 TODD: I just wanted you to know that. *(GENE turns sharply; looks*
14   *at TODD.)*
15
16   **SCENE NINE**
17
18   *(GENE sits at the table, smiling. A small gift-wrapped package is*
19   *on the table. TODD bursts in, effusive.)*
20 TODD: I just got word! We're already into a second printing.
21   That's extremely unusual on a publication day.
22 GENE: Ah!
23 TODD: And three reviews came out — all raves!
24 GENE: Lovely.
25 TODD: *(Reading)* "When a book receives as much hype as *Drift*
26   has, and when, in addition, its author looks more like a
27   model for cologne than like Herman Melville, this critic is
28   naturally inclined to skepticism. That proves unfounded
29   here, however, because *Drift* is a knockout, far and away
30   the best first novel of the season, perhaps the decade." Do
31   you believe it?
32 GENE: Very nice.
33 TODD: I have to thank you.
34 GENE: Oh, no ...
35 TODD: No, I do. I know things weren't always ... pleasant ...

1   between us, but look what it got you to do! Gene, I can say
2   it now. I was amazed how you worked! Once you got started,
3   it took you, what, three weeks? And that from scratch! You
4   ditched all the material you had before and just started. I
5   used to listen, I can tell you this now, I listened at the door
6   to the typewriter clattering away, nonstop, it just *thundered*
7   out of you!
8 GENE: Yes.
9 TODD: When I go on talk shows, Gene — I want you to know
10   this — I'm always asked, "How do you write?" And do you
11   know what I say? I say, "A demon lives with me." I mean,
12   you. I want you to know that. For vanity's sake . . .
13 GENE: You're very kind.
14 TODD: This review starts by quoting the entire opening
15   paragraph! "I live alone. There are no neighbors. There is
16   no neighborhood. Brick has vanished. Tree and sky, too.
17   When I peer through the narrow, grimy shaft that is my
18   window, I see horizon and murk." He says it's the most
19   memorable opening since, "Call me Ishmael."
20 GENE: *(Indicating package)* This is for you.
21 TODD: What?
22 GENE: For you.
23 TODD: What?
24 GENE: A present.
25 TODD: *(Touched)* Gene!
26 GENE: Open it.
27 TODD: I don't know what to say . . .
28 GENE: I wanted to give you this for publication day. A momento.
29 TODD: *(Unwraps it.)* A book. *Layaway.* Thank you.
30 GENE: I found it that day I was a bad boy . . . remember . . . It's
31   very obscure. Canadian. It was out-of-print but it called to
32   me. I used the phone when you were out. I was so moved, I
33   tracked the author down and spoke to him.
34 TODD: Really?
35 GENE: I hope you don't mind.

353

1   TODD: Of course not. I'm very touched that you'd think of me.
2   GENE: Read some.
3   TODD: Now?
4   GENE: Yes, please. It's one of my favorite books, ever. I think
5   I'm the only one who's ever read it, but it may gain shortly
6   in prestige.
7   TODD: *(Reads.)* "I live alone. There are no neighbors. There is no
8   neighborhood . . ."
9   GENE: That resonates, doesn't it?
10   TODD: *(Reading on in horror)* "Brick has vanished. Tree and sky,
11   too. When I peer through the narrow, grimy shaft that is
12   my window . . ."
13   GENE: So Canadian.
14   TODD: ". . . I see horizon and murk . . ."
15   GENE: Do you like it?
16   TODD: *(Flipping in horror through the book)* Every word . . . You
17   stole every word!
18   GENE: The author has such a strong voice, don't you think?
19   Truly distinctive. It comes right out of him. He's sickly, he
20   told me. Stooped and scarred. Unpleasant looking. He
21   should be calling any minute. Be kind to him. *(TODD doubles*
22   *over, clutches himself, lets out an almost silent cry.)* I hear he's in
23   tremendous pain. *(GENE looks at TODD.)*
24   *(Fadeout)*
25
26
27
28
29
30
31
32
33
34
35

SELECTED BIBLIOGRAPHY

The following textbooks and suggested readings are recommended for the beginning student who may like to review the contemporary theatre in terms of practice and principle. The suggested readings provide a more immediate discussion and evaluation of the current theatre as it is related to performance and production techniques. There is also an effort made here to direct the reader toward the more innovative and imaginative practices at work in the contemporary theatre. The valuable insights and observations provided should also promote a more mature understanding of the contemporary theatre at work at this very special point in time.

Abel, Lionel. *Meta Theatre*. New York: Hill and Wang, 1963.

Ball, William. *A Sense of Direction: Some Observations on the Art of Directing*. New York: Drama Book Publishers, 1984.

Barton, Robert. *Acting: Onstage and Off*. New York: Holt, Rinehart and Winston, 1989.

Blau, Herbert. *Eye of Prey: Subversions of the Post Modern*. Bloomington: Indiana University Press, 1987.

Brockett, Oscar. *History of the Theatre*. 5th Edition. Boston: Allyn and Bacon, 1987.

Carnovsky, Morris. *The Actor's Eye*. New York: Performing Arts Journal Publications, 1984.

Cohen, Robert. *Acting One*. Mountain View, California: Mayfield Publishing, 1992.

Cohen, Robert. *Theatre*. Palo Alto, California: Mayfield Publishing, 1981.

Colyer, Carlton. *The Art of Acting*. Colorado Springs, CO: Meriwether Publishing Ltd., 1989.

Hart, Lynda. *Making a Spectacle: Feminist Essays on Contemporary Women's Theatre*. Ann Arbor: University of Michigan Press, 1989.

Hill, Errol. *The Theatre of Black Americans*. Englewood Cliffs, New Jersey: Prentice-Hall, 1980.

Inverso, Mary Beth. *The Gothic Impulse in Contemporary Drama*. Ann Arbor: University of Michigan Press, 1990.

Kirby, Michael. *A Formalist Theatre*. Philadelphia: University of Pennsylvania Press, 1987.

Lessac, Arthur. *Body Wisdom: Use and Training of the Human Body*. New York: Drama Book Specialists, 1988.

Meisner, Sanford and Dennis Longwell. *On Acting*. New York: Vintage Books, 1987.

O'Neill, R. H. and N. M. Boretz. *The Director as Artist: Play Direction Today*. New York: Holt, Rinehart and Winston, 1987.

Owen, Mack. *The Stages of Acting*. New York: Harper-Collins Publishers, 1993.

Schechner, Richard and Willa Appel. *By Means of Performance: Intercultural Studies in Theatre and Ritual*. New York: Cambridge University Press, 1990.

Turner, Victor. *From Ritual to Theatre: The Human Seriousness of Play*. New York: Performance Arts Journal Publications, 1982.

Worthen, William. *The Idea of the Actor: Drama and the Ethics of Performance*. Princeton: Princeton University Press, 1984.

CHAPTER SEVEN

PLAYING "AUDITION" SCENES

"On the stage he was natural, simple, affecting;
'Twas only that when he was off he was acting."

— Oliver Goldsmith, *Retaliation*

The serious study of acting suggests that there must be more involved in this creative, personal art form than mere imitation or invention. Indeed, the successful performance is carefully researched, staged and voiced with a "blueprint" that is at once creative and competent and yet also polished and positive. Although playscripts may vary and performance styles may suggest a variety of approaches, the actor should discover an individual, personal technique that promotes a consistent method of preparation and orchestration of the character that communicates truthfulness and honesty to an audience. That is why it is essential for the actor to understand basic theatrical techniques related to both the "audition" and the "call back" process and to be knowledgeable of the playscript from which the audition scene or monolog is taken as well as to have an in-depth understanding of character relationships in the selected call back scene.

Before discussing the specific performance approach the actor needs to pursue in preparing for both the audition and the call back scene, let's review the basic principles associated with open calls or tryouts for a production. Long before the actual auditions are posted for call, the director has already begun the dramatic visualization of the playscript and looks to the audition as a simple, efficient mechanism to become familiar with a number of actors in an initial attempt to discover "who" most closely resembles the director's concept of the characters in the playscript being cast. In this exploratory audition process the director evaluates each actor's vocal and physical attributes to determine those who are most appropriate for the subsequent "call back" readings with other potential cast members.

Because there are as many methods of conducting auditions as there are imaginative directors, the actor should have cultivated an orderly personal system of preparation and rehearsal that will address any possible audition scenario. For example, the actor who is disciplined and firmly rooted within a framework of detailed character analysis, scene evaluation and creative interpretation should have little difficulty with auditions that call for the traditional three-minute contrasting scenes that consist of one dramatic and one comedic episode or monolog. There may need to be, however, additional preparation devoted to such audition procedures as the "interview" that may follow the prepared scene, the "improvisation" that may be requested or the "movement" demonstration that is generally a part of the occasion.

The actor should consider the audition as a performance in which a number of talents — voice, body, intellect, sensitivity, interpretation — are on display *simultaneously*. It is essential, therefore, that your "presence" radiates the mimetic instinct, or the ability to imitate the characters in the selected scene or monolog as if they were other human beings rather than as names or words on a page. There should also be an indescribable "life spirit" present in the audition that not only stimulates the imagination of the viewer but also enriches the character portrait being drawn in the audition performance so that what is seen and heard is honest, natural, spontaneous and familiar. The style of audition performance, therefore needs to be carefully rehearsed to reflect a relaxed and yet distinctly personal manner that will be memorable to the director when the "call back" process begins to determine the casting of the playscript.

Remember, further, that the audition process is very similar to a job interview and that you are *performing* answers to the questions asked by the director. It is important to respond with a scene or monolog that portrays carefully drawn characters based upon authentic observation, to bring vitality and credibility to the performance and to avoid overly precise use of the voice, exaggerated movement or theatrical posing. Regardless of the rather limited time allocated to the initial audition, it is essential that the actor draw upon personal traits as well as detailed "memory book" observations to give added dimension and flair to the performance portrait audition. It is also imperative in the initial audition to establish a stage presence that is memorable for its radiant aura that suggests here is a character portrait that is both accurate and authentic in addition to being electric!

THE AUDITION BLUEPRINT

The actor should approach the audition scene or monolog with careful research to discover the complexities of the playscript in terms of structure, language and characterization so that performance and staging possibilities may then be explored. At first, it is well to read the scene or monolog appreciatively, with an ear for character interpretation and an eye for creative staging clues. The first reading should develop an indication of the character's intellectual and emotional thought, and should suggest whether the actor is sensitive to the description. The first reading should also reveal the primary action detailed in the scene or monolog, and whether the actor possesses the degree of association and familiarity necessary to perform the description with honesty and naturalness. This initial reading may even evoke creative ideas for the staging or the movement of the characters that will give vitality and tempo to the selected scene or monolog.

A second reading of the scene or monolog should be more critical and objective than the first, and should concentrate on discovering the inherent "meaning" being conveyed in the words and the actions of the characters. This analytical reading should consider the character's word choice, point of view and attitude in the selection and may also include a critical evaluation of the character's mood and relationship with others in the selection. The second reading invariably produces performance ideas that promote active possibilities for role-playing and fuller use of potential vocal and physical approaches to characterization that may help to detail the visual and aural involvement of the character in the selected scene or monolog.

For example, an initial reading of Henrik Ibsen's playscript *A Doll's House* may suggest to the actor that the best staging device to highlight the implication that marriage for Nora and Torvald Helmer has become a "childish plaything" is to perform the scene with the characters using whining, pouting voices to convey the immaturity of their relationship or to invent "childish games" for the characters to play as they each compete for attention and individual control of the situation. A second reading of the playscript, however, reveals a noticeable change in Nora Helmer's language and action as she begins to assert herself and to strike the "independent woman" pose. In Act II she begins to use compound sentences and more descriptive, concrete words; and appears to avoid repetition of the masculine endings for words. The pattern of change continues in Act III, and the discerning actor now notices that Nora communicates her frustration and despair in compound-complex sentences, refutes her earlier views as expressed in Act I and engages in active word play and confrontation with her husband.

The critical evaluation of the second reading of Ibsen's playscript should suggest performance adjustments that must now be made as a more detailed interpretation of the selected scene or monolog begins to emerge. Continued reading helps to polish the interpretation of the scene or monolog and provides the actor with a precise catalog of character thoughts, emotions and responses that distinguish the individual dramatization. When incorporated with critical insight, frequent re-readings of a scene or a monolog should provide the inspiration for character movement that provokes a theatrically stimulating response, should sharpen the character portrait being drawn, should define the physical activity that clarifies the action being described, should enrich the use of the voice to give added dimension to the performance and should suggest ideas for appropriate costumes or the use of hand props to more accurately define character.

Audition Expectations

As valuable as all of these preliminary research resources may be for the audition, however, the actor's most important resource remains imagination and creativity. There will no doubt be audition situations in which the most careful analysis and preparation cannot provide the clue necessary to understand why you may *not* be cast in a production or reviewed favorably by the director in the "call back" selection process. It is important to understand, therefore, that imagination and creativity provide the spark that illuminates both the character and the scene or the monolog and that the actor has a limited amount of time to confirm or to contradict the appropriateness of the preliminary character portrait being sketched in the audition.

It is very important to approach the audition in a calm, relaxed manner rather than as a hectic competition with other equally prepared and talented performers. Remember that the director has already begun the process of visualizing the playscript and that your audition is primarily to demonstrate your "acting personality" and to showcase your performance skills in character analysis, scene evaluation and interpretation. Your performance audition should be spontaneous and true-to-life rather than contrived or artificial so that what emerges is a flexible, well-disciplined actor who would be capable of achieving the indescribable character the director has already begun to imagine as he devises his own blueprint for the production.

The audition expectations should also include attention to the basic ingredients of scene study performance evaluation. The director or agent present in the audience will surely have judgments to make regarding your presentation of how the character looks, speaks and moves. It will be important, therefore, to have ease and freedom of movement, to project vocal variety as well as vocal control and to demonstrate an emotional honesty and concentration that suggests realistic, stage-worthy performance. The actor's preparation for the audition should also include sensory and emotional responses that help to enrich the tempo of the scene or monolog being performed. Alertness to events in everyday life and casual observation may also provide the gesture, the attitude, the voice, the mannerism or the movement that will give distinction and individuality to the selected scene or monolog.

THE SELECTED MONOLOGS

The following monologs are representative of the audition material the actor might select for performance as part of the tryout process. As part of the initial preparation for performance it will be necessary to read the individual playscript as well to determine the context in which the scene is to be played to best reveal the character's intention. It will also be important to rehearse the vocal delivery of the material so that the monolog flows with a sense of tempo that underscores the mood and the attitude of the character. Remember that the monolog is an intimate, fleeting glance at an individual character in a given moment of time in the playscript and that you must strive to "focus" that moment directly toward the audience for its most immediate, meaningful impact. Assume a performance attitude that is concerned with simplicity and subtlety as you perform each monolog as if it were being played for the "first" time. Concentrate only on the "present" and devote all of your energy and thought to the detailed character portrait that has emerged from the dialog and the action of the monolog. Also pay special attention to your choice of costume and personal appearance and what each might say about the character in the monolog. Leave nothing to random chance or to distraction as you share the character with the audience and remember that the monolog should capture an incisive portrait of a truly unique individual rather than attempt to disguise ordinary human features.

In the preliminary rehearsal period of the monolog it would be a good performance idea to review each of the previous chapters of the scene study book to select appropriate vocal and physical exercises to repeat before the audition is scheduled. In the audition itself it will be important to suggest good variety in the type of characters you choose from the classical and the Shakespearean periods to contrast with the more modern and contemporary monologs. So make a concerted effort to also review the general characteristics associated with each performance style described in the scene study book before you allow your own individual, personal performance technique to reveal itself in the audition. Perhaps the often quoted Polonius, Shakespeare's statesman of practical advice in *Hamlet*, most clearly expresses what is desired in the truly inspired audition and in the truly creative actor:

> *"To thine own self be true,*
> *And it must follow as the night the day,*
> *Thou canst not then be false to any man."*

(I, iii)

from **Antigone** (442 B.C.)

Sophocles

The classical heroine Antigone has acted bravely in pursuing a course of action that she knows will bring her inevitable suffering: she refuses to obey the law of her uncle the King, Creon, and attempts to bury her brother in a ceremonial ritual that will allow his spirit to ascend to the gods in spite of the fact that he attempted to overthrow the kingdom of Creon and seize power for himself. Antigone is now being led away by guards to be walled up in a vaulted tomb and sealed forever against the light of day.

ANTIGONE: Tomb, my bridal-chamber, eternal prison in the caverned rock, when I come to you I shall find mine own, those many who have perished, who have seen Persephone. Last of all I take that way, and fare most miserably of all, my days so few! But I cherish good hope that my coming will be welcome to my father, and pleasant to my own mother, and to you, my brother, pleasing too; for each of you in death I washed with my own hands, and dressed for your graves; and I poured drink-offerings over you.

And you too, Polynices; for you also in death I
tended, and for that I win such recompense as this.
Yet the just will say I did rightly in paying you these
honors. Not for my children, if I had been a mother,
nor for my husband, if his dead body were rotting before me, would I have chosen to suffer like this in violent defiance of the citzens. For the sake of what law
do I say this? If my husband had died, there would
have been another man for me; I could have had a child
from another husband if I had lost my first child. But
even with my mother and father both hidden away in
Hades, no other brother could ever have come into
being for me. For it was thus I saw the higher law; but
Creon calls me guilty, brother, and leads me captive
on the way to death. No bridal bed, no bridal song have
been mine, no joy of marriage, no children at my breast;
but thus forlorn and friendless I go living to the grave.

Yet what law of heaven did I offend? Ah, why
should I look to the gods anymore, for I see they do
not hear me, but let me suffer the punishment of the
impious for doing a pious deed. If my fate indeed is
pleasing to the gods, when I have suffered my doom
no doubt I shall learn my sin; but if the sin is with my
judges, I wish them no measure of evil greater than
they have now measured out to me. Your words call
death to hurry for me. O, land of my fathers! O, my city
Thebes! O, ye gods! They hurry me now, they are in
haste to have done with me. Behold me, princes of my
Thebes, the last of the house of your kings — see what
I suffer, and by whom — because I feared to forget the
fear of heaven!

Creon's denial of Polynices' funeral rites — a fate reserved for
the worst of criminals — provokes eternal sorrow and tragedy for the
King as the momentum of Antigone's defiance reaches the level of
horror and poignancy. In the following pathetic description the Messenger details what has now befallen Creon's son, Haemon, and Anti-

gone in the cold nuptial chamber they now share as spiritual lovers. There is also a soul searing vision of the heartbroken King as he recoils in horror from the pitiful sight that follows.

MESSENGER: Neighbors of the house of Cadmus, dwellers within these sacred walls, there is no state of mortal life that I would ever praise or pity, for none is beyond swift change. Fortune raises men up and fortune casts them down from day to day, and no man can foretell the fate of things established. For Creon was blest in all that I count happiness: he had honor as our savior; power as our king; pride as the father of princely children. Now all is ended. For when a man is stripped of happiness, I count him not with the living — he is but a breathing corpse. Let a man have riches heaped in his house, and live in royal splendor; yet I would not give the shadow of a breath for all, if they bring no gladness.

I will tell you what I saw, I will hide nothing of the truth. I would gladly tell you a happier tale, but it would soon be found out false. Truth is the only way. I guided your lord the King to the furthest part of the plain, where the body of Polynices, torn by dogs, still lay unpitied. There we prayed to the goddess of the roads, and to Pluto, in mercy to restrain their wrath. We washed the dead with holy rites, and all that was left of the mortal man we burned with fresh-plucked branches; and over the ashes at last we raised a mound of his native earth.

That done, we turned our steps toward those fearsome caves where in a cold nuptial chamber, with couch of stone, that maiden had been given as a bride of Death. But from afar off, one of us heard a voice wailing aloud, and turned to tell our master.

And as the King drew nearer, the sharp anguish of broken cries came to his ears. Then he groaned and said like one in pain, "Can my sudden fear be true? Am

364

I on the saddest road I ever went? That voice is my son's! Hurry, my servants, to the tomb, and through the gap where the stones have been torn out, look into the cell — tell me if it is Haemon's voice I hear, or if my wits are tortured by the gods."

At these words from our stricken master, we went to make that search; and in the dim furthest part of the tomb we saw Antigone hanging by the neck, her scarf of fine linen twisted into a cruel noose. And there, too, we saw Haemon — his arms about her waist, while he cried out upon the loss of his bride, and his father's deed, and his ill-starred love.

But now the King approached, and saw him, and cried out with horror, and went in and called with piteous voice, "Unhappy boy, what a deed have you done, breaking into this tomb! What purpose have you? Has grief stolen your reason? Come forth, my son! I pray you — I implore!" The boy answered no word, but glared at him with fierce eyes, spat in his face, and drew his cross-hilted sword. His father turned and fled, and the blow missed its mark. Then that maddened boy, torn between grief and rage and penitence, straightway leaned upon his sword, and drove it half its length into his side; and in the little moment before death, he clasped the maiden in his arms, and her pale cheek was red where his blood gushed forth.

Corpse enfolding corpse they lie; he has won his bride, poor lad, not here but in the halls of Death; to all of us he has left a terrible witness that man's worst error is to reject good counsel.

from **Medea** (431 B.C.)

Euripides

Jason, the classical explorer, has abandoned his wife, Medea, in order to make a more profitable and political marriage with the

younger daughter of Creon, ruler of Corinth. Medea has been condemned to exile, and yet rages with desire for revenge. She had been
endowed with the supernatural powers of a sorceress and used that
power to help Jason succeed in his quest for the golden fleece. Now
that he has abandoned her, Medea is consumed with jealousy and
plots her retribution against Jason.

JASON: Needs must I now, it seems, turn orator, and, like a
good helmsman on a ship with close-reefed sails,
weather that wearisome tongue of thine. Now, I
believe, since thou wilt exaggerate thy favours, that to
Cypris alone of gods or men I owe the safety of my
voyage. Thou hast a subtle wit enough; yet were it a
hateful thing for me to say that the Love-god
constrained thee by his resistless shaft to save my life.
However, I will not reckon this too nicely; 'twas kindly
done, however, thou didst serve me. Yet for my safety
hast thou received more than ever thou gavest, as I
will show. First, thou dwellest in Hellas, instead of thy
barbarian land, and hast learnt what justice means
and how to live by law, not by the dictates of brute
force; and all the Hellenes recognize thy cleverness,
and thou hast gained a name; whereas, if thou hadst
dwelt upon the confines of the earth, no tongue had
mentioned thee. Give me no gold within my halls, nor
skill to sing a fairer strain than ever Orpheus sang,
unless therewith my fame be spread abroad! So much
I say to thee about my own toils, for 'twas thou didst
challenge me to this retort. As for the taunts thou
urgest against my marriage with the princess, I will
prove to thee, first, that I am prudent herein, next
chastened in my love, and last a powerful friend to
thee and to thy sons; only hold thy peace. Since I have
here withdrawn from Iolcos with many a hopeless
trouble at my back, what happier device could I, an
exile, frame than marriage with the daughter of the
king? 'Tis not because I loathe thee for my wife — the

thought that rankles in thy heart; 'tis not because I am smitten with desire for a new bride, nor yet that I am eager to vie with others in begetting many children, for those we have are quite enough, and I do not complain. Nay, 'tis that we — and this is most important — may dwell in comfort, instead of suffering want (for well I know that every whilom friend avoids the poor), and that I might rear my sons as doth befit my house; further, that I might be the father of brothers for the children thou hast borne, and raise these to the same high rank, uniting the family in one — to my lasting bliss. Thou, indeed, hast no need of more children, but me it profits to help my present family by that which is to be. Have I miscarried here? Not even thou

The "sorceress" Medea rages with desire for revenge after her husband Jason abandons her. Consumed with jealousy, Medea plots her revenge to alienate Jason and to secure her retribution. (From the Kansas State University production of Medea.)

367

wouldst say so unless a rival's charms rankled in thy bosom. No, but you women have such strange ideas, that you think all is well so long as your married life runs smooth; but if some mischance occur to ruffle your love, all that was good and lovely erst you reckon as your foes. Yea, men should have begotten children from some other source, no female race existing; thus would no evil ever have fallen on mankind.

Although there may be a certain degree of honesty in Jason's defense that he is marrying the Corinthian princess in order to consolidate not only his own position in their new home but also that of Medea and their children, the insane violence that follows is horrifying. Medea kills Creon and his daughter through her poisoned gifts of a robe and a chaplet and now contemplates slaying her own children to render Jason abjectly desolate and alone in the world.

MEDEA: O my babes, my babes, ye have still a city and a home, where far from me and my sad lot you will live your lives, reft of your mother for ever; while I must to another land in banishment, or ever I have had my joy of you, or lived to see you happy, or ever I have graced your marriage couch, your bride, your bridal bower, or lifted high the wedding torch. Ah me! A victim of my own self-will. So it was all in vain I reared you, O my sons; in vain did suffer, racked with anguish, enduring the cruel pangs of childbirth. 'Fore Heaven I once had hope, poor me! High hope of ye that you would nurse me in my age and deck my corpse with loving hands, a boon we mortals covet; but now is my sweet fancy dead and gone; for I must lose you both and in bitterness and sorrow drag through life.

And ye shall never with fond eyes see your mother more, for o'er your life there comes a cloud. Ah me! Why do ye look at me so, my children? Why smile that last sweet smile? What am I to do? My heart gives way when I behold my children's laughing eyes? O, I cannot! Farewell to all my former schemes. I will take the

368

children from the land. Why should I wound their sire
by wounding them, and get me a twofold measure of
sorrow? No, I will not do it. And yet, what possesses
me? Can I consent to let those foes of mine escape from
punishment, and incur their mockery? Out upon my
craven heart! To think that I should even have let the
soft words escape my soul. Into the house, children!
And whosoever feels he must not be present at my
sacrifice must see to it himself. I will not spoil my
handiwork!

O, do not do this deed! Let the children go,
unhappy one, spare the babes! For if they live, they
will cheer thee in our exile there. Nay, by the fiends of
hell's abyss, never will I hand my children over to their
foes to mock and flout. Die they must in any case, and
since 'tis so, why I, the mother who bore them, will
give the fatal blow. In any case their doom is fixed and
there is no escape. Fain would I say farewell to them.
O my babes, my babes, let your mother kiss your hands.
Ah! Hands I love so well, O lips most dear to me! O
noble form and features of my children, I wish ye joy,
but in that other land, for here your father robs you
of your home. O the sweet embrace, the soft young
cheek, the fragrant breath! My children! Go, leave me!
I cannot bear to look longer upon ye; my sorrow wins
the day. At last I understand the awful deed I am to
do; but passion, that cause of direst woes to mortal
man, hath triumphed o'er my sober thoughts.

My friends, I am resolved upon the deed; at once
will I slay my children and then leave this land, without
delaying long enough to hand them over to some more
savage hand to butcher. Needs must they die in any
case; and since they must, I will slay them — I, the
mother that bare them. O heart of mine, steel thyself!
Why do I hesitate to do the awful deed that must be
done? Come, take the sword, thou wretched hand of

mine! Take it, and advance to the post whence starts thy life of sorrow. Away with cowardice! Give not one thought to thy babes, how dear they are or how thou art their own mother. This one brief day forget thy children dear, and after that lament; for though thou wilt slay them yet they were thy darlings still, and I am a lady of sorrows.

(MEDEA slowly moves toward the house with sword held high.)

from As You Like It (1599)
William Shakespeare

In the magical forest of Arden, Rosalind, an attractive young maiden wounded by the sad arrows of a failed love, innocently stumbles upon the saucy shepherdess Phebe and her fellow shepherd Silvius. Now disguised as the dashing male Ganymede, Rosalind rebukes the advances of the country bumpkin Phebe and lectures her on the true meaning of love. Phebe, now "love sick" for the handsome Ganymede, speaks of the infatuation she has for him/her with her companion in the following tender dialog.

PHEBE: Think not I love him, though I ask for him.
'Tis but a peevish boy. Yet he talks well.
But what care I for words? Yet words do well
When he that speaks them pleases those that hear.
It is a pretty youth — not very pretty —
But sure he's proud; and yet his pride becomes him.
He'll make a proper man. The best thing in him
Is his complexion; and faster than his tongue
Did make offence, his eye did heal it up.
He is not very tall; yet for his years he's tall.
His leg is but so-so; and yet 'tis well.
There was a pretty redness in his lip,
A little riper and more lusty-red
Than that mixed in his cheek. 'Twas just the difference
Betwixt the constant red and mingled damask.
There be some women, Silvius, had they marked him

In parcels as I did, would have gone near
To fall in love with him; but for my part,
I love him not, nor hate him not. And yet
Have I more cause to hate him than to love him.
For what had he to do to chide at me?
He said mine eyes were black, and my hair black;
And now I am remembered, scorned at me.
I marvel why I answered not again.
But that's all one. Omittance is no quittance.
I'll write to him a very taunting letter,
And thou shalt bear it. Wilt thou, Silvius?

In the Epilogue that concludes this comic playscript, Rosalind addresses the audience to offer one last theatrical laugh. Her speech is full of wit and yet the tone is not particularly biting. There is a gentle sweetness and honesty in her call to the men and women of the audience to embrace the mystery of her previous disguise and to bid her farewell now that all understand the proper conduct of true lovers!

ROSALIND: It is not the fashion to see the lady in the
      Epilogue.
   But it is no more unhandsome than to see the lord in the
      Prologue.
   If it be true that good wine needs no bush, 'tis true that a
   Good play needs no epilogue. Yet to good wine they do
      use good
   Bushes, and good plays prove the better by the help of good
   Epilogues. What a case am I in then, that am neither a
      good epilogue
   Nor cannot insinuate with you in the behalf of a good
      play! I am
   Not furnished like a beggar, therefore to beg will not
      become me.
   My way is to conjure you; and I'll begin with the women.
      I charge you,
   O women, for the love you bear to women — as I perceive
      by your

371

Simpering none of you hates them — that between you
    and the women
The play may please. If I were a woman I would kiss as
    many of
You as had beards that pleased me, complexions that
    liked me, and
Breaths that I defied not. And I am sure, as many as
    have good
Beards, or good faces, or sweet breaths will for my kind
    offer,
When I make curtsy, bid me farewell!

from A Midsummer Night's Dream (1596)

William Shakespeare

In the woods near Athens late at night, Oberon, the King of
the mystical sprites and fairies, confronts Titania, his Queen of the
eternal darkness, and demands possession of a small "changeling
child" that had been stolen from an ancient Indian lord. Titania
refuses to surrender the child to Oberon, who now begins to plot his
revenge as a proud and vain ruler. He summons his faithful servant,
Puck, and instructs the trickster to become the agent of his rage.

OBERON: Well, go thy way! Thou shalt not from this
    grove
    Till I torment thee for this injury.
    My gentle Puck, come hither. Thou rememb'rest
    Since once I sat upon a promontory
    And heard a mermaid on a dolphin's back
    Uttering such dulcet and harmonious breath
    That the rude sea grew civil at her song
    And certain stars shot madly from their spheres
    To hear the sea-maid's music?
        That very time I saw, but thou couldst not,
    Flying between the cold moon and the earth
    Cupid, all armed. A certain aim he took
    At a fair vestal throned by the west,

372

And loosed his love-shaft smartly from his bow
As it should pierce a hundred thousand hearts.
But I might see young Cupid's fiery shaft
Quenched in the chaste beams of the wat'ry moon,
And the imperial vot'ress passed on,
In maiden meditation, fancy-free.
Yet marked I where the bolt of Cupid fell.
It fell upon a little western flower —
    Before, milk-white; now, purple with love's
Wound — and maidens call it love-in idleness.
Fetch me that flower; the herb I showed thee once.
The juice of it on sleeping eyelids laid
Will make or man or woman madly dote
Upon the next live creature that it sees.
Fetch me this herb, and be thou here again
Ere the leviathan can swim a league.
    Having once this juice,
I'll watch Titania when she is asleep,
And drop the liquor of it in her eyes.
The next thing then she waking looks upon —
Be it on lion, bear, or wolf, or bull,
On meddling monkey, or on busy ape —
She shall pursue it with the soul of love.
And ere I take this charm from off her sight —
As I can take it with another herb —
I'll make her render up her page to me.
But who comes here? I am invisible,
And I will overhear their conference.

As the agent of Oberon's revenge, Puck sets in motion all of the mischief and misunderstanding that adds to the joy and entertainment of the comic plot. Even though his deceits may have humorous consequences, there is still an air of terror and tension that surrounds Puck as he flies from one malicious mission to another. Having administered Oberon's magic potion, inducing Titania to fall in love with the rustic Bottom — who has been transformed into an ass as well — Puck scurries back to Oberon to report the news.

Oberon, the mystical ruler of sprites and fairies, achieves his own measure of spirited revenge on Titania, his Queen, with the help of his faithful servant, Puck. Here, Titania falls hopelessly in love with the "ass" Bottom after the mischievous Puck secretly administers a magic potion while she was asleep. (From the Western Michigan University production of A Midsummer Night's Dream.*)*

PUCK: My mistress with a monster is in love.

Near to her close and consecrated bower

While she was in her dull and sleeping hour

A crew of patches, rude mechanicals,

That work for bread upon Athenian stalls,

Were met together to rehearse a play

Intended for great Theseus' nuptial day

The shallowest thick skin of that barren sort,

Who Pyramus presented, in their sport

Forsook his scene and entered in a brake,

When I did him at this advantage take.

An ass's nose I fixed on his head.

Anon his Thisbe must be answered,

And forth my mimic comes. When they him spy —

As wild geese that the creeping fowler eye,

Or russet-pated choughs, many in sort,
Rising and cawing at the gun's report,
Sever themselves and madly sweep the sky —
So, at his sight, away his fellows fly;
And at our stamp here o'er and o'er one falls.
He "Murder" cries, and help from Athens calls.
Their sense thus weak, lost with their fears thus strong,
Made senseless things begin to do them wrong.
For briers and thorns at their apparel snatch;
Some sleeves, some hats — from yielders all things
    catch.
I led them on in this distracted fear,
And left sweet Pyramus translated there;
When in that moment, so it came to pass,
Titania waked and straightway loved an ass!

from Henry VI, Part 3 (1591)

William Shakespeare

On a rugged battlefield near the outskirts of Wakefield, "Captain Margaret," stern and crude Queen of England, leads her troops in the capture of Richard, Duke of York, who is trying to seize King Henry's crown. Queen Margaret displays a sadistic and mocking tone as she drags the terrified York to a molehill for his "mock coronation." Her theatrical taunts and sneers are startling moments of dramatic history and help disguise her true bloody intentions.

QUEEN MARGARET: Brave warriors, Clifford and North-
    umberland,
    Come make him stand upon this molehill here,
    That wrought at mountains with outstretched arms
    Yet parted but the shadow with his hand.
    What — was it you that would be England's king?
    Was't you that revelled in our Parliament,
    And made a preachment of your high descent?
    Where are your mess of sons to back you now?
    The wanton Edward and the lusty George?

And where's that valiant crookback prodigy,
Dickie, your boy, that with his grumbling voice
Was wont to cheer his dad in mutinies?
Or with the rest where is your darling Rutland?
Look, York, I stained this napkin with the blood
That valiant Clifford with his rapier's point
Made issue from the bosom of thy boy.
And if thine eyes can water for his death,
I give thee this to dry thy cheeks withal.
Alas, poor York, but that I hate thee deadly
I should lament thy miserable state.
I prithee, grieve, to make me merry, York.
What — hath thy fiery heart so parched thine
Entrails that not a tear can fall for Rutland's death?
Why art thou patient, man? Thou shouldst be mad,
And I, to make thee mad, do mock thee thus.
Stamp, rave, and fret, that I may sing and dance.
Thou wouldst be fee'd, I see, to make me sport.
York cannot speak unless he wear a crown.
A crown for York, and, lords, bow low to him.
Hold you his hands whilst I do set it on.
   (Places paper crown on YORK's head.)
Ay, marry, sir, now looks he like a king,
Ay, this is he that took King Henry's chair,
And this is he was his adopted heir.
But how is it that great Plantagenet
Is crowned so soon and broke his solemn oath?
As I bethink me, you should not be king
Till our King Henry had shook hands with death.
And will you pale your head in Henry's glory,
And rob his temples of the diadem
Now, in his life, against your holy oath?
O 'tis a fault too, too, unpardonable.
Off with the crown,
   (She knocks the crown from his head.)
      and with the crown his head,
And whilst we breathe, take time to do him dead.

376

The great Shakespearean characters and memorable speeches have more often than not attracted the most novel performances and the most imaginative interpretations in the history of theatre. The original performance practice of young men playing female roles in Shakespeare's playscripts was later abandoned as attractive, romantic actresses of the 18th century quietly rose to stardom in such roles as Ophelia, Lady Macbeth and Desdemona. In the mid-19th century, however, it became a fashionable theatre treat to witness female stars like Sarah Bernhardt and Charlotte Cushman bring fresh insights and sensitive points of view to their own interpretations of such traditional male roles as Hamlet or Puck.

In that tradition of women playing male roles — termed "breeches roles" in the historical period — here is a challenging audition monolog from *As You Like It* that is certain to gain attention. As the speech begins, the world-weary and melancholy Jaques (Ja'kis) laments the bitter and cynical view of a world in which human vanity corrupts and destroys. A malcontent rarely given to expressions of pleasure or laughter, Jaques spins a masterful tale of human existence and sardonic vision that captures the essence of man's inevitable, fateful reality.

JAQUES: **All the world's a stage,**
And all the men and women merely players.
They have their exits and their entrances,
And one man in his time plays many parts,
His acts being seven ages. At first the infant,
Mewling and puking in the nurse's arms.
Then the whining schoolboy with his satchel
And shining morning face, creeping like snail
Unwillingly to school. And then the lover,
Sighing like furnance, with a woeful ballad,
Made to his mistress' eyebrow. Then, a soldier,
Full of strange oaths, and bearded like the pard,
Jealous in honor, sudden, and quick in quarrel,
Seeking the bubble reputation
Even in the cannon's mouth. And then the justice,
In fair round belly with good capon lined,
With eyes severe and beard of formal cut,
Full of wise saws and modern instances;

377

And so he plays his part. The sixth age shifts
Into the lean and slippered pantaloon,
With spectacles on nose and pouch on side,
His youthful hose, well saved, a world too wide
For his shrunk shank, and his big, manly voice,
Turning again toward childish treble, pipes
And whistles in his sound. Last scene of all,
That ends this strange, eventful history,
Is second childishness and mere oblivion,
Sans teeth, sans eyes, sans taste, sans everything.

from The Beaux' Stratagem (1707)
George Farquhar

The English 18th-century comedy of manners offers a vivid
reflection of life in which "sentimental" characters appear unnatur-
ally good and their problems too easily overcome. Pathetic situations
were usually ideal opportunities to reveal the essential goodness of
a character and in the monolog that follows Mrs. Sullen affects the
manner and demeanor of "acceptable taste" as she discusses marriage
and the "right conduct" one should observe in polite society.

MRS. SULLEN: Country pleasures! Racks and torments!
Dost think, child, that my limbs were made
for leaping of ditches, and clambering over stiles? Or
that my parents, wisely foreseeing my future happiness in country pleasures, had early instructed me in
the rural accomplishments of drinking fat ale, playing
at whisk, and smoking tobacco with my husband? Or
of spreading of plasters, brewing of diet-drinks, and
stilling rosemary-water, with the good old gentlewo-
man, my mother-in-law?

Not that I disapprove rural pleasures, as the poets
have painted them; in their landscape, every Phyllis
has her Corydon, every murmuring stream, and every
flow'ry mead, gives fresh alarms to love. Besides, you'll
find that their couples were never married.

But yonder I see my Corydon, and a sweet swain

it is, heaven knows!

Come, Dorinda, don't be angry, he's my husband, and your brother; and, between both, is he not
a sad brute? O Sister, Sister! If ever you marry, beware
of a sullen, silent sot, one that's always musing, but
never thinks. There's some diversion in a talking bock-
head; and since a woman must wear chains, I would
have the pleasure of hearing 'em rattle a little.

Now you shall see, but take this by the way.

He came home this morning at his usual hour of
four, wakened me out of a sweet dream of something
else by tumbling over the tea-table, which he broke all
to pieces; after his man and he had rolled about the
room like sick passengers in a storm, he comes flounce
into bed, dead as a salmon into a fishmonger's basket;
his feet cold as ice, his breath hot as a furnace, and his
hands and his face as greasy as his flannel night-cap.
O, matrimony! He tosses up the clothes with a barbarous swing over his shoulders, disorders the whole economy of my bed, leaves me half naked, and my whole
night's comfort is the tuneable serenade of that wake-
ful nightingale, his nose!

Oh, the pleasure of counting the melancholy
clock by a snoring husband! But now, Sister, you shall
see how handsomely, being a well-bred man, he will
beg my pardon.

from The Miser (1668)
Molière

French comedy of manners ridicules trifle customs and
human nature that are pretentious and hypocritical. The biting
satire and wit of the comic playwrights of the 17th century,
especially Molière, exposed the foibles and follies of the church,
society and prominent leaders in the historical times. In
this comic monolog that follows, Harpagon (The Miser) is
enraged when he discovers that the secret treasure he has
buried was unearthed and that he is now penniless!

HARPAGON: Stop thief! Stop thief! Stop assassin! Stop murderer! Justice! Divine Justice! I am ruined! I've been murdered! He cut my throat, he stole my money! Who can it be? What's become of him? Where is he? Where is he hiding? What shall I do to find him? Where shall I run? Where shall I not run? Isn't that he there? Isn't this he here? Who's this? *(Sees his own shadow and grabs his own arm.)* Stop! Give me back my money, you rogue. Ah! It is myself! My mind is unhinged, and I don't know where I am, who I am, or what I am doing. *(Falls to his knees.)* Alas! My poor money, my poor money, my dear friend, they have taken you from me. And since they carried you off, I've lost my support, my consolation, my joy. Everything is at an end for me; I have no more to do in this world! I cannot live without you! It's finished. I can do no more. *(Lies down.)* I am dying. I am dead. I am buried! Isn't there anybody who would like to bring me back to life by returning my dear money or by telling me who took it? *(Rising to his knees)* What did you say? It was nobody. *(Stands.)* Whoever did the job must have watched very closely for his chance; for he chose exactly the time when I was talking to my treacherous son. *(Takes his hat and cane.)* I'll go and demand justice. I'll order them to torture everyone in my house for a confession: the maids, the valets, my son, my own daughter — and myself too! What a crowd of people! Everybody I cast my eyes on arouses my suspicion, and everything seems to be the thief. Eh! What are you talking about there? About the man that robbed me? Why are you making that noise up there? Is my thief there? *(Kneels and addresses the audience.)* Please, if anyone has any information about my thief, I beg you to tell me. Are you sure he isn't hidden there among you? They all look at me and laugh. *(Stands.)* You will probably see that they all had a part in this robbery. Here, quick, commissaries, archers,

provosts, judges, tortures, scaffolds and executioners!
I want to have everybody hanged! And if I don't recover
my money, I'll hang myself afterward!

from The Beggar's Opera (1728)
John Gay

A number of recent adaptations of this popular "ballad opera" have portrayed the character Macheath as the fearless leader of a leather jacket, daredevil gang of motorcycle rascals in order to make it address more contemporary social issues.

This "ballad opera" popularized London low-life in the 18th century and set the tone for later heroic dramas and musicals that glamorized the lives of hardened criminals, beggars and vagabonds of the night. As the fearless leader of a rowdy gang of cutthroats and pickpockets, Macheath loves his ale and his pleasure; and not the least of his many pleasures is the bevy of bawdy "street ladies" who display their social graces and lovely forms with such cunning and seductive artistry!

MACHEATH: I must have women! There is nothing unbends the mind like them.

Dear Mrs. Coaxer, you are welcome. You look charmingly today. I hope you don't want the repairs of quality, and lay on paint.

Dolly Trull! Kiss me, hussy! Are you as amorous as ever? You are always so taken up with stealing hearts, that you don't allow yourself time to steal anything else. Ah, Dolly, thou wilt ever be a coquette.

Mrs. Vixen, I'm yours; I always loved a woman of wit and spirit. They make charming mistresses, but plaguey wives.

Betty Doxy! Come hither, turtledove. Do you drink as hard as ever? You had better stick to good wholesome beer; for in troth, Betty, strong waters will in time ruin your constitution. You should leave those to your betters.

What! And my pretty Jenny Diver too! As prim and demure as ever! There is not any prude, though ever so high bred, hath a more sanctified look, with a more mischievous heart. Ah! Thou art a dear artful hypocrite.

Mrs. Slammekin! As careless and genteel as ever! All you fine ladies, you know your own beauty, affect an undress.

But see, here's Suky Tawdry come to contradict what I was saying. Everything she gets one way, she lays out and then back. Why, Suky, you must keep at least a dozen tally-men.

Molly Brazen! *(Throws her a kiss.)* **That's well done!**
I love a free-hearted wench. Thou hast a most agreeable
assurance, girls, and art as willing as a turtle.
    But hark! I hear music. The harper is at the door.
"If music be the food of love, play on." Ere you seat
yourselves, ladies, what think you of a dance?

from **All for Love** (1677)
John Dryden

This elegant "blank verse" tragedy is a more restrained version
of William Shakespeare's classic *Antony and Cleopatra* and presents
the lovely, seductive Cleopatra at her most cunning and dramatic.
Surrounded by armed soldiers, she pleads in rousing speech that
alternates between a daring defense and an arrogant dismissal that
Antony not leave her. The melodramatic public presentation provides
an especially attractive setting for Cleopatra to be the center of
attention as well as the object of adulation.

CLEOPATRA: **Yet may I speak?**
How shall I plead my cause, when you, my judge,
Already have condemn'd me?
                            Shall I bring
The love you bore me for my advocate?
That now is turn'd against me, that destroys me;
For love, once past, is, at the best forgotten;
    but oft'ner sours to hate.
                         'Twill please my lord
To ruin me, and therefore I'll be guilty.
But, could I once have thought it would have pleas'd you,
That you would pry, with narrow searching eyes,
Into my faults, severe to my destruction,
And watching all advantages with care,
That serve to make me wretched?
                       You seem griev'd
(And therein you are kind) that Caesar first
Enjoy'd my love, though you deserv'd it better.

I grieve for that, my lord, much more than you;
For, had I first been yours, it would have sav'd
My second choice: I never have been his,
And ne'er had been but yours. But Caesar first,
You say, possess'd my love. Not so, my lord:
He first possess'd my person, you, my love:
Caesar lov'd me, but I lov'd Antony.
If I endur'd him after, 'twas because
I judg'd it due to the first name of men;
And, half constrain'd, I gave, as to a tyrant,
What he would take by force.
How often have I wish'd some other Caesar,
Great as the first, and as the second young,
Would court my love, to be refus'd for you!
You leave me, Antony; and yet I love you,
Indeed I do: I have refus'd a kingdom —
That's a trifle:
For I could part with life, with anything,
But only you.

                                 Oh, let me die with you!
Is that a hard request?
No, you shall go; your int'rest calls you hence;
Yes, your dear int'rest pulls too strong, for these
Weak arms to hold you here.

                              Go; leave me, soldier
(For you're no more a lover); leave me dying:
Push me pale and panting from your bosom,
And, when your march begins, let one run after,
Breathless almost for joy, and cry, "She's dead."
The soldiers shout; you then, perhaps, may sigh,
And muster all your Roman gravity:
Ventidius chides; and straight your brow clears up,
As I had never been.
Here let me breathe my last: envy me not
This minute; I'll die apace,
As fast as e'er I can, and end your trouble.

from **Cyrano de Bergerac** (1898)

Edmund Rostand

The honest, courageous and romantic Cyrano is a brilliant musician, talented poet, agile swordsman and philosopher extraordinaire in 17th-century France. There is only one apparent defect in this otherwise perfect person: an *enormous* nose that provokes ridicule and laughter. This deformity, however, has helped to inspire the biting wit and the daring insolence which is characteristic of Cyrano's heroic struggle to resist conformity and to cultivate a romantic victory over the dull and the ordinary.

CYRANO: **Take notice, boobies all,**

Who find my visage's center ornament
A thing to jest at — that it is my wont —
An if the jester's noble — ere we part
To let him taste my steel, and not my boot!
Know that I am proud possessing such appendice.
Tis well known, a big nose is indicative
Of a soul affable, and kind, and courteous,
Liberal, brave, just like myself, and such
As you can never dare to dream yourself,
Rascal contemptible! Show your heels, now!
Or tell me why you stare so at my nose!
Well, what is there so strange to the eye?
How now? Is't soft and dangling, like a bird?
Is it crook'd, like an owl's beak?
Do you see a wart upon the tip? Or a fly,
That takes the air there? What is there to stare at?
You might have said a thousand things, like this, by
Varying the tone. Aggressive: "Sir, if I had such a nose
I'd amputate it!" Friendly: "When you sup it must annoy
You, dipping in your cup; you must need a special shape!"
Descriptive: " 'Tis a rock! . . . a peak! . . . a cape!
A cape! Forsooth! 'Tis a peninsula!"
Gracious: "You love the little birds, I think?
I see you've managed with a fond research
To find their tiny claws a roomy perch!"

Considerate: "Take care, with your head bowed low
By such a weight, lest head o'er heels you go!"
Tender: "Pray get a small umbrella made,
Lest its bright color in the sun should fade!"
Cavalier: "The last fashion, friend, that hook?
To hang your hat on? 'Tis a useful crook!"
Emphatic: "No wind, O majestic nose,
Can give *thee* cold — save when the mistral blows!"
Dramatic: "When it bleeds, what a Red Sea!"
Admiring: "Sign for a perfumery!"
Simple: "When is the monument on view?"
Rustic: "Call that thing a nose? Ay, marry, no!
'Tis a dwarf pumpkin, or a prize turnip!"
Military: "Point against cavalry!"
Practical: "Put it in the lottery!
Assuredly 'twould be the biggest prize!"
Or, parodying the lover Pyramus' sighs,
"Behold the nose that mars the harmony
Of its master's phiz! blushing its treachery!"
Such, my dear sir, is that you might have said,
Had you the least of wit or letters.
But, of wit you have not an atom, and of letters
There are only three that spell *you* out — A-S-S!

from The Lower Depths (1902)

Maxim Gorky

Already famous as a writer of realistic short stories and novels, Maxim Gorky won a dramatic reputation as spokesman for the Russian lower classes and exerted enormous influence in the effort to improve their social condition. His romantic heroes, rebels and outcasts are treated with dignity and humanity, even though they are ultimately defeated by a cruel and harsh reality. In this monolog the emotional Satine reminds his fellow outcasts of man's great potential for happiness and survival.

SATINE: *(Banging on the table with his fist)* **Shut up, you brutes, numbskulls! That's enough about the old man!**

(In a calmer tone) **You're the worst of all. You understand nothing — and lie. The old man is not a faker. What's truth? Man — that's the truth! He understood this — you don't. You're dull, like a brick. I understand the old man — I do. Certainly he lied — but it was out of pity for others — I know it — I've read about it. They lie beautifully, excitingly, with a kind of inspiration. There are lies that soothe, that reconcile one to his lot. There are lies that justify the load that crushed a worker's arm — and hold a man to blame for dying of starvation — I know lies! People weak in spirit — and those who live on the sweat of others — these need lies — the weak find support in them, the exploiters use them as a screen. But a man who is his own master, who is independent and doesn't batten on others — he can get along without lies. Lies are the religion of slaves and bosses. Truth is the god of the free man.**

Why shouldn't a cheat speak well sometimes, when the decent people — speak like cheats? Yes, I've forgotten a lot, but I still know some things. The old man had a head on his shoulders. He had the same effect on me as acid on an old, dirty coin. Let's drink to his health! Fill the glasses! The old man lives from within — he looks at everything through his own eyes. I asked him once: Grandpa, what do people live for? *(Trying to imitate the old man's voice and manner)* **"They live for something better to come, my friend. Let's say, there are cabinetmakers. They live on, and all of them are just trash. But one day a cabinetmaker is born — such a cabinetmaker as has never been seen on this earth — there's no equal to him — he outshines everybody. The whole cabinetmaking trade is changed by him — and in one jump it moves twenty years ahead. Likewise, all the rest — locksmiths, say — cobblers and other working people — and peasants, too — and even the masters — they all live for something better to**

come. They live a hundred — and maybe more years for a better man."

(SATINE continues to imitate the old man's voice and manner.) "Everybody, my friend, everybody lives for something better to come. That's why we have to be considerate of every man — at every moment. Who knows what's in him, why he was born and what he can do? Maybe he was born for our good fortune — for our greater benefit. And most especially we have to be considerate of youngsters. Kids need plenty of elbowroom. Don't interfere with their life. Be kind to them." *(In his own voice)* Yes, sir. When I'm drunk I like everything. A man can believe or not believe — it's his own affair. A man is free — he pays for everything himself — for belief and disbelief, for love, for intelligence, and that makes him free. Man — that's the truth!

What is man? It's not you, nor I, nor they — no. It's you, I, they, the old man, Napoleon, Mohammed — all in one. *(He outlines the figure of a man in the air.)* You understand? It's tremendous! In this are all the beginnings and all the ends. Everything in man, everything for man. Only man exists, the rest is the work of his hands and his brain. Man! It's magnificent! It has a proud ring — Man! We have to respect man, not pity him, not demean him. Let's drink to man! It's good to feel oneself a man. I'm a jailbird, a murderer, a cheat — granted! When I walk down the street, people look at me as at a crook — they sidestep and glance back at me — and often say "Scoundrel!" or "Work, work!" Work? For what? So that I have what my body needs and to feel satisfied? *(Laughs.)* I've always despised people whose main thought in life is to feel satisfied. That's not important — no! Man is above that! Man is above satisfaction!

from **The Cherry Orchard** (1904)

Anton Chekhov

Chekhov's playscripts occupy a special place in the world of the theatre because they provide character portraits that are three-dimensional and matchless in their decency, intelligence and gentleness — in spite of the obvious selfishness and narrow-mindedness they also display at times. Here, the poor but idealistic student Trofimov expresses his point of view on human nature and politics as they are reflected in Czarist Russia at the beginning of the 20th century.

TROFIMOV: Humanity progresses, perfecting its powers. Everything that is beyond its ken now will one day become familiar and comprehensible; only we must work, we must with all our powers aid the seeker after truth. Here among us in Russia the workers are few in number as yet. The vast majority of the intellectual people I know, seek nothing, do nothing, are not fit as yet for work of any kind. They call themselves intellectual, but they treat their servants as inferiors, behave to the peasants as though they were animals, learn little, read nothing seriously, do practically nothing, only talk about science and know very little about art. They are all serious people, they all have severe faces, they all talk of weighty matters and air their theories, and yet the vast majority of us — ninety-nine percent — live like savages, at the least thing fly to blows and abuse, eat piggishly, sleep in filth and stuffiness, bugs everywhere, stench and damp and moral impurity. And it's clear all our fine talk is only to divert our attention and other people's. Show me where to find the creches there's so much talk about, and the reading-rooms? They only exist in the novels: in real life there are none of them. There is nothing but filth and vulgarity and apathy. I fear and dislike very serious faces. I'm afraid of serious conversations. We should do better to be silent.

from **The Sea Gull** (1896)

Anton Chekhov

The lament that Chekhov expressed for the loss of innocence and gentleness that gave way to the dark and depressing clouds swelling over Russia prior to the revolution are indicative of his own respect for human dignity. The impending sense of doom and despair is translated to the stage in the character of Nina, who had left home to find success on the stage but found failure instead. Here she unburdens herself to a young, sensitive writer who still loves her deeply in spite of her attraction for another man.

NINA: Why do you say you kiss the ground I walk on? I ought to be killed. I'm so tired. If I could rest — rest. I'm a sea gull. No, that's not it. I'm an actress. Well, no matter now. He didn't believe in the theatre, all my dreams he'd laugh at, and little by little I quit believing in it myself, and lost heart. And there was the strain of love, jealousy, constant anxiety about my little baby. I got to be small and trashy, and played without thinking. I didn't know what to do with my hands, couldn't stand properly on the stage, couldn't control my voice. You can't imagine the feeling when you are acting and know it's dull. I'm a sea gull. No, that's not it. Do you remember, you shot a sea gull? A man comes by chance, sees it, and out of nothing else to do, destroys it. That's not it — *(Puts her hand to her forehead.)* What was I — ? I was talking about the stage. Now I'm not like that. I'm a real actress, I act with delight, with rapture. I'm drunk when I'm on the stage, and feel that I am beautiful. And now, ever since I've been here, I've kept walking about, kept walking and thinking, thinking and believing my soul grows stronger every day. Now I know, I understand that in our work — acting or writing — what matters is not fame, not glory, not what I used to dream about. It's how to endure, to bear my cross, and have faith. I have faith and it all doesn't hurt me so much, and when I think of my calling I'm not afraid of life.

from **There Shall Be No Night** (1940)

Robert E. Sherwood

A product of the Depression, Sherwood struggled to create a serious, realistic theatre that addressed significant social and ethical issues. In this monolog Miranda is reading the last letter written by her husband, the life-long pacifist, who finally realized the price of liberty and gave his own life in the pursuit of freedom after he received news of the death of his only son who defended his homeland of Finland against Russian invasion.

MIRANDA: *(Reading)* **"In this time of our own grief it is not easy to summon up the philosophy which has been formed from long study of the sufferings of others. But I must do it, and you must help me." You see — he wanted to make me feel that I'm stronger — wiser. "I have often read the words which Pericles spoke over the bodies of the dead, in the dark hour when the light of Athenian democracy was being extinguished by the Spartans. He told the mourning people that he could not give them any of the old words which tell how fair and noble it is to die in battle. Those empty words were old, even then, twenty-four centuries ago. But he urged them to find revival in the memory of the commonwealth which they together had achieved; and he promised them that the story of their commonwealth would never die, but would live on, far away, woven into the fabric of other men's lives. I believe that these words can be said now of our own dead, and our own commonwealth. I have always believed in the mystic truth of the Resurrection. The great leaders of the mind and the spirit — Socrates, Christ, Lincoln — were all done to death that the full measure of their contribution to human experience might never be lost. Now — the death of our son is only a fragment in the death of our country. But Erik and the others who gave their lives are also giving to mankind a symbol — a little symbol, to be sure, but a clear one — of man's**

unconquerable aspiration to dignity and freedom and purity in the sight of God. When I made that radio speech" — you remember? — "I quoted from St. Paul. I repeat those words to you now, darling. 'We glory in tribulations; knowing that tribulation worketh patience; and patience, experience; and experience, hope.' There are men here from all different countries. Fine men. Those Americans who were at our house on New Year's Day — and that nice Polish officer, Major Rutkowski — they are all here. They are waiting for me now, so I must close this, with all my love."

from **Oh, Dad, Poor Dad, Mama's Hung You in the Closet and I'm Feelin' So Sad** (1960)

Arthur Kopit

The setting for this absurd comedy is a lavish hotel room on a secluded Caribbean island. Jonathan, "a boy 17 years old but now dressed like a child of 10," is entertaining Rosalie, a girl some two years older than he, in a series of half-stated notions and comic turns intended to be sensational. Off-stage observers include Jonathan's mother, Madame Rosepettle, and her husband, who is dead, stuffed and hung in the closet!

JONATHAN: Well, would you like me to tell you how I made my telescope in case you find some lenses and tubing? Would you like that? Well, I made it out of lenses and tubing. The lenses I had because Ma-Ma-Mother gave me a set of lenses so I could see my stamps better. I have a fabulous collection of stamps, as well as a fantastic collection of coins and a simply unbelievable collection of books. Well, sir, Ma-Ma-Mother gave me these lenses so I could see my stamps better. She suspected that some were fake so she gave me the lenses so I might be ... able to see. You see? Well, sir, I happen to have nearly a billion stamps. So far I've looked closely at 1, 352, 769. I've discovered three actual fakes! Number 1, 352, 767 was a fake.

Number 1, 352, 768 was a fake, and number 1, 352, 769 was a fake. They were stuck together. Ma-Mother made me feed them im-mediately to her flytraps. Well . . . *(He whispers)* one day, when Mother wasn't looking . . . that is, when she was out, I heard an airplane flying. An airplane . . . somewhere . . . far away. It wasn't very loud, but still I heard it. An airplane. Flying . . . some-where, far away. And I ran outside to the porch so that I might see what it looked like. The airplane. With hundreds of people inside it. Hundreds and hundreds and hundreds of people. And I thought to myself, if I could just see . . . if I could just see what they looked like, the people, sitting at their windows looking out . . . and flying. If I could see . . . *just* once . . . if I could see *just once* what they looked like . . . then I might . . . know what I . . . what I . . . *(Slight pause)* So I . . . built a telescope in case the plane ever . . . came back again. The tubing came from an old blowgun. *(He reaches behind the bureau and produces a huge blowgun, easily a foot larger than he.)* Mother brought this back from her last hunting trip to Zanzibar. The lenses were the lenses she had given me for my stamps. So I built it. My telescope. A telescope so I might be able to see. And . . . *(He walks to the porch)* . . . and . . . and I *could* see! I could! I COULD! I really could. For miles and miles I could see. For miles and miles and *miles*! *(He begins to lift it up to look through but stops, for some reason, before he's brought it up to his eye.)* Only . . . *(He hands it to Rosalie. She takes it eagerly and scans the horizon and the sky. She hands it back to him.)* There's nothing out there to see. That's the trouble. You take the time to build a telescope that can sa-see for miles, then there's nothing out there to see. Ma-Mother says it's a lesson in Life. *(Pause)*

from **The Homecoming** (1965)

Harold Pinter

In an old and dreary house in North London lives Max, an aging head-of-the-household, and his son Lenny, a small-time pimp whose dreams of a successful life have long since evaporated. Into this dull environment comes Max's eldest son, Teddy, who has been living in America for six years teaching philosophy in a university. The "homecoming" celebration has an added attraction of Ruth, Teddy's wife, who is visiting the family she has never met. In this monolog Lenny shares intimate thoughts with Ruth to demonstrate his "sensitivity."

LENNY: I mean, I'm not saying that I'm not sensitive. I am, really. I mean, I am very sensitive to atmosphere, but I tend to get desensitized, if you know what I mean, when people make unreasonable demands on me. For instance, last Christmas I decided to do a bit of snow-clearing for the Borough Council, because we had a heavy snow over here that year in Europe. I didn't have to do this snow clearing — I mean I wasn't financially embarrassed in any way — it just appealed to me, it appealed to something inside me. What I anticipated with a good deal of pleasure was the brisk cold bite in the air in the early morning. And I was right. I had to get my snowboots on and I had to stand on a corner, at about five-thirty in the morning, to wait for the lorry to pick me up, to take me to the allotted area. Bloody freezing. Well, the lorry came, I jumped on the tailboard, headlights on, dipped, and off we went. Got there, shovels up, and off we went, deep into the December snow, hours before cockcrow. Well, that morning, while I was having my midmorning cup of tea in a neighbouring cafe, the shovel standing by my chair, an old lady approached me and asked me if I would give her a hand with her iron mangle. Her brother-in-law, she said, had left it for her, but he'd left it in the wrong room, he'd left it in the front room. Well, naturally, she wanted it in the back room. It was a

present he'd given her, you see, a mangle, to iron out
the washing. But he'd left it in the wrong room, he'd
left it in the front room, well that was a silly place to
leave it, it couldn't stay there. So I took time off to give
her a hand. She only lived up the road. Well, the only
trouble was when I got there I couldn't move this
mangle. It must have weighed about half a ton. How
this brother-in-law got it up there in the first place I
can't even begin to envisage. So there I was, doing a
bit of shoulders on with the mangle, risking a rupture,
and this old lady just standing there, waving me on,
not even lifting a little finger to give me a helping hand.
So after a few minutes I said to her, now look here,
why don't you stuff this iron mangle up your arse?
Anyway, I said, they're out of date, you want to get a
spin drier. I had a good mind to give her a workover
there and then, but as I was feeling jubilant with the
snow clearing I just gave her a short-arm jab to the
belly and jumped on a bus outside. Excuse me, shall I
take this ashtray out of your way?

from **Wandering** (1966)

Lanford Wilson

The essential seriousness of this excellent audition piece for
three performers is its almost cartoon-like approach to describing the
vivid episodes of a young man's life as he moves from adolescence to
maturity. As the title suggests, the young man is aimless and
uncertain as he wanders from one attraction to another; but there is
also the suggestion that his travels result in subsequent meaning
and purpose as he becomes aware of the many directions life may
take if only one chooses the right path.

For purposes of smooth transition, a description of the suggested
environments in which the action takes place is included for
performance consideration. The actors should retire to the "Attention"
position when not speaking and should face the audience in the
presentational style of delivery as appropriate. The episodes should

be performed in a rather rapid pace, with the performers changing roles as quickly and as obviously as the playscript indicates. The actors are also encouraged to enrich their audition performance by suggesting the many changes of locale within the playscript by rotating a single bench or chair so that it symbolizes the different environments called for in the episodes.

SUGGESTED LOCALES

UNIT I: *A Living Room*

Him is the young son, He is the angry Father, and She is the disappointed Mother. He is right of the chair facing left; She is left of the chair facing right; and Him is seated in the chair center stage.

UNIT II: *A Business Office*

He is the gruff-voiced employer, She is the gum-chewing secretary and Him is the nervous job applicant. He sits in a chair with his feet upon the desk. Him stands nervously downstage left and She is upstage center pantomiming the taking of notes.

UNIT III: *A Doctor's Office*

She is the physician, Him is the patient and He is the laboratory assistant. She stands upstage of the examination table, Him stands left of the desk and He stands down right of the desk holding a specimen jar.

UNIT IV: *A Confessional*

He is the priest, She is a statue of the Virgin Mary and Him is the penitent. He sits in a chair center stage and speaks with an Irish or Italian accent, Him kneels at the side of the chair stage right and She poses on the desk upstage left.

UNIT V: *A Draft Center*

Him is the inductee, He is a Southern general and She is off-stage right. Him stands shaking down center, and He sits in a chair upstage left. Him addresses the general by speaking directly to the audience.

UNIT VI: *A Clearing in the Park*

He is off-stage left as the voice of God, She is a sweet young girl of 16 and Him is a young lover. Him and She stand down right holding hands and looking above the heads of the audience, smiling and giggling.

UNIT VII: *A Battlefield*

Him and She are medics, and He is a wounded soldier who screams and then stumbles forward into their arms. They are all downstage center and face the audience throughout the episode.

UNIT VIII: *A Business Office*

Him is now the gruff-voiced employer and She is an older gum-chewing secretary. He is now the brash, youthful salesman. Him sits in a chair with his feet upon the desk, She is upstage center pantomiming the taking of notes and He enters to stand nervously downstage left.

UNIT IX: *A Cemetery*

Him lies on the bench with his head facing center stage, as the deceased. She is the mournful wife and sits in a chair facing the bench. He is the scheming friend and stands behind the chair with his hand gently resting on her shoulder.

UNIT X: *Limbo*

They stand in a straight line near the downstage center playing area facing the audience. He is right, Him is center and She is left. They speak to the audience as robots and as the characters indicated in the suggested directions. Him tries to cover his ears whenever he is not speaking.

The vivid portrayal of a young man's journey in search of himself provides a challenging ensemble selection for three performers. The simplicity of each episode only masks the more serious undertone as the young man moves from adolescence to maturity in his "wandering" toward self-recognition.

UNIT I
"A Living Room"

SHE: Where have you been?

HIM: Wandering around.

SHE: Wandering around. I don't know why you can't be a man; you just wait till the Army gets a hold of you, young man.

HE: They'll make a man of you —.

SHE: Straighten you out.

HE: A little regimentation.

SHE: Regulation.

HE: Specification.

SHE: Indoctrination.

HE: Boredom.

SHE: You'll get up and go to bed.

HE: Drill; march.

SHE: Take orders.

HE: Fight.

SHE: Do what they tell you.

HE: Keep in step.

SHE: Do your part.

HE: Kill a man.

SHE: You'll be a better person to live with, believe me. As a matter of fact, your father and I are getting damned tired of having you around.

HE: Looking after you.

SHE: Making your bed.

HE: Keeping you out of trouble.

SHE: How old are you, anyway?

HIM: Sixteen.

HE: Sixteen — well, my God.

SHE: Shouldn't you be drafted before long?

HIM: Two years.

SHE: You just better toe the mark.

399

UNIT II
"A Business Office"

HE: How long at your present address?

HIM: Six months.

HE: Any previous experience as an apprentice?

HIM: No, sir.

HE: Where did you live before that?

HIM: I was just wandering around.

HE: Not good. Draft status?

HIM: Well, I haven't been called but —

HE: We like fighters on our team, fellow.

HIM: Well, actually I'm a conscientious —

UNIT III
"A Doctor's Office"

SHE: Sit down. Roll up your sleeve. Take off your shirt. Stick out your tongue. Bend over, open your mouth, make a fist, read the top line. Cough. *(HIM coughs.)* Very good.

HIM: Thank you.

SHE: Perfect specimen.

HIM: I do a considerable amount of walking.

UNIT IV
"A Confessional"

HE: I don't follow you.

HIM: I don't believe in war.

HE: There's no danger of war. Our country is never an aggressor.

HIM: But armies, see — I don't believe in it.

HE: Do you love your country?

HIM: No more than any other, the ones I've seen.

HE: That's treason.

400

HIM: I'm sorry.

UNIT V
"A Draft Center"

HE: Quite all right, we'll take you.

HIM: I won't go.

HE: Service is compulsory.

HIM: It's my right.

HE: You'll learn.

HIM: I don't believe in killing people.

HE: For freedom?

HIM: No.

HE: For love?

HIM: No.

HE: For money?

HIM: No.

HE: We'll teach you.

HIM: I know, but I won't.

HE: You'll learn.

HIM: I can't.

HE: You're going.

HIM: I'm not.

HE: You'll see.

HIM: I'm sure.

HE: You'll see.

HIM: I'm flat-footed.

HE: You'll do.

HIM: I'm queer.

HE: Get lost.

UNIT VI
"A Clearing in the Park"

SHE: I'm lost.

HIM: I'm sorry.

401

SHE: Aren't you lost?

HIM: I wasn't going anyplace in particular.

SHE: That's unnatural.

HIM: I was just wandering.

SHE: What will become of you?

HIM: I hadn't thought of it.

SHE: You don't believe in anything.

HIM: But you see, I do.

HE: I see.

HIM: It's just that no one else seems to believe — not really.

HE: I see.

HIM: Like this pride in country.

HE: I see.

HIM: And this pride in blood.

HE: I see.

HIM: It just seems that pride is such a pointless thing. I can't believe in killing someone for it.

SHE: Oh, my God, honey, it isn't killing. It's merely nudging out of the way.

HIM: But we don't need it.

SHE: Think of our position, think of me, think of the children.

HIM: I am.

SHE: You're shiftless is what it is.

HIM: I'm really quite happy; I don't know why.

SHE: Well, how do you think I feel?

UNIT VII
"A Battlefield"

HIM: Not too well, really.

SHE: Where does it hurt?

HE: Nothing to worry about.

SHE: Yes, sir.

HE: Thank you.

UNIT VIII
"A Business Office"

SHE: And that's all for the morning. Mr. Trader is on line six.

HIM: Thank you. Send Wheeler in.

HE: How are you, old boy?

HIM: Not well, I'm afraid.

SHE: Don't be. It isn't serious.

HE: Just been working too hard.

SHE: Why don't you lie down.

HE: Best thing for you.

UNIT IX
"A Cemetery"

SHE: I know, but he was quite handsome — a gentle man.

HE: Bit of a radical though — not good for the family.

SHE: I know.

HE: You're better off.

SHE: I have a life of my own.

HE: ... you have a life of your own.

SHE: He was such a lost lamb.

HE: Never agreed with anyone.

SHE: Arguments everywhere we went.

HE: What kind of disposition is that?

SHE: I don't know what I ever saw in him.

HE: You need someone who knows his way around.

SHE: I do.

HE: I do.

UNIT X
"Limbo"

(Pause)

SHE: *(In the voice of the Mother)* I don't know why you can't be
a man.

HE: *(In the voice of the Father)* **Keep in step.**

SHE: *(In the voice of the Mother)* **Toe the mark.**

HE: *(In the voice of the Employer)* **Draft status?**

SHE: *(In the voice of the Doctor)* **Stick out your tongue.**

HE: *(In the voice of the General)* **You'll learn.**

SHE: *(In the voice of the Sweet Young Girl)* **What'll become of you?**

HE: *(In the voice of God)* **I see.**

SHE: *(In the voice of the Sweet Young Girl)* **Think of the children.**

HE: *(In the voice of the Scheming Friend)* **Best thing for you.**

SHE: *(In the voice of the Mournful Wife)* **I do.**
    (Pause)

HE: *(In the voice of God)* **I see.**

HIM: *(Faces audience and speaks in a normal voice.)* **I mean, that can't be the way people want to spend their lives.**

SHE: *(In the voice of the Secretary)* **Trader on line six.**

HIM: *(In the voice of Him as the Boss)* **Thank you.**

HE: *(In the voice of the Brash Salesman)* **Just been working too hard.**

SHE: *(In the voice of the Mournful Wife)* **I do.**
    (Pause)

SHE: *(In the voice of the Mother)* **Where?**

HIM: *(In the voice of Him as the young man in his youth)* **Wandering.**

HE: *(In the voice of the Father)* **I see.**

HIM: *(Faces audience and speaks in a normal voice.)* **They'll believe anything anyone tells them.**

HE: *(In the voice of God)* **I see.**

HIM: *(Faces audience and speaks in a normal voice)* **I mean, that can't be the way people want to spend their lives.**

SHE: *(In the voice of the Secretary)* **That's all for the morning.**

HIM: *(In the voice of Him as the Boss)* **Quite happy.**

HE: *(In the voice of the Scheming Friend)* **Best thing for you.**

SHE: *(In the voice of the Mournful Wife)* **I do.**

HE: *(In the voice of the Scheming Friend)* **I do.**
    (Pause)

SHE: *(In the voice of the Mother)* **Where have you been?**

(Pause)

HIM: *(Faces audience, kneels and pleads in a sad, mournful voice.)* **Can it?**

(Blackout)

from **Cousins** (1979)

Horton Foote

The Robedaux family relatives have all gathered — in person and in memory — to comfort Horace Robedaux's mother after an emergency operation. As the family circle, especially the eccentric cousins, draws bravely together to face the inevitable life-and-death struggle of Mother Robedaux there are warm moments of remembrance as well as recollections of the good old days. In the monolog that follows, cousin Lewis enters in a drunken stupor and reminisces about his own bitter past and the loss of family ties.

LEWIS: **My mama died, you know, when I was three. She had it fixed so my daddy couldn't get hold of her inheritance. It came directly to me and my brother. My granddaddy said he gets the credit for fixing it that way. No matter how many wives and children my daddy had he couldn't give our land to them to divide it amongst them. Brother says that hurt Daddy so, when he found out how Mama had made out her will, that he just gave up and died, too. Granddaddy says it wasn't so. He says my daddy wasn't much to start with and if he had ever gotten his hands on what my brother and I had we would have wound up with nothing. As it is, I've got a thousand acres of fine cotton land and so has my brother. But like Brother Vaughn says, a loss of a mother is a terrible thing. I know one night we were all on our way to Houston, drunk, and we stopped by Richmond on the way there and we went out to this bootlegger we knew about in the country to get us some whiskey and when we went inside there was strangers there and we didn't know a soul, not a**

living soul . . . except for one man who reminded me later he was my cousin. My fifth cousin, I think he said. And Brother Vaughn can talk, you know, when he has a mind to, and he says to all those people there: "Good people . . . good people. You don't know us and we don't know you. But here is an old boy before you that lost his mother when he was three. And that's a sad, terrible thing. Now, I have a mother and I trust the rest of you have, this old boy doesn't." Well, I tell you those men couldn't do enough for me. They all felt so bad, they said, about my mother dying. They all had to buy me a drink of whiskey and Brother Vaughn a drink of whiskey because he was my good friend. Well, sir, they bought us so much whiskey and we got so drunk we never did get to Houston. We just spent the whole day and night out in the country in Richmond drinking whiskey until we both passed out and some good, kind person put us to bed. Anyway, that's the kind of friend Brother Vaughn was.

from Act Without Words (1980)
Samuel Beckett

Desert. Dazzling light. The scenic image is simple: a solitary mime performs an extended scenario of suffering and rejection as he confronts the unknown isolated in both time and space. The radical simplification of the dramatic events that follow is typical of the theatre of the absurd and presents imaginative performance opportunities for movement and nonverbal communication that should make for a memorable audition performance that calls for precisely choreographed actor focus, gesture and subtext.

The man is flung backwards on stage from right wing.
  He falls, gets up immediately, dusts himself, turns aside, reflects.
Whistle from right wing.
He reflects, goes out right.
Immediately flung back on stage he falls, gets up

Precisely choreographed movement and gesture helps to promote a truly imaginative audition piece that involves suggestive "subtext" as well as "nonverbal" communication in the development of the character being depicted.

immediately, dusts himself, turns aside, reflects.

Whistle from left wing.

He reflects, goes out left.

Immediately flung back on stage he falls, gets up immediately, dusts himself, turns aside, reflects.

Whistle from left wing.

He reflects, goes toward left wing, hesitates, thinks better of it, halts, turns aside, reflects.

A little tree descends from flies, lands. It has a single bough some three yards from ground and at its summit a meager tuft of palms casting at its foot a circle of shadow.

He continues to reflect.

Whistle from above.

He turns, sees tree, reflects, goes to it, sits down in its shadow, looks at his hands.

A pair of tailor's scissors descends from flies, comes to rest before tree, a yard from ground.

He continues to look at his hands.

Whistle from above.

He looks up, sees scissors, takes them and starts to trim his nails.

The palms close like a parasol, the shadow disappears.

He drops scissors, reflects.

A tiny carafe, to which is attached a huge label inscribed WATER, descends from flies, comes to rest some three yards from ground.

He continues to reflect.

Whistle from above.

He turns, sees cube, takes it up, carries it over and sits it down under carafe, tests its stability, gets up on it, tries in vain to reach carafe, renounces, gets down, carries cube back to its place, turns aside, reflects.

A second smaller cube descends from flies, lands.

He continues to reflect.

Whistle from above.

He turns, sees second cube, looks at it, at carafe, goes to second cube, takes it up, carries it over and sets it down under carafe, tests its stability, gets up on it, tries in vain to reach carafe, renounces, gets down, takes up second cube to carry back to its place, hesitates, thinks better of it, sets it down, goes to big cube, takes it up, carries it over and puts it on small one, tests their stability, gets up on them, the cubes collapse, he falls, gets up immediately, brushes himself, reflects.

He takes up small cube, puts it on big one, tests their stability, gets up on them and is about to reach carafe when it is pulled up a little way and comes to rest beyond his reach.

He gets down, reflects, carries cubes back to their place, one by one, turns aside, reflects.

A third still smaller cube descends from flies, lands.

He continues to reflect.

Whistle from above.

He turns, sees third cube, looks at it, reflects, turns aside, reflects.

The third cube is pulled up and disappears in flies.

Beside carafe a rope descends from flies, with knots to facilitate ascent.

He continues to reflect.

Whistle from above.

He turns, sees rope, reflects, goes to it, climbs up it and is about to reach carafe when rope is let out and deposits him back on ground.

He reflects, looks around for scissors, sees them, goes and picks them up, returns to rope and starts to cut it with scissors.

The rope is pulled up, lifts him off ground, he hangs on, succeeds in cutting rope, falls back on ground, drops scissors, falls, gets up again immediately, brushes himself, reflects.

409

The rope is pulled up quickly, and disappears in flies.

With length of rope in his possession he makes a lasso with which he tries to lasso carafe.

The carafe is pulled up quickly and disappears in flies.

He turns aside, reflects.

He goes with lasso in his hand to tree, looks at bough, turns and looks at cubes, looks again at bough, drops lasso, goes to cubes, takes up small one, carries it over and sets it down under bough, goes back for big one, takes it up and carries it over under bough, makes to put it on small one, hesitates, thinks better of it, sets it down, takes up small one and puts it on big one, tests their stability, turns aside and stoops to pick up lasso.

The bough folds down against trunk.

He straightens up with lasso in his hand, turns and sees what has happened.

He drops lasso, turns aside, reflects.

He carries back cubes to their places, one by one, goes back for lasso, carries it over to cubes and lays it in a neat coil on small one.

He turns aside, reflects.

Whistle from right wing.

He reflects, goes out right.

Immediately flung back on stage he falls, gets up immediately, brushes himself, turns aside, reflects.

Whistle from left wing.

He does not move.

He looks at his hands, looks around for scissors, sees them, goes and picks them up, starts to trim his nails, stops, reflects, runs his finger along blade of scissors, goes and lays them on small cube, turns aside, opens his collar, frees his neck and fingers it.

The small cube is pulled up and disappears in flies, carrying away rope and scissors.

He turns to take scissors, sees what has happened.

He turns aside, reflects.

He goes and sits down on big cube.

The big cube is pulled from under him. He falls. The big cube is pulled up and disappears in flies.

He remains lying on his side, his face towards auditorium, staring before him.

The carafe descends from flies and comes to rest a few feet from his body.

He does not move.

Whistle from above.

He does not move.

The carafe descends further, dangles and plays about his face.

He does not move.

The carafe is pulled up and disappears in flies.

The bough returns to horizontal, the palms open, the shadow returns.

Whistle from above.

He does not move.

The tree is pulled up and disappears in flies.

He looks at his hands.

(End)

from **Yesterday's News** (1981)

Peter Barnes

This is one of *seven* 15-minute monologs written by the author as part of his "Barnes' People" collection of character sketches. In each of the extended monologs the characters share intimate details of their lives, address the audience directly about their thoughts and offer personal testimonies of their views on a wide range of mundane and serious topics. In this monolog the character Anna offers a candid and critical interpretation of her life and anticipates the suspenseful future now that she is 113 years old!

ANNA: Young man, if lobsters were just ten times bigger and carried guns, they'd be given respect instead of boiling water. I'm one hundred and thirteen years old and an O.B.E. I'm so old I have to be fumigated. That's why you're here, isn't it? You want to get my story down on that machine. Sometimes sentences are just a noise to the old but I can still hold my water. I've got a personal maid and nurse. I can pay so I'm not treated like old rope. There's a lot of sad sights if you're old and the steam's running out. It's to do with the mind. But I'm different. I'm different, young man.

I've had congratulations from all over the world, and a telegram from the Queen. She's coming to see me. If it's formal I'll wear my Marie Antoinette bonnet. She'll hear about Mrs. Allen. I don't think the Queen knows much about her. And I'll tell her the wonder is not that such things should be, it's that they should be such things and not such other things.

Give me a drink. If it's wet I'll drink it when the mood's on me and the dancers in hobnail boots start thumping away in my head. I've drunk everything in my time. Once I even tried metal polish and hard cider, that's a real thirst-quencher and better than having your arm cut off. It sent Percy McKell away blind ... or was it self-abuse? My memory isn't what it was when ...

If you're old you lose your sense of time. You find yourself wondering what came first and what followed this and that and what happened when, how and why? It makes no difference. But the difference is what makes life worth living.

How can a little old lady like me fight the fading of memory? But I try, I try. I remember saying to my husband, George, "I've a confession to make. I've been sleeping with another man." And he said, "Me too, turn over." Oh, I remember the horse-drawn buses and the Zeppelin raids and the Silvertown explosion and the long skirts and bustles and the ladies with lace handkerchiefs and lavender —.

I don't want to lie calmly in my grave and dream.

I still like life with its sweet and bitter wonders. It's hard when your face is hairy and your teeth are out and your eyes have sunk into your head. It's better than having your body rot in a clean winding sheet but it's hard even if you've got charm. And I've got charm. Always have had. My mother said it's better to have charm than beauty and better to have money than anything.

My mother was a remarkable woman for her height. I owe everything to her. She taught me to always pay my way. I never owed anything to anyone, that's what puts years on your life.

I was an adventuress but I should've been an accountant. I've always liked working with figures. There's no hypocrisy there. Cheating, yes, but no hypocrisy. My mother set me up in business when I was about thirteen. I was gorgeous, wasn't I? We took furnished rooms at 12 Lissom Grove. The landlady was passionately fond of me. My mother had lots of gentlemen callers and they looked at me like beggars at a sunbeam. But my mother said, "God forbid my daughter should make the same mistakes I did. She's not going to sell herself cheap."

Finally she dressed me in a white satin gown without any sleeves to show off my arms and introduced me to an old man who kept rubbing his hands together when he looked at me: the rich know where the good wine lies.

He came to my room that night after paying the full price of admission — one hundred pounds: I wasn't being sold cheap. My mother told me to put up some kind of fuss. It was expected of a nice young lady. So I threw him out of the bed and broke two of his ribs — though he didn't notice at the time, except when he moved. I cried, "Ooh, ooh, you'll split me in two." The old man smiled proudly through his pain. With the help of cochineal and tomato ketchup I managed to re-sell my maidenhead at least twenty times before I was eighteen. There are no good girls, only frightened men. I learnt very early that large sums of money are to be made in the love market, but there are no rules because the price of love is governed by desire, and nothing is more easy to manipulate than desire as I found out to my cost when I ran off with a singer from the chorus of *The Gondoliers*. I soon became pregnant and he lost his job. I was going to drown myself but I decided to wait for the warm weather. I've been rich and I've been poor — believe me rich is better. I'm not talking about the warm poverty of softies like you, young man, where you shelter under a leaky roof, on the edge of destitution because you temporarily lack money. I'm talking about the cold poverty of the poor where there's no bread for starving kids and the sick ones moan and there's no medicine for 'em and no help. That sort of poverty isn't just a lack of money, it's something positive, a disease more terrible than leprosy and the poor should be shunned like lepers. I had to cure myself before I rotted away. I abandoned my lover on Crewe station and my twin baby girls in the vestibule of a nearby church. I found out later they were taken to a Foundling Hospital where they died within a month of something called marasmus. Well, lessons have to be paid for and it's all yesterday's news.

When the world turns honest I'll take the veil. I went back to mother and met George. He was an eligible bachelor — I forget to ask eligible for what? He had a receding chin and brain but he came from a good background. My mother said he had royal blood in his veins. I didn't care if he had a royal flush in his kidneys. I married him to please her though I knew insanity ravaged his family from time to time.

He always carried a soap container in his pocket

and when he shook hands with someone he would go straight out and wash them. In restaurants he drank coffee through a straw so as not to touch the cup with his lips.

We had two good years until the money ran out and he expected me to provide for both of us. "What do you call a man who is kept by his wife?" I asked. "Lucky," he replied. He didn't think it wrong for a woman to prostitute herself for her husband provided he approved. Neither did I but I hated working for a sleeping partner. I had to be rid of him but it was hard then, the scales were weighted against women. Unfortunately for George his family had never approved of divorce. I didn't want to leave him because he could always return to me and my money. He had to leave me. Luckily, George's favourite meal was mushrooms. I picked them myself. Somehow they got mixed with some weed killer. Now there are more efficient methods but in those days we had to make do. Poor George, there's no man so good that someone isn't delighted to be at his deathbed.

There was talk, of course, about George's death. Yesterday's news. Murder's an ugly word — but bankruptcy is uglier. I think I made the right choice. One's values remain the same no matter how long you live; the hair on your chin grows longer but your principles don't change. But I'll admit my method with George had disadvantages. Killing and such can have a bad effect on one's character if you're not careful.

After a woman indulges herself, it can be downhill all the way. From then on I thought nothing of lying, cheating, being lazy and rude. You start in a small way, wasting a wastrel and end up by being rude to your mother. And that's when I started drinking. Nothing to do with conscience, young man. I've managed to survive one hundred and thirteen years without a conscience. What's it for? Nobody's even been able to tell me. Can conscience put hot food in your stomach and money in your pocket? I don't believe in conscience.

A conscience wouldn't have helped us in two world wars. *(Singing)* "Good-bye Dolly, I must leave you though it breaks my heart to go."

They were good times for me. I bought and sold anything. I had lots of German friends and they paid well for information — it *was* the Germans we were fighting wasn't it, not the Czechs? Young man, the recruiting sergeant is always waiting at the corner trying to sell you a uniform or a flag. Don't buy!

The twenties were the best. I had the most exclusive house in London. Our prospectus listed sadism, masochism, voyeurism — it was good value for money for the overheads were high and profit margins slim so I had a sideline in white slavery and snow. I imported cocaine and exported girls to establishments in Cairo and Valparaiso. Human beings are forced into sin as fish are forced into water. But everybody's against vice when they aren't practicing it. I was the most notorious madame in London for a year or two. They called me a loose woman. I told them not to worry, I'd be tight before the evening was over. But it's all yesterday's news. The truth was I kept a well-run house. We had our accidents, of course, like when Bishop Mallard was found asphyxiated in our Eastern room. He lay dead on the six-inch Persian carpet with his trousers off beside the naked body of one of my girls. In the passion of the moment he'd accidentally kicked open a gas jet with his foot. He seemed happy enough. I don't know about the girl.

We catered for parties too, with special rates for Rotarians, Freemasons, sales conventions and the like. I tried to give them a good show. Once we had two naked

416

girls running round a couch and some idiot we borrowed from a lunatic asylum in South Lambeth chasing
them. The real idiots were down in the audience.

I had to be like a tiger. Young man, I think you
are lovely. Greed was the motive that kept me going.
They're always insulting greed. All I can say is God
help the ungreedy — the poor and the starving mil-
lions. I'm a grabber. When I grabbed I prospered. When
I stopped grabbing I struck trouble.

Horatio Bottomly gave me some good advice. If
you meet a man who wants to share his good fortune
with you — run. He's a cook who's trying to swindle
you out of your honest savings. *(Singing)* "Oh hear me
sigh. I'm old, I'm old. Lie with me before I die."

Teddy was thirty years younger than me. It seems
ever since I can remember everybody's been younger
than me. Strapping chap. Very tall, well-shaped, dark
skin, always in the best of humour — everybody's
friend. I was fool enough to spend my money on him
and he was smart enough to help me. The greatest
chiseler since Michaelangelo. Oh, but his jingle jobs
filled me to overflowing. He left and it was heartbreak
hill for me. But the nice thing about tears is they come
out in the wash. I had to start up again: gambling,
blackmail, swindling — if there was a demand for it I
was there.

Now I never give anything away. I'm a mean,
selfish old mother-monster. But I'm still here because
I've lived every day, every hour, every minute of my
one hundred and thirteen years for myself alone.

You've got lovely hair, young man. I was going to
tell the Queen the story of Mrs. Allen, wasn't I? She
was a charlady in one of my brothels.

After her husband died, her neighbours said she'd
come home drunk and was an unfit mother. So the
authorities took away her little four-year-old girl and

417

put her in a home. Some time after I gave Mrs. Allen a hat of mine which she loved. She said her neighbours wanted to take the hat away too just because she loved it. So one evening she got hold of a hammer and nail, put on the hat, stood in front of a mirror, put the nail in the middle of her head and hammered it into her skull. They couldn't take the hat away from her as they took away her baby. It shows you shouldn't brood on yesterday's news; 'tisn't healthy. No, I don't sit in the corner and worry. I'm still interested in myself. That's what keeps me going. You've got lovely hair, young man. The sentences are sounding like a lot of noise now. I'm tired. I want to be right for the Queen. You've got enough now, haven't you? Prostitution, white slavery, drugs, murder, blackmail — passed like passing water. Now it's about as wicked as smoking a cigarette, as interesting as watching celery grow. Yesterday's news...

from The Marriage of Bette and Boo (1985)
Christopher Durang

The comic genius of Christopher Durang's absurdism frequently dramatizes the imagination as it might be realized in dreams and explores the world of the subconscious to reveal the interior of man through visual objects and symbols. This savage comedy of domestic family life depicts the bizarre Bette, whose marriage to the ineffectual Boo, is characterized by her series of tragic miscarriages and his chronic drunkness. In this monolog we listen to Father Donnally offer this perceptive counsel at a parish retreat.

FATHER DONNALLY: Young marrieds have many problems to get used to. For some of them this is the first person of the opposite sex the other has even known. The husband may not be used to having a woman in his bathroom. The wife may not be used to a strong masculine odor in her boudoir. Or then the wife may not cook well enough. How many marriages have floundered on the rocks of ill-cooked bacon? *(Pauses.)* I used to amuse friends by imitating bacon in a saucepan. Would anyone like to see that? *(FATHER DONNALLY looks around. After a while, FATHER DONNALLY falls to the ground and does a fairly good — or if not good, at least unabashedly peculiar — imitation of bacon, making sizzling noises and contorting his body to represent bacon becoming crisp. Toward the end, he makes sputtering noises into the air. Then he stands up again. All present applaud with varying degrees of approval or incredulity.)* I also do coffee percolating. *(He does this.)* Pt. Pt. Ptptptptptptptptpt. Bacon's better. But things like coffee and bacon are important in a marriage, because they represent things that the wife does to make her husband happy. Or fat. *(Laughs.)* The wife cooks the bacon, and the husband brings home the bacon. This is how St. Paul saw marriage, although they probably didn't really eat pork back then, the curing process was not very well worked out in Christ's time, which is why so many of them followed the Jewish dietary laws even though they were Christians. I know I'm glad to be living now when we have cured pork and plumbing and showers rather than back when Christ lived. Many priests say they wish they had lived in Christ's time so they could have met him; that would, of course, have been very nice, but I'm glad I live now and that I have a shower. *(EMILY, bothered by what he's just said, raises her hand.)* I'm not ready for questions yet, Emily. *(EMILY lowers her hand; he sips his wine.)* Man and wife as St. Paul saw it. Now the woman should obey her husband, but that's not considered a very modern thought, so I don't even want to talk about it. All right, don't obey your husbands, but if chaos follows, don't blame me. The tower of Babel as an image of chaos has always fascinated me —.

Now I don't mean to get off the point. The point is

husband and wife, man and woman. Adam and rib. I don't want to dwell on the inequality of the sexes because these vary from couple to couple — sometimes the man is stupid, sometimes the woman is stupid, sometimes both are stupid. The point is man and wife are joined in holy matrimony to complete each other, to populate the earth and to glorify God. That's what it's for. That's what life is for. If you're not a priest or a nun, you normally get married. *(EMILY raises her hand.)* Yes, I know, you're not married, Emily. Not everyone gets married. But my comments today are geared toward the *married* people here. *(EMILY lowers her hand.)* Man and wife are helpmates. She helps him, he helps her. In sickness and in health. Anna Karenina should not have left her husband, nor should she have jumped in front of a train. Marriage is not a step to be taken lightly. The church does not recognize divorce; it does not permit it, if you insist for legal purposes, but in the eyes of the church you are still married and you can never be unmarried, and that's why you can never remarry after a divorce because that would be bigamy and that's a sin and illegal as well.

(Breathes.) So, for God's sake, if you're going to get married pay attention to what you're doing, have conversations with the person, figure out if you *really* want to live with that person for years and years and years, because you can't change it. Priests have it easier. If I don't like my pastor, I can apply for a transfer. If I don't like a housekeeper, I can get her fired. *(Looks disgruntled.)* But a husband and wife are *stuck* together. So know what you're doing when you get married. I get so *sick* of these people coming to me after they're married, and they've just gotten to know one another *after* the ceremony, and they've discovered they have nothing in common and they hate one another. And they want me to come up with a

solution. *(Throws up his hands.)* **What can I do? There is no solution to a problem like that. I can't help them! It puts me in a terrible position. I can't say get a divorce, that's against God's law. I can't say go get some on the side, that's against God's law. I can't say just pretend you're happy and maybe after a while you won't know the difference because, though that's not against God's law, not that many people know how to do that, and if I suggested it to people, they'd write to the Bishop complaining about me and then he'd transfer me to some godforsaken place in Latin America without a shower, and all because these people don't know what they're doing when they get married.** *(Shakes his head.)* **So I mumble platitudes to these people who come to me with these insoluble problems, and I think to myself, "Why didn't they** *think* **before they got married? Why does no one ever** *think***? Why did God make people stupid?"** *(Pause)* **Are there any questions?**

from **Dancing at Lughnasa** (1990)

Brian Friel

Winner of the 1991 Tony Award for "Best Dramatic Play," this is a "memory" drama told from the point of view of Michael, who recalls the year 1936 when he was seven years old living in a typical Irish cottage with his unwed mother and several loving aunts. Michael, the man, is present to the audience but not to the rest of the characters in the play and wanders in and out of the individual scenes to comment upon the celebration of life that is being observed.

MICHAEL: **The following night Vera McLaughlin arrived and explained to Agnes and Rose why she couldn't buy their hand-knitted gloves anymore. Most of her home knitters were already working in the new factory and she advised Agnes and Rose to apply immediately. The Industrial Revolution had finally caught up with Ballybeg.**

They didn't apply, even though they had no other means of making a living, and they never discussed their situation with their sisters. Perhaps Agnes made the decision for both of them because she knew Rose wouldn't have got work there anyway. Or perhaps, as Kate believed, because Agnes was too stubborn to work in a factory. Or perhaps the two of them just wanted . . . away.

Anyhow, on my first day back at school, when we came into the kitchen for breakfast, there was a note propped up against the milk jug: "We are gone for good. This is best for all. Do not try to find us." It was written in Agnes's resolute hand. Of course, they did try to find them. So did the police. So did our neighbors who had a huge network of relatives all over England and America. But they had vanished without trace. And by the time I tracked them down — twenty-five years later, in London — Agnes was dead and Rose was dying in a hospice for the destitute in Southwark.

The scraps of information I gathered about their lives during those missing years were too sparse to be coherent. They had moved about a lot. They had worked as cleaning women in public toilets, in factories, in the underground. Then, when Rose could no longer get work, Agnes tried to support them both — but couldn't. From then on, I gathered, they gave up. They took to drink; slept in parks, in doorways, on the Thames Embankment. Then Agnes died of exposure. And two days after I found Rose in that grim hospice — she didn't recognize me, of course — she died in her sleep.

Father Jack's health improved quickly and he soon recovered his full vocabulary and all his old bounce and vigor. But he didn't say Mass that following Monday. In fact, he never said Mass again. And the neighbors stopped inquiring about him. And his name never again appeared in the *Donegal Enquirer*. And of course there was never a civic reception with bands and flags and speeches.

But he never lost his determination to return to Uganda and he still talked passionately about his life with the lepers there. And each new anecdote contained more revelations. And each new revelation startled — shocked — stunned poor Aunt Kate. Until finally she hit on a phrase that appeased her: "His own distinctive spiritual search." "Leaping around a fire and offering a little hen to Uka or Ito or whoever is not religion as I was taught it and indeed know it," she would say with a defiant toss of her head. "But then Jack must make his own distinctive search." And when he died suddenly of a heart attack — within a year of his homecoming, on the very eve of the following La Lughnasa* — my mother and Maggie mourned him sorely. But for months Kate was inconsolable.

My father sailed for Spain that Saturday. The last I saw of him was dancing down the lane in imitation of Fred Astaire, swinging his walking stick, Uncle Jack's ceremonial tricorn at a jaunty angle over his left eye. When he got to the main road he stopped and turned and with both hands blew a dozen theatrical kisses back to Mother and me. He was wounded in Barcelona — he fell off his motorbike — so that for the rest of his life he walked with a limp. The limp wasn't disabling but it put an end to his dancing days; and that really distressed him. Even the role of maimed veteran, which he loved, could never compensate for that. He still visited us occasionally, perhaps once a year. Each time he was on the brink of a new career. And each time he proposed to Mother and promised me a new bike. Then the war came in 1939; his visits

*Lughnasa (loo'-na-sa) is Gaelic for "August" and is the name of a festival celebrated in Ireland since pagan times to guarantee good harvest and celebrate life.

423

became more infrequent; and finally he stopped coming altogether.

Sometime in the mid-fifties I got a letter from a tiny village in the south of Wales; a curt note from a young man of my own age and also called Michael Evans. He had found my name and address among the belongings of his father, Gerry Evans. He introduced himself as my half-brother and he wanted me to know that Gerry Evans, the father we shared, had died peacefully in the family home the previous week. Throughout his final illness he was nursed by his wife and his three grown children who all lived and worked in the village.

My mother never knew of that letter. I decided to tell her — decided not to — vacillated for years as my father would have done; and eventually, rightly or wrongly, kept the information to myself!

from **Trophies** (1992)

John Wooten

The most recent monolog in the collection of contemporary drama, this excerpt focuses upon a troubled family shattered by a freak accident that left the youngest son crippled and disillusioned. The elder son, David, also reveals his own hidden and troublesome thoughts of frustration and despair in this candid, honest conversation with his father that follows the traditional holiday argument they inevitably share. The dialog also mirrors David's own sense of disillusionment in the "games" he and his father play with each other.

DAVID: I was up there getting my stuff together and as I packed everything in my suitcase, ready to storm out of here and never come back, it occurred to me what Bobby and Laura said. How it gets worse for them when I come home. How I use them to get at you. And I sat down and looked around the room I grew up in. I tried to remember what it was like being a little kid. I tried to shut my eyes and force time to reverse, to take a different path. I mean, that's what we both want, isn't it? Time to rewind itself? Anyway, I thought of how my visits home have grown uglier, shorter and less frequent. I started thinking maybe I've been unfair, maybe what they said was true. I was tempted to unpack the suitcase, run downstairs and declare I wouldn't be leaving. I was here for the duration, here to save this family! *(No response)* But that would be proving Laura and Bobby wrong. And as much as I hate to admit it and as much as it hurts, I'm afraid I can't do that. And as pathetic as that makes me feel, I don't think I can stop behaving this way. *(No response)* You see, when I was sitting up there, I couldn't reverse time, no, but I could see time. Feel it. Almost like I was there again. I saw a man in front of a television set and he was like a statue, his eyes wouldn't move. And next to him I saw a little boy, very young, and he was speaking to this statue, asking it questions. It was clear he was the boy's hero and the longer the man remained still and distant, the more frequent and desperate the questions became. But still all I could hear was the little boy's voice. I saw other things, but this one was the most vivid. The boy continued to try to chisel away but to no avail. And his longing grew to such a point that he wanted this frozen hero of his to lash out, hit him, kick him, anything. Anything to let him know he was there, let him know he existed. *(Short pause)* Then this vision, the little boy and the statue vanished. *(Pause)* Stupid kid, huh? You and I both know there's no such thing as heroes. *(No response)* Anyway, I couldn't rewind time. But what I saw made me realize I no longer hate you, Dad. I don't hate you because I don't think I love you anymore. *(DAVID takes a deep breath. MR. STONE remains motionless.)*

(Fade out)

SELECTED BIBLIOGRAPHY

The following textbooks and suggested readings are recommended for the beginning student who may like to review the audition process in terms of practice and principle. The suggested readings provide useful information related to the preparation and rehearsal of audition scenes or monologs and also include valuable references and resource materials related to career opportunities, casting agents and arts' agencies. There is also an effort made here to direct the reader toward the more practical and realistic sources related to auditions at both the regional and the national level.

Bert, Norman. *The Scenebook for Actors.* Colorado Springs, CO: Meriwether Publishing Ltd., 1992.

Campbell, Douglas and Diana Devlin. *Looking Forward to a Career: The Theatre.* Minneapolis: Dillon Press, 1970.

Cohen, Robert. *Acting Professionally.* Palo Alto, California: Mayfield, 1975.

Colyer, Carlton. *The Art of Acting.* Colorado Springs, CO: Meriwether Publishing Ltd., 1989.

Dalrymple, Jean. *Careers and Opportunities in the Theatre.* New York: E. P. Dutton, 1969.

Ellis, Roger. *Scenes and Monologs From the Best New Plays.* Colorado Springs, CO: Meriwether Publishing Ltd., 1993.

Engel, Lehmann. *Getting Started in the Theatre.* New York: Macmillan, 1973.

Gelb, Michael. *Body Learning.* 2nd ed. London: Henry Holt, 1996.

Hunt, Gordon, *How to Audition: For TV, Movies, Commercials, Plays and Musicals.* 2nd edition. HarperCollins, New York, 1995.

Kluger, Garry Michael. *Fifty Professional Scenes for Student Actors.* Colorado Springs, CO: Meriwether Publishing Ltd., 1997.

Lawrence, Eddie. *57 Original Auditions for Actors.* Colorado Springs, CO: Meriwether Publishing Ltd., 1983.

Savan, Bruce. *Your Career in the Theatre.* Garden City, New York: Doubleday Books, 1961.

Shurtleff, Michael. *Audition: Everything an Actor Needs to Know to Get the Part.* Studio City, CA: Players Press Inc., 1984.

Yakim, Moni. *Creating a Character: A Physical Approach to Acting.* New York: Applause Theatre Book Publications, 1993.

About the Author

Gerald Lee Ratliff is an award-winning author of numerous articles and textbooks in performance approaches to the study of classroom literature. He has held national and international offices as President of the Eastern Communication Association (1993), Theta Alpha Phi (1986), American Association of Arts' Administrators (1998), and Deputy Director General of the (Cambridge, England) International Biographical Centre (1999). He has also served on the advisory boards of the Association for Communication Administration, American Council of Academic Deans, International Arts Association, and Society of Educators and Scholars.

In addition, he was awarded the "Distinguished Service Award" from both the Eastern Communication Association (1993) and Theta Alpha Phi (1992); was selected a Fulbright Scholar to China (1990) and a U.S.A. delegate of the John F. Kennedy Center for the Performing Arts to Russia (1991); elected "Fellow" of the (London) International Schools of Theatre Association (1991); and has received multiple "Outstanding Teacher" awards for pioneering creative approaches to classroom instruction. Currently, he is associated with The State University of New York, College at Potsdam.

Order Form

Meriwether Publishing Ltd.
P.O. Box 7710
Colorado Springs, CO 80933
Telephone: (719) 594-4422
Website: www.meriwetherpublishing.com

Please send me the following books:

_____ **Playing Scenes — A Sourcebook for** $17.95
Performers #BK-B109
by Gerald Lee Ratliff
How to play great scenes from modern and classical theatre

_____ **The Theatre Audition Book** #BK-B224 $16.95
by Gerald Lee Ratliff
Playing monologs from contemporary, modern,
period and classical plays

_____ **Playing Contemporary Scenes** #BK-B100 $16.95
edited by Gerald Lee Ratliff
Thirty-one famous scenes and how to play them

_____ **Introduction to Readers Theatre** #BK-B234 $16.95
by Gerald Lee Ratliff
A guide to classroom performance

_____ **Outstanding Stage Monologs and** $15.95
Scenes from the '90s #BK-B236
edited by Steven H. Gale
Professional auditions for student actors

_____ **Audition Scenes for Student Actors** #BK-B232 $15.95
edited by Roger Ellis
Selections from contemporary plays

_____ **The Scenebook for Actors**   #BK-B177 $15.95
edited by Norman A. Bert
Collection of great monologs and dialogs for auditions

These and other fine Meriwether Publishing books are available at
your local bookstore or direct from the publisher. Prices subject to
change without notice. Check our website or call for current prices.

Name: _____

Organization name: _____

Address: _____

City: _____ State: _____

Zip: _____ Phone: _____

❏ **Check enclosed**

❏ **Visa / MasterCard / Discover #** _____
                                              Expiration
                                              date: _____
Signature: _____
        (required for credit card orders)

Colorado residents: Please add 3% sales tax.
Shipping: Include $2.75 for the first book and 50¢ for each additional book ordered.

❏ *Please send me a copy of your complete catalog of books and plays.*